HANDBOOK OF KEY ECONOMIC INDICATORS

Second Edition

R. Mark Rogers

McGRAW-HILL

New York   San Francisco   Washington, D.C.   Auckland   Bogotá
Caracas   Lisbon   London   Madrid   Mexico City   Milan
Montreal   New Delhi   San Juan   Singapore
Sydney   Tokyo   Toronto

Library of Congress Cataloging-in-Publication Data

Rogers, R. Mark.
    Handbook of key economic indicators / R. Mark Rogers.—2nd ed.
      p.   cm.
    Includes bibliographical references and index.
    ISBN 0-07-054045-4
    1. Economic indicators—United States. 2. Business cycles—United States—Statistics.
3. United States—Economic conditions—Statistics.   I. Title.
HC103.R64   1998
330.973´0021—dc21   97-51903
                                                                                CIP

McGraw-Hill

A Division of The McGraw·Hill Companies

1 2 3 4 5 6 7 8 9 0 DOC/DOC 9 0 2 1 0 9 8 7

ISBN 0-07-054045-4

The sponsoring editor for this book was *Stephen Isaacs,* the editing supervisor was *John M. Morriss,* and the production supervisor was *Suzanne W. B. Rapcavage.* Composition by *BookMasters, Inc.*

Printed and bound by R. R. Donnelley & Sons Company.

McGraw-Hill books are available at special quantity discounts to use as premiums and sales promotions, or for use in corporate training programs. For more information, please write to the Director of Special Sales, McGraw-Hill, 11 West 19th Street, New York, NY 10011. Or contact your local bookstore.

This book is printed on recycled, acid-free paper containing a minimum of 50% recycled de-inked fiber.

To Graceann and Alexander

CONTENTS

PREFACE

The first edition of *Handbook of Key Economic Indicators* explained the use of key traditional economic news releases. Since the release of the first edition, in 1994, there have been many important changes in key economic data and in the way that many traditional economic series are used. The second edition discusses and analyzes these changes. New material evaluates changes in household employment data based on 1994 revisions, the effect of the switch in real GDP from a constant dollar to a chained dollar basis, the 1998 revisions to CPI data and further planned changes, the Boskin report on the CPI, and revisions to the composite indicators that were part of the handover of these indicators to the Conference Board by the Commerce Department. New sections have been added for initial unemployment claims, productivity and unit labor costs, and employment cost indexes. Finally, data have been updated throughout the *Handbook*. Many thanks to those who have offered suggestions over the years to make this edition even more valuable to its users.

Why is following economic releases important? For investors and traders, the answer is obvious: Economic releases move markets. And the markets—including bonds, stocks, foreign exchange, and commodities—usually move quickly. However, market analysts sometimes make mistakes, initially focusing on wrong interpretations of economic news. Traders and investors want a quick buy or sell verdict based on some hurried rule-of-thumb analysis. Yet the data are complex and initial impressions can be at odds with more in-depth analysis. The problem is that markets can turn on a dime once it becomes evident that for a given economic release the initial, superficial interpretation is wrong. Of course, the change in reaction to the data can be for a number of reasons: A minor, unimportant subcomponent may have experienced a large monthly change and affected the overall number; a "technical factor" may have affected the overall number; there was a change in definition; previous data were revised; or there may have been problems seasonally adjusting the data.

Market analysts crave rules of thumb for quick buy or sell directions. But rules of thumb can be mistaken; there is no substitute for in-depth knowledge and experience for learning what to look for in economic indicators to portray the current health of the economy.

This book is written to meet the needs of market watchers—traders, investors, and financial analysts—and even academics who want to move beyond the superficial, to become knowledgeable in understanding the true content of each month's economic news. Academics often get caught up in simply using data as inputs for statistical models without a clear understanding of definitions, method-ologies, or changes in methodologies. In turn, many studies misuse data or ignore key facets that can have a significant bearing on empirical analysis. This book is also written to be useful to researchers seeking to avoid such pitfalls.

While there are numerous books explaining financial instruments, there are only a handful of quality books that explain nonfinancial economic indicators. Since these books take a "dictionary" approach—many indicators, but with only very basic information— the *Handbook of Key Economic Indictors* focuses most closely on the nonfinancial economic indicators and then on the financial markets. In-depth methodologies and analytics are detailed for each indicator. In particular, this book concentrates on explaining the nonfinancial economic indicators that can move financial markets on a regular basis. Those chosen are generally acknowl-edged by the financial community as the key economic indicators. These are mostly government-produced indicators that cover all of the major segments of the economy. The breadth of coverage is seen in the table of contents, with sections on employment, personal income, and consumer spending; monthly inflation in-dicators; the manufacturing sector; international trade; construction activity; gross domestic product; and the Commerce Department's composite indicators.

This book is written primarily for market analysts and investors who want to improve their expertise and ability to correctly gauge the strength and direction of the economy. In essence, to fully understand financial markets, one must be knowl-edgeable about key economic series. As already noted, the series chosen cover all major real sectors and key inflation measures. It is the combination of real sector developments and inflation news and monetary and fiscal policy changes that move financial markets. Additionally, it is often news about inflation or the real sector (e.g., unemployment) that leads to changes in monetary policy. The bottom line is that financial market behavior cannot be fully understood without a broad aware-ness of nonfinancial economic indicators. Some basic approaches to using the data are discussed in the Introduction.

This work is based on my many years of experience as an analyst and econ-omist at the Federal Reserve Bank of Atlanta, tracking the data and watching mar-ket reactions to the numbers. It is also based on reading hundreds of pages of technical papers on methodologies and talking with dozens of government econ-omists and statisticians in person and over the telephone.

Because many economic indicators are interrelated, this book is best used through more than one reading, making cross-references between chapters. Each month, news about key economic indicators that move the markets can be com-pared with each chapter's key features about the data. This book helps to develop an analyst's awareness of both key and subtle features of the data contained in a given economic indicator. Each chapter explains not only methodologies behind the indicators, but also what to look for each month.

At the end of the chapters are key questions for analyzing each monthly economic report. These questions get to the heart of the issue of how economic in-dicators are currently portraying the economy. Each chapter discusses the method-ologies, the basic characteristics, and even some quirks in the data, providing insight into these questions each month. Over time, as one relates the methodologies to actual news releases and to the key questions, thinking about and analyzing economic indicators will become second nature.

This book reflects the work of many dedicated professionals who have worked in the private sector or in various government statistical agencies and policy institutions. The author thanks them for their many considerations over the years and hopes that this publication does justice to their work. Many have contributed indirectly to the author's effort and this is appreciated. The author would particularly like to thank those who commented specifically on earlier drafts or offered suggestions. Of course, the author accepts full responsibility for any errors in the manuscript.

Special thanks are due to Steve Andrews, Cynthia Bansak, Steve Berman, Daniela Biliotti, Michael Boldin, Janice Breuer, Mary Cho, Gerald Donahoe, Robert Eisenbeis, David Fondalier, Charles Gilbert, Daniel Ginsburg, George Green, Eve Gu, Harvey Hamel, Ethan Harris, Steve Haugen, Steven Henderson, James Holmes, Craig Howell, Linda Hoyle, Curt Hunter, Robert Keleher, Pam Kelly, James Kennedy, Frank King, Don Luery, Haydn Mearkle, Patricia Nielsen, Ronald Piencykoski, Lois Plunkert, Brooks Robinson, Charles Robinson, George Roff, Mary Rosenbaum, Mary Lee Seifert, Dixon Tranum, Irving True, and Sheila Tschinkel.

The views in this book are the sole responsibility of the author and do not necessarily reflect the views of the Federal Reserve Bank of Atlanta or the Board of Governors of the Federal Reserve System.

R. Mark Rogers

INTRODUCTION

THE MONTHLY FORECAST CYCLE

Each month financial markets make judgments about the strength of the economy and base many of their positions in the markets on these interpretations. Over the course of the month, with each release of economic data, new information is added to the data banks (whether actual or intuitive) of market analysts. Due to the intensively competitive nature of the primary financial markets, data are assimilated rapidly. In turn, market perceptions change—sometimes quite sharply. For example, a significantly stronger-than-expected employment or consumer price index (CPI) report can affect expectations regarding possible changes in interest rates by the Federal Reserve System. As a result, bonds and stocks are immediately repriced.

Prior to the release of economic indicators, participants take positions in the market that are based on their expectation of what the data for various indicators suggest is the direction of the economy, bond prices, and prices for other financial assets. Sophisticated participants explicitly prepare forecasts for the indicators and then determine their market position, either "going long" (buying) or "going short" (selling) various financial instruments.

Financial analysts use every piece of readily available data to try to determine the current state of the economy. Various statistical agencies sometimes use earlier released data from other agencies to derive portions of their own series. For example, the Bureau of Economic Analysis (BEA) uses employment and earnings data from the Bureau of Labor Statistics (BLS) to derive large segments of the wages and salaries component in personal income.

A number of earlier released data series have a statistically significant behavioral relationship to later released data. A prime example of this is the producer price index (PPI), which is generally released about a week before that month's consumer price index is made public. Analysts try to understand long-term relationships between economic data in order to better project trends in the economy and in financial markets.

The following section summarizes how financial markets use monthly data to forecast concurrent later-released monthly data. The use of the word "forecast" is somewhat of a awkward word to use since the actual forecast is generally for data of the same month. Still, given the differences in the timing of releases and the rapid assimilation of information in the financial markets, the term does apply. Table I–1, which shows the most watched economic data, gives a good idea of the timing involved in this forecast cycle. Various bond houses and investment firms regularly compile and publish calendars for upcoming releases. Subscriptions to their newsletters are often free. The

TABLE I–1

The Monthly Release Schedule for October-November 1997

Date	Indicator	For Month, Week, or Quarter
October		
1	Construction expenditures	August
1	Purchasing managers' index, NAPM report	September
1	Conference Board's composite indicators	August
2	Manufacturers' shipments, inventories, and orders	August
2	Initial unemployment claims	September 25
3	Employment report	September
6	Auto sales, AAMA report	September
8	Wholesale trade	August
9	Initial unemployment claims	October 4
10	Producer price index	September
14	Atlanta Fed manufacturing survey	September
14	Richmond Fed manufacturing survey	September
15	Advance monthly retail sales	September
16	Consumer price index	September
16	Initial unemployment claims	October 11
16	Philadelphia Fed manufacturing survey	October
16	Business inventories and sales	August
17	Housing starts and permits	September
17	Industrial production and capacity utilization rate	September
21	U.S. International trade in goods and services	August
23	Initial unemployment claims	October 18
28	Employment cost index	Third Quarter
29	Advance report on durable goods	September
30	New one-family house sales	September
30	Initial unemployment claims	October 25
31	Gross domestic product	Third quarter
November		
3	Personal income, outlays, and saving	September
3	Purchasing managers index, NAPM report	October

Commerce Department also puts a schedule of releases on its electronic bulletin board (EBB). The specific links between the various series, and various long-term considerations, are discussed in more detail in later chapters.

KEY MONTHLY INDICATORS AND THEIR USE IN CONCURRENT FORECASTING

Construction Expenditures

These Census Bureau data are modified by the BEA and then used as major inputs in the BEA's estimates for residential and nonresidential fixed investment in the gross domestic product (GDP) accounts. Market analysts use these monthly series to help project these components of GDP for the upcoming release.

Purchasing Managers Index

This indicator and its components of the purchasing managers' index—compiled by the National Association of Purchasing Management (NAPM)—are basically ordinal net measures of "better," "worse," or "same" conditions by respondents and are not quantitative (i.e., do not have a dollar value) in the same sense that surveys by the Census Bureau are. However, the total index and components provide some insight for:

1. The manufacturing component of industrial production
2. Manufacturing employment
3. Producer prices
4. Manufacturers' inventories
5. New factory orders

Specifically, simple regression models use NAPM data for forecasting the upcoming releases for manufacturing employment and industrial production.

Also, the vendor performance component of the NAPM index is one of the components in the Conference Board's index of leading indicators.

Manufacturers' Shipments, Inventories, and Orders

Since the nondefense capital goods component of manufacturers' shipments provides a key input into the GDP component for investment in producers' durable equipment, money market economists use this indicator to project that component in GDP for the month's gross national product release. Also, the inventory number provides some initial insight into the strength in inventories prior to the release of overall business inventories. A portion of the orders data goes into the Conference Board's index of leading indicators.

Initial Unemployment Claims

The initial unemployment claims data are released on a timely basis every week and are primarily used by money market analysts to project the upcoming unemployment rate in the Household Survey.

Employment Report

This Labor Department release provides the first broad measure on the state of the economy for any given month and is probably the most closely watched of all reports. It provides key forecast information, as follows:

1. Aggregate production hours (based on production employment and the average workweek in manufacturing) are used to project the manufacturing component of industrial production.

2. Average hourly earnings, payroll employment, and average weekly hours are used to estimate major portions of the wages and salaries component of personal income.

3. The average manufacturing workweek enters the Conference Board's index of leading indicators. Payroll employment also enters Conference Board's coincident indicators index.

The first two sets of data are followed because in the predicted series they are actual methodological components used by the source agencies for their figures—at least for the initial estimates. The Federal Reserve Board uses labor hours models for initial estimates of a significant number of the components in industrial production. Also, the BEA directly derives much of their wage income data from the payroll data.

Unit New Auto Sales

These industry data are produced by the American Automobile Manufacturers Association (AAMA) and used by market analysts to estimate the auto component in retail sales. Also, this series more closely correlates with the auto component of durables personal consumption expenditures as derived for the personal consumption expenditures part of the BEA's personal income report.

Retail Sales

Data are generally used to project major subcomponents of personal consumption expenditures for durables and nondurables for the personal income report. The retail sales data are also used as a proxy for the missing months of data for personal consumption in GDP.

Producer Prices

Market analysts use regression analysis (or even simple estimates) based on producer prices to project the consumer price index for the latest release. There is no tie between the BLS methodologies in terms of inputs for producer prices and consumer prices. The connection is simply statistical. In other words, the BLS does not use the PPI in its estimates for the CPI, but market analysts try to use historical patterns between the two to make forecasts.

Business Inventories

Most estimates for the inventory component of GDP are based on monthly business inventory figures. The inventory data are taken from the Census Bureau for use by the BEA in the GDP accounts. Various adjustments to put data in current market value, as well as the deflation from current dollars to constant dollars (both of which are done at fine levels of detail), make for a very loose statistical relationship between the overall monthly figures and the quarterly inventory number.

Monthly International Trade in Goods and Services

The Census Bureau and BEA data on monthly international trade are used to help estimate real net exports for the upcoming GDP release.

ANALYZING THE MONTHLY INDICATORS

There are many ways to analyze economic indicators—from highly to very sophisticated statistical techniques. However, for investors, market analysts, and policy makers, some facets of interpretation are common to all methods. First, there are two basic time perspectives: the perceived phase of the business cycle and the latest economic news release. Financial markets "move" when the latest economic news indicates that earlier perceptions about the current strength of the economy (the business cycle) are not quite correct. Since financial instruments (bonds, stocks, and other securities) are priced according to market perceptions of the strength of the economy, changes in perception lead to repricing.

The next key point is that market analysis of economic indicators revolves around determining the strength of the economy and the accuracy of earlier perceptions. Certainly, the latest news is incorporated into how the markets view the strength of the economy, but more importantly, analysts often discount news releases if the data are aberrant for special considerations. That is, the latest changes for an economic indicator may reflect special or temporary factors rather than true underlying strength or weakness. Basically, the latest economic news for any given month may not be a good indicator of the current state of the economy, and sophisticated analysts are aware of this. It is important to be able to differentiate between substantive movements in data and mere technical "noise." Monthly data are erratic at times and financial markets must be able to have some sort of benchmark against which to judge whether the latest news provides useful information.

The basic steps in such an analysis are determining benchmark expectations for various indicators for different stages of the business cycle; determining what makes this business cycle different from the past and how these factors alter one's views on reasonable expectations for economic activity; and evaluating the latest economic release in terms of earlier expectations. This can be quite complex, but it should include an evaluation of (1) the key components for each indicator, (2) the components that are frequently erratic for technical reasons but that are unrelated to underlying economic strength, and (3) the closeness of the discounted data to expectations for the perceived phase of the business cycle. If recent news does not meet expectations, then the change in an indicator's strength should be applied to the analysis of related sectors of the economy.

Benchmark Expectations: Learning from Past Business Cycles

Ongoing analysis of the economy requires some basis for determining what expectations are reasonable for an indicator in the current and upcoming phases of the business cycle. History is always a good starting point (Table I–2). These are some reasonable questions to ask: What is the typical growth rate for personal income during recovery? How much do auto sales rise in recovery? How much do housing starts typically rebound during recovery? To begin to answer these questions one should compare and average previous business cycle movement for individual economic indicators.

For example, one could obtain seasonally adjusted data for housing starts over the last four recoveries and expansions and create one series for each economic rebound such that the trough of the previous recession is the base period for that series (see Table I–3). If data are put into quarterly form (to cut down on the number of observations and also to make them comparable with quarterly GDP figures), then the trough of the 1982 recession was the third quarter of that year (based on real GDP levels). To compare relative growth across business cycles, each recovery must be rebased so that the trough value is 1 (or 100, depending on one's preferences).

Since the quarterly average for housing starts in the third quarter of 1982 was 1.12 million units annualized, subsequent values for the post-1982 series all must be divided by this value to rebase the entire series (see Table I–4). For this realigned and rebased series, levels subsequent to the base period—the trough—indicate cumulative growth in activity since the trough. Similarly, the quarterly trough of the 1974–75 recession was the first quarter of 1975, with the value of housing starts at 0.98 million units annualized. This is the divisor for the post-1975

TABLE I–2

Post–World War II Business Cycle Peaks and Troughs

Monthly		Quarterly	
Peak	Trough	Peak	Trough
November 1948	October 1949	1948 Q4	1949 Q4
July 1953	May 1954	1953 Q2	1954 Q2
August 1957	April 1958	1957 Q3	1958 Q1
April 1960	February 1961	1960 Q1	1960 Q4
December 1969	November 1970	1969 Q3	1970 Q4
November 1973	March 1975	1973 Q4	1975 Q1
January 1980	July 1980	1980 Q1	1980 Q2
July 1981	November 1982	1981 Q3	1982 Q3
July 1990	March 1991	1990 Q2	1991 Q1

Note: Monthly peaks and troughs are official monthly dates set by the National Bureau of Economic Research (NBER). Quarterly peaks and troughs are unofficial and are based on real GDP levels, with the lowest level closest to the quarter inclusive of the monthly peaks and trough being defined as the peak and trough quarters. Because real GDP represents average activity for a given quarter, quarterly peaks and troughs do not always include the monthly peak and trough dates.

TABLE I–3

Housing Starts in Millions of Units, Annualized

| Trough | Quarters Past Trough | | | | | |
	1	2	3	4	5	6
1991Q1	**1991Q2**	**1991Q3**	**1991Q4**	**1992Q1**	**1992Q2**	**1992Q3**
0.89	1.01	1.04	1.09	1.24	1.15	1.18
1982Q3	**1982Q4**	**1983Q1**	**1983Q2**	**1983Q3**	**1983Q4**	**1984Q1**
1.12	1.28	1.63	1.66	1.80	1.73	1.94
1975Q1	**1975Q2**	**1975Q3**	**1975Q4**	**1976Q1**	**1976Q2**	**1976Q3**
0.98	1.07	1.25	1.34	1.44	1.45	1.56

TABLE I–4

Housing Starts Data Rebased, (Trough = 1.00)

| Trough | Quarters Past Trough | | | | | |
	1	2	3	4	5	6
1991Q1	**1991Q2**	**1991Q3**	**1991Q4**	**1992Q1**	**1992Q2**	**1992Q3**
1.00	1.13	1.17	1.21	1.39	1.29	1.32
1982Q3	**1982Q4**	**1983Q1**	**1983Q2**	**1983Q3**	**1983Q4**	**1984Q1**
1.00	1.15	1.46	1.48	1.61	1.55	1.73
1975Q1	**1975Q2**	**1975Q3**	**1975Q4**	**1976Q1**	**1976Q2**	**1976Q3**
1.00	1.10	1.28	1.37	1.48	1.48	1.59

recovery series for cyclical comparisons. With starts realigned to troughs and re-based to 1, comparisons can readily be made for relative growth since troughs. For example, the post-1975 and post-1982 recoveries had starts in the sixth quarter of growth that were, respectively, 59 percent and 73 percent higher than their trough levels of starts. In contrast, the post-1991 period had starts only 32 percent higher six quarters after the recession bottom.

With data realigned, growth rates can be compared over different phases of the business cycle. For example, the residential investment component of real GDP can be compared with realigned and rebased series for each recovery. For housing starts, comparing levels over the business cycle is a standard type of analysis. However, for components of real GDP, growth rates are often more interesting. Once real residential investment series have been created and realigned for each recovery, quarterly annualized growth rates can be calculated and averaged for whatever time period is of interest. One might want to calculate the average quarterly annualized percent change for the first six quarters of recovery and expansion. Or one might be interested in average growth rates for the second year of economic growth.

Such calculations provide guides to what are reasonable growth rates for a given indicator. Upper and lower growth rates over several business cycles tend to set boundaries for reasonable projections unless there are very significant reasons for exceeding outlier growth rates. Similar tables can be constructed for post–peak economic activity. These types of cyclical comparisons are useful for heavily judgmental analyses as well as for doing a "reality check" on econometric projections.

For example, owing to demographic factors (the aging of baby boomers and the movement of the smaller "baby-bust" generation into home-buying years) and an overbuilt multifamily sector, many economists expected housing to have a below-average recovery in 1991. Based on the data in Table I–5, housing investment averaged 30.1 percent annualized growth in the first four quarters of recovery in the previous four major recoveries. A reasonable forecast would have projected post-trough growth in 1991 to be below 30.1 percent for the first year. Indeed, actual growth of 14.4 percent was close to the lowest pace that occurred during the post-1969 recovery.

Previous business cycles are a good starting point for analyzing the current business cycle. But what is the next step?

What's Different about This Business Cycle?

Every business cycle is different. An analyst must always ask what's different about the current recovery, expansion, or recession compared to the past. Importantly, how will these changes affect what one should expect for strength in various sectors?

The recovery and expansion following the 1990–91 recession provides excellent examples of how business cycles differ from each other by sector. Demographic factors play key roles in consumer spending and housing. Baby boomers have aged past prime home-buying years and the smaller baby-bust generation is now the major force in this market. Baby boomers are more inclined to save than during the 1980s—both for retirement and for children's college expenses. Personal consumption is thereby dampened. In contrast to the post-1982 recovery, there was an excess of multifamily housing. Employment levels and manufacturing output are being hurt by long-term defense cutbacks. Computer inventory and tracking systems have radically changed inventory investment decisions while expanded worldwide trade and competition have affected almost every facet of the economy—from consumer prices to employment, labor-management relations, inventory control, and investment decisions.

In accessing reasonable expectations for a given component of the economy, one must ask what long-term fundamentals have changed.

- How are various sectors, such as housing and personal consumption, affected by demographic changes (for example, the aging of the large baby-boom population segment)?

- Have any key regulatory changes resulted in additional costs or more liberal rules for business?

- How have international markets for U.S. products changed? For example, is a greater share of U.S. exports going to Latin America and Asia, thereby lessening dependence on the European economies?

- Is the dollar weaker or stronger compared to this phase in the previous business cycle?
- Are foreign economies stronger or weaker than in previous U.S. business cycles? Which countries are different?
- Has fiscal policy changed and what sectors are affected?
- While interest rates are an obvious factor to be considered, have financial regulations or supervision changed such that credit conditions are different?
- Are energy costs higher or lower relative to other cost factors?

The Latest Monthly News Release

As soon as new monthly data for an indicator are released, financial markets use the information to corroborate earlier perceptions about the current strength of the economy and to formulate any changes in market views of future strength of the economy. Before the release of a key economic indicator, market participants form opinions on what is expected for the change in the indicator's value. Analysts base their projections on many differing methodologies. When possible, if an indicator is based on earlier released information, analysts look at the earlier data to form projections. Such is usually the case for industrial production, personal income, the Conference Board's index of leading indicators, and portions of real GDP.

Another method is to examine the statistical relationship between earlier released data and an indicator. An earlier released series may have an economically meaningful relationship even though it is not an input into the later indicator. For example, changes in the producer price index are used to project changes in the consumer price index. Also, the purchasing managers' index compiled by NAPM is used to provide insight into movement in industrial production.

More complex econometric and flow of expenditure models are used to project merchandise trade balances and inventory changes as production and consumption flows are tracked. Finally, numerous methods of technical analysis are applied to past values of a series in order to track certain trends.

Many different types of data and analyses help form expectations about soon-to-be-released economic data. Because of the importance of these expectations in setting the price of financial instruments, a number of electronic vendors of real-time trading data (bid and ask prices for bonds, foreign currencies, futures prices, etc.) conduct their own surveys of projections by market participants.

Each vendor maintains running calendars of recent and pending releases, showing recent performance of economic indicators, the median expectations of the survey panel, and the range of forecasts for upcoming economic indicators. These surveys are usually taken roughly 5 to 10 days prior to a news release. Survey results are posted on vendors' calendar pages for use by their clients. Similarly, bond houses, major banks, economic consultants, and others publish weekly calendars that include their own projections. These various forecasts form the standard against which actual data are compared for evaluating earlier perceptions of the strength of the economy. One caveat: expectations change daily; by the date

TABLE I–5

Recovery and Expansion in Chain-Weighted Real GDP

	Average Annualized Growth Rates Following Recession Troughs of:					
	1960Q4	1970Q4	1975Q1	1982Q3	1991Q1	Average
Gross Domestic Product						
1st 4 quarters	6.4	4.3	6.4	5.2	2.1	4.9
2nd 4 quarters	4.0	7.3	3.3	6.7	2.5	4.7
3rd 4 quarters	5.2	4.2	4.1	3.7	3.1	4.1
4th 4 quarters	5.2	—	6.2	2.6	2.8	4.2
Personal Consumption Expenditures, Total						
1st 4 quarters	4.1	5.3	6.4	6.1	2.2	4.8
2nd 4 quarters	4.5	7.1	4.5	4.6	2.7	4.7
3rd 4 quarters	3.9	1.9	3.5	5.4	3.6	3.7
4th 4 quarters	6.1	—	4.0	3.9	2.5	3.0
Personal Consumption Expenditures, Durables						
1st 4 quarters	4.8	23.0	18.1	18.7	4.0	13.7
2nd 4 quarters	10.8	13.5	7.3	11.9	5.7	9.9
3rd 4 quarters	7.5	2.5	3.5	15.2	9.3	7.6
4th 4 quarters	7.1	—	6.8	11.7	4.0	7.4
Personal Consumption Expenditures, Nondurables						
1st 4 quarters	3.3	1.5	5.4	3.6	1.1	3.0
2nd 4 quarters	2.7	6.4	3.8	3.3	1.8	3.6
3rd 4 quarters	1.7	0.5	2.5	2.2	3.1	2.0
4th 4 quarters	6.1	—	3.6	3.0	2.2	3.7
Personal Consumption Expenditures, Services						
1st 4 quarters	5.2	4.3	4.3	5.2	2.5	4.3
2nd 4 quarters	4.7	5.9	4.3	4.0	2.6	4.3
3rd 4 quarters	5.1	3.2	4.6	5.2	2.7	4.2
4th 4 quarters	5.8	—	3.8	2.9	2.4	3.7
Business Fixed Investment						
1st 4 quarters	4.3	4.5	1.3	1.6	−1.9	2.0
2nd 4 quarters	6.1	12.7	10.2	19.2	6.2	10.9
3rd 4 quarters	9.2	11.6	8.9	3.3	8.6	8.3
4th 4 quarters	10.9	—	17.9	−4.2	11.1	8.9
Producer's Durable Equipment						
1st 4 quarters	9.4	8.3	2.1	8.8	2.5	6.2
2nd 4 quarters	6.2	17.6	15.0	20.2	10.3	13.9
3rd 4 quarters	12.6	13.7	11.5	3.3	12.6	10.8
4th 4 quarters	11.0	—	17.3	1.4	12.6	10.6

TABLE I–5 (*Continued*)

	Average Annualized Growth Rates Following Recession Troughs of:					
	1960Q4	1970Q4	1975Q1	1982Q3	1991Q1	Average
Nonresidential Structures						
1st 4 quarters	−2.6	−1.1	0.0	−7.7	−9.7	−4.2
2nd 4 quarters	6.1	5.0	2.0	18.1	−2.6	5.7
3rd 4 quarters	4.5	8.2	4.0	3.7	−0.6	3.9
4th 4 quarters	10.6	—	19.3	−12.4	8.0	6.4
Residential Investment						
1st 4 quarters	10.1	26.9	26.5	56.8	14.4	27.0
2nd 4 quarters	4.9	13.4	19.7	7.9	11.2	11.4
3rd 4 quarters	16.9	−9.6	12.6	1.7	10.6	6.4
4th 4 quarters	−1.3	—	4.0	14.3	0.4	4.3
Government CE&GI Total						
1st 4 quarters	5.8	−2.2	1.2	4.3	−0.3	1.7
2nd 4 quarters	4.8	0.4	−0.9	2.2	−0.6	1.2
3rd 4 quarters	2.0	−0.1	1.1	7.2	−0.6	1.9
4th 4 quarters	0.9	—	3.4	5.4	1.4	2.8
Government CE&GI Federal						
1st 4 quarters	5.3	−7.5	−0.9	8.0	−4.0	0.2
2nd 4 quarters	6.8	−1.5	0.2	0.1	−2.1	0.7
3rd 4 quarters	−1.5	−3.7	1.3	9.1	−4.8	0.1
4th 4 quarters	−3.1	—	2.9	6.0	−1.0	1.2
Government CE&GI State and Local						
1st 4 quarters	6.6	2.8	2.8	1.1	2.5	3.2
2nd 4 quarters	2.2	2.4	−1.6	4.4	0.6	1.6
3rd 4 quarters	7.2	3.1	0.9	5.5	2.3	3.8
4th 4 quarters	6.1	—	3.8	5.2	3.0	4.5
Exports						
1st 4 quarters	2.5	−4.3	3.3	−0.8	10.8	2.3
2nd 4 quarters	3.1	24.6	3.5	9.1	2.3	8.5
3rd 4 quarters	16.5	20.0	2.8	0.1	5.0	8.9
4th 4 quarters	10.4	—	17.2	9.7	12.6	12.5
Imports						
1st 4 quarters	10.7	3.4	15.2	16.2	8.7	10.8
2nd 4 quarters	7.9	21.6	17.2	21.4	8.5	15.3
3rd 4 quarters	2.5	0.5	8.3	5.4	10.3	5.4
4th 4 quarters	7.7	—	3.1	11.3	13.0	8.8

* Average of growth rates for recoveries from 1960 through 1991 (not inclusive of post-1980 recovery). For the fourth four quarters, the average does not include the recovery and expansion that followed the 1970Q4 trough, since recession sets in during those four quarters. Includes annual revisions of July 1997.

Note: Inventory investment is not included in this table because analysis of that component generally is in dollar values, not in percent changes.

of an indicator's actual release, the consensus expectation may have changed because of new information and may differ from earlier published survey data.

Market participants are interested in whether newly released data provide new information about the economy. If the actual release meets expectations (assuming there are no quirks in the figures), then there is no new information relative to expectations. If actual data differ from expectations, then the question is whether the divergence is substantive or merely statistical noise. Therefore, financial analysts find it prudent to learn which indicators are reliable. A good analyst must learn which components of a series are critical for measuring the true strength of an indicator and which ones are minor. Many series also have specific components that are notoriously volatile, reflecting merely random rather than meaningful changes in the economy for a given month.

Within the series for personal income, the wages and salaries component is quite large and generally indicative of changes in consumer purchasing power. In contrast, personal farm income is very volatile owing to farm subsidy payments, which vary significantly over the course of a year; an experienced analyst would therefore focus more on wages and salaries than on overall personal income, which is pushed around by volatile farm income. Similarly, aircraft orders typically are large and irregular and cause overall new factory orders to seesaw; the impact of aircraft orders in a particular month is usually discounted by financial markets, but over many months they must certainly be tracked and evaluated for their impact on the economy.

Finally, when actual release data differ from expectations, the impact on other data series and the economy must be evaluated. Such an evaluation can be complex and is made by analysts using both experience in following the data over the years and formal economic models. The *Handbook* discussion on this topic will elaborate only on the sectors affected and on typical cyclical behavior of series. Each chapter contains a summary section describing an indicator's key roles, listing the principal long-term factors affecting the economic indicators, and encapsulating earlier discussions on key factors to watch with each month's release of economic news. These include the primary components and sources of volatility for each indicator.

In order to determine the impact of an economic news release on financial markets, economic and financial analysts need to be aware of various types of information before an indicator's release and understand what information to extract from the release.

Before an indicator's release, learn:

- Each series' key components
- Some of the usual irregularities
- Typical growth rates (or levels, for some series) over various phases of the business cycle
- Market expectations for an indicator's upcoming release
- Financial markets' typical reactions to unusually strong or weak data

After an indicator's release, ask:

- If a release differs from expectations, are the reasons significant or mere technicalities? What happened with the major components?
- Does the latest news release corroborate your view of the current phase of the business cycle? Are demands on financial markets as expected?
- Does the latest news indicate unexpected imbalances within the economy? Which sectors are affected?
- Is good news really "good news," or is it "bad news" in that monetary authorities react with a policy change? Similarly, is a weak economic indicator actually "good news" for financial markets?

CHAPTER 1

THE EMPLOYMENT REPORT

The first major economic release each month is the employment report prepared by the U.S. Department of Labor, Bureau of Labor Statistics (BLS). This report generally is released on the first Friday of the month following the reference month. It contains the closely watched unemployment rate and the even more important nonfarm payroll job data. From these latter figures come key inputs in estimates for industrial production and personal income, one component in the Conference Board's composite index of leading indicators as well as one in the coincident index, and it even has inputs for some minor series in GDP. Because of its early release date, its use in estimating other indicators, and its broad coverage of many sectors in the economy, the employment report sets the tone for how subsequent monthly economic releases are likely to portray the health of the economy. This, in turn, impacts various financial markets. The employment data are viewed as being particularly important indicators of the health of consumer spending since job creation is a key source of growth in personal income.

The employment report actually contains data from two separate, independent surveys. The first of these is the *Household Survey,* which contains employment data supplied by the Bureau of the Census from its Current Population Survey. The Household Survey measures job statistics from the workers' perspective and provides data on the work status of individuals in interviewed households. The *Establishment Survey*—also referred to as the Payroll Survey—is conducted as a mail-in survey by the BLS. It is basically a job count based on employers' records; it also includes questions on earnings, and hours worked.

The employment report first appears in the news release "The Employment Situation." It is also published in the U.S. Labor Department's *Employment and Earnings* and is found in secondary sources, such as the Commerce Department's *Survey of Current Business* and the Federal Reserve Board's *Federal Reserve Bulletin.*

THE HOUSEHOLD SURVEY

The Household Survey contains key statistics on the labor force, employment, unemployment, and persons not in the labor force. (See summary tables at the end of this chapter.) Data are derived from a scientifically selected sample of households that are representative of the civilian noninstitutional population of the United States.[1] The sample size was cut from about 60,000 to 50,000 in January 1996 as a result of federal government budget cuts. Stratification of the sample takes into account urban and rural population distributions as well as different types of industry representation. The Household Survey excludes persons under 16 years of age as well as the institutional population (inmates of penal and mental institutions, sanitariums, and homes for the aged, infirm, and needy).

In order to reduce the burden of reporting, a selected household is interviewed on a rotating basis rather than every month. For the initial interview, a household visit is made; follow-up interviews are by telephone. A household is interviewed for the first four months after being selected to be in the sample, omitted from the interview sample for the next eight months, and then interviewed for four consecutive months before being dropped from the sample. The 4-8-4 rotation scheme is used not only to reduce the reporting burden but also to reduce discontinuities in the data as a result of month-to-month and year-to-year overlap. While specific panels rotate every four months, there is significant overlap in the survey sample each month. Only part of the sample is changed each month. On a month-to-month basis, 75 percent of the sample is common to both months and on a year-ago basis, 50 percent of the sample overlaps.

The Household Survey reflects employment status for the calendar week including the 12th day of the month, and the actual survey is conducted during the following week. Once the survey is completed, the data are weighted in order to reflect the overall population intended.

The key concepts used to classify labor force activity are employment, unemployment, persons in the labor force, and persons not in the labor force. Of course, the unemployment rate is derived from some of the above series.

Before going into how various series are defined, it is important to note that beginning with the Household Survey's January 1994 report, the data reflect a major revision in the Census Bureau's Current Population Survey. Broad classifications remain constant in definition, but questions that determine which classifications respondents fall into have changed significantly for some series. (See "Impact of the 1994 Revisions," below.) Importantly, data before and after the redesign are not directly comparable despite an apparent constancy in most broad definitions. Note, for example, the impact on the classification of employed and unemployed persons. The first important definition is that of employed.

> Employed persons comprise (1) all those who, during the survey week, did any work at all as paid employees, or in their own business, profession, or on their own farm, or who worked 15 hours or more as unpaid workers in a family-operated enterprise; and (2) all those who did not work but had jobs or businesses from which they were temporarily absent due to illness, bad weather, vacation, labor-management dispute, or various personal reasons—whether or not they were paid by their employers for the time off and whether or not they were seeking other jobs.[2]

For the level of employed, each person who holds a job is counted only once regardless of how many jobs are held. However, starting in 1994, employed persons are asked how many jobs are held, making possible comparisons with establishment data on payroll positions.

> Unemployed persons include those who did not work at all during the survey week, were looking for work, and were available for work during the reference period (except for temporary illness). Those who had made specific efforts to find work within

the preceding four-week period—such as by registering at a public or private employment agency, writing letters of application, canvassing for work, etc.— are considered to be looking for work. Persons who were waiting to be recalled to a job from which they had been laid off or were waiting to report to a new job within 30 days need not be looking for work to be classified as unemployed.[3]

The civilian labor force is defined as the sum of employed civilians and persons classified as unemployed. The total labor force includes members of the Armed Forces stationed in the United States. All persons who are 16 years of age and older and do not meet the criteria either for employed or for unemployed are defined as "not in the labor force." Both the level of unemployed and the labor force appear to have been significantly affected by the 1994 household survey redesign, as discussed further below.

The civilian unemployment rate is the number of civilians unemployed as a percentage of the civilian labor force. Of course, the overall unemployment rate uses the overall labor force figure as the denominator. The numerator is the same since by definition if one is in the Armed Forces, then one is employed. For this reason, the overall unemployment rate is marginally lower—about one-tenth of a percentage point on average—than the civilian unemployment rate.

There is an additional useful classification for a portion of the working-age population: discouraged workers. These are individuals who want a job but for various reasons have been discouraged from continuing to actively seek employment. Because discouraged workers are not actively seeking employment, they are not considered to be part of the labor force. While they are not employed, they also are not counted as unemployed.

However, the BLS's definition of discouraged workers changed with the January 1994 household report. Prior to 1994, to be classified as discouraged, a respondent had only to (1) tell the interviewer that he or she wanted a job and (2) express discouragement in providing reasons for not looking. Beginning in 1994, there are added qualifications.

> To be classified as discouraged, an individual has to want a job, provide a discouraged reason for not looking, have looked in the last year (or since last working), and be available to work (where one's own temporary illness does not disqualify an individual from being available).[4]

The new definition of discouraged worker lowers the estimate of discouraged workers significantly; the measurement now includes the objective requirements that an individual had to have looked for a job in the last year and also had to be available for work. These new requirements rule out respondents who say they want a job merely because they feel it is socially desirable and those who say they want a job but are really not available to work for such reasons as keeping house or tending ill relatives.

Household data, including the unemployment rate, are available by sex, age, race, Hispanic ethnicity, industry, occupation, and for some combinations of these characteristics. Unemployment rates are available by reason of unemployment, including job losers, job leavers, reentrants to the labor force, and new entrants to the labor force.

The household data for employment are also broken down into full-time and part-time status. Those indicating they work a schedule of 35 hours or more per week are full-time, and those working 1 to 34 hours per week are considered part-time. Part-time workers are generally divided into those working part-time for economic reasons and those working part-time for noneconomic reasons. The questions in the survey determining economic and noneconomic reasons changed significantly with the 1994 redesigned survey.

Prior to 1994, part-time workers were asked why they usually worked part-time. These reasons were classified as either economic or noneconomic. Economic reasons included slack work, material shortage, plant or machine repair, new job started during week, job terminated during week, and could find only part-time work. Noneconomic reasons were legal or religious holiday, labor dispute, bad weather, own illness, on vacation, too busy with housework or other personal business, and did not want full-time work. Respondents were merely told possible answers and economic or noneconomic status was deduced from the answer given.

Beginning in 1994, the requirements for being classified as working part-time for economic reasons became more stringent. Individuals who usually work part-time are explicitly asked if they want to work full-time and whether they are available to work full-time if offered the hours. In the earlier survey, this information was inferred from the answers provided for not working full-time. With the redesigned survey, the reasons differ from the earlier survey. Economic reasons for working part-time are limited to two categories: "slack work/business conditions" and "could only find part-time work." Categories for noneconomic reasons are: "seasonal work," "child-care problems," "other family/personal obligations," "health/medical limitations," "school/training," "retired/Social Security limit on earnings," and "full-time workweek is less than 35 hours."

Annual Revisions

For all household series, each month's data are final in that there are no revisions in later months' releases except for annual revisions, which update seasonal factors. Unadjusted data generally are not revised in the annual revisions. Each month the BLS uses population controls independent of the Census Bureau data to weight individual responses from the Household Survey. Weights by various social strata are based on population estimates produced by the Census Bureau. Generally, these population estimates have been very close to decennial census figures, and there has been no reestimation of household survey data. An exception was made in regard to the 1980 census, because the yearly population estimate differed significantly from the actual census count. In early 1982, population counts and other household survey statistics were matched to the 1980 census, and the data were refitted back to 1970.

The BLS does revise the population controls that are used to weight the household survey sample-based data. Generally, these revisions in controls are infrequent and only carry forward, generally with no historical revisions in the data. The most recent revision to the population controls went into effect with the

January 1997 data. This change reflected two projected components of population change: undocumented migration to the United States and emigration of legal residents from the United States. These revisions specifically affected both components by age, sex, race, and Hispanic origin and the estimated population 16 years and over. Essentially, these revisions in the population controls created a break in the household data series. The changes led to a substantial increase in the Hispanic-origin share of net undocumented immigration, with the greatest effect for males 16 to 39 years old. The share of non-Hispanic whites was revised down. Overall, the civilian noninstitutional population was raised by about 470,000, primarily men. Labor force and employment levels were increased by about 320,000 and 290,000, respectively.

Impact of the 1994 Redesign

The employment data in the January 1994 Household Survey reflect a redesigned Current Population Survey. The new survey is based on the same definitions of key series—such as employed, unemployed, and labor force—but the questions designed to classify the respondents have changed. The data, therefore, are not completely comparable to earlier data. While earlier data were not revised, as usually occurs with the release of January household survey data, seasonal factors were revised several years back. Seasonal adjustment revisions do not affect the underlying unadjusted data. The prior survey had been in use since 1967, when the last significant changes were made. The BLS redesigned the survey for several reasons: to incorporate more precise measurement methods (particularly for discouraged workers), to implement more efficient and less error-prone data collection procedures, and to modify survey questions to reflect social changes. These changes include the more prominent role of women in the labor force, the growing importance of part-time workers, and the greater importance of the service sector.

Prior to 1994, most data collection was based on paper questionnaires, with interviewers following written instructions on the form in order to determine which questions to ask each respondent. For example, a person not working during the reference week is asked a different set of follow-up questions from those asked of a respondent who is working. Subsequent answers continue to affect the set of questions asked. Owing to the somewhat complex sequencing of alternative questions, an interviewer would occasionally ask improper follow-up questions. Computer-assisted telephone interviewing and the computer-assisted personal interviewing (CATI/CAPI) ensures that the proper sequence of questions is asked, especially since follow-up questions are based on earlier, keyed-in answers.

From July 1992 to December 1993, the BLS tested the new procedures in a so-called Parallel Survey and compared them with the techniques then in use. The Parallel Survey has also been referred to as the CATI/CAPI Overlap (CCO). The old Current Population Survey had a sample size of 58,900 households; the Parallel Survey had a sample size of 12,000. The following are key differences between the new and old survey designs based on statistical inferences from the Parallel

TABLE 1–1

Employment and Unemployment Questions in Old and New Current Population Survey

Old CPS (pre-1994)	*Current CPS*
	1. Does anyone in this household have a business or a farm?
1. What were you doing most of LAST WEEK? (working or something else?) (keeping house or something else) (going to school or something else)	2. LAST WEEK, did you do ANY work for (either) pay (or profit)? **Parenthetical filled in if there is a business or farm in the household.**
If answer indicates "with a job, but not at work" (either temporarily or on lay-off), ask 4. If answer indicates "working," skip 2. All others, ask 2.	**If 1 is "yes" and 2 is "no," ask 3.** 3. LAST WEEK, did you do any unpaid work in the family business or farm?
2. Did you do any work at all LAST WEEK, not counting work around the house? (Note: If farm or business operator in household, ask about unpaid work.)	**If 2 and 3 are both "no," ask 4.** 4. LAST WEEK (in addition to the business), did you have a job, either full- or part-time? Include any job from which you were temporarily absent.
3. Did you have a job or business from which you were temporarily absent or on layoff LAST WEEK?	**Parenthetical filled in if there is a business or farm in the household.**
If "no," ask 5. If "yes," ask 4.	
4. Why were you absent from work LAST WEEK?	**If 4 is "no," ask 5.** 5. LAST WEEK, were you on layoff from a job?
	If 5 is "yes," ask 6. If 5 is "no, ask 8. 6. Has your employer given you a date to return to work?
	If "no," ask 7. 7. Have you been given any indication that you will be recalled to work within the next 6 months?
	If "no," ask 8.
5. Have you been looking for work during the past 4 weeks?	8. Have you been doing anything to find work during the last 4 weeks?
If "yes," ask 6.	**If "yes," ask 9.**
6. What have you been doing in the last 4 weeks to find work?	9. What are all of the things you have done to find work during the last 4 weeks?
Individuals can be classified as "at work" at question 1 or 2. Individuals can be classified "employed, temporarily absent" with the combination of 1 and 4.	**Individuals are classified as employed if they say "yes" to questions 2, 3, or 4.**
Individuals can be classified as unemployed with combinations of 1 and 4, 3 and 4, 1 and 6, or 5 and 6.	**Individuals are classified as unemployed if they say "yes" to 5 and either 6 or 7, or if they say "yes" to 8 and provide a job search method that could have brought them into contact with a potential employer in 9.**

Note: Bold text lines are instructions to interviewer.

Survey and the old CPS design. It should be noted that the BLS developed preliminary estimates of the impact of the new questionnaire on household data but later revised its estimates of the impact.

Based on one year of data (September 1992 to August 1993), preliminary analysis indicated that differences should be a crude baseline for comparing new and old CPS data. Also, a New Parallel Survey began in 1994. A small sample was given the old CPS questions to see how more recent economic conditions would have shown up in the data, as compared with the new CPS. Unfortunately, the New Parallel Survey was stopped after only a few months; budget constraints were cited for not continuing the study. Curiously, the New Parallel Survey for some of the months gave results that were opposite of what was expected. For example, at times the unemployment rate differential went in the opposite direction from that indicated in the initial Parallel Survey. Unofficial speculation was that giving a different questionnaire to the same sample was confusing to the participants and invalidated the data. Regardless, there has been no direct study of the difference between the old and new surveys since the New Parallel Survey was stopped.

Some indirect comparisons have been made, including one study by Richard Tiller and Michael Welch of the BLS. They compared other monthly labor sector variables that are available prior to and after January 1994 with the old unemployment rate. These variables were regressed against the old unemployment rate prior to 1994 and then used to "forecast" the old rate in the post-1993 period. Basically, employment type data that were available for new and old Household survey periods were used to estimate new period unemployment rates based on old period relationships between these data series. Model variables included unemployment insurance claims, the employment level from the current employment statistics (CES) program, the civilian noninstitutional population, a time-varying trend term, and seasonal components. Based on this and similar models, the BLS now says that the new unemployment rate is 0.1 to 0.3 percent lower than the old unemployment rate, in contrast to the 0.5 percent estimate based on the initial Parallel Survey.

THE ESTABLISHMENT SURVEY

The Establishment Survey is based on a cooperative effort between the BLS and state employment security agencies. Under the current employment statistics (CES) program, data are collected each month from a sample of about 390,000 nonagricultural establishments (including civilian government).[5] The CES data provide information on employment, hours, and earnings at the national, state, and local level. The data are sorted by industry and economic sector aggregated from industry data. (For a comparison of the Household and Establishment Surveys, see Table 1–2).

In the Establishment Survey, employment represents the number of persons on the payroll on a full-time or part-time basis in nonagricultural establishments during the pay period that includes the 12th of the month. The data include temporary workers. For federal government workers, employment represents the number of persons employed during the last full pay period of the calendar month.

TABLE 1–2

Household and Establishment Employment Data

Household Survey	Establishment Survey
Door-to-door and telephone interviews conducted by Census for BLS	Mail-in, CATI, and TDE survey by BLS*
Survey is for week that includes the 12th day of the month	Survey is for pay period that includes the 12th day of the month
Sample of 50,000 households	Sample of about 390,000 business establishments
Includes farm sector and some unpaid workers	Includes nonfarm and paid workers only
Includes self-employed, proprietors, and some unpaid family workers	Excludes self-employed, proprietors, and all unpaid workers
Civilian and noncivilian employment counts	Civilian employment only
Covers ages 16 and older	Counts jobs regardless of age
Measures work and labor force status of individuals	Acts as a job count from the employer perspective
Data oriented toward socioeconomic characteristics	Data generally organized by industry
Used to derive unemployment rates	No unemployment measures
Individual counted only once for level of employed	Multiple jobs are counted separately
Data are not affected by work stoppages†	Strikes show up as job losses until strikers return to work
Tallies part-time and full-time employed separately	No differentiation between part-time and full-time jobs

*CATI stands for computer-assisted telephone interview and TDE stands for touch-tone data entry.

†For the level of employed, job holders are counted only once, but in 1994, the CPS began tracking how many jobs individuals hold.

Importantly, since workers can hold jobs in more than one establishment, persons who appear on multiple payrolls are counted more than once. Workers are counted only once within an establishment even if they hold two jobs.

Workers are counted as being on the payroll if they are on paid leave (such as sick leave, paid holiday, or paid vacation) or if they are paid for only part of the specified pay period. However, if a worker receives no pay during the specified pay period, then he or she is not considered employed. The key to the Establishment Survey definition of being employed is whether the person was a paid employee during the survey period. Since proprietors, the self-employed, and un-paid family workers are not paid employees, they are not included in the payroll employment figures. Salaried officers of corporations are part of the employment data, while household domestic workers are not. The government sector includes only civilian workers, although employees of the Central Intelligence Agency and National Security Agency are explicitly excluded from the survey.[6]

The Establishment Survey data are revised in the two monthly releases im-mediately following the initial estimate. The first two estimates are referred to as "preliminary" and the third as "final." Revisions are due to late received reports. New seasonal factors are usually introduced in the employment report for the month of May as part of annual revisions and updated in November.

Organization of Establishment Data

For the Establishment Survey, data are primarily organized and analyzed by in-dustry and aggregated sectors of production. (See summary tables at the end of the chapter.) By sectors, overall nonfarm payroll employment is broken down into goods-producing and service-producing sectors. The goods-producing sector cov-ers manufacturing, construction, and mining. In 1997, the goods-producing sector accounted for 20.2 percent of Establishment Survey jobs, while service-producing had the lion's share, at 79.8 percent (see Chart 1–1).

For the goods-producing sector, the most closely watched detail is for man-ufacturing, which is readily divided into durables and nondurables and two-digit Standard Industrial Classification (SIC) industries.[7] Durables industries include lumber and wood; furniture; stone, clay, and glass; primary metals, fabricated met-als; industrial machinery and equipment ("nonelectrical machinery"); electronic and other electrical equipment ("electrical machinery"); transportation equipment;

CHART 1–1
Establishment Survey Employment (Percent Shares in 1997.)

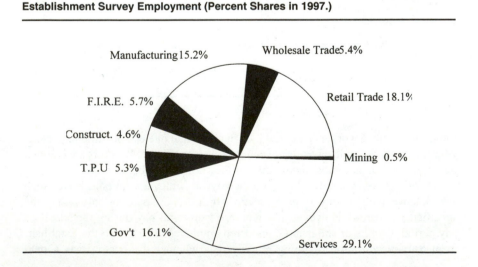

instruments; and miscellaneous durables. Nondurables industries are food, tobacco products, textiles, apparel, paper and allied products, printing and publishing, chemicals, petroleum and coal products, rubber and plastics, and leather and leather products. Of course, BLS classifies manufacturing (and nonmanufacturing as well) employment data available in greater detail than the two-digit SIC level.

For mining, the only subcomponent of general interest is oil and gas extraction employment. Within construction, only the subcomponent for general building contractors is published in the press release, but other components such as highway construction and special trades are also available.

Service-producing industries encompass all non-goods-producing industries. More specifically, this sector includes transportation and public utilities; wholesale trade; retail trade; finance, insurance, and real estate (FIRE); narrowly defined services; and government.

There are some interesting details about some of the service-producing subcomponents. Retail trade employment—like retail sales data—is *not* dominated by department store or general merchandise store employment. The largest component series is for eating and drinking establishments, which constitute about one-third of retail trade. The next largest is food store (grocery stores) employment—about one-sixth of retail trade—followed by miscellaneous retail by general merchandise.

The narrowly-defined-services component is often confused with the broader category of service-producing employment. The former includes health services, business services, hotel and other lodging, private educational services, auto repair, amusement, and others.

As mentioned earlier, the government component includes only civilian employment. At the state and local level, education workers (e.g., teachers) make up the vast majority of government employment.

Average Workweek and Average Hourly Earnings

Data on average weekly hours, average hourly earnings, and average weekly earnings are series that are a part of the Establishment Survey. These three series are all actually based on other payroll data. The hours and earnings series are derived from reported gross payrolls and corresponding paid hours specifically for production workers, construction workers, and nonsupervisory workers. These series cover only what are broadly defined as nonsupervisory workers. As will be discussed later, the data for nonsupervisory workers are important for projecting various monthly indicators.

First, what do these series cover? For manufacturing, the definition of production workers includes employees up through the level of working supervisors who are directly involved in the manufacture of the establishment's product. Executive, professional workers, and routine office workers are excluded. Production workers in mining are defined similarly. In the construction industry, production workers cover employees up through the level of working supervisors who work directly on the construction project at the work site or in shops or yards in activity normally performed by one in a construction trade. Executives, professionals, and office workers are excluded. For the service-producing industries, similar data are compiled for nonsupervisory workers and are basically defined as all workers except those in top executive and managerial positions.

Average weekly hours is a published series derived from the number of production or nonsupervisory workers and unpublished data on total hours. Total hours are paid hours and reflect not just hours worked but also paid standby time and paid time for vacation, sick leave, and holidays. Premium pay periods (such as overtime or holidays) are included but are not converted to straight-time equivalent.

The concept of average hourly earnings differs from an average wage rate since aggregate payrolls include both premium pay and pay for holidays, vacations, and sick leave paid directly by the employer to employees for the pay period reported. Also by definition, these earnings exclude irregular bonuses, various fringe benefits, and the employer's share of payroll taxes. Also, average hourly earnings for specific detailed industries are impacted by occupational shifts between high- and low-wage skills. Average hourly earnings at the aggregate level are also impacted by shifts in employment distribution among the component industries.

Annual Revisions to Payroll Data

Once a year—typically with a June release date—the Labor Department calibrates its initial Establishment Survey data on employment to more complete benchmarks. The initial three-monthly estimates for national payroll employment figures are based on a large survey of about 380,000 business establishments. This survey is a sample from the statistical "universe" for payroll data: administrative records from the unemployment insurance (UI) tax files. The insurance records filed by nearly all employers with state employment security agencies provide an almost full population count for payroll employment. However, the UI data come out with a long lag—about six or seven months—so these are not used in the initial monthly establishment reports.

Once these data are available, they are used to benchmark the month of March of the previous year. For example, in June of 1997, the establishment employment level was adjusted to the UI level for the month of March 1996. Adjustments are made for a few industries not covered by the UI program—such as railroads. BLS benchmarks only the March level for each year and interpolates the employment levels between March benchmarks with the patterns of monthly changes from the current employment statistics—CES Establishment Survey data.

A new trend is created when the difference between the original CES estimate for March employment and the UI-based figure is spread gradually over the entire March-to-March period. BLS refers to this as the *wedge period,* when month-to-month numbers are interpolated. The benchmarks, of course, create a new trend for the employment numbers only up to the latest benchmark month. Levels subsequent to the latest benchmark March are still based on the monthly percent changes in the Establishment Survey. Since only *levels* in the postbenchmark period are affected, and not percent changes in general, the postbenchmark *trend* remains the same as prior to the benchmark.

The annual revisions also incorporate the reestimation of new seasonal factors going back through the previous five calendar years. After employment revisions have been completed, other series are recomputed that have employment series as inputs. These include average hourly earnings, average weekly hours, and diffusion indexes. (See Table 1–8 at the end of this chapter for summary of average hourly earnings, 1978–1996.)

Annual revisions incorporate data from a broader stratification of establishments, since these data essentially come from the universe of establishments. However, as discussed below, the BLS attempts to adjust for these differences prior to the revisions. The CES sample survey consists mainly of large firms. This increases coverage of the universe at a smaller cost and reduces sampling error. Smaller firms are included in the monthly sample but not to the same degree as in the UI pool of firms. However, at the national level, payroll data are stratified by firm size and data are weighted to compensate for low representation of small firms in the CES sample. A problem arises because of the BLS's need to estimate a portion of payroll employment attributable to net growth in firms and because of changes in growth rates for small firms over the business cycle. To get full estimates for total employment, data must be adjusted for growth in the number of firms and their employers, since new firms are not fully represented in the CES survey.

Importantly, statistical analysis shows that the BLS sample is biased toward including mature, well-established firms. An adjustment for changes in business start-up and failure rates is needed over the business cycle since universe information on new business start-ups is not timely. Just as private-sector economists have difficulty predicting the magnitude of recovery and recession, the BLS has had trouble estimating growth in employment for new firms entering and leaving the economy. Newer firms tend to gain employment more rapidly in periods of expansion but also tend to go out of business more readily during recessions. BLS attempts to correct for this problem with a regression based "bias adjustment" (sometimes referred to as the "birth bias adjustment") for small-firm entry and exit. This problem tends to be compounded during recessions as firms fail more quickly than on average. Importantly, as seen in Table 1–3, during periods of moderate employment growth, on a net basis the average monthly gains "attributed to" bias adjustments can account for most of the overall increase in nonfarm payroll employment.

KEYS TO ANALYZING THE MONTHLY REPORTS

Key Components

The primary use of the employment report is to gauge the *current strength of the economy*. First, analysts usually try to get an overall impression from the unemployment rate and the total payroll job gains or losses. Second, more specific information is gleaned for projecting industrial production and personal income. Analysts even try to determine business expectations based on hiring in specific industries such as retail trade or construction.

TABLE 1–3

Employment Benchmarks and Bias Adjustments for Total Private Industries, March 1985–1995 (in thousands)[a]

	Benchmark		Average Monthly Bias		Over-the-Year Employment
Year	Employment[b]	Revision[c]	Added[d]	Required[e]	Change[f]
1985	79,446	−131	152	141	3,075
1986	81,204	−400	149	116	1,758
1987	83,173	21	98	99	1,969
1988	86,180	−310	114	88	3,007
1989	89,015	−93	131	123	2,835
1990	90,546	−261	85	63	1,531
1991	88,790	−583	61	12	−1,756
1992	88,347	−130	33	22	−443
1993	89,790	288	83	107	1,443
1994	92,730	688	115	171	2,940
1995	96,175	511	144	187	3,445

[a]Data in this table exclude government employment because there is no bias adjustment for this sector.

[b]Universe counts for March of each year are used to make annual benchmark adjustments to the employment estimates. About 98 percent of the benchmark employment is from unemployment insurance administrative records, and the remaining 2 percent is from alternate sources. Data represent benchmark levels as originally computed.

[c]Benchmark revision is the difference between the final March sample-based estimate and the benchmark level for total private employment.

[d]The average amount of bias adjustment each month over the course of an interbenchmark period, i.e., from April of the prior year through March of the given year.

[e]The difference between the March benchmark and the March estimate derived solely from the sample without bias adjustment, converted to a monthly amount by dividing by 12.

[f]Over-the-year employment change is March-to-March changes in the benchmark employment level.

Source: Bureau of Labor Statistics, *Employment and Earnings,* February 1997, p. 161.

For the Household Survey, analysts focus on the *civilian unemployment rate* simply because it is an apparently straightforward measure of the health of the economy. It is a indicator of strength in the real sector as well as an indicator of labor cost pressure affecting inflation. Low unemployment is generally associated with a strong economy and rising inflation potential.

Some caution is appropriate when comparing unemployment rates over various historical periods. This rate is affected as much by labor force growth as by employment growth and this fact is often overlooked. Over the 1970s, labor force growth surges as more women and minorities entered the labor force and as baby boomers reached working age. Since the late 1980s, labor force growth has slowed owing to the maturation of the baby boomers, the baby-bust generation reaching working age, and participation rates for the labor force peaking (see Chart 1–2).

The change in *overall payroll jobs* gives an equally important view of the strength of the economy. It is the number of jobs, not just the number of unemployed, that plays a key role in the health of the consumer sector. Financial analysts actually pay more attention to changes in payroll employment than to the unemployment rate because of the Establishment series' greater reliability. On a monthly basis, the payroll data are

CHART 1–2

Household Employment and the Unemployment Rate

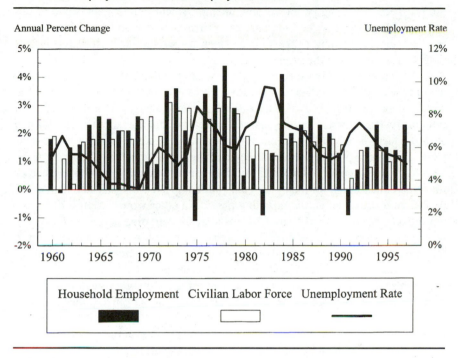

Annual Percent Change   Unemployment Rate

| Household Employment | Civilian Labor Force | Unemployment Rate |

viewed as somewhat more dependable than the Household Survey employment figures because of the significantly larger Establishment Survey, and monthly changes
in payroll employment are less volatile than household employment. The payroll data
also give important information on subsequent economic indicators.

In analyzing either the unemployment rate (including household employment) or the payroll figures, one should try to discount any special factors that may
be causing unusual monthly changes in the data. The types of special factors are
varied but are usually recurrent throughout a business cycle. Two of the more common special factors include strike activity and seasonal adjustment problems.

In addition to the unemployment rate in the Household Survey, one should also
look at recent *changes in the labor force participation rate and the employment-to-
population ratio* to help see if there is much slack in labor supply. Doing so does require some educated guessing as to whether there is some motivation among potential
workers to change their willingness to work. Historical perspective is also important:
participation rates in the late 1990s and 2000s cannot be expected to continue to rise
as they did during the 1970s and 1980s. In the 1970s and 1980s women and minorities were able to increase their participation rates, but there is a limit to this process.

Among the Household Survey data, there is a relatively recent alleged indicator of potential wage pressures. During periods of probable labor market
tightness, the indicator is *job leavers' share of overall unemployed.* The unemployed are classified as either job losers or job leavers. Theoretically, workers are

more willing to quit their jobs voluntarily if they are confident of obtaining a job with another firm. Doing so would indicate that workers are less insecure about job prospects. If during periods of low unemployment, job leavers' share of unemployed rises, this may be an indication of firms having to bid more for workers in short supply, thereby suggesting stronger wage pressures. Research is still scanty in documenting these relationships.

What are some of the special factors that can mask the true strength or weakness in the employment data? As already mentioned, *strike activity* can affect the payroll data. The level of strike activity has declined sharply over the 1980s and into the 1990s, but strike activity can still affect the data if a large firm such as an auto producer or major communications company is experiencing a work stoppage. Changes in payroll data are affected in the first month with the week of the 12th following the start of the strike and the first such month following the end of the strike. In addition, for the payroll data to be impacted, the affected firm's pay period must occur within the reporting period. In other words, payroll data may not reflect strike activity if a strike begins after the reporting period and ends before the next reporting period. Strike activity can be followed by subscription to the weekly publication *Current Work Stoppages,* which is compiled by the Bureau of Labor Statistics. Household data are not affected by strike activity.

Seasonal adjustment procedures can also create temporary distortions in the data since cyclical changes necessarily create divergences from assumed seasonal patterns. This phenomenon is hardly limited to employment data but is also seen in any series with large seasonal patterns, such as construction or manufacturing data.

With the payroll employment data, two components that are more frequently affected are retail trade and construction. There are strong seasonal movements at the beginning and end of the Christmas season and also at the start and end of summer. If the economy is particularly weak going into the holiday season, the hiring of temporary sales people might be below the levels assumed by seasonal factors and November retail trade employment could be weak on a seasonally adjusted basis. For the following January, the seasonal factor would assume that normal hiring increases had occurred in November and December and a typical number of layoffs would be incorporated into the seasonally adjusted data. Following weak unadjusted increases before Christmas, below average layoffs would occur in January. On a seasonally adjusted basis, January might see an increase in retail trade employment but not by the same magnitude as the November decline if employment is cyclically declining over this period. The January rise in this series during a cyclical downturn makes sense only as an effect of seasonal factors that do not "work" very well when the business cycle is not following the trend path that the seasonal factors are based on.

For construction, the winter months have large seasonal factors to adjust the unadjusted payroll employment levels upward. If weather is particularly favorable in a given February, for example, unadjusted employment might edge up and the seasonal factors would lead to an increase in adjusted data. Similarly, seasonal factors for construction employment over spring and early summer assume strong seasonal hiring, and a weak economy over these months would show sluggishness in adjusted construction data. Difficult-to-interpret months occur subsequent to such movement as seasons end. For the construction example, if hiring is strong early in the season but returns to a trend level at the end of the season, then the magnitude of layoffs would be greater than assumed by seasonal factors. In turn, the seasonally adjusted data would look weak.

For the household data, probably the most recurring seasonal adjustment problem involves the student population in the 16- to 19-year-old age bracket, and the 20- to 24-year-old age group to a lesser degree. Summer hiring does typically rise on an unadjusted basis in June, but the labor force rises dramatically as high school and college students seek summer employment. The seasonally adjusted labor force data assume a large jump in June and a similar decline in September. Given these very large factors, it does not take much deviation in either month to cause volatility in the seasonally adjusted labor force data for these age cohorts and, in turn, the respective unemployment rates.

The Four-Week versus the Five-Week Effect

Hstorically, market reaction to specific releases of Establishment Survey data were affected by the "four-week versus five-week effect." Until mid-1996, this phenomenon played a key role in increasing monthly volatility in the data. What was the underlying phenomenon? It was a problem related to the complexities in seasonally adjusting data. Typically, seasonal adjustment procedures take into account variations in "trading days." However, Establishment Survey data differ from, for example, retail sales data. Retail sales data cover a calendar month, whereas Establishment Survey data cover periods related to the 12th of each month and the number of weeks between surveys can be four or five weeks, depending on when the 12th falls for the current and prior months. Normal seasonal flows can be magnified when the number of weeks between surveys deviates from what is "expected" by seasonal factors. The number of weeks between surveys varies between four and five weeks depending on whether the survey in the "previous" month is "early" or the "current" month is "late" in the calendar month. Because five-week months depend only on how the 12th falls each month, there is no constancy for which months have five weeks between survey periods. In effect, there is some apparent randomness for which months seasonal factors "expect" a five-week intersurvey period. Each month's seasonal factors (for both surveys) are based on that month's data over the previous three years and any given month could have anywhere from zero to three instances with five-week intersurvey periods.

However, which months have four or five weeks since the prior survey is known with certainty. Beginning with annual revisions and initial monthly estimates for May 1996, released on June 7, 1996, the BLS implemented a new seasonal adjustment procedure to take into account the effect of varying weeks between survey periods. The new seasonal adjustment procedure was based on X-12 autoregressive integrated moving average (ARIMA) software developed by the Bureau of the Census. The X–11 procedure in simplified terms smooths unadjusted data by applying a seasonal factor to unadjusted data. The seasonal factor for a given month is based on the ratio of a given month to a moving average—after X-11 discounts on their values. The primary difference between X-12 and X-11 is that X-12 also takes into account variations in the number of weeks in a given month for a survey period based on a particular date each month. For the new X-12 data, historical data were revised only from January 1988 forward. Prior data remain seasonally adjusted using the X-11 ARIMA procedure, not taking into account varying time intervals between surveys. The BLS's internal research clearly showed that the X-12 procedure lowered monthly volatility in the payroll data.[8] The X-12 procedure used 11 separate variables to measure intervals between surveys to "filter" the original data. Only 11 variables were needed as there are always 4 weeks between February and March surveys.

Use in Projecting Other Monthly Indicators

For making concurrent projections, industrial production and personal income are the primary economic indicators forecast with data from the employment report. Employment data also enter into estimates for the Commerce Department's indexes of leading and coincident indicators. For a given month, specific employment data released by the BLS during the first week of the month are used by other statistical agencies in the estimates for specific indicators released later in the month.

First, the Federal Reserve Board uses aggregate weekly hours of production workers in manufacturing for primary input in initial estimates of the manufacturing portion of industrial production (IP).[9] This estimation is done at the industry level and for industries that do not yet have information on actual output. About three-fourths of the manufacturing index is projected with production hours data for the initial release.

Output is essentially modeled as a function of aggregate production hours and productivity growth. Aggregate production worker hours is defined as the product of production workers and the average workweek for manufacturing. The BLS produces a specific table in the employment report for "indexes of aggregate weekly hours of production or nonsupervisory workers on private nonfarm payrolls by industry." Private forecasters who roughly duplicate the Federal Reserve's procedure can do so with the product of the published production worker and average weekly hours series, but percent changes in this derived series do vary slightly from those produced by the published indexes of aggregate production hours. The difference is primarily attributable to the fact that the index data are calculated from employment and hours figures that are kept to greater decimal precision than the one decimal place for published numbers.

Regressions for these types of models are usually just percentage changes in manufacturing output (or sometimes overall IP) regressed against percent changes in aggregate production worker hours and a constant term. That is, a percent change in industrial production for manufacturing is a function of a percent change in production worker hours and a constant term:

$$\%(\text{IPmfg}) = f[\%(\text{aggregate production hours}), \text{constant}]$$

Sometimes a productivity variable is added to the model and may be as simple as the percent change in lagged values of the ratio of manufacturing output to production hours. Otherwise, the productivity effect is often assumed to show up in the constant term.

For the BEA's estimates of personal income, the earnings data play a key role. For the private wages and salaries components of personal income, the average weekly earnings numbers are the primary inputs. These data are published in a separate table in the employment report and are the product of average weekly hours, average hourly earnings, and production workers. However, these earnings figures are just for production workers and the salaries portion of wages and salaries is derived separately (though it is not publicly available separately). Hence, this is one source of error in the simple models used to mimic the BEA process. Private forecasts are usually based on the percent change in personal income (or more appropriately wages and salaries or even private wages and salaries) being regressed against the percent change in aggregate weekly earnings:

%(Wages and salaries) = f[%(aggregate weekly earnings, constant)]

The last major indicators that employment report data are used for as inputs are for various components in the Conference Board's indexes of leading, coincident, and lagging indicators.[10] These three composite indicators track changes in the business cycle. In the financial markets, the index of leading indicators is the most closely followed of the three. This index currently is derived from 11 data series, of which average weekly hours for manufacturing is one component. Manufacturing output and the number of labor hours used as input—that is, the average workweek—generally lead the business cycle. For the leading index, there is another employment component—average weekly initial claims for unemployment insurance, but this data series is not part of either the Establishment or Household Surveys. It is produced through a separate state cooperative program.

For the index of composite indicators, the nonagricultural payroll total employment series is one of four components. Also, two of the other three components of the coincident index are heavily impacted by the payroll survey: industrial production and real personal income less transfer payments. The indicator for average duration of unemployment in weeks is one of seven components in the lagging index and comes from the Household Survey.

Finally, some employment report data are used in estimates of some GDP components. For example, the BEA uses industry earnings data for early estimates for personal consumption of some health care services. Also, employment in various financial industries is used to derive estimates for real changes in personal consumption for certain financial services related to interest on checking accounts.

KEY ROLES IN THE ECONOMY AND UNDERLYING FUNDAMENTALS

Employment is a fundamental force behind the consumer sector. Consumer willingness to spend is heavily dependent on the level of employment as well as on perceptions of job stability. The nonfinancial media generally focuses on the civilian unemployment rate. Over the business cycle the unemployment rate typically leads the economy going into recession but usually lags during recovery. Nonfarm payroll employment is a coincident indicator and reflects the current strength of the economy. Financial markets pay attention to payroll employment because of that indicator's inherent reflection of consumer purchasing power. Related to this issue, it is important to watch the distribution of job gains and losses in low-wage versus high-wage industries. In addition to being an important indicator of the current strength of manufacturing, manufacturing employment is watched because it is in a high-wage sector.

Employment is affected by basic demand factors for the economy. Employment tracks the economy on a coincident basis but with less cyclical movement. Certainly, employment is affected by overall demand, but cyclical movement is tempered by average weekly hours being more responsive to changes in output. During recession, hours are cut back before employees are laid off. Hours rise more rapidly than jobs during recovery because a work schedule is easier and quicker to change by managers than is the size of the workforce. Additionally, there are fixed costs to hiring and laying off workers.

Other factors affecting employment trends are worker productivity, the relative cost of capital, and the overall cost of labor. While worker productivity is affected by available capital equipment per worker, the quality of the worker is also a consideration. Low wages are not the only consideration for hiring; the educational level of the workforce is also key. As the United States faces greater import competition and as U.S. output shifts toward higher value goods and services (requiring higher levels of technology), the educational level of the workforce is becoming more critical in maintaining a comparative advantage with other countries.

If labor costs are rising, an employer has the option of considering capital substitution for labor. This is encouraged if the cost of capital equipment is declining (i.e., interest rates as well as the price of the equipment). Finally, employers consider all costs when hiring labor. Total costs include not just wages but a wide variety of benefits. These include vacation, retirement, life and disability insurance, and health care coverage. Business decisions to hire are affected not just by current employment costs but also by anticipated changes in (or fears of) government-mandated benefits for employees.

KEY SOURCES OF MONTHLY VOLATILITY

For the household data, the smaller sample is the basic source of monthly volatility in seasonally adjusted data for both primary series—employed and unemployed. The movement of students into and out of the labor force also create seasonal adjustment problems because the timing of entry and exit is erratic relative to the survey week during critical months. For the overall unemployment rate, only changes greater than 0.1 percent are statistically significant.

For seasonally adjusted nonfarm payroll employment, unseasonal weather can affect a number of components, particularly construction and retail trade.

Strike activity may also affect employment levels during the month a work stoppage begins and ends, depending on timing relative to the survey period. While the four-week versus five-week effect has largely been eliminated by the X-12 seasonal adjustment procedure, there may still be some residual effect.

For average hourly earnings, federal government employees generally get pay increases in January. These data do not seasonally adjust well. Average hourly earnings are generally erratic in the government component that month and can affect the overall figure.

KEY QUESTIONS IN ANALYZING THE NEWS RELEASE

The Household Survey

- Did the unemployment rate fall (rise) beause of a rise (decline) in household employment or because of a drop (increase) in the labor force?
- Was there unusual seasonal movement before or after Christmas or before or after summer?
- For students entering the work force, did the survey period occur unusually early or late in May or in June?
- For part-time workers, was the change within the normal range of high volatility or was there an obvious continuation of an uptrend or downtrend?
- Was an unusually large increase or decrease in household employment due to the introduction of population controls, which takes place each January?
- Have there been notable changes in job leavers' share of total unemployed—possibly indicating greater or less optimism about job prospects?

The Establishment Survey

- How strong was the change in overall nonfarm payroll employment?
- Were there significant revisions to the previous two months of data for the change in nonfarm payroll employment?
- Was there adequate growth in the goods-producing sectors—especially manufacturing and construction—or was growth in lower-wage services jobs—retail trade in particular?
- For projecting the month's industrial production figure—for manufacturing in particular—how strong were production worker jobs and the average workweek in manufacturing?
- To estimate growth in current month's personal income—the private wages and salaries component in particular—how strong were establishment employment, the average workweek, and average hourly earnings for the private sector?

- For projecting upcoming industrial production and personal income, is the survey period representative of the entire month for employment, hours worked, and earnings? Were these data series affected by adverse weather, holidays, or strikes?
- Was construction employment affected by atypical weather—e.g., unusually wet during the normal construction season or unseasonably warm in late winter?
- For retail trade employment, how much of the change was in the large components for eating and drinking establishments and grocery stores as opposed to department stores?
- At the end of the Christmas selling season, does unusually strong (or weak) retail trade employment reflect weaker- (or stronger-)than-normal hiring at the start of the season?

RELATED EMPLOYMENT DATA:
STATE UNEMPLOYMENT CLAIMS

The state unemployment claims report is a key weekly report followed by the financial markets. This report is released every Thursday. The data are for the prior week, ending on Saturday; they are released only five days after the reference week. Financial markets like to watch this weekly report because it is such a timely indicator for the labor markets and gives a hint of the strength of the monthly employment situation report produced by the Bureau of Labor Statistics.

One should note that the state unemployment claims report is not a part of or source data for the monthly unemployment rate or for any other series in the monthly employment situation. The claims data are collected and published by the Employment and Training Administration (ETA), not the Bureau of Labor Statistics. Both agencies, however, are part of the U.S. Department of Labor. There are two reports: an advance report and a more comprehensive report the following week. The advance report has national data, while the revised report includes state data. Annual revisions to the data are made each January.

The data for the claims reports are based on state programs for unemployment insurance. They do not reflect claims made under federal programs. The data are primarily counts of (1) initial claims, and (2) the total number receiving state unemployment benefits. Initial claims are that—applications. An application does not mean that a claimant will receive benefits. Local agencies compile the data over each weekend and then forward them to the state. The state then forwards the data to the ETA. Applicants make claims through their employer, not through the agency directly. Additionally, state data are by residence of the claimant. More detailed computation is required to derive state data, resulting in the one-week lag in reporting. State data, in turn, are reported by claimants' residence.

The importance of the state unemployment claims data is that they are an early indicator of strength or weakness in the upcoming monthly employment report. There is moderate correlation between changes in direction of the covered unemployed insurance rate and the civilian unemployment rate. This also holds true for initial unemployment claims once the trend growth in the labor force has been discounted. Basically, financial analysts use the claims data to forecast the current-month civilian unemployment rate. As seen in Chart 1–3, these two series do tend to move together, although there can be divergent movement in some months. Additionally, the initial claims series is part of the Conference Board's index of leading indicators.

But the data are very volatile. This is typical for a weekly frequency series. Seasonal adjustment is difficult for a weekly series. Also, "emergency" programs can skew the data. During a lengthy recession, emergency programs for the long-term unemployed may be offered as an alternative choice to the regular program of state benefits. These emergency programs can affect the preference of a worker away from the regular program. During the latter part of the 1990–91 recession, an emergency program led the regular program applications to weaken, not because the economy had improved, but because the benefits were better.

A regular analyst of this report should track not only the latest weekly number but also the four-week average so as to discount some of the volatility. Since the long-term growth of the economy and labor force affects the "typical" level of application (one should expect the trend to be upward regardless of recession), focusing on the rate of insured unemployment helps to eliminate some of the long-term growth effect from the data.

CHART 1–3

Civilian Unemployment Rate versus Insured Unemployment as a Percent of Covered Employment

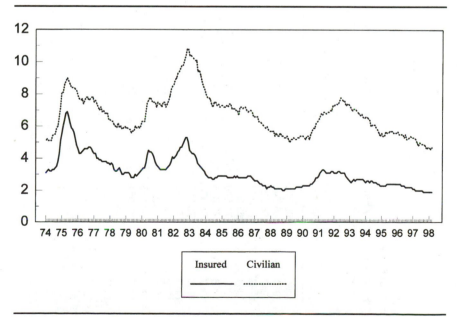

TABLE 1–4
Household Survey Employment (Annual Data in Millions)

	Civilian Employment	Number Unemployed	Civilian Labor Force	Civilian Unemployment Rate*	Not In Labor Force	Noninstitutional Population, 16+
1960	65.785	3.874	69.659	5.6	47.586	117.245
1961	65.744	4.706	70.450	6.7	48.320	118.770
1962	66.702	3.918	70.619	5.5	49.534	120.153
1963	67.760	4.053	71.812	5.6	50.604	122.416
1964	69.301	3.776	73.077	5.2	51.408	124.485
1965	71.070	3.354	74.424	4.5	52.089	126.513
1966	72.878	2.867	75.745	3.8	52.313	128.058
1967	74.376	2.972	77.348	3.8	52.526	129.873
1968	75.913	2.797	78.710	3.6	53.317	132.027
1969	77.875	2.830	80.705	3.5	53.629	134.335
1970	78.669	4.127	82.796	5.0	54.290	137.086
1971	79.355	5.022	84.376	6.0	55.840	140.216
1972	82.135	4.876	87.011	5.6	57.114	144.125
1973	85.051	4.359	89.411	4.9	57.686	147.097
1974	86.803	5.173	91.976	5.6	58.145	150.121
1975	85.830	7.940	93.770	8.5	59.383	153.153

TABLE 1–4 (Continued)
Household Survey Employment (Annual Data in Millions)

	Civilian Employment	Number Unemployed	Civilian Labor Force	Civilian Unemployment Rate*	Not In Labor Force	Noninstitutional Population, 16+
1976	88.753	7.398	96.151	7.7	59.999	156.149
1977	92.017	6.967	98.984	7.0	60.049	159.033
1978	96.046	6.187	102.233	6.1	59.678	161.911
1979	98.825	6.135	104.961	5.8	59.904	164.865
1980	99.303	7.671	106.974	7.2	60.772	167.746
1981	100.400	8.276	108.676	7.6	61.454	170.130
1982	99.529	10.715	110.244	9.7	62.027	172.271
1983	100.822	10.694	111.515	9.6	62.700	174.216
1984	105.003	8.529	113.532	7.5	62.851	176.383
1985	107.154	8.313	115.467	7.2	62.738	178.206
1986	109.601	8.245	117.846	7.0	62.741	180.587
1987	112.439	7.414	119.853	6.2	62.900	182.753
1988	114.974	6.697	121.671	5.5	62.942	184.613
1989	117.327	6.524	123.851	5.3	62.542	186.393
1990	118.796	7.061	125.857	5.6	63.307	189.164
1991	117.713	8.640	126.352	6.8	64.572	190.925
1992	118.488	9.611	128.099	7.5	64.706	192.805
1993	120.259	8.927	129.185	6.9	65.652	194.838
1994	123.069	7.976	131.045	6.1	65.770	196.815
1995	124.903	7.408	132.311	5.6	66.273	198.584
1996	126.708	7.230	133.938	5.4	66.652	200.591
1997	129.557	6.728	136.285	4.9	66.848	203.133

Source: U.S. Department of Labor, Bureau of Labor Statistics, Employment and Earnings, March 1998. Annual averages are from seasonally adjusted monthly data.

TABLE 1–5
Household Survey Employment (Annual Percent Changes)

	Civilian Employment	Number Unemployed	Civilian Labor Force	Civilian Unemployment Rate	Not In Labor Force	Noninstitutional Population, 16+
1960	1.8	3.8	1.9	5.6	1.3	1.7
1961	-0.1	21.5	1.1	6.7	1.5	1.3
1962	1.5	-16.7	0.2	5.5	2.5	1.2
1963	1.6	3.4	1.7	5.6	2.2	1.9
1964	2.3	-6.8	1.8	5.2	1.6	1.7
1965	2.6	-11.2	1.8	4.5	1.3	1.6
1966	2.5	-14.5	1.8	3.8	0.4	1.2
1967	2.1	3.7	2.1	3.8	0.4	1.4
1968	2.1	-5.9	1.8	3.6	1.5	1.7
1969	2.6	1.2	2.5	3.5	0.6	1.7
1970	1.0	45.8	2.6	5.0	1.2	2.0
1971	0.9	21.7	1.9	6.0	2.9	2.3
1972	3.5	-2.9	3.1	5.6	2.3	2.8
1973	3.6	-10.6	2.8	4.9	1.0	2.1
1974	2.1	18.7	2.9	5.6	0.8	2.1
1975	-1.1	53.5	2.0	8.5	2.1	2.0

TABLE 1–5 (*Continued*)
Household Survey Employment (Annual Percent Changes)

	Civilian Employment	Number Unemployed	Civilian Labor Force	Civilian Unemployment Rate	Not In Labor Force	Noninstitutional Population, 16+
1976	3.4	−6.8	2.5	7.7	1.0	2.0
1977	3.7	−5.8	2.9	7.0	0.1	1.8
1978	4.4	−11.2	3.3	6.1	−0.6	1.8
1979	2.9	−0.8	2.7	5.8	0.4	1.8
1980	0.5	25.0	1.9	7.2	1.4	1.7
1981	1.1	7.9	1.6	7.6	1.1	1.4
1982	−0.9	29.5	1.4	9.7	0.9	1.3
1983	1.3	−0.2	1.2	9.6	1.1	1.1
1984	4.1	−20.2	1.8	7.5	0.2	1.2
1985	2.0	−2.5	1.7	7.2	−0.2	1.0
1986	2.3	−0.8	2.1	7.0	0.0	1.3
1987	2.6	−10.1	1.7	6.2	0.3	1.2
1988	2.3	−9.7	1.5	5.5	0.1	1.0
1989	2.0	−2.6	1.8	5.3	−0.6	1.0
1990	1.3	8.2	1.6	5.6	1.2	1.5
1991	−0.9	22.4	0.4	6.8	2.0	0.9
1992	0.7	11.2	1.4	7.5	0.2	1.0
1993	1.5	−7.1	0.8	6.9	1.5	1.1
1994	2.3	−10.7	1.4	6.1	0.2	1.0
1995	1.5	−7.1	1.0	5.6	0.8	0.9
1996	1.4	−2.4	1.2	5.4	0.6	1.0
1997	2.2	−6.9	1.8	4.9	0.3	1.3

* Level for civilian unemployment rate.

Source: U.S. Department of Labor, Bureau of Labor Statistics.

TABLE 1–6

Establishment Survey Employment (Annual Data in Millions)

	Total Employment	Goods- Producing	Manufacturing	Construction	Mining	Service- Producing
1960	54.170	20.437	16.799	2.926	0.712	33.733
1961	53.980	19.856	16.326	2.857	0.672	34.124
1962	55.534	20.448	16.854	2.944	0.650	35.086
1963	56.640	20.637	16.996	3.006	0.635	36.003
1964	58.270	21.004	17.276	3.093	0.634	37.266
1965	60.752	21.926	18.062	3.231	0.632	38.827
1966	63.883	23.159	19.213	3.319	0.627	40.724
1967	65.798	23.309	19.448	3.248	0.614	42.489
1968	67.889	23.735	19.780	3.348	0.606	44.154
1969	70.383	24.361	20.168	3.573	0.620	46.021
1970	70.889	23.585	19.371	3.589	0.624	47.305
1971	71.215	22.934	18.623	3.699	0.612	48.281
1972	73.667	23.666	19.153	3.886	0.628	50.001
1973	76.779	24.889	20.153	4.094	0.642	51.891
1974	78.273	24.803	20.081	4.026	0.697	53.470
1975	76.940	22.600	18.321	3.528	0.752	54.340
1976	79.380	23.352	18.997	3.576	0.779	56.029
1977	82.469	24.344	19.687	3.845	0.812	58.125
1978	86.692	25.580	20.511	4.221	0.849	61.112
1979	89.826	26.461	21.044	4.459	0.959	63.365
1980	90.418	25.668	20.288	4.353	1.028	64.750
1981	91.161	25.503	20.172	4.192	1.139	65.658
1982	89.552	23.819	18.783	3.909	1.128	65.732
1983	90.145	23.329	18.433	3.943	0.952	66.816
1984	94.404	24.718	19.375	4.378	0.965	69.686
1985	97.387	24.843	19.250	4.667	0.927	72.544
1986	99.344	24.536	18.948	4.810	0.777	74.809
1987	101.953	24.673	18.998	4.958	0.717	77.280
1988	105.202	25.123 *	19.315	5.096	0.712	80.079
1989	107.883	25.253	19.391	5.171	0.691	82.630
1990	109.404	24.909	19.075	5.125	0.709	84.495
1991	108.255	23.749	18.405	4.655	0.689	84.506
1992	108.591	23.232	18.106	4.492	0.634	85.359
1993	110.707	23.352	18.077	4.665	0.609	87.355
1994	114.145	23.904	18.322	4.982	0.600	90.241
1995	117.195	24.273	18.525	5.167	0.581	92.922
1996	119.517	24.430	18.457	5.399	0.574	95.088
1997	122.264	24.774	18.538	5.632	0.574	97.520

Source: U.S. Department of Labor, Bureau of Labor Statistics.

TABLE 1–6 (*Continued*)
Establishment Survey Employment (Annual Data in Millions)

Transportation and Public Utilities	Wholesale Trade	Retail Trade	FIRE	Services	Government
4.005	3.153	8.240	2.628	7.378	8.329
3.904	3.142	8.196	2.688	7.619	8.576
3.906	3.208	8.359	2.754	7.981	8.877
3.903	3.259	8.520	2.830	8.277	9.214
3.952	3.347	8.812	2.911	8.660	9.585
4.036	3.477	9.237	2.977	9.036	10.064
4.159	3.608	9.637	3.058	9.498	10.764
4.269	3.701	9.905	3.185	10.046	11.383
4.318	3.791	10.307	3.337	10.567	11.834
4.443	3.920	10.785	3.512	11.169	12.193
4.517	4.007	11.035	3.646	11.548	12.552
4.482	4.014	11.337	3.772	11.796	12.879
4.542	4.127	11.820	3.908	12.274	13.331
4.656	4.291	12.314	4.046	12.856	13.727
4.725	4.448	12.538	4.148	13.444	14.167
4.543	4.430	12.628	4.165	13.894	14.679
4.583	4.562	13.193	4.271	14.550	14.870
4.713	4.724	13.790	4.467	15.303	15.129
4.923	4.985	14.555	4.724	16.252	15.673
5.136	5.221	14.971	4.974	17.112	15.950
5.147	5.293	15.018	5.160	17.890	16.243
5.165	5.375	15.173	5.297	18.615	16.032
5.082	5.295	15.159	5.340	19.021	15.834
4.952	5.283	15.585	5.466	19.662	15.868
5.156	5.568	16.509	5.684	20.745	16.024
5.233	5.727	17.314	5.948	21.927	16.394
5.247	5.761	17.880	6.272	22.957	16.692
5.362	5.848	18.421	6.533	24.109	17.008
5.512	6.030	19.025	6.629	25.500	17.383
5.614	6.187	19.477	6.669	26.904	17.779
5.776	6.173	19.601	6.709	27.930	18.306
5.755	6.081	19.282	6.647	28.335	18.406
5.718	5.997	19.355	6.602	29.047	18.640
5.811	5.982	19.775	6.756	30.192	18.839
5.985	6.163	20.504	6.895	31.573	19.122
6.134	6.378	21.187	6.807	33.112	19.304
6.260	6.483	21.619	6.899	34.380	19.446
6.424	6.656	22.135	7.052	35.593	19.660

TABLE 1–7

Establishment Survey Employment (Annual Percent Changes)

	Total Employ- ment	Goods- Producing	Manu- facturing	Con- struction	Mining	Service- Producing
1960	1.7	0.1	0.7	−2.5	−2.7	2.7
1961	−0.4	−2.8	−2.8	−2.3	−5.6	1.2
1962	2.9	3.0	3.2	3.0	−3.2	2.8
1963	2.0	0.9	0.8	2.1	−2.3	2.6
1964	2.9	1.8	1.6	2.9	−0.2	3.5
1965	4.3	4.4	4.5	4.5	−0.3	4.2
1966	5.2	5.6	6.4	2.7	−0.8	4.9
1967	3.0	0.6	1.2	−2.1	−2.2	4.3
1968	3.2	1.8	1.7	3.1	−1.2	3.9
1969	3.7	2.6	2.0	6.7	2.2	4.2
1970	0.7	−3.2	−4.0	0.5	0.6	2.8
1971	0.5	−2.8	−3.9	3.1	−2.0	2.1
1972	3.4	3.2	2.8	5.0	2.7	3.6
1973	4.2	5.2	5.2	5.3	2.3	3.8
1974	1.9	−0.3	−0.4	−1.7	8.5	3.0
1975	−1.7	−8.9	−8.8	−12.4	7.9	1.6
1976	3.2	3.3	3.7	1.4	3.7	3.1
1977	3.9	4.3	3.6	7.5	4.2	3.7
1978	5.1	5.1	4.2	9.8	4.5	5.1
1979	3.6	3.4	2.6	5.6	12.9	3.7
1980	0.7	−3.0	−3.6	−2.4	7.2	2.2
1981	0.8	−0.6	−0.6	−3.7	10.8	1.4
1982	−1.8	−6.6	−6.9	−6.8	−0.9	0.1
1983	0.7	−2.1	−1.9	0.9	−15.6	1.6
1984	4.7	6.0	5.1	11.0	1.4	4.3
1985	3.2	0.5	−0.6	6.6	−4.0	4.1
1986	2.0	−1.2	−1.6	3.1	−16.1	3.1
1987	2.6	0.6	0.3	3.1	−7.7	3.3
1988	3.2	1.8	1.7	2.8	−0.7	3.6
1989	2.5	0.5	0.4	1.5	−3.0	3.2
1990	1.4	−1.4	−1.6	−0.9	2.6	2.3
1991	−1.1	−4.7	−3.5	−9.2	−2.8	0.0
1992	0.3	−2.2	−1.6	−3.5	−8.0	1.0
1993	1.9	0.5	−0.2	3.9	−3.9	2.3
1994	3.1	2.4	1.4	6.8	−1.5	3.3
1995	2.7	1.5	1.1	3.7	−3.2	3.0
1996	2.0	0.6	−0.4	4.5	−1.1	2.3
1997	2.3	1.3	0.4	4.3	−0.1	2.6

Source: U.S. Department of Labor, Bureau of Labor Statistics.

TABLE 1–7 (*Continued*)
Establishment Survey Employment (Annual Percent Changes)

Transportation and Public Utilities	Wholesale Trade	Retail Trade	FIRE	Services	Government
−0.2	2.0	2.6	3.1	4.1	3.4
−2.5	−0.3	−0.5	2.3	3.3	3.0
0.1	2.1	2.0	2.5	4.8	3.5
−0.1	1.6	1.9	2.8	3.7	3.8
1.3	2.7	3.4	2.9	4.6	4.0
2.1	3.9	4.8	2.3	4.3	5.0
3.0	3.8	4.3	2.7	5.1	7.0
2.7	2.6	2.8	4.2	5.8	5.8
1.2	2.5	4.1	4.8	5.2	4.0
2.9	3.4	4.6	5.2	5.7	3.0
1.7	2.2	2.3	3.8	3.4	2.9
−0.8	0.2	2.7	3.5	2.1	2.6
1.3	2.8	4.3	3.6	4.1	3.5
2.5	4.0	4.2	3.5	4.7	3.0
1.5	3.6	1.8	2.5	4.6	3.2
−3.9	−0.4	0.7	0.4	3.3	3.6
0.9	3.0	4.5	2.5	4.7	1.3
2.8	3.5	4.5	4.6	5.2	1.7
4.4	5.5	5.5	5.8	6.2	3.6
4.3	4.7	2.9	5.3	5.3	1.8
0.2	1.4	0.3	3.7	4.5	1.8
0.3	1.6	1.0	2.7	4.1	−1.3
−1.6	−1.5	−0.1	0.8	2.2	−1.2
−2.6	−0.2	2.8	2.4	3.4	0.2
4.1	5.4	5.9	4.0	5.5	1.0
1.5	2.9	4.9	4.7	5.7	2.3
0.3	0.6	3.3	5.4	4.7	1.8
2.2	1.5	3.0	4.2	5.0	1.9
2.8	3.1	3.3	1.5	5.8	2.2
1.9	2.6	2.4	0.6	5.5	2.3
2.9	−0.2	0.6	0.6	3.8	3.0
−0.4	−1.5	−1.6	−0.9	1.5	0.5
−0.6	−1.4	0.4	−0.7	2.5	1.3
1.6	−0.3	2.2	2.3	3.9	1.1
3.0	3.0	3.7	2.0	4.6	1.5
2.5	3.5	3.3	−1.3	4.9	1.0
2.1	1.6	2.0	1.4	3.8	0.7
2.6	2.7	2.4	2.2	3.5	1.1

TABLE 1–8
Average Hourly Earnings

	1978	1979	1980	1981	1982	1983	1984	1985	1986	1987
Levels, Dollars										
Total private	5.69	6.16	6.66	7.25	7.68	8.02	8.32	8.57	8.76	8.98
Mining	7.62	8.49	9.16	10.02	10.79	11.28	11.63	11.98	12.47	12.54
Construction	8.63	9.25	9.92	10.80	11.62	11.94	12.13	12.32	12.48	12.70
Manufacturing	6.17	6.69	7.28	7.99	8.50	8.83	9.19	9.53	9.73	9.91
Transportation, public utilities	7.57	8.16	8.87	9.70	10.32	10.79	11.12	11.40	11.70	12.02
Wholesale trade	5.87	6.39	6.95	7.55	8.08	8.53	8.88	9.15	9.34	9.59
Retail trade	4.20	4.53	4.88	5.25	5.48	5.74	5.85	5.94	6.03	6.11
FIRE	4.89	5.27	5.78	6.31	6.78	7.29	7.63	7.94	8.35	8.73
Services	4.99	5.36	5.85	6.41	6.92	7.31	7.59	7.90	8.17	8.49
Yearly, Percent Change										
Total private	8.5	8.2	8.2	8.9	5.9	4.4	3.7	3.0	2.3	2.5
Mining	9.8	11.5	7.9	9.3	7.7	4.5	3.1	3.0	4.1	0.6
Construction	6.7	7.2	7.3	8.9	7.6	2.7	1.6	1.6	1.3	1.8
Manufacturing	8.7	8.5	8.7	9.8	6.3	3.9	4.1	3.8	2.1	1.8
Transportation, public utilities	8.3	7.8	8.7	9.4	6.4	4.6	3.0	2.5	2.7	2.8
Wholesale trade	9.1	8.7	8.9	8.6	7.0	5.7	4.1	3.0	2.1	2.7
Retail trade	9.0	8.0	7.7	7.5	4.4	4.7	1.9	1.6	1.5	1.4
FIRE	7.7	7.8	9.7	9.1	7.5	7.5	4.7	4.1	5.2	4.4
Services	7.4	7.4	9.2	9.5	8.0	5.6	3.8	4.0	3.5	3.9

TABLE 1-8 (Continued)
Average Hourly Earnings

	1988	1989	1990	1991	1992	1993	1994	1995	1996	1997
Levels, Dollars										
Total private	9.27	9.65	10.00	10.31	10.57	10.83	11.11	11.43	11.81	12.26
Mining	12.81	13.27	13.68	14.19	14.54	14.61	14.89	15.30	15.60	16.12
Construction	13.06	13.53	13.77	14.00	14.15	14.37	14.71	15.07	15.44	15.98
Manufacturing	10.18	10.48	10.83	11.18	11.45	11.74	12.06	12.37	12.78	13.17
Transportation, public utilities	12.24	12.57	12.92	13.19	13.43	13.56	13.78	14.13	14.43	14.88
Wholesale trade	9.98	10.38	10.78	11.15	11.40	11.74	12.06	12.43	12.86	13.43
Retail trade	6.31	6.52	6.75	6.93	7.12	7.29	7.49	7.69	7.98	8.34
FIRE	9.05	9.52	9.97	10.39	10.83	11.35	11.83	12.32	12.78	13.30
Services	8.88	9.38	9.83	10.22	10.55	10.78	11.04	11.39	11.79	12.28
Yearly, Percent Change										
Total private	3.3	4.0	3.7	3.1	2.5	2.4	2.6	2.9	3.3	3.8
Mining	2.1	3.6	3.1	3.7	2.5	0.5	1.9	2.8	1.9	3.4
Construction	2.8	3.5	1.8	1.7	1.1	1.5	2.4	2.5	2.5	3.5
Manufacturing	2.7	3.0	3.3	3.3	2.4	2.5	2.7	2.6	3.3	3.1
Transportation, public utilities	1.8	2.7	2.8	2.1	1.8	0.9	1.6	2.5	2.2	3.1
Wholesale trade	4.0	4.1	3.9	3.4	2.2	3.0	2.7	3.1	3.5	4.4
Retail trade	3.2	3.4	3.4	2.7	2.7	2.4	2.8	2.6	3.8	4.4
FIRE	3.8	5.2	4.6	4.3	4.2	4.8	4.2	4.1	3.8	4.1
Services	4.6	5.6	4.8	4.0	3.2	2.2	2.4	3.1	3.5	4.2

Source: U.S. Department of Labor, Bureau of Labor Statistics. Based on annual averages of seasonally adjusted monthly data.

NOTES FOR CHAPTER 1

1. This is the sample size as of August 1997. The sample size has changed over the years, peaking at 60,000 in the period from April 1989 to October 1994. The sample size was 58,000 from November 1994 to August 1995; 56,300 from September 1995 to December 1996. See "Characteristics of the CPS Sample," *Monthly Labor Review,* February 1997, Table 1-A, p. 145.
2. U.S. Department of Labor, Bureau of Labor Statistics, Labor Force, Employment, and Unemployment from the Current Population Survey," *BLS Handbook of Methods,* September 1992, Bulletin 2414, p. 4.
3. Ibid.
4. U.S. Department of Labor, Bureau of Labor Statistics, *Briefing Materials on the Redesigned Current Population Survey,* November 16-17, 1993, p. 13.
5. This is the survey size as of April 1997.
6. Roy H. Webb and William Whelpley, "Labor Market Data," *Macroeconomic Data: A User's Guide,* 1990, Federal Reserve Bank of Richmond, p. 18.
7. Industrial classification refers to the grouping of reporting establishments into industries on the basis of their major product or activity as determined by the establishments' percent of total sales or receipts. Data are currently classified in accordance with the *Standard Industrial Classification Manual,* Office of Management and Budget, 1987. The two-digit reference is in regard to the level of aggregation of data. Industries can be narrowly or broadly defined as at the two-digit level, as listed in the main text.
8. See U.S. Department of Labor, Bureau of Labor Statistics, "Current Employment Statistics Survey: Refining Seasonal Adjustment Procedures to Account for Varying Survey Intervals: The Effect of 4 or 5 Weeks," Mimeo, March 8, 1996.
9. The other sectoral components in industrial production are mining and public utilities.
10. These composite indexes were revised to their current form with the March 3, 1989, release for January 1989 estimates.

BIBLIOGRAPHY

Bowie, Chester E., Lawrence S. Cahoon, and Elizabeth A. Martin. "Overhauling the Current Population Survey: Evaluating Changes in the Estimates," *Monthly Labor Review,* U.S. Department of Labor, September 1993, pp. 29–33.

Bregger, John E., and Cathryn S. Dippo. "Overhauling the Current Population Survey: Why Is It Necessary to Change?" *Monthly Labor Review,* U.S. Department of Labor, September 1993, pp. 3–9.

Bureau of Labor Statistics, U.S. Department of Labor. *Briefing Materials on the Redesigned Current Population Survey,* November 16–17, 1993.

———. "Current Employment Statistics Survey: Refining Seasonal Adjustment Procedures to Account for Varying Survey Intervals: The Effect of 4 or 5 Weeks," Mimeo, March 8, 1996.

———. Employment, Hours, and Earnings from the Establishment Survey," Ibid., pp. 13–27.

———. "Explanatory Notes," *Employment and Earnings,* November 1992, pp. 130–158.

———. "Labor Force, Employment, and Unemployment from the Current Population Survey," *BLS Handbook of Methods,* April 1988, Bulletin 2285, pp. 3–12.

————. "Revisions in the Current Population Survey Effective January 1997," *Employment and Earnings,* February 1997, p. 3.

————. "Revision of Payroll Survey Employment Estimates to March 1991 Benchmarks," News release, June 3, 1992.

Green, Gloria. "Comparing Employment Estimates from Household and Payroll Surveys," *Monthly Labor Review,* U.S. Department of Labor, December 1969, pp. 9–20.

Polivka, Anne E., and Jennifer M. Roghgeb. "Overhauling the Current Population Survey: Redesigning the CPS Questionnaire," *Monthly Labor Review,* U.S. Department of Labor, September 1993, pp. 10–28.

Tiller, Richard, and Michael Welch. "Predicting the National Unemployment Rate That the 'Old' CPS Would Have Produced," Bureau of Labor Statistics, CPS Bridge Team Technical Report 2, Revised March 15, 1994.

Webb, Roy H., and William Whelpley. "Labor Market Data," *Macroeconomic Data: A User's Guide,* Federal Reserve Bank of Richmond, 1990, pp. 17–24.

CHAPTER 2

THE PERSONAL INCOME REPORT

The personal income report, which also includes personal outlays and saving, is produced by the Bureau of Economic Analysis (BEA) in tandem with the GDP release. Personal income and its components are part of the quarterly GDP national income and product accounts (NIPA), but are released as a separate set of monthly indicators the next business day after the GDP report. This is generally during the fourth week of the month following the reference month.

Personal income is a broad measure of household income. It is important because it is one of the primary measures of the health of the economy: it reflects the ability of consumers to make purchases. Over the long run or business cycle in particular, personal income is considered to be the primary determinant of household spending, which is one of the main reasons that data on personal income are closely tracked. Also, personal consumption accounts for about two-thirds of final demand in the economy and is part of the personal income report. The importance of personal income is demonstrated by the fact that it is one of the four components of the index generally used to define turning points in the business cycle—the Conference Board's index of coincident indicators.[1]

Since the personal income report is an integral part of the effort to produce data for the national income and product accounts, data are derived for both the income and product (or expenditure) sides of the NIPA accounting ledger. On the expenditure side, the personal income report details the disposition of personal income. Disposition of personal income gives us data series for personal outlays (mainly personal consumption), personal taxes, and personal saving. Through the accounting process, disposable personal income is also derived.

The monthly report is known as *Personal Income and Outlays* but these data are also published in the Commerce Department's *Survey of Current Business* and in the *Federal Reserve Bulletin,* a secondary source. Data for personal income, outlays, taxes, and saving are available in both monthly and quarterly form, not seasonally adjusted and seasonally adjusted, and in both current- and constant-dollar series. As is the case for most NIPA series, personal income and disposition data are expressed in annualized rates—that is, the income level should that month's income flow continue at the same rate for an entire year.

Monthly personal income and disposition of income series are subject to revision until the quarter inclusive of the reference month is closed out for GDP revisions. This means that monthly data can be revised for two to four months after the initial release depending on whether the reference month is early or late in a given quarter. Annual revisions are usually released in July, along with GDP revisions, and typically cover the previous three calendar years and earlier monthly releases of the current year. See summary tables of personal income and disposition from 1970 to 1997 at the end of this chapter.

PERSONAL INCOME AND DISPOSITION: OVERVIEW

Personal income is derived by the BEA from a number of sources. Early estimates for both the income and expenditure sides are often based on different sources from later estimates in annual or benchmark revisions.

As mentioned above, personal income is part of the NIPA system. Specifically, the BEA has created a Personal Income and Outlay Account in which the total personal income equals total disposition of personal income. That is, the dollar value of sum of all personal income components equals all of the uses of personal income. This is seen on the two sides of the ledger (see Table 2–1). As shown, the three basic uses or ways to dispose of personal income are: paying taxes, making outlays, and saving.

Components and Sources of Personal Income:

The first key series in this report is, of course, total personal income. According to the *Survey of Current Business,* personal income is "the income received by persons from all sources, that is from participation in production, from transfer payments from government and business, and from government interest, which is treated like a transfer payment."[2]

Personal income includes wage and salary disbursements, other labor income, proprietors' income (farm and nonfarm) after inventory valuation and capital consumption adjustments, rental income of persons (with capital consumption adjustment), dividends, personal interest income, and transfer payments to persons from both business and government. After these income estimates are summed, personal contributions for social insurance are subtracted to define total personal income.

Wage and Salary Disbursements
By far the largest component of personal income is wage and salary disbursements. For example, this component was 56 percent of nominal personal income in 1997. It broadly covers monetary earnings of employees. Wage and salary disbursements "consists of the monetary remuneration of employees, including the compensation of corporate officers; commissions, tips, and bonuses; and receipts in kind that represent income to the recipients."[3]

Wage and salary data are derived at the industry level and then aggregated. Data are generally analyzed at a moderate level of aggregation, such as for commodity-producing industries (including manufacturing), distributive industries, and service industries. These are for the private sector. There is also a separate wage and salary component for government and government enterprises.

TABLE 2–1

Personal Income and Its Disposition*

	Billions of Current Dollars	
	1996	*1997*
Personal income	6,495.2	6,874.4
Wage and salary disbursements	3,632.5	3,877.2
Private industries	2,989.9	3,211.8
Commodity-producing industries	909.1	960.1
Manufacturing	674.7	705.9
Distributive industries	823.3	876.0
Service industries	1,257.5	1,375.6
Government	642.6	665.4
Other labor income	407.6	416.6
Proprietors' income with inventory evaluation and capital consumption adjustments (CCA)	520.3	544.7
Farm	37.2	40.9
Nonfarm	483.1	503.8
Rental income of persons with CCA	146.3	148.1
Personal dividend income	291.2	321.5
Personal interest income	735.7	768.8
Transfer payments to persons	1,068.0	1,121.1
Less: Personal contributions for social insurance	306.3	323.6
Disposition of Personal Income		
Personal income	6,495.2	6,874.4
Less: Personal tax and nontax payments	886.9	987.9
Equals: Disposable personal income	5,608.3	5,886.6
Less: Personal outlays	5,368.8	5,661.0
Personal consumption expenditures	5,207.6	5,488.6
Interest paid by persons	145.2	154.5
Personal transfer payments to the rest of world (net)	15.9	17.9
Equals: Personal saving	239.6	225.6
Addenda: Personal saving as percentage of disposable personal income	4.3	3.8

*Disposable personal income in chained (1992) dollars equals the current-dollar figure divided by the implicit price deflator for personal consumption expenditures.

Source: U.S. Department of Commerce, *Survey of Current Business,* February 1998.

Sources for data vary by components. For most private-sector wage and salary disbursements, annual estimates are based on wage data from reports filed with state employment security agencies by employers. For industries not subject to state unemployment insurance taxes—namely, for farms, railroads, private households, and nonprofit membership organizations—a variety of other sources are used. For manufacturing, earnings are divided between wages and salaries according to the ratio of production worker earnings to total earnings (based on information from the Census Bureau's Annual Survey of Manufactures and, to a lesser degree, from BLS monthly production worker data.) Annual wages and salaries data for federal civilian employees are obtained primarily from the Office of Personnel Management, while military wages and salaries figures come from the Department of Defense.

Monthly estimates for most private industries are derived by extrapolation using changes in the product of BLS data on employment, hours, and earnings from wages. This information is part of BLS's monthly employment report. For manufacturing, salaries are estimated separately. Other monthly wage and salary component estimates, such as for government, are largely simple extrapolations primarily based on recent employment and earnings trends.

Other Components of Personal Income

"Other labor income" is basically employer contributions to private pensions and private welfare funds. Group health insurance is over half of this component, and pensions and workers' compensation are large subcomponents. This category also includes supplemental unemployment and directors' fees. However, this personal income component does not include contributions to publicly administered funds, such as social security, nor does it include civilian government employees retirement funds. Annual data for other labor income series primarily come from the IRS and the U.S. Department of Health and Human Services. Monthly estimates for other labor income are extrapolations based on BLS employment figures.

Proprietors' income with inventory valuation and capital consumption adjustments is the monetary and in-kind incomes of proprietorships and partnerships after taking into account two special factors. To more accurately measure profits, Proprietors' income is originally available in a form that includes inventory changes and depreciation charges but these allowances do not necessarily reflect appropriate economic accounting to measure current income. Instead, these figures have usually been distorted by inflation and tax laws. Therefore, the inventory valuation adjustment is the difference between changes in inventories valued in current period prices and the value reported on a historical basis. The capital consumption adjustment (CCA) is the difference between depreciation based on tax returns and those based on economic service lives, straight-line depreciation, and replacement cost. This personal income component excludes interest and dividend income received by proprietors as well as most rental income. If the primary business of the person receiving rental income is real estate, then the rental income is included.

Annual estimates for proprietors' income are derived from several sources, including the IRS and the U.S. Department of Agriculture (USDA). Monthly estimates of farm income are based on annual projections for farm income published by the USDA with monthly interpolations to account for natural disasters and any unusual changes in prices, crop yields, or subsidy payments. Monthly estimates for the nonfarm component are extrapolations and interpolations by industry and are estimated using a variety of data for projections, including Census Bureau data for retail sales and value of new single-family housing put-in-place.

Rental income of persons with capital consumption adjustment contains both monetary and imputed components. The monetary component is personal income from the rental of real property; as noted above, however, the income of persons primarily earning their income in the real estate business is allocated to proprietors' income. Rental income also includes an imputed component for net rental income of owner-occupants of nonfarm dwellings. These owner-occupants are treated in a strict economic sense as renting their houses to themselves and deriving imputed income and an equal amount of personal consumption of housing services (after taking into account intermediate goods and services used in maintaining the houses). Finally, this personal income component includes royalties paid to persons from patents, copyrights, and rights to natural resources.

Annual estimates for the monetary net rental income components are primarily based on data from the Census Bureau's Annual Housing Survey (AHS) for income from residential properties and from the IRS for income from nonresidential properties. The Census Bureau data provide information on the number of housing units and average rent per unit, but the BEA must make its own estimates for various expenses netted against rent from residential properties. Some rental income from farm realty to nonfarm landlords come from the Department of Agriculture, and royalty income is derived from IRS data. For the imputed net rental income of owner-occupied nonfarm residential properties, estimates are based on housing units from the AHS and on BEA estimates for the imputed rents and expenses. However, the imputed rent figures are derived from actual rents for tenant-occupied units with comparable housing characteristics. Monthly estimates for rent components are interpolations of annual estimates for past years and extrapolations of past years for months of the current year, with adjustments for natural disasters and changes in property tax rates.

Dividends are "payments in cash or other assets, excluding stock, by corporations organized for profit to stockholders who are U.S. persons."[4] Annual estimates for dividends are from IRS data for corporate income tax returns, with various adjustments by the BEA. These adjustments include Federal Reserve and other federal banks and dividends to U.S. persons from the rest of the world. Exclusions are made for capital gains and return of capital distribution, dividends paid to other U.S. corporations (these profits remain in the business sector), and for dividends paid to non-U.S. residents and to pension plans. Following the most recent IRS tabulation, annual data are derived from data from the Federal Trade Commission for manufacturing, mining, and trade industries; from various regulatory agencies for transportation and utilities industries; and from a BEA sample of publicly reporting companies for other industries.[5] Monthly estimates are interpolations for historical years and extrapolations from recent months based on the BEA's sample of publicly reporting corporations.

Personal interest income is monetary and in-kind (imputed) interest income of persons from all sources. Monetary personal interest income is derived as a net flow of interest paid and received by consumers with the government and business sectors. Mortgage payments by consumers are excluded from these calculations since, for home purchases, consumers are treated as business entities.

The imputed component is for earnings (1) from life insurance carriers and private noninsured pension plans and (2) from "services furnished without payment by financial intermediaries except life insurance carriers and private noninsured pension plans."[6] For personal interest income, about 45 percent is imputed interest income. Roughly 60 percent of this is accrued interest income on insurance policies and pension funds. For these funds, interest is counted the year it is earned, rather than the year it is withdrawn or paid out, and an imputation is required. The rest of the imputed interest income is interest returns made by financial institutions on personal accounts above the monetary interest actually paid to individuals. Basically, this is the imputed income paying for various financial services such as checking accounts, no-fee travelers checks, and so forth. Combined with monetary interest received by individuals, this is basically the opportunity cost of holding the funds in these accounts. The BEA assumes that individuals implicitly earn the market rate even though not all of it is received in actual monies. On the expenditure side of the NIPA ledger, the BEA also creates imputed personal consumption for these financial services, which equals the income component.

The methodology for estimating annual interest income is somewhat complex but is based on data from the IRS, the Treasury Department, the Federal Trade Commission, the Federal Deposit Insurance Corporation, the Census Bureau, and the Federal Reserve. Recent monthly estimates are extrapolations based on debt outstanding from regulatory agencies and on recent interest rates.

Transfer payments to persons generally are monetary payments for which current services are not rendered. These transfer payments are from both government and business. For businesses, transfers are for gifts to nonprofit institutions and for bad debt from the consumer sector. Government transfer payments are made under a number of programs, including federal old-age, survivors, disability, and hospital insurance; supplementary medical insurance; unemployment insurance for federal and state employees and for railroad employees; government retirement and railroad retirement; workers' compensation; veterans benefits and veterans life insurance; food stamps; black lung; supplemental security income; direct relief; and earned income credit. Government payments to nonprofit institutions are also included. These are to nonprofit institutions serving households, for example, the Red Cross or universities offering scholarships funded by government.

Corporate transfers are estimated with data from the IRS; preliminary annual and monthly figures are extrapolations. Federal government transfers are based primarily on the Budget of the United States, Treasury Department data, and various agency data for specific programs. For state and local government transfer payment series, estimates are dependent upon Census Bureau surveys and reports from federal agencies funding specific nonfederal programs. Recent monthly figures are extrapolations.

Personal contributions for social insurance are the payments made by employees, the self-employed, and other persons participating in the applicable programs (for example, the food stamp program does not involve personal contributions) listed under transfer payments. Annual estimates for contributions to federal programs are based on data from the Social Security Administration and the Treasury Department, among others. Yearly data for contributions to state and local programs are derived from figures from the Census Bureau and from the Department of Labor. Monthly estimates for contribution subcomponents are based on monthly wages and salaries estimates and applicable tax rates.

Personal Taxes and Nontax Payments: Components and Sources

Personal tax and nontax payments are "tax payments (net of refunds) by persons (except personal contributions for social insurance) that are not chargeable to business expense, and contain other personal payments to general government that it is convenient to treat like taxes."[7] At the federal level, the subcomponents are for income taxes, estate and gift taxes, and "other." Personal income taxes have been about 97 to 98 percent of the federal tax and nontax payment totals. At the state level, income taxes also provide the bulk of personal taxes and nontax payments, running at roughly at 75 percent of the total. The rest is a variety of nontaxes and "other." Sales taxes and property taxes are considered to be indirect business taxes and are not part of the disposition of personal income. Since homeowners are treated as businesses, property taxes are treated as taxes on business and are moved from the household sector to the business sector.

Personal taxes and nontax payments do not cover all sources of receipts for government. The concept of overall receipts differs significantly from that of personal taxes and nontax payments. Government receipts also come from such sources as direct corporate taxes, indirect taxes on businesses and consumers, contributions for social insurance, and grants-in-aid.

Annual data for federal personal income tax withholdings are derived from Treasury Department figures, while state and local taxes data are based on the Census Bureau's *Quarterly Summary of State and Local Taxes*. Monthly data are interpolations for past years and extrapolations for recent months. For income taxes (at all levels), extrapolations are based on wage and salary estimates and changes in tax rates.

Disposable Personal Income

Personal income less personal tax and nontax payments equals disposable personal income. *Disposable personal income* is the concept that most economists use as a measure of consumer spending capacity. It is from this measure of income that consumers can choose to either spend or save and is used as a base for the calculation of the personal saving rate.

Personal Outlays: Components and Sources

There are three definitional ways in which consumers can spend or make outlays. Personal outlays consist of personal consumption expenditures (PCEs), interest paid by consumers to business, and personal transfer payments to foreigners (net). PCEs usually make up over 95 percent of personal outlays (current dollars) and, together with interest paid to business, typically account for over 99 percent of personal outlays.

Personal consumption expenditures generally are viewed as purchases of goods and services made by consumers for their own use (see Table 2–2). However, housing purchases by individuals are classified as fixed investment in the NIPA accounts; in this activity, consumers are treated as businesses. A more detailed definition of PCEs includes "Goods and services purchased by individuals, operating expenses of nonprofit institutions serving individuals, and the value of food, fuel, clothing, housing, and financial services received in kind by individuals. Net purchases of used goods are also included."[8]

Personal consumption expenditures are broken down by major type of product. The three broad categories are durables, nondurables, and services. Consumer *durables* are defined as those goods with expected lifetimes of three years or longer. Durables include motor vehicles and parts, furniture and household equipment, and "other durables." Durables purchases tend to be very cyclical because these purchases can be postponed during difficult times and because of the interest rate sensitivity caused by the need to finance most big ticket items.

Under *nondurables* are food, clothing and shoes, gasoline and oil, fuel oil and coal, and "other nondurables." Nondurables are not very cyclical because they are necessities for the most part. These purchases generally track population growth.

Finally, the *services* category covers housing services, household operation (including electricity and gas), transportation, medical care, and "other services."

TABLE 2–2

Personal Consumption Expenditures; 1997

	Dollar Amount (Billions)	Percent Share of Total
Total personal consumption expenditures	5,488.6	100.0
Durable goods	659.4	12.0
Motor vehicles and parts	262.9	4.8
Furniture & household equipment	267.6	4.9
Other	128.9	2.3
Nondurable goods	1,592.7	29.0
Food	776.4	14.1
Clothing and shoes	277.6	5.1
Gasoline and oil	124.6	2.3
Fuel oil and coal	10.9	0.2
Other	403.3	7.3
Services	3,236.5	59.0
Housing	826.4	15.1
Household operation	328.7	6.0
Electricity and gas	127.2	2.3
Other household operation	201.5	3.7
Transportation	236.3	4.3
Medical care	855.0	15.6
Other	990.1	18.0

Source: U.S. Department of Commerce, *Survey of Current Business*, February 1998.

The housing services component is basically use of dwellings, including owner-occupied nonfarm, tenant nonfarm, farm, and lodging such as hotels and motels. Transportation services' largest subcomponent is mainly for repair, rental, and leasing, with other significant subcomponents for public transportation and for insurance. "Other services" is largely personal business services (including brokerage, banking, insurance, and legal services), but it also has services subcomponents for personal care, recreation, education, and religion. By dollar volume, most services are necessities, are not very cyclical, and follow population growth.

Also, services include sizable components that are imputed rather than for which monetary payment is made. Imputed items are basically series reflecting opportunity costs, and a corresponding income series is derived for each expenditure series. The largest imputed components in services PCEs are space rent for owner-occupied housing (nonfarm and farm), employer-paid health and life insurance premiums, and services furnished without payment by financial intermediaries other than life insurance carriers and private noninsured pension plans. There are also a few imputed PCE series for nondurables but they are very minor: employer-provided food, clothing, and lodging, for example. There are no imputed components in durables PCEs.

There are a variety of sources for PCE data. For durables and nondurables, preliminary estimates for most components are based on data from the Census Bureau's monthly survey of retail trade using the retail-control method (as discussed in Chapter 3). Estimates for purchases of autos and trucks are largely based on estimates from trade sources, such as *Ward's Automotive Reports* and the American Automobile Manufacturers Association. Estimates of consumption of gasoline and oil come from the Energy Information Administration and the Bureau of Labor Statistics. The remaining minor durables and nondurables series come from various miscellaneous sources. Consumption of food furnished to employees is derived from employment data from the BLS and from federal outlays data from the Office of Management and Budget. Various federal agencies report data for expenditures by U.S. residents abroad (net).

Annual data for these durable and nondurable series often come from the same preliminary sources. Other sources for annual data are the quinquennial census and the Census Bureau's merchandise trade, among others.

Services expenditures are based on dozens of government and private sector sources for preliminary and annual estimates: for example, wage and salary data from the BLS for estimating physician, dentist, and other medical professional services; brokerage services based on transactions data from trade sources; hospital services and electricity use from private organizations.

However, preliminary estimates for a noticeable number of services subcomponents are extrapolations or judgment series because of the lack of timely data. Among these are farm housing rent; numerous medical services; financial services furnished without payment by banks, credit agencies, and investment companies; domestic services; some entertainment services; and some educational services. Annual estimates for services PCEs are generally based on trade reports and reports from numerous government agencies.

Although less closely followed by the financial community's media, PCEs are also organized by "type of expenditure" (durables, nondurables, and services are categorized by "major type of product"). The major expenditure type categories are food and tobacco; clothing, accessories, and jewelry; personal care; housing; household operation; medical care; personal business; transportation; recreation; education and research; religious and welfare activities; and foreign travel and other, net.

Interest Paid by Consumers to Business

Interest paid by consumers to business is, basically, installment credit payments. It covers payments on revolving credit, auto finance payments, personal bank loans, finance companies, and even insurance policy loans, among others. However, this category does not include mortgage payments or payments on home improvement loans because homeowners are treated as businesses in the national income and product accounts.

Personal Transfer Payments to Foreigners (Net)

Personal transfer payments to foreigners (net) is the final component of personal outlays. These are a variety of payments between U.S. residents and foreign residents and include goods, services, and financial claims. Included are cash and goods distributed abroad by various United States nonprofit organizations; some foreign government pensions forwarded to the United States; and numerous financial transfers between private residents, including through banks, communications companies, and the U.S. Postal Service. Quarterly and annual data are based on reports to the BEA by U.S. banks, nonprofit organizations, and U.S. and foreign government agencies and publications.

Personal Saving and Definitional Constraints

Personal saving is a residual series. It is simply disposable personal income less personal outlays (not just PCEs). While personal income, taxes, and outlays are all derived from many independent sources, there are no sources used specifically for the purpose of estimating personal saving. Personal saving is derived through an accounting identity after personal income, taxes, and outlays are estimated.

The personal saving rate is the ratio of personal saving to disposable personal income. Because personal saving is an accounting derivative of several large components, the personal saving rate is quite volatile. Small movements in personal income, taxes, and outlays can lead to relatively large movements in the much smaller personal saving series and, in turn, the personal saving rate.

FARM SUBSIDIES

As mentioned above, farm income in the personal sector is included under proprietors' farms income. Federal subsidies are the primary source of volatility in this component. There are two basic types of farm subsidies in the United States:

price subsidies and payments from the Conservation Reserve Program. Price subsidies are deficiency payments to farmers and are the difference between a target price (set by Congress) for a given crop and the market price. The Conservation Reserve Program is used to reduce acreage planted for various crops; the federal government makes a "rental payment" for not planting.

Farm subsidy payments are not seasonally adjusted since there is some variation in the timing of payments. Typically, farm program legislation is written for five-year periods and the timing of subsidy payments has varied with different five-year plans. Currently, Conservation Reserve Program payments are usually made in October, while deficiency payments are crop-dependent for the timing. The Agriculture Department now makes an estimate for a given year's deficiency, and an advance payment is made at the time that farmers sign up for the program. The advance is one-half of the expected deficiency and the remainder is paid after the end of the crop season. From February to May there are usually heavy final payments for the previous year and for advances for the coming year.

NATURAL DISASTERS

Natural disasters can have a major impact on personal income and some impact on personal consumption. The biggest impact on personal income is in terms of depreciation expenses—that is, capital consumption. Damage to assets directly lowers personal income components for rental income and proprietors' income. For initial estimates the BEA makes an upward adjustment for its estimate of depreciation expenses that would be included on an accounting basis in IRS data (from which the BEA extrapolates initial figures). The BEA also raises its estimates for the adjustments to capital consumption allowances for rental income and proprietors' income. These adjustments transform the accounting-based depreciation to an economic basis. These higher depreciation expenses and capital consumption adjustments are made on an incurred basis and affect the month in which a natural disaster occurs. For example, Hurricane Andrew, which hit south Florida and Louisiana in late August 1992, caused a large decline in personal income for August 1992 primarily owing to dramatic falls in proprietors' income (farm and nonfarm) and rental income. A modest part of the decline was due to the loss of revenues, but the vast majority was a result of accelerated depreciation and adjustments to capital consumption allowances.

For the farm sector, the impact of natural disasters on proprietors' income is heavily dependent on the type of natural disaster. (The farm sector is represented in personal income only in the farm proprietors' income subcomponent—that is, farm income of personal income.) Disasters affect farm income through higher capital consumption because of damage to structures and equipment and revenues lost due to damage to crops and livestock. Not all natural disasters affect farm facilities, however. Hurricanes damage property whereas a drought does not.

When there is asset damage, farm income is adjusted by two factors: There is higher consumption of fixed capital, which is raised by the market value of structures and equipment destroyed or damaged. Property insurance expenditures are lowered by insurance indemnities earned (incurred as opposed to received). Basically, farm income is reduced by the amount of uninsured property losses. There is a one-time adjustment for farm residential and service structures.

The third and final adjustment to farm income is for crop (and livestock, if applicable) losses. Crops represent current income and are not considered assets. In contrast to asset damage, crop losses frequently are not recognized all at once. Crop revenues are usually heavily seasonal, and the BEA distributes estimated revenues (based on projections from the U.S. Department of Agriculture) over the entire year. Once crop damages have occurred, revenues for the rest of the year are usually lowered. This is a general rule; allocation of crop losses is very dependent upon the type of disaster (e.g., hurricane versus extended drought) as well as the types of crops affected.

Wage and salary figures are usually adjusted to a small degree to take into account the impact of natural disasters. Taxes and contributions to social insurance, which are initially estimated using wage and salary estimates and appropriate tax rates, are also affected by disasters owing to this methodological tie to wages and salaries. Adjustments to wages and salaries are made regardless of whether the relevant month's payroll employment and earnings data from the BLS capture the impact (that is, whether the disaster is before or after the survey week for that month's employment reports).

The only major effect on personal consumption typically occurs for services consumption for property insurance. However, the impact is only the current dollar component, which is on a net basis: premiums paid less benefits received. A jump in benefits received causes a decline in this services component; benefits are estimated on an incurred basis. In contrast, the constant-dollar subcomponent for this insurance is based on gross payments, which are then deflated. Hence, benefits paid do not affect the constant-dollar services series. Monthly real figures continue to be based on trend, while the nominal data are significantly affected by natural disasters.

For rental income, natural disasters typically cause some accelerated depreciation for the imputed series for owner-occupied housing as well as for the other types of rental income. However, there is usually no impact on housing services consumption for owner-occupied housing. Normally, the impact of natural disasters on the local housing stock is negligible relative to the U.S. stock and no adjustment is made to this imputed consumption component. For Hurricane Andrew, a minor adjustment was made to the imputed housing services component in services personal consumption. This was the first natural disaster to be large enough to cause such an adjustment in this outlays component.

Generally, no other special adjustments are made for estimates of personal consumption expenditures at times of natural disasters. Data from standard sources, such as retail sales and industry reports on motor vehicle sales, are used "as is" in deriving other PCE subcomponents. If a natural disaster affects retail sales data, then that impact will carry through to PCE figures. There are no special adjustments. However, the impact on national data is rarely discernable owing to the size of the U.S. economy relative to the area affected by a natural disaster.

In sum, natural disasters can dramatically affect personal income at the national level because of the effect of accelerated depreciation (and loss of farm income when applicable). Generally, there is no noticeable impact on real PCEs, but nominal PCEs can be negatively affected through insurance benefits received (on an incurred basis) being lowered by a drop in net insurance premiums.

KEYS TO ANALYZING THE MONTHLY REPORT

Because consumer spending is so critical to the health of the economy, the monthly personal income report is closely watched by financial markets. Analysts look to see whether there are changes in the underlying ability of consumers to spend through changes in income growth and whether consumer support for the economy is in the process of changing. Over the business cycle, personal income is a coincident indicator, tracking peaks and troughs and providing the fuel for consumer spending—a major force in the economy. Within personal consumption, nondurables and services growth is relatively stable, being largely dependent on population growth. Nondurables such as clothing also appears to be very price-sensitive and affected by the cost of imports. Durables are interest-rate sensitive and dependent on demographics to the extent that housing (and, in turn, household durables) and automobile markets are affected.

For measuring the current strength of consumer spending power, the broadest measure of personal income is not always the best indicator of monthly changes in consumers' ability to spend. Total personal income can be affected by temporary factors that do not really affect the typical consumer. The most frequent distortion is probably caused by gyrations in farm proprietors' income, as government subsidy payments are large and irregular and are not seasonally adjusted. This problem of farm subsidy payments can be avoided by watching changes in nonfarm personal income, which is less volatile than total personal income. By definition, nonfarm personal income equals total personal income less farm proprietors' income, farm wages, farm other labor income and agricultural net interest.

However, nonfarm personal income also includes a number of components that do not quickly translate into consumer purchasing power. For example, dividend income is usually not a major factor in affecting near-term spending. Monthly gyrations are of minor importance (although longer changes in the trend can affect consumers' willingness to spend). Natural disasters also impact personal income significantly because of depreciation expenses (see section below) but have less impact on spending patterns. The wages and salaries component of personal income avoids most of these problems and is a good measure of consumer ability to spend since it is directly tied to the health of the labor sector. The wages and salaries series is methodologically tied to payroll employment, hours worked, and hourly earnings. Its importance in personal income is underscored by the fact that it was almost 56 percent of personal income in 1997.

The argument is often made that disposable personal income is the best measure to track because it takes into account changes in taxes as well as changes in gross earnings. It is what consumers can spend. By definition, disposable personal income is the measure from which consumers can choose to spend or save. However, in tracking recent monthly data, disposable personal income has the same volatility problems as total personal income. Therefore, unless there are noticeable changes in tax rates or withholdings over the time period under study, the wages and salaries component is probably the best indicator of the near-term health of the consumer.[9]

For personal consumption expenditures, the durables and nondurables series largely reflect the appropriate retail sales series[10] and unit new auto and light truck sales. The services series are derived from a wide array of industry sources, although early estimates are largely extrapolations.

Most of the volatility in durables PCEs is attributable to changes in sales of autos and light trucks and to how the BEA includes the sales in PCEs. Even though motor vehicles have long lives and in reality depreciate slowly over time, the BEA assumes that motor vehicles are fully depreciated at the time of purchase. In fact, the BEA counts basically the entire purchase price as the amount entering into the personal consumption data.[11] Neither the amount of down payment nor the monthly payment is a factor.

The primary consideration by the BEA for choosing to fully depreciate a vehicle at time of sale is that this accounting method does not change the BEA's overall measure of GDP, since a fully depreciated vehicle is shifted from one GDP account (perhaps inventories) to another (durables PCEs) without incorrectly measuring overall production. The BEA agrees that using some type of depreciation schedule would be more technically correct but would complicate the accounting procedures without improving the overall measure of GDP. However, in a true economic sense, some distortions remain in the monthly personal consumption figures and in personal saving.

Because personal saving is a residual of disposable personal income and personal outlays, the method of calculating personal consumption affects personal saving and the personal saving rate. For months when motor vehicle sales rise over previous rates, the personal saving rate declines significantly (assuming no change in recent trends in disposable personal income) because motor vehicle sales are fully depreciated at the time of purchase. Similarly, a relative decline in auto and light truck sales leads to an upswing in the personal saving rate. Studies indicate that the BEA method of treating durables as fully depreciated at the time of sale does raise the volatility of the personal saving rate.[12]

The personal saving rate is quite volatile on a monthly basis since it is a small residual of several much larger components. Small movements in personal income, outlays, or even taxes lead to larger relative movement in the level of personal saving. It is primarily for this reason that the BEA only reports a three-month average for the personal saving rate even though the data are available for calculating the most recent month.

Despite popular opinion to the contrary, monthly movements in the personal saving rate do not directly reflect changes in consumers' monetary saving at financial institutions. The BEA measure of personal saving is not a measure of saving at financial institutions and should not be construed as such. The earlier mentioned effect of auto purchases on personal saving is a clear example of a divergence between popular concepts of financial flows versus those measured in the BEA data. The practical interpretation of the impact of a surge in durables consumption is not necessarily that consumers "dipped into their savings" but that consumers assumed further debt. A decline in the level of personal saving in the personal income accounts does not directly reflect activity in personal savings accounts. To get a measure of saving at financial institutions, the "flow of funds" data published by the Federal Reserve Board is more appropriate.

KEY ROLES IN THE ECONOMY AND UNDERLYING FUNDAMENTALS

Personal income is primarily a coincident indicator (once transfer payments are excluded). It cyclically tracks employment but with larger cyclical movement because of greater adjustments to changes in output with hours worked—which in turn affects aggregate earnings. However, for its impact on consumer spending, disposable income is less cyclical because of the stabilizing impact of progressive income taxes. Over the business cycle, durables PCEs are seen as a leading indicator, since durables, particularly motor vehicles, are interest rate sensitive.

Over the long run, personal consumption is affected by both growth and shifting preferences in saving. For individuals, preferences in saving are generally influenced by what stage in life one is in—as stated in the life cycle hypothesis. The basic life cycle hypothesis states that a consumer is more inclined to spend income (and less inclined to save) during youth and during old age. Before income-producing years, a consumer dissaves (consumes more than earns), and during youth, a typical consumer simply does not worry about saving. In retirement, a consumer consumes by drawing down wealth. It is during middle age—when income earning capabilities are at their peak—that consumers have the greater propensity to save for retirement and other long-term needs.

From the overall economy's perspective, the impact of the life cycle hypothesis is seen if there is an uneven distribution of the population in terms of age. For example, as the baby-boom generation ages, its life cycle phase dominates consumer spending habits. Currently, most baby boomers are in the midlife phase, saving for kids' college education and for their own retirement. However, business cycle movement usually dominates long-term factors. Nonetheless, long-term factors affect the magnitude of business cycle peaks and troughs as well as long-term trends.

KEY SOURCES OF MONTHLY VOLATILITY

Personal Income

Wages and salary disbursements closely reflect changes in employment, the average workweek, and average hourly earnings (that is, these are aggregate earnings from the BLS establishment survey). However, wage and salary disbursements can diverge from earnings owing to BEA adjustments if the employment report's survey period does not appear to be representative of the entire month. Strikes or significant differences in weather during the months are factors that can cause BEA to make adjustments. Wage and salary data are also affected by irregular bonus payments (generally other than regular commissions) that are often made in certain industries such as automobile and finance. Also, while trends in government wages and salaries are relatively even, pay raises for federal workers or Postal Service employees often lead to spikes in the data.

While it is important to understand sources of volatility in the large wages and salaries component, probably the largest overall source of volatility in total personal income is from the farm proprietors' income component. Farm subsidy payments are not seasonally adjusted, even when entered as a component of seasonally adjusted personal income. Natural disasters also cause significant changes in personal rent income and in proprietors' income, more so because of depreciation effects than temporary loss of revenues.

Personal Consumption

Personal consumption changes on a monthly basis for many very practical and technical reasons. Retailers frequently have consumer incentives (sales). For any given month or two, consumers may binge, get bills in the mail a month later, and cut back accordingly for a few months. Spending responds to the latest news in the economy about layoffs as well as favorable developments on interest rates. These sources of volatility are very real, but extracting this information requires tracking the data over years and cross-checking with other series such as consumer installment credit. When PCEs are rising quickly it is logical to ask whether sales are being funded by credit.

The number of technical factors behind monthly volatility that can be somewhat verified are few. First, some industries are relatively obvious when special incentives are given. For durables, one must track not only changes in prices (rebates) for autos, but also whether dealers are pushing leases more so than on average. Leases go under producers' durable equipment for the purchase amount rather than under durables PCEs. For nondurables, price changes affect apparel purchases significantly. Price changes are also a factor in nondurables PCEs because oil prices that can move sharply at times.

Finally, the two most volatile components of services PCEs are utilities and brokerage services. These can be tracked prior to release date reasonably well by following weekly or monthly utility production and stock market volume for the month. Unseasonable weather generally causes the largest deviations in services PCEs.

KEY QUESTIONS IN ANALYZING THE NEWS RELEASE

- How strong was the wages and salaries component?
- Were wages and salaries affected by special bonus pay in the current month or in the previous month (as in the auto industry)?

- Were January data affected by government pay increases in the wages and salaries component or by cost-of-living adjustments (COLAs) for transfer payments?
- Were overall personal income figures affected by large changes in farm subsidy payments (which are not seasonally adjusted)?
- How strong was nonfarm personal income?
- If disposable income is weak, was it due to softness in personal income growth or a rise in tax payments?
- Were any significant changes in tax payments due to temporary changes in withholdings or atypical patterns in tax returns?
- For sharp swings in personal consumption, how were the changes allocated between durables, nondurables, and services?
- Were durables gains or losses due to the promotion or discontinuation of special incentives or rebates for motor vehicles?
- Especially for apparel or for gasoline, were nondurables changes due to price changes (either higher prices or discounting)?
- Were services temporarily affected by atypical weather (utilities usage) or by swings in the stock market (brokerage fees)?
- For the personal saving rate, were changes due to changes in outlays or in disposable personal income?
- Did a swing in durables personal consumption affect the personal saving rate (since durables, especially autos, are considered fully consumed at the time of purchase)?

TABLE 2–3

Personal Income and Components, 1970–1997 ($ Billions)

Year	Personal Income, Total	Wage and Salary Disbursement	Other Labor Income	Proprietors' Income, Total with CCA	Farm Proprietors' Income with CCA
1970	836.1	551.5	32.5	78.0	14.8
1971	898.9	583.9	36.7	83.9	15.5
1972	987.3	638.7	43.0	95.2	19.5
1973	1,105.6	708.7	49.2	113.3	32.6
1974	1,213.3	772.6	56.5	111.3	25.9
1975	1,315.6	814.6	66.0	116.5	24.2
1976	1,455.4	899.5	79.7	127.5	18.7
1977	1,611.4	993.9	94.7	140.8	18.0
1978	1,820.3	1,120.8	110.1	162.1	22.9
1979	2,049.7	1,255.9	124.3	177.3	26.6
1980	2,285.7	1,377.7	139.8	168.0	13.8
1981	2,560.4	1,517.6	153.0	178.3	23.7
1982	2,718.7	1,593.9	165.4	169.9	16.4
1983	2,891.7	1,685.3	177.2	181.7	6.0
1984	3,205.5	1,855.1	188.9	237.9	24.8
1985	3,439.6	1,995.9	203.1	257.4	24.9
1986	3,647.5	2,116.6	216.0	267.8	25.2
1987	3,877.3	2,272.7	235.4	292.9	32.4
1988	4,172.8	2,453.6	251.7	322.9	28.2
1989	4,489.3	2,598.1	273.1	345.0	36.8
1990	4,791.6	2,757.5	300.6	361.0	36.3
1991	4,968.5	2,827.6	322.7	362.9	30.2
1992	5,277.2	2,986.4	351.3	423.8	37.1
1993	5,519.2	3,089.6	385.1	450.8	32.4
1994	5,791.8	3,240.7	405.0	471.6	36.9
1995	6,150.8	3,429.5	406.8	488.9	23.4
1996	6,495.2	3,632.5	407.6	520.3	37.2
1997	6,874.4	3,877.2	416.6	544.7	40.9

Sources: U.S. Department of Commerce, including "Personal Income and Outlays: July 1997," News Release, August 29, 1997. *Survey of Current Business,* February 1998.

TABLE 2–3 (*Continued*)

Personal Income and Components, 1970–1997 ($ Billions)

Rental Income, Personal	Dividend Income, Personal	Interest Income, Personal	Transfer Payments to Persons	Personal Contributions for Social Insurance
24.7	23.5	69.2	84.6	27.9
25.8	23.5	75.8	100.1	30.7
25.7	25.5	81.8	111.8	34.5
27.4	27.6	94.1	127.9	42.6
27.5	29.6	112.4	151.3	47.9
26.6	29.2	123.0	190.2	50.4
26.3	35.0	134.6	208.3	55.5
24.7	39.5	155.7	223.3	61.2
26.5	44.3	184.5	241.6	69.8
28.4	50.5	223.5	270.7	81.0
35.3	57.5	274.7	321.4	88.6
45.7	67.2	337.2	365.9	104.5
47.6	66.9	379.2	408.1	112.3
47.2	77.4	403.2	439.4	119.7
51.0	79.4	472.3	453.6	132.7
49.1	88.3	508.4	486.5	149.0
42.3	105.1	543.3	518.6	162.1
45.5	101.1	560.0	543.3	173.7
55.7	109.9	595.5	577.6	194.2
52.4	130.9	674.5	626.0	210.8
61.4	142.9	704.4	687.8	223.9
68.4	153.6	699.3	769.9	235.8
79.4	159.4	667.2	858.2	248.4
105.7	185.3	651.0	912.0	260.3
124.4	204.8	668.1	954.7	277.5
132.8	251.9	718.9	1,015.0	293.1
146.3	291.2	735.7	1,068.0	306.3
148.1	321.5	768.8	1,121.1	323.6

TABLE 2–4

Personal Income and Disposition, 1970–1997 ($ Billions)

Year	Personal Income, Total	Personal Tax and Nontax Payments	Disposable Personal Income	Personal Outlays	Personal Saving	Personal Saving Rate
1970	836.1	109.0	727.1	666.1	61.0	8.4
1971	898.9	108.7	790.2	721.6	68.6	8.7
1972	987.3	132.0	855.3	791.6	63.6	7.4
1973	1,105.6	140.6	965.0	875.4	89.6	9.3
1974	1,213.3	159.1	1,054.2	956.6	97.6	9.3
1975	1,315.6	156.4	1,159.2	1,054.8	104.4	9.0
1976	1,455.4	182.4	1,273.0	1,176.7	96.4	7.6
1977	1,611.4	210.0	1,401.4	1,308.9	92.5	6.6
1978	1,820.3	240.2	1,580.1	1,467.6	112.6	7.1
1979	2,049.7	280.2	1,769.5	1,639.5	130.1	7.4
1980	2,285.7	312.4	1,973.3	1,811.5	161.9	8.2
1981	2,560.4	360.2	2,200.2	2,001.1	199.1	9.1
1982	2,718.7	371.4	2,347.3	2,141.8	205.5	8.8
1983	2,891.7	369.3	2,522.4	2,355.5	167.0	6.6
1984	3,205.5	395.5	2,810.0	2,574.4	235.7	8.4
1985	3,439.6	437.7	3,002.0	2,795.8	206.2	6.9
1986	3,647.5	459.9	3,187.6	2,991.1	196.5	6.2
1987	3,877.3	514.2	3,363.1	3,194.7	168.4	5.0
1988	4,172.8	532.0	3,640.8	3,451.7	189.1	5.2
1989	4,489.3	594.8	3,894.4	3,706.7	187.7	4.8
1990	4,791.6	624.8	4,166.8	3,958.1	208.7	5.0
1991	4,968.5	624.8	4,343.7	4,097.4	246.4	5.7
1992	5,277.2	650.5	4,626.7	4,341.0	285.6	6.2
1993	5,519.2	690.0	4,829.2	4,580.7	248.5	5.1
1994	5,791.8	739.1	5,052.7	4,842.1	210.6	4.2
1995	6,150.8	795.1	5,355.7	5,101.1	254.6	4.8
1996	6,495.2	886.9	5,608.3	5,368.8	239.6	4.3
1997	6,874.4	987.9	5,886.6	5,661.0	225.6	3.8

68

TABLE 2–5
Personal Income: Outlays and Subcomponents, 1970–1997 ($ Billions)

Year	Outlays	Total PCEs	Durables PCEs	Nondurables PCEs	Services PCEs	Interest Paid	Transfer Payments (Net)
1970	666.1	648.1	85.0	272.0	291.1	16.8	1.2
1971	721.6	702.5	96.9	285.5	320.1	17.8	1.3
1972	791.6	770.7	110.4	308.0	352.3	19.7	1.3
1973	875.4	851.6	123.5	343.1	384.9	22.4	1.4
1974	956.6	931.2	122.3	384.5	424.4	24.2	1.3
1975	1,054.8	1,029.1	133.5	420.6	475.0	24.5	1.2
1976	1,176.7	1,148.8	158.8	458.2	531.8	26.7	1.2
1977	1,308.9	1,277.1	181.1	496.9	599.0	30.7	1.2
1978	1,467.6	1,428.8	201.4	549.9	677.4	37.5	1.3
1979	1,639.5	1,593.5	213.9	624.0	755.6	44.5	1.4
1980	1,811.5	1,760.4	213.5	695.5	851.4	49.4	1.6
1981	2,001.1	1,941.3	230.5	758.2	952.6	54.6	5.2
1982	2,141.8	2,076.8	239.3	786.8	1,050.7	58.8	6.2
1983	2,355.5	2,283.4	279.8	830.3	1,173.3	65.5	6.5
1984	2,574.4	2,492.3	325.1	883.5	1,283.6	74.7	7.4
1985	2,795.8	2,704.8	361.1	927.6	1,416.1	83.2	7.8
1986	2,991.1	2,892.7	398.7	957.2	1,536.8	90.4	8.1
1987	3,194.7	3,094.5	416.7	1,014.0	1,663.8	91.5	8.7
1988	3,451.7	3,349.7	451.0	1,081.1	1,817.6	92.9	9.1
1989	3,706.7	3,594.8	472.8	1,163.8	1,958.1	102.4	9.6
1990	3,958.1	3,839.3	476.5	1,245.3	2,117.5	108.9	9.9
1991	4,097.4	3,975.1	455.2	1,277.6	2,242.3	111.9	10.4
1992	4,341.0	4,219.8	488.5	1,321.8	2,409.4	111.7	9.6
1993	4,580.7	4,459.2	530.2	1,370.7	2,558.4	108.2	13.3
1994	4,842.1	4,717.0	579.6	1,428.4	2,709.1	110.9	14.2
1995	5,101.1	4,957.7	608.5	1,475.8	2,873.4	128.5	14.8
1996	5,368.8	5,207.6	634.5	1,534.7	3,038.4	145.2	15.9
1997	5,661.0	5,488.6	659.4	1,592.7	3,236.5	154.5	17.9

NOTES FOR CHAPTER 2

1. More specifically, the relevant component is personal income excluding the transfer payments subcomponent, and it is in 1992 dollars.
2. James C. Byrnes et al; "Monthly Estimates of Personal Income, Taxes, and Outlays," *Survey of Current Business,* U.S. Department of Commerce, November 1979, p. 19.
3. Ibid.
4. Ibid., p. 22.
5. Ibid.
6. See the table "Imputations in the National Income and Product Accounts" in any July *Survey of Current Business.*
7. Byrnes et al, "Monthly Estimates, op. cit., p. 23.
8. Carol S. Carson, "GNP: An Overview of Source Data and Estimating Methods," *Survey of Current Business,* U.S. Department of Commerce, July 1987, p. 105.
9. For initial estimates, the tax and nontax payments component is based on estimates of actual withholdings rather than on estimates of taxes owed. Changes in the withholding schedules for federal personal income taxes lowered personal taxes (and raised disposable personal income) in the second quarter of 1992 even though the tax rates were unchanged.
10. See Chapter 3, "Retail Control Series and PCEs."
11. The BEA fully depreciates all durables at the time of purchase, but motor vehicle sales are probably the most prominent for economy watchers.
12. See R. Mark Rogers, "Measuring the Personal Savings Rate: Some Technical Perspectives," *Economic Review,* Federal Reserve Bank of Atlanta, July-August 1990, p. 47.

BIBLIOGRAPHY

Byrnes, James C., et al. "Monthly Estimates of Personal Income, Taxes, and Outlays," *Survey of Current Business,* U.S. Department of Commerce, November 1979, pp. 18–38.

Carson, Carol "GNP: An Overview of Source Data and Estimating Methods," *Survey of Current Business,* U.S. Department of Commerce, July 1987, pp. 103–126.

Rogers, R. Mark. "Measuring the Personal Savings Rate: Some Technical Perspectives," *Economic Review,* Federal Reserve Bank of Atlanta, July-August 1990, pp. 38–49.

U.S. Department of Commerce, "Annual Revisions of the U.S. National Income and Product Accounts," *Survey of Current Business,* July 1992, pp. 6–43.

U.S. Department of Commerce, "Updated Summary Methodologies," *Survey of Current Business,* August 1996, pp. 81–103.

CHAPTER 3

RETAIL SALES

The retail sales series is probably the most closely followed indicator used for judging the strength of the consumer sector. In popular analysis, it also tends to be used as a broad yardstick for the health of the economy. Although this series is not a direct component of GDP, the data do figure prominently in the derivation of personal consumption expenditures within GDP, even though there are substantial differences between the series. Importantly, the retail sales series covers a broader portion of consumer spending than just department store sales, as is often portrayed by the media.

The monthly retail sales series is released by the Commerce Department around the middle of the month following the reference month. These data are published as part of the Census Bureau's Current Business Reports. Retail sales data are actually released each month with the initial release entitled Advance Monthly Retail Sales. This is the midmonth release and contains only sales data. Generally the next working day, retail inventories are made available, but for the prior reference month. About two weeks later, retail sales data for the month prior to the advance sales data are released as part of the publication *Monthly Retail Trade: Sales and Inventories*. These numbers do differ somewhat from the earlier released data owing to differences in the samples: the advance figures are based on about 3,250 establishments, while the later data are derived from the full monthly panel of about 12,500 sampling units. Sampling units can be multi-establishment companies, parts of companies, or single establishments. Data on selected groups' retail sales for the years 1980–1997 appear in the summary table at the end of this chapter.

KEY CONCEPTS

Retail sales reflect sales of merchandise for cash or credit by establishments that sell primarily to the public.[1] Some wholesale and service transactions enter the data since some establishments that are primarily engaged in retail trade also have some wholesale and service customers. Payments made on layaway, and rentals also are part of the sales figures. Manufacturers' rebates are not included, while retailer rebates are.[2] Sales and excise taxes collected directly from customers and paid directly to a local, state, or federal tax agency are excluded. While the sales figures include wholesale and service transactions made by retailers, retail transactions made by manufacturers, wholesalers, or service establishments are not included.

To be classified as a retail establishment, a store generally must have a fixed place of business and operate to sell to the general public. Firms may also buy or receive merchandise as well as act as a retailer, but they must be considered a retailer by the industry. Some processing of products may occur as long as it is not the primary function. These characteristics are general; there are some exceptions.

Retail sales data are organized by kind of business or establishment rather than by type of goods sold. Of course, many businesses, such as apparel stores, do sell a narrow range of goods, while others, such as department stores or drug stores, sell a wide variety of items. In effect, kind-of-business classifications are not the same as commodity classifications. An establishment is classified according to its primary source of receipts.

SURVEY METHODOLOGY AND REVISIONS

The Census Bureau asks approximately 13,300 retail businesses to report in the monthly Current Retail Sales Survey. Of this number, about 4,000 are also asked to participate in the Current Retail Inventory Survey. About 3,000 large retail firms are selected with certainty to report their sales each month and other large firms less regularly. The remaining businesses, selected by Employer Identification (EI) Number, are asked to report sales four times a year about 6,100 single unit firms and 2,200 small multi-unit firms (in any given month). Each rotating panel reports data for the latest two months in order to lessen the reporting burden, but there also is overlap between panels. Each panel is representative of the overall survey sample, with the entire sample stratified according to the most recent Census of Retail Trade, which occurs every five years. Since some firms go out of business and new ones begin business, updating of businesses in the survey is based on information from the Internal Revenue Service and the Social Security Administration and from annual surveys. The full sample of 31,000 companies available for the monthly surveys is updated quarterly to reflect business "births" and "deaths."

The advance estimate for a given month is based primarily on a subsample of the initial panel's data. Because of time constraints in meeting the release deadline, data from only about 3,400 firms are used instead of the full sample of about 13,300. The advance retail sales estimate is derived by applying the ratio of current month sales to previous month sales from the advance subsample to the estimate of sales levels for the previous month based on the full sample. For example, if the advance subsample reports sales up 0.2 percent (reflecting a ratio of 1.002) and the preliminary estimate for June is $1,000 million, then the July advance estimate would be $1,002 million.

The use of a small subsample does play a role in the relatively large revisions that often occur following the initial estimate. However, the major contributing factor may be that the initial panel's figures for their own firms' sales data are often estimates because they generally do not yet have access to the book value of sales when their reports to the Census Bureau are due. When the book value data are not available, the respondent is asked to provide an estimate for the full month.

Importantly, the retail firms with the largest impact on sales are included in both surveys, thereby reducing the effect of the smaller sample on revisions in data from the advance report to the preliminary report. The majority of reported sales for the advance report are based on records of the full month or the sum of four or five weeks.

"Preliminary" and "final" estimates (second and third estimates) incorporate full-panel samples rather than the 3,400 reporting unit subsample. These figures are weighted averages of data reported for those months and estimates based on ratios to earlier reported months. A small portion of respondents also report estimated sales for the preliminary estimates. Nonetheless, given that a high percentage of reported sales are based on actual data for both the preliminary and final estimates, the responses from a second rotating panel of retailers likely contributes more to the revision from the preliminary estimate to the final estimate of monthly sales.

Annual revisions to retail sales are based on an annual survey of about 22,000 firms selected from the monthly retail trade panels.

MAJOR RETAIL SALES GROUPS

The major groups (kinds of business) in retail sales are based on classifications in the 1987 edition of the *Standard Industrial Classification Manual.* Chart 3–1 gives some indication of the importance of each category.

Each kind of business category is defined by its primary activity. There are often many types of sales incorporated in a given component. Some of the more important examples of this are automotive dealers, service stations, and drugstores.

The *building materials group* includes building materials (such as lumber, paint, glass, and wallpaper), hardware, nursery stock, lawn and garden supplies,

CHART 3–1
Retail Sales (Percent Shares in 1997)

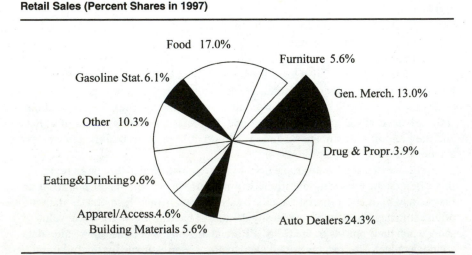

and mobile homes. Some of these establishments also sell housewares, household appliances, and, to a small degree, electronics.

Automobile dealers primarily sell new motor vehicles, but a significant portion of receipts also come from sales of used cars, boats, recreational trailers, motorcycles, auto accessories, and tires. Some stores classified as auto accessory stores also sell a wide variety of goods, such as household appliances, electronics, sporting goods, housewares, and hardware. In each case, however, the majority of the sales are automotive-related.

Furniture group stores include stores primarily selling furniture (including sleep equipment), floor covering, household appliances, and radio and television, music, electronics, and computers to the general public.

The *miscellaneous durable goods stores group* includes all retail durable goods stores not classified in the building materials, automotive, or furniture groups. This includes used merchandise stores, sporting goods stores and bicycle shops, bookstores, jewelry stores, hobby shops, camera and photographic supply stores, gift, novelty, and souvenir shops, luggage and leather goods stores, optical goods stores, and "miscellaneous retail stores not classified elsewhere."

The *general merchandise stores group* sell a broad line of nondurables. Stores in this group include department stores, variety stores, and miscellaneous general merchandise stores. Department stores have been accounting for the vast majority of sales in this group and are the most closely followed series. Mail-order houses, direct-selling establishments and a few other related kinds of businesses are no longer classified under general merchandise but are now under miscellaneous durable goods stores.

The Census Bureau officially defines department stores as follows:

Establishments normally employing 50 people or more, having sales of apparel and soft goods combined amounting to 20 percent or more of total sales, and selling each of the following lines of merchandise:

1. Furniture, home furnishings, appliances, and radio, and TV sets.

2. A general line of apparel for the family.

3. Household linens and dry goods.

To qualify as a department store, sales of each of the lines listed above must be less than 80 percent of total store sales. An establishment with total sales of $10 million or more is classified as a department store even if sales of one of the merchandise lines listed above exceed the maximum percent of total sales, provided that the combined sales of the other two groups are $1 million or more.[3]

The *food stores group* includes retail stores that primarily sell food for home preparation and consumption. This definition excludes restaurants which fall under the category of eating and drinking places. All but a very small percentage of food store sales are from grocery stores. Minor food store components are meat and fish (seafood) markets and retail bakeries. Very minor components include fruit stores and vegetable markets; candy, nut, and confectionery stores; dairy products stores; and "other miscellaneous" food stores.

The *apparel and accessory stores group* covers stores that primarily sell clothing and related accessories. The major components are: men's and boys' clothing and furnishings stores, women's ready-to-wear stores, women's accessory and specialty stores, children's and infants' wear stores, family clothing stores, shoe stores, and "miscellaneous apparel and accessory stores."

Gasoline service station sales include not only gasoline sales but also all other types of sales ranging from miscellaneous items such as soft drinks and snacks, to larger items such as tires, and even repair services. Gasoline sales, however, are the bulk of sales for this group.

Eating and drinking places are establishments that primarily sell *prepared* foods and drinks. Naturally, the two broad components of this group are eating places and drinking places. Under eating places, further classification is based on establishments selling a full menu of items versus a limited line of refreshments and prepared foods. Restaurants have full menus, waiter service, and seating for at least 15 customers. Fast-food stores are not restaurants by technical definition but fall under the category of refreshment places. Drinking establishments are defined by the primary activity of selling alcoholic beverages for consumption on the premises.

The *drug stores and proprietary stores group* consists almost entirely of drugstores by sales volume. Drugstores sell prescription drugs as well as many other related goods. These stores are not defined by prescription drug sales being the primary source of receipts but rather by trade designation. Proprietary stores do not sell prescription drugs but sell items such as health and beauty aids.

Liquor stores mainly sell packaged alcoholic beverages.

KEYS TO ANALYZING THE MONTHLY REPORT

Overview and Key Components

The nonfinancial media usually focus on department store sales since this series typifies the concept of retail sales often held by the public. However, department store sales are only one of several major components. The retail sales series truly covers a wide array of consumer spending, and analysis of retail sales should examine all major components to ascertain the health of the consumer sector. Nonetheless, some components are more important than others. Of course, sales by auto dealers are important because of their volume and because of their cyclical nature. Additionally, department store sales, while not a majority of stores, are still a sizable component. But a more appropriate series to follow for department store type sales is the general merchandise, apparel, furniture (GAF) series (discussed below). For projecting personal consumption components of durables and nondurables within real GDP, an analyst should become familiar with the concept of the retail control series. In the overall economy, retail sales have much the same role as personal consumption expenditures, except for the definitional differences; for example, there is no basic services component in retail sales. However, like wholesale sales and manufacturers' shipments, retail sales are better suited for tracking inventory and sales flows than are personal consumption expenditures and are collected by the Census Bureau on a similar statistical basis. Hence, retail sales data should be closely watched along with inventories (and even exports and imports) in order to project trends in production.

The Auto Component

The auto sales component of retail sales is fairly sizeable. From 1990 through 1997, auto sales averaged 23 percent of total retail sales. Analysts have paid close attention in trying to interpret trends in this component. As is often the case, economists have looked to another data source—unit new auto sales in this case—for additional insights. However, the typical methodology used is not appropriate, given the way these two data series are derived.

Typically, unit new auto sales and the auto component of retail sales move together on a monthly basis. When they do not, analysts are often quick to point out that the divergence is due to significant price changes. For example, if unit sales rise by 3 percent in one month while the auto component of retail sales is unchanged, the presumption is that auto dealers cut prices sharply to get the increase in sales volume. In fact, this may have occurred but cannot be proven with the two data series. These series are compiled by two completely different sources and the coverage of each series is significantly divergent.

First, the unit new sales data come from the American Automobile Manufacturers Association (formerly the Motor Vehicle Manufacturers Association) in Detroit, Michigan. The data are from an industry sample that is very close to being the full universe. That is, the data do not just *represent* all sales; for all practical purposes, they *are* all sales. There is almost no measurement or sampling error.[4]

In contrast, the auto component of retail sales comes from survey data collected by the Census Bureau. As is the case with any data derived from small sample surveys, there is sampling error. For any given month, sampling error can cause the variations in sales that often are alleged to be caused by dealer changes in prices.

The second factor that precludes any reliable monthly comparison between the unit auto data and Census series is that the auto component of retail sales is actually sales *by* auto dealers and includes sales other than automobiles. The biggest difference is that auto dealer sales figures include parts and repair. In recent years, these have become an increasingly large share of dealers' sales. Auto dealers' sales also include items such as used autos, recreational vehicles (RVs), recreational and utility trailers, motorcycles, and boats. Automobile repairs are included but only if the shops are maintained by an establishment selling new cars. These other items are not individually broken down in the figures reported to Census by auto dealers.

For two very different reasons, rarely can any significant price inferences be made between the two series on a monthly basis. To do so risks attributing sales with a trend that does not exist. As an aside there are relatively easy ways of looking at price movement for autos.

Although the data usually come out a few days later, price trends for autos are best derived from consumer price data. Also, producer price data for motor vehicles come out at about the same time as retail sales and can be used to corroborate any suspicions about price trends associated with the two auto sales series.

There is one important inference that can be made by comparing these two auto sales series. As is discussed in Chapter 13, the Commerce Department uses the unit new auto sales data in its personal consumption estimate for durables within GDP. Should the unit auto data be noticeably stronger (or weaker) than the auto component in retail sales, then the unit sales generally suggest that the durables personal consumption in constant dollars will be stronger (or weaker) for that month than implied by the Census auto sales data. This type of analysis is further elaborated in the section on "retail control," below.

Links between General Merchandise, Department Store, Chain Store, and GAF Sales

Contrary to common public perceptions, department store sales are only a small portion of retail sales. In 1997, this component's share of the total was only 10.4 percent. Of course, the general merchandise category is slightly broader than the department store definition, since variety stores and some miscellaneous general merchandise stores are also included. See Chart 3–1 for the relative importance of this sales group.

Even though general merchandise is a small component of retail sales, analysts often focus on this concept for forecasting purposes. Various national department stores (unofficial definition) release their monthly sales figures to the public about 10 days prior to the release of the Census Bureau's retail sales data. This data comes from firms such as Sears, Wal-Mart, Kmart, J. C. Penney, and others.

The difficulties in using these data to forecast retail sales are many: The announced percent changes from these so-called chain stores are year to year, not month-to-month. Some firms open new stores or close old ones, and "same-store sales" are not always available. And, of course, general merchandise sales are a small part of retail sales. Incidentally, the media usually refers to these figures as "chain store sales." However, a number of these firms—such as Kmart and Wal-Mart—come under the "discount department stores" subcomponent rather than the Census definition of "national chain department stores." Common usage and Census definitions differ.

Since the concept of department store sales is somewhat ingrained in the public's consciousness, there is a broader definition that covers this. This is the general merchandise, apparel, furniture sales (GAF) category. Simply put, GAF includes stores that specialize in department store *types* of merchandise: general merchandise stores, apparel and accessories, furniture group sales, and miscellaneous shopping goods stores. Even with this definition, this popular concept of retail sales still was just a little over one-fourth of the total of officially defined retail sales in 1997.

The Retail Control Series and PCEs

One of the primary objectives of many money market economists in analyzing the retail sales report is to derive an estimate for personal consumption expenditures (PCEs) for the same month as the latest retail sales data. The PCE data are released by the Commerce Department about two weeks later. Economists usually remove the auto component and substitute some version of unit new auto sales to "move" the forecast for monthly PCEs. However, the appropriate mover for PCEs is known as the retail control series. The retail control series is total retail sales less autos and building materials group.

The retail control series concept is based on two considerations. First, not all retail sales series conceptually apply to personal consumption expenditures. Second, some key PCE series are estimated better with source data other than retail sales.

In terms of matching concepts, retail sales of course can only be used to estimate portions of goods PCEs. Also, retail sales data include some components that are less related to consumer expenditures and more related to residential investment. The series for building materials and supply stores are excluded in the retail control concept because they reflect home ownership costs and are tied more to residential investment than to personal consumption. This group includes building materials stores, hardware stores, garden supply stores, and mobile home dealers.

In the early official definition of retail control, both auto dealers and service station sales were *also* omitted since they were estimated for their respective PCE components with source data separate from retail sales. However, the definition has changed somewhat in recent years. Over the 1980s, service station sales had a noticeable and rising share of sales that were for items other than gasoline. Since service station sales are not broken down between gasoline and nongasoline sales, the overall service station sales figures have been used to move the nongasoline components of service station sales for PCEs. Currently, the retail control series does not exclude service station sales.

Further elaboration is useful for explaining how the auto dealers component is treated to obtain the control series. First, there is a broadly defined auto dealers series. The broad series is the sum of the narrow series plus two other subcomponents: "other auto dealers" and "auto and home supply stores." These last two subcomponents are part of the control series, while the narrowly defined auto dealers series is excluded. "Other auto dealers" are primarily stores that sell motorcycles, boats, and RVs. For the advance release of retail sales data, the complicating factor is that only the broad auto dealers component and the subcomponent for auto and home supply stores are available. Therefore, the BEA must use a ratio method (from earlier data) to estimate the narrowly defined auto dealers component for exclusion until more detailed data become available. Table 3–1 details some of the differences between retail sales and PCEs.

KEY SOURCES OF MONTHLY VOLATILITY

Retail sales are affected by a number of factors in any given month. These are variability in the significant auto dealer component, various price factors, and seasonal considerations. One of the problems with the auto dealer component is rather

TABLE 3–1

Differences between Retail Sales and PCEs

Components in Retail Sales but Not in PCEs

---

1. Survey estimates of new and used motor vehicles and parts sales, including imports, business sales, and government purchases
2. Building materials, hardware, garden supplies, and mobile home dealer sales

Components in PCEs but Not in Retail Sales

---

1. Services
2. Unit new motor vehicle sales from manufacturers data
3. Dealers' margins on used car sales (which are implicitly part of used car sales in the retail sales series)
4. Gasoline and oil sales, based on Department of Transportation and Department of Labor data
5. Food and fuel produced and consumed on farms
6. Food and clothing received as compensation in kind
7. Expenditures abroad by U.S. residents
8. Personal remittances in kind to foreigners

Source: R. Mark Rogers, "Retail Sales: A Primer," *Economic Review,* Federal Reserve Bank of Atlanta, April 1985, p. 29. This table differs from the earlier published version since retail service station sales had been excluded previously from PCEs to allow substitution of another source. Service station sales from retail sales are now part of the PCE control series.

straightforward: the sample size is small. Some variability in this component is due to sampling difficulties rather than to other technical factors or changes in demand. Other factors affecting auto dealer sales are discussed in more detail below.

Price Factors

In interpreting the "real" strength in each month's retail sales report, price is always a factor. An analyst must always know if an industry is having greater or less than average discounting in price. The auto industry frequently offers rebates and other discounts. In turn, the practice of looking at nonauto sales has been adopted partly in order to "remove" the auto industry's volatile price behavior. However, some other retail sales components have very erratic and sharp price movements.

The two primary components with volatile price behavior are apparel stores and service stations. Apparel sales have very strong seasonal price swings, and if inventories are out of line with desired levels, prices can swing dramatically, thereby making real estimates of sales difficult to ascertain by forecasters. If sales are stronger than normal early in a clothing season, a normal amount of discounting may not take place late in the season. This will push clothing prices up on a seasonally adjusted basis. Also, the timing of the introduction of seasonal clothing can vary from year to year and earlier (or later) introduction can also cause large monthly swings in prices and complicate estimates for real sales.

The other key series is for service station sales, which are primarily gasoline sales. Price volatility is also high, owing to relatively inelastic demand and supplies that can be quickly affected by political decisions within OPEC, strikes, and temporary shutdowns at refineries for maintenance. These price considerations mask the real strength not only in gasoline sales but also in broader retail sales aggregates such as nondurables and nonauto sales. Coincidentally, apparel sales are also under nondurables; this means that price effects can play a large role in monthly movement in that broad category. In essence, price considerations for these two components—apparel and gasoline—mean that nonauto retail sales should not be taken as an accurate barometer of consumer spending without first examining and discounting price factors in at least these subcomponents.

Seasonal Considerations

Retail sales are very seasonal for many components. Deviations from average patterns can lead to sharp month-to-month changes in the data once the data are put into seasonally adjusted form. Seasonal adjustment assumes stability in seasonal patterns but this is not always the case. Abnormal weather during the Christmas selling season can dramatically affect seasonally adjusted data since volume is relatively strong this time of year. For example, early snowstorms in November in the Northeast or rainstorms in other regions can lead to weak sales that month and tremendous catch-up the next month. Warm weather in January can depress winter apparel sales, or an early summer can really boost clothing sales in the spring. Finally, sales around Easter and Thanksgiving are difficult to adjust seasonally since sales are typically relatively strong in many components but the date of these holidays—particularly Easter—varies from year to year.

RETAIL INVENTORY AND REGIONAL DATA

Monthly Retail Trade includes data on inventories and inventory-to-sales ratios by kinds of business categories. Inventories are estimated on an end-of-month basis. An end-of-period basis is standard for inventory data rather than period averages. The inventory data come from a subsample of the monthly sales sample. However, inventories are valued at cost for both inventories on hand at retail stores and at warehouses that maintain merchandise primarily for distribution to retail stores within the same organization.[5]

Monthly Retail Trade also includes moderately detailed monthly sales figures by Census regions. For selected large states, monthly sales figures are published for totals, durables for the states where the sampling error is sufficiently low, nondurables, department store sales, and the GAF total. For specific metropolitan areas, department store sales and GAF totals are available. Some metropolitan areas also have data for nondurables. None of the regional data are published in seasonally adjusted form owing to the relatively high level of imputation and sampling error. These regional and subregional series are first available in the publication that is released about eight weeks after the end of the reference month.

KEY QUESTIONS IN ANALYZING THE NEWS RELEASE

- How were sales excluding autos?
- How do unit new auto sales and light truck sales add to the picture?
- Did price changes affect apparel store and service station sales?
- Were previous months—especially for the control series—revised significantly?
- Did atypical weather affect sales, especially for apparel, department store, and hardware sales?
- Are changes in housing starts affecting sales of hardware and building materials as well as furniture and household furnishings?

TABLE 3–2
Retail Sales: Selected Major Sales Groups, 1980–1997*

					Annual Percent Changes				
	1980	1981	1982	1983	1984	1985	1986	1987	1988
Total	6.6	8.8	2.9	9.4	10.0	7.0	5.5	6.2	7.1
Total excluding autos	10.3	8.3	2.2	7.1	7.8	6.0	4.8	6.6	6.7
Durable goods stores	-2.4	8.7	3.4	16.3	16.2	9.7	8.6	6.3	9.2
Building materials, hardware, garden supplies and mobile home dealers	0.4	2.8	-2.7	14.8	14.5	6.2	8.6	7.9	9.1
Automotive dealers	-7.9	10.8	5.8	19.5	18.6	11.0	7.8	4.8	8.6
Furniture group stores	4.0	6.6	-0.7	16.7	12.6	11.3	10.9	3.5	8.8
Nondurable goods stores	11.3	8.8	2.6	6.2	6.8	5.6	3.7	6.1	5.9
General merchandise	4.9	10.9	3.2	8.7	10.9	6.0	6.8	7.1	5.3
Food group	11.0	7.4	4.2	4.0	6.2	5.0	4.2	4.1	4.8
Gasoline service stations	27.7	9.9	-5.4	5.5	4.5	5.5	-9.6	2.2	5.0
Apparel and accessory stores	6.7	10.1	2.9	7.5	7.4	9.0	8.0	4.8	6.7
Eating and drinking places	9.5	9.2	6.4	8.4	6.9	5.7	8.9	10.2	9.1
Drug and proprietary stores	8.4	10.1	7.2	11.5	8.2	7.1	7.5	7.1	6.6

Source: U.S. Department of Commerce.

TABLE 3–2 (*Continued*)
Retail Sales: Selected Major Sales Groups, 1980–1997*

	1989	1990	1991	1992	1993	1994	1995	1996	1997
Total	6.7	4.9	0.6	4.8	6.5	7.4	4.6	4.9	4.4
Total excluding autos	7.5	6.2	1.8	3.7	5.0	5.7	4.0	4.2	4.3
Durable goods stores	4.9	1.8	-2.9	7.9	10.6	12.5	6.2	6.9	5.1
Building materials, hardware, garden supplies and mobile home dealers	1.9	2.4	-3.6	10.2	8.6	11.6	3.5	5.9	7.3
Automotive dealers	3.9	0.3	-3.9	9.0	12.4	13.7	6.4	7.1	4.6
Furniture group stores	7.7	0.3	0.0	5.0	9.0	12.4	7.9	4.7	5.9
Nondurable goods stores	7.8	6.8	2.6	3.1	4.2	4.4	3.5	3.6	3.9
General merchandise	7.7	4.9	5.1	8.2	7.8	6.9	5.9	4.5	5.8
Food group	7.1	6.1	1.7	0.3	2.4	3.6	2.9	3.1	2.2
Gasoline service stations	11.7	12.7	-0.7	-0.6	1.3	2.5	3.2	5.8	1.2
Apparel and accessory stores	9.2	4.1	1.6	6.2	3.6	2.2	0.9	2.9	2.7
Eating and drinking places	6.3	6.9	2.2	2.8	6.8	4.7	3.9	1.8	3.4
Drug and proprietary stores	10.0	11.3	7.1	2.7	2.6	2.8	4.7	5.5	8.7

NOTES FOR CHAPTER 3

1. Definitions of terms are based primarily on information from the appendix in *Monthly Retail Trade.*
2. Since the respondents are asked to report their operating receipts, they should include the amounts that they receive from their customers. If the customers get some of their costs back from the manufacturer because of a rebate, the retailer is not involved in that transaction. If the retailer offers a rebate, that in effect is a reduction in the amount of the operating receipts.
3. U.S. Department of Commerce, *Monthly Retail Trade: Sales and Inventories,* December 1992, Appendix E, p. E-3.
4. As discussed in Chapter 4, the 10-day sales do include estimates for Chrysler although full-month data are actual counts from the manufacturer.
5. U.S. Department of Commerce, *Monthly Retail Trade: Sales and Inventories,* December 1992, Appendix A, p. A-4.

BIBLIOGRAPHY

Rogers, R. Mark. "Retail Sales: A Primer," *Economic Review,* Federal Reserve Bank of Atlanta, April 1985, pp. 28–33.

U.S. Department of Commerce, *Monthly Retail Trade: Sales and Inventories,* December 1992.

U.S. Department of Commerce, Census Bureau, "Advanced Monthly Retails Sales Survey," Census Web mimeo, April 15, 1997.

U.S. Department of Commerce, Census Bureau, "Monthly Retail Trade Survey," Census Web mimeo, April 15, 1997.

U.S. Department of Commerce, Census Bureau, "Annual Retail Trade Survey," Census Web mimeo, April 15, 1997.

CHAPTER 4

UNIT NEW AUTO SALES AND OTHER RELATED MOTOR VEHICLE DATA

The unit new auto sales series is the primary indicator of the strength of the auto sector. Autos are important in tracking the economy because over the business cycle changes in auto demand can be quite dramatic. Sales are very sensitive to interest rates and are also affected by consumer confidence, which is a general barometer of the economy. Essentially, auto sales is a leading indicator of the economy because of these factors. Also, unit new auto sales are important as an economic indicator because of the series' use in the auto component in personal consumption expenditures. It is less well known, but these data also end up in producers' durable equipment and in other GDP components. Auto sales and inventories also provide an indication of the sustainability of auto production levels.

In addition to being a leading indicator, auto production is still a sizable part of the U.S. economy. In terms of real GDP, auto output's share (chain dollars) peaked at 2.7 percent in 1965 but was still very significant in 1997, with a 1.7 percent share. Combined auto and truck output reached 4.2 percent of real GDP in 1977 and is still sizable, with a 3.5 percent share in 1997.[1] (See Tables 4–1 and 4–2 at the end of this chapter.) Swings in auto output can be sharp and cause noticeable changes in growth rates for real GDP for any given quarter. Understanding these effects on the economy is the primary reason for following auto sales. Other related data on the motor vehicle industry are also useful. Of secondary importance are data for auto production and inventories. As is discussed below, these monthly series are not always consistently defined relative to each other. Finally, in recent years, sales of light trucks have increased and warrant much more attention than in the past.

UNIT NEW AUTO SALES DATA

For the automobile industry, the monthly data most closely followed by the general economics community is the series referred to as unit new auto sales. Data are released each month by the BEA around the third business day of the month for the previous month's sales figures and are available as unpublished data from the BEA. Data for this series come primarily from the American Automobile Manufacturers Association (formerly the Motor Vehicle Manufacturers Association) and *Ward's Automotive Reports*. The BEA combines the various components and seasonally adjusts the data. The AAMA is a trade association for U.S. domestic auto produc-ers and is based in Detroit. *Ward's* is a commercial, for-profit publisher of auto-motive industry news and data and *Ward's* is also based in Detroit.

As an overview of BEA's unit new auto sales data, data for domestic sales come primarily from the AAMA while information on import sales are reported by *Ward's*. As an industry news source *Ward's* also tracks domestic sales, which are frequently seen in many of their statistics. With domestic sales, the AAMA is generally the original data source, while *Ward's* is the original collection point for import sales across the United States.

Initially, data are released only for totals and a breakdown between domes-tics and imports. Sales of domestic units are closely watched to determine if manu-facturers need to raise or lower production levels to keep up with sales and to keep inventories at desired quantities. Unit sales are also divided into components by sector: consumer, business, and government. However, these components are pub-lished with a lag of two months. This breakdown is based on estimates using the privately compiled *Polk* auto registration data, located in Detroit Michigan. How-ever, early figures for the consumer, business, and government sectors are avail-able at the end of the month of the initial release as a by-product of GDP component derivation. These numbers are available by subscription to unpub-lished computer tables produced by the BEA. Before *Polk* registration data be-come available, these sectoral expenditure components are derived from industry contacts, trends, and a variety of miscellaneous sources.

For the GDP accounts, new unit auto sales data are used in the motor vehicle components for (1) personal consumption of durables, (2) purchases of producers'

CHART 4–1

Unit New Auto and Light Truck Sales

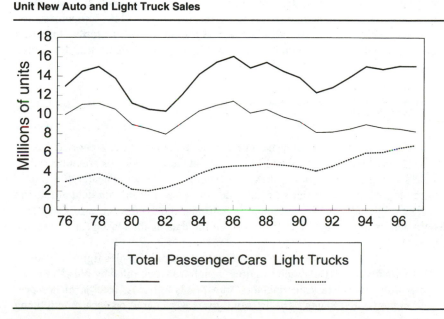

durable equipment, and (3) government purchases. This is in contrast to the typical assumption by many economy watchers that these sales essentially are to consumers only. In fact, there is not perfect timing in the changes in overall unit auto sales and the relevant personal consumption component because the consumer sector's share in unit new sales does vary. In particular, business purchases for fleets can change sharply, especially since U.S. auto producers have taken large ownership positions in major car rental firms.

Leased vehicles create special problems in allocating sales between consumer and business sectors. Sales are allocated according to *Polk* registration data, and leased sales are still registered to businesses even though the vehicles are for consumer use. Essentially, cars leased by consumers are counted as sales to the business sector and show up in producers' durable equipment in the GDP accounts. This also means that shifts in preferences by car buyers between leasing and purchasing affect the relative strength of autos in consumer durables expenditures compared to business investment in producers' durable equipment. However, the monthly value of motor vehicle leases to consumers is allocated to personal consumption of services.

BEA's domestic sales are for what the industry refers to as sales from North American production. For some time, General Motors, Ford, and Chrysler have had plants in Canada and Mexico for U.S. makes sold in the United States. Currently, Honda and Toyota also have foreign nameplates that have been transplanted to the United States and subsequently have had some production shifted to Canada. Sales of these are counted as "domestics" because auto producers primarily keep sales data in terms of North American operations. The *Survey of Current Business* defines sales of domestic vehicles as "sales in the United States of domestic-nameplate vehicles and "transplant" vehicles manufactured in North America—that is, Canada, the United States, and Mexico. Domestic-nameplate vehicles are those manufactured at factories owned by U.S. companies, and transplant vehicles are those manufactured at foreign-owned factories. Imported vehicles are those manufactured outside North America and sold in the United States."[2]

TEN-DAY SALES

Prior to the end of 1993, domestic motor vehicle manufacturers reported 10-day sales figures. In early December 1993, Ford and General Motors announced they would no longer report sales figures on a 10-day basis, ending nearly 40 years of economic tradition. Chrysler stopped reporting these intramonth data at the end of 1990 (although *Ward's* continued to estimate the 10-day sales of Chrysler). Major auto manufacturers cited volatility in the data as the reason for ending the reports.

For historical reference, as a precursor to the monthly sales figures, industry analysts watched the 10-day sales figures, which were compiled by *Ward's* for domestics only. Domestic sales include "transplants," that is, foreign makes produced in the United States.[3] The 10-day figures were based on each month being divided into three sales periods with the first two having 10 days each and with the final period of the month consisting of the remaining days of the month. The last period can be as short as 8 days or as long as 11 days. but for a given month they are always the same except for February in leap years.

Seasonal adjustment procedures removed most of the differences in sales rates caused by different lengths in the final sales period for specific months. However, differences often occurred in the number of business days per period owing to the timing of weekends each month and annual holidays such as Easter and Thanksgiving, which do not have a set month or day of month for observance. Despite the use of sophisticated seasonal adjustment programs, these factors made the sales data volatile. This was further compounded by the shortness of the 10-day period, which could be significantly affected by random events such as unseasonable weather. For example, over such a short time span, special promotions (rebates, subsidized interest rates, etc.) can cause significant differences.

Consequently, comparisons of sales with the 10-day period dates were somewhat unreliable, especially in the short run. Typically, 10-day data were compared on a year-ago basis, often using unadjusted data. Even though year-ago percentages frequently appeared in headlines in the news media, they did not always indicate the latest direction in sales. For this, the more appropriate comparison was with period-to-period data in seasonally adjusted form. Given the volatility of the 10-day sales numbers, determination of current trends had to be based on several periods—perhaps three to four weeks of seasonally adjusted data.

The monthly averages of the 10-day sales for domestics did not quite match the BEA monthly domestics figures. First, Chrysler stopped reporting 10-day sales in 1991, and *Ward's* then estimated Chrysler's sales. Not all transplant producers reported 10-day sales either, so *Ward's* estimated their sales also. Beginning in 1989, *Ward's* shifted some vehicles to the light-truck category that previously were considered passenger cars. The BEA did not make this change; consequently, BEA's figures for domestic passenger cars tended to run slightly higher.

TRUCK SALES

Over the 1980s, truck sales became more important to the consumer sector as pickup trucks became more popular; this was also true for mini-vans. The truck share of motor vehicles' contribution to GDP has risen from about 22 percent in 1970 to 53 percent in 1997. To correctly assess the impact of the motor vehicle sector on the economy, one must watch sales of trucks as well as passenger cars.

Data for light-weight truck sales actually covers both trucks and buses (vans and minivans) weighing 10,000 pounds and under. The series officially published by the BEA is "trucks and buses, retail sales, 0–10,000 lbs GVW [gross vehicle weight], domestics" (and a matching series for imports). Figures are both seasonally and not seasonally adjusted and are available as unpublished tables from the Commerce Department.

In contrast to the passenger car data, seasonally adjusted truck data are not annualized and are in thousands of units rather than millions. Therefore, in order to compare the truck data with unit figures for new passenger car sales, the seasonally adjusted truck figures must be multiplied by 12 and then divided by 1,000. This gives sales in millions of units, seasonally adjusted, annualized.

As is the case for passenger car data, unit sales for light-trucks and buses are used not just in NIPA estimates for personal consumption but also for investment in producers' durable equipment and, to a lesser extent, for government purchases and exports.

PRODUCTION DATA

Monthly output figures for motor vehicles that are comparable to the unit sales data are most readily available from the Federal Reserve Board of Governors as part of the monthly industrial production releases. In addition to the standard indexes based for the year 1992 being set equal to 100, data are also available in terms of annualized production rates for units of vehicles. The most often cited terminology is "assembly rate," which is in millions of units annualized and seasonally adjusted. Production rates for both passenger cars and trucks can be compared to seasonally adjusted annualized sales rates to see if unit production rates are sustainable. That is, one can see if production has been running above or below a sales pace that might be considered sustainable given the current economic conditions—including inventory levels and import penetration.

Federal Reserve assembly rates for passenger cars are released with the monthly industrial production report, while truck data are unpublished but are generally available from electronic data vendors.

The Federal Reserve assembly rates average a little below the BEA sales rates because the Fed's data are U.S. production and exclude Canadian and Mexican output of domestic makes. *Ward's* also publishes weekly production figures for U.S. and Canadian car and truck output. The BEA unit sales data cover North American operations.

The BEA also releases unpublished monthly data (in computer printout form) for unit production rates on a BEA basis. The BEA data differ from Federal Reserve data primarily in terms of the seasonal factors used. Both series are based on the same monthly reports from auto manufacturers. The unpublished data (which can be subscribed to) also contains the Federal Reserve production figures as well as additional BEA estimates for nominal and real-dollar values for output, and unit and dollar values for sales.

For the "current" and upcoming quarter, *Ward's* publishes production schedules, which are announced by the manufacturers. While the production schedules frequently change during each quarter, they do provide good information on the near-term direction for motor vehicle production.

KEY QUESTIONS IN ANALYZING THE NEWS RELEASE

- How do the latest autos sales figures compare to recent months?
- Are data being compared on the same statistical basis; that is, are units sold on a seasonally adjusted basis?
- How strong were domestic sales compared to import sales?
- Are domestic sales in line with production rates?
- Were recent sales affected by special incentives either for the current month or for the previous month?
- How strong were light truck sales?
- Did the shift from traditional autos to light trucks include vans and minivans?
- Has there been a shift from sales to businesses to sales to consumers or vice versa in recent months?
- Has a shift between sales to consumers or businesses been affected by changes in preferences for leasing by consumers since leases remain counted as business purchases?
- Have motor vehicle sales been affected by fleet sales to car rental agencies?

TABLE 4–1
Unit New Auto Sales, 1970–1997
(Millions, Annual Totals)

	Total	Domestic Origin	Import Origin	Consumer Purchases	Business Purchases	Government Purchases
1970	8.403	7.119	1.283	6.252	2.056	0.094
1971	10.228	8.662	1.566	7.611	2.510	0.107
1972	10.873	9.253	1.621	8.230	2.523	0.120
1973	11.350	9.589	1.762	8.423	2.811	0.116
1974	8.774	7.362	1.412	6.084	2.565	0.126
1975	8.538	6.951	1.587	5.907	2.508	0.123
1976	9.994	8.492	1.502	7.036	2.822	0.137
1977	11.046	8.971	2.075	7.657	3.253	0.136
1978	11.164	9.164	2.000	7.540	3.474	0.150
1979	10.559	8.230	2.329	7.172	3.246	0.141
1980	8.982	6.581	2.401	6.100	2.758	0.124
1981	8.534	6.209	2.326	5.639	2.781	0.114
1982	7.980	5.758	2.221	5.295	2.583	0.101
1983	9.179	6.793	2.386	6.047	3.020	0.112
1984	10.390	7.952	2.439	6.591	3.662	0.137
1985	10.978	8.205	2.774	7.092	3.754	0.132
1986	11.406	8.215	3.191	7.579	3.701	0.126
1987	10.171	7.081	3.090	6.625	3.413	0.132
1988	10.546	7.539	3.006	6.746	3.664	0.135
1989	9.777	7.078	2.699	6.288	3.356	0.134
1990	9.300	6.897	2.403	5.677	3.477	0.147
1991	8.175	6.137	2.038	4.424	3.648	0.103
1992	8.214	6.277	1.938	4.566	3.529	0.119
1993	8.518	6.734	1.784	4.646	3.758	0.113
1994	8.990	7.255	1.735	4.610	4.257	0.124
1995	8.636	7.129	1.507	4.316	4.177	0.144
1996	8.527	7.254	1.273	4.065	4.328	0.134
1997	8.245	6.885	1.360	3.880	4.233	0.131

Source: Bureau of Economic Analysis, U.S. Department of Commerce.

TABLE 4–2
Unit New Auto and Light Truck Sales, 1970–1997

	Millions				
	Total Autos and Light Trucks	Total Domestic Autos and Light Trucks	Total Light Trucks	Domestic Light Trucks	Imported Light Trucks
1970	—	8.528	—	1.408	—
1971	—	10.362	—	1.700	—
1972	—	11.369	—	2.116	—
1973	—	12.102	—	2.513	—
1974	—	9.538	—	2.176	—
1975	—	9.006	—	2.055	—
1976	12.966	11.225	2.971	2.733	0.239
1977	14.486	12.087	3.440	3.116	0.324
1978	14.973	12.633	3.809	3.469	0.340
1979	13.768	10.970	3.209	2.740	0.469
1980	11.192	8.312	2.211	1.730	0.480
1981	10.564	7.794	2.030	1.586	0.444
1982	10.363	7.729	2.384	1.971	0.413
1983	12.119	9.273	2.941	2.480	0.461
1984	14.197	11.150	3.807	3.198	0.609
1985	15.442	11.838	4.464	3.634	0.831
1986	16.050	11.891	4.645	3.676	0.969
1987	14.855	10.858	4.684	3.777	0.907
1988	15.433	11.729	4.887	4.190	0.697
1989	14.522	11.195	4.745	4.117	0.629
1990	13.854	10.848	4.554	3.951	0.603
1991	12.303	9.737	4.128	3.601	0.528
1992	12.846	10.510	4.631	4.233	0.398
1993	13.867	11.718	5.350	4.984	0.366
1994	15.013	12.883	6.023	5.627	0.395
1995	14.725	12.823	6.089	5.694	0.395
1996	15.048	13.343	6.521	6.089	0.432
1997	15.026	13.099	6.781	6.214	0.567

Source: BEA.

NOTES FOR CHAPTER 4

1. U.S. Department of Commerce, Bureau of Economic Analysis, NIPA data.
2. Ralph W. Morris, "Motor Vehicles, Model Year 1996," *Survey of Current Business,* U.S. Department of Commerce, November 1996, p. 37.
3. Monthly BEA data for domestics also include transplants.

BIBLIOGRAPHY

Economic Indicators: The Motor Vehicle's Role in the U.S. Economy, Motor Vehicle Manufacturers Association, Detroit, Michigan, 1991, 1992, pp. .

Morris, Ralph W. "Motor Vehicles, Model Year 1996," *Survey of Current Business,* U.S. Department of Commerce, November 1996, pp. 35–40.

CHAPTER 5

THE CONSUMER PRICE INDEX

OVERVIEW

The consumer price index (CPI) is one of the most important economic indicators published by the government because this series provides one of the broadest, most followed measures of inflation. It is used as a tool for analysis for both monetary and fiscal policy. Businesses and labor unions use the CPI for contract escalation clauses, and the federal government uses it for Social Security payments. Federal income tax brackets and standard deductions are also affected by the movement of the CPI.

Inflation as measured by the CPI is important to market analysts largely because expected inflation affects the prices of financial securities, notably bond prices. Changes in bond prices are, in effect, changes in interest rates. If the expected rate of inflation rises, financial markets generally bid bond prices lower. Lower bond prices are equivalent to higher interest rates. Essentially, when expected inflation rises, investors demand a higher rate of return for new issues of debt.

For holders of existing debt, CPI inflation data are important because changes in interest rates for new debt affect the market value of old debt. If old debt is sold on the market for cash, the interest rate on it must be competitive with interest rates on new debt. When inflation rates rise, rates on existing debt placed on the market also rise; that is, prices for existing debt fall. Rising inflation cuts into the market value of old debt, which are assets, if interest rates are rising at the same time. Typically, this is the case as investors seek to maintain real rates of return.

The consumer price index is a measure of changes in prices for purchases made by urban consumers only. It was initially begun in World War I to help calculate cost-of-living adjustments in wages in highly industrialized areas that were hard-hit by wartime inflation.[1] There are two basic versions: the original urban wage earners and clerical workers (CPI-W) index and the broader, more representative, all-urban consumers (CPI-U) index. The all-urban index was introduced in 1978; based on the 1990 census count, it covers about 80 percent of the total population of the United States. The CPI-W covers 32 percent of the U.S. population. As of 1998, data were collected from 19,000 retail establishments and 57,000 housing units in 85 urban geographic areas in the United States.

The all-urban index is based on the expenditures of all urban consumer units (the official definition of "household").[2] Income levels or employment status do not affect inclusion. Excluded from the index population are rural residents outside metropolitan areas, all farm residents, the military, and individuals in institutions.[3] The consumer price index for wage earners and clerical workers is also based on urban households, but these consumer units must meet two additional employment-related requirements: More than one-half of the consumer unit's income must be earned from clerical or wage occupations, and at least one of the members has to have been employed for 37 or more weeks in an eligible occupation during the last 12 months.

The two indexes use the same methodology and survey and differ only in terms of how the individual components are weighted. For example, wage earners spent an average of 40 percent of total expenditures on housing in the 1982–1984 period, compared to 42.6 by all urban consumers. For transportation, wage earners spent an average of 20.9 percent, versus 18.7 percent by the broader group.[4] Today the all-urban index is generally more closely followed by the media, although the wage earners index is still used in contract price escalation clauses and Social Security cost-of-living adjustments.

The CPI measures a fixed market basket of goods and services, currently over 360 categories of items. Prices include sales taxes and other indirect taxes (i.e., gasoline taxes). Basic price data are collected monthly (bimonthly for some cities) from individual retail and service establishments, while house rents are collected on a rotating basis (six subsets repriced once every six months).

The market basket defining the CPI generally is not altered to reflect changes in consumer spending patterns. However, about once every 10 years, the basket is redefined, based on the Consumer Expenditure Survey (which is conducted by the Census Bureau for the BLS). With the 1987 revision of the CPI, the index was set at 100, using the base period 1982–84. Thus, the market basket reflected the spending habits of urban consumers over the 1982–1984 period as shown in Consumer Expenditure Surveys for those years. For 1989, the CPI averaged 124.0, indicating that its market basket cost 24 percent more in 1989 than in 1982–1984 on average.[5] Despite the updating of expenditure weights in 1998, the index base period remains 1982–84.

It is important to understand that the consumer price index is *not* a cost-of-living index. The metropolitan-area CPIs are in index form, not in absolute dollars; therefore, intercity or interregional cost-of-living comparisons are not possible. The CPI simply measures the cost of maintaining the same purchases over time for each geographic area.

Regarding the CPI as a measure of a constant standard of living based on "utility" or well-being, authors Aizcorbe, Cage, and Jackman argue as follows:

> A CLI [cost-of-living index] is defined as the ratio of the minimum expenditures required to attain a particular level of satisfaction in two price situations, a comparison period and the base period. The CPI, a modified Laspeyres index, holds the standard of living constant (in the span between major revisions) by keeping quantities fixed, but allows prices to vary. In addition, over an extended period of time the CPI is a chain index, because the expenditure pattern of consumers is updated and sequentially linked into the index at approximately 10-year intervals. The restriction imposed on the CPI, by keeping the quantities fixed and not allowing substitution among goods in response to relative price change, results in a substitution effect, or a divergence between the CPI (or any other index with fixed quantity weights) and the CLI. In the case of a Laspeyres index, the effect is such that it is greater than or equal to the true cost of living. Indeed, as is well known, a Laspeyres index is an upper bound to the true CLI.[6]

As hinted, the indexing methodology of the CPI leads to a mild overstatement of the inflation rate if it is intended that it measure changes in the cost of maintaining a constant level of consumer satisfaction. There are other reasons why the CPI likely overstates the cost of living; these are discussed in the section on the Boskin report.

TIMING OF RELEASES AND REVISIONS

The CPI is released monthly by the Bureau of Labor Statistics in the U.S. Department of Labor. The data are typically provided to the public during the second or third full week after the month to which they refer. Published data appear in the BLS's *Monthly Labor Review,* in the BLS's *CPI Detailed Report* (which is quite voluminous), and in secondary sources such as the Commerce Department's *Survey of Current Business* and the *Federal Reserve Bulletin.* Table 5–1 lists the schedule of publication for various metropolitan regions.

TABLE 5–1

Consumer Price Index Frequency of Publication for Metropolitan Areas

---

Effective January 1998, indexes for various metropolitan regions are published on the following schedule:

Monthly
   New York, Northern New Jersey, Long Island: NY-NJ-CT-PA
   Chicago, Gary, Kenosha: IL-IN-WI
   Los Angeles, Riverside, Orange County: CA

Bimonthly, in odd months (January, March, May, July, September, November)
   Boston, Brockton, Nashua: MA-NH-ME-CT
   Washington, Baltimore: DC-MD-VA-WV
   Cleveland, Akron: OH
   Atlanta: GA
   Dallas-Fort Worth, TX

Bimonthly, in even months (February, April, June, August, October, December)
   Philadelphia, Wilmington, Atlantic City: PA-NJ-DE-MD
   San Francisco, Oakland, San Jose: CA
   Houston, Galvenston, Brazoria: TX
   Detroit, Ann Arbor, Flint: MI
   Miami, Fort Lauderdale: FL
   Seattle, Tacoma, Bremerton: WA

Semiannually (January and July)
   Pittsburgh: PA
   Kansas City: MO-KS
   Minneapolis, St. Paul: MN-WI
   Tampa, St. Petersburg, Clearwater: FL
   Denver, Boulder, Greeley: CO
   Portland, Salem: OR-WA
   Cincinnati, Hamilton: OH-KY-IN
   Milwaukee, Racine: WI
   Anchorage: AK
   Honolulu: HI
   San Diego: CA

Source: U.S. Department of Labor, *Monthly Labor Review,* December 1996, p. 28.

Annual revisions for seasonally adjusted data are generally released in February and cover the previous five calendar years. Unadjusted data are not revised after the initial month's release. When the data are rebased, previous percentage changes are maintained except for differences created by rounding error. Also, with rebasing, component weights are not changed in earlier years, although the index levels are changed to be consistent with the new base year. The maintaining of earlier percentage changes is desirable primarily owing to the need for consistency by users of the CPI for contract purposes. For this reason, unadjusted data are not revised after the initial release except in the rare occurrence of an error in reporting or processing that meets stated correction policy. Contracts with price escalation clauses generally use the unadjusted data, since there are no seasonal factors to be revised each year, as is the case for seasonally adjusted CPI series for the subsequent five calendar years after the initial release.

SCOPE OF THE CPI

Because it is not practical to measure prices in all consumer transactions, the CPI is based on a set of statistically designed samples. The result is a CPI that is representative of prices paid for all urban areas of the United States. The samples are:[7]

- Urban areas selected from all U.S. urban areas
- Consumer units within each selected urban area
- Outlets from which these consumer units purchased goods and services
- Specific, unique items—goods and services—purchased by these consumer units
- Housing units in each urban area for the shelter component of the CPI

For the CPI, price data for goods and services are collected in 85 urban geographic areas and from about 19,000 retail and service establishments. In 1998, the rent data sample sizes were 36,000 renters and 26,000 owners. At publication time, BLS stated that it hoped to include 50,000 renters in its 1999 housing sample. Each month prices for food, fuels, and a few other items are obtained in all 85 urban geographic areas. For most other goods and services, prices are collected monthly in the 5 largest urban areas, bimonthly in the remaining 80 areas. A portion of the housing sample is collected each month.

The basic bundle of goods and services included in the CPI is determined by the Census Bureau's Consumer Expenditure Survey. However, to choose the establishments that are surveyed, a Point-of-Purchase Survey (POPS) is used.[8] This household interview survey asks consumers to provide information about nonrental purchases made over a specific recall period or time span. The survey, taken over a four-to-six–week period each spring, asks consumers by purchase category how much was spent at each outlet. From this information outlets are then selected for BLS's monthly price surveys, with the probability of being selected proportional to expenditures reported in the POPS for each outlet. Prior to the 1998 CPI revision, one-fifth of the CPI pricing areas had their outlet samples reselected each year. Even though the basket of goods in the CPI is fixed between major revisions, the places surveyed have been and are updated on an ongoing basis to track consumer changes in outlet preferences. With the 1998 CPI revision, a computer-assisted telephone interview replaced the in-person household interview. Additionally, a portion of outlets for the CPI categories are reselected each year for each sampling unit. As of 1998, area rotation was replaced by outlet and item rotation by expenditure category. Reselection is quarterly for some items and outlets. Updating items and outlets undergoes a full rotation every four or five years at every primary sampling area.

The various surveys used in producing the CPI may be a little confusing. They can be summarized as follows:

1. The Consumer Expenditure Survey, conducted by the Census Bureau, is used to determine the weights for the components in the CPI.

2. The Point-of-Purchase Survey, also produced by the Census Bureau, is used to select outlets—stores and other retail establishments—to be priced.

3. The CPI survey, conducted by BLS, actually selects and prices the goods and services.

4. The housing units are selected from information provided by the 1990 census, combined with ongoing new permit sample.

MAJOR EXPENDITURE CATEGORIES

CPI data are primarily organized by expenditure category and reflect the organization of the Consumer Expenditure Survey. Prior to 1998, the seven major expenditure categories were food and beverages, housing, apparel and upkeep, transportation, medical care, entertainment, and "other goods and services." Table 5–2 shows the relative importance of the major expenditure categories. As of 1998, the major expenditure categories (formally called "product groups") covered include food and beverages, housing, apparel, transportation, medical care, recreation, education and communication, and "other goods and services." Product groups are broken down into 70 expenditure classes (ECs), 211 item strata, and 305 entry-level items (ELIs). Prior to the 1998 revision, there were 69 expenditure classes, 207 item strata, and 364 ELIs. ELIs are the ultimate sampling units from which unique items are selected for actual pricing. With the 1998 revisions, numerous ELIs were combined, either because individual ELIs were too small in terms of relative share of the CPI (as in the case of beef and veal) or because they were too intertwined with another ELIs (as in the case of hospital medical care services).

Within the food and beverages product group, two examples of expenditure classes are "cereals and cereal products" and "bakery products." Under the first is the item stratum "rice, pasta, and cornmeal," which includes the ELI "rice." Expenditure classes are often put into common groups. For example, "meats" is a

TABLE 5–2
Consumer Price Index: The Seven Major Expenditure Groups*

Expenditure Category	Relative Importance, December 1996
All items	100.000
Food and beverages	17.484
Food	15.913
Food at home	10.040
Food away from home	5.873
Alcoholic beverages	1.571
Housing	41.203
Shelter	28.194
Renters' costs	7.994
Rent, residential	5.731
Other renters' costs	2.263
Homeowners' costs	20.000
Owners' equivalent rent	19.616
Household insurance	0.383
Maintenance and repairs	0.200
Fuel and other utilities	7.102
Fuels	3.878
Fuel and other household fuel commodities	0.424
Gas (piped) and electricity	3.453
Other utilities and public services	3.224
Household furnishings and operation	5.908
Apparel and upkeep	5.330
Transportation	17.140
Private transportation	15.499
New vehicles	4.955
New cars	3.952
Used cars	1.278
Motor fuel	3.171
Maintenance and repairs	1.533
Other private transportation	4.562
Public transportation	1.642
Medical care	7.346
Medical care commodities	1.273
Medical care services	6.073
Entertainment	4.352
Other goods and services	7.145

*Pre-1998 revisions.

combination of the expenditure classes of "beef and veal," "pork," "poultry," "fish and seafood," and "other meats." As such, "meats" is a grouping that falls in between product groups and expenditure classes.

Under the apparel product group, two examples of expenditure classes are "women's apparel" and "girls' apparel." Under the first is the item stratum "women's underwear, nightwear, and accessories," which includes the ELI "women's hosiery."[9]

TABLE 5–3

Consumer Price Index: The Eight Major Expenditure Groups*

Expenditure Category	Relative Importance Dec. 1997
All items	100.000
Food and beverages	16.310
Food	15.326
Food at home	9.646
Food away from home	5.680
Alcoholic beverages	0.983
Housing	39.560
Shelter	29.788
Rent of primary residence	6.885
Lodging away from home	2.327
Owners' equivalent rent of primary residence	20.199
Tenants' and household insurance	0.377
Fuel and utilities	4.942
Fuels	4.018
Fuel oil and other fuels	0.261
Gas (piped) and electricity	3.757
Household furnishings and operations	4.831
Apparel	4.944
Transportation	17.578
Private transportation	16.240
New and used motor vehicles	7.899
New vehicles	5.063
Used cars and trucks	1.880
Motor fuel	2.995
Motor vehicle parts and equipment	0.560
Motor vehicle maintenance and repair	1.603
Public transportation	1.338
Medical care	5.614
Medical care commodities	1.222
Medical care services	4.392
Recreation	6.145
Education and Communication	5.528
Education	2.615
Communication	2.913
Other goods and services	7.145

*Based on 1998 group revisions.

Source: U.S. Department of Labor, *News Release: Consumer Price Indexes,* January 1998.

THE 1998 CPI REVISION

Major revisions in the CPI occur about every 10 years, with the most visible portion of the revision being a change in the market basket of goods and services upon which the CPI is based. This is done so as to take into account changes in consumer spending patterns reflecting numerous factors, including relative price changes, real income changes, new products, demographic changes, and changes in consumer preferences. With the introduction of new expenditure weights and samples, the substitution bias problem should be mitigated.

The latest CPI revision is known as the 1998 revision since the new expenditure weights (based on the 1993–1995 CES) are introduced with the release of January 1998 CPI figures. However, this major revision is actually being introduced to the public in stages, starting in 1997 and ending in 2000.[10] Notably, the base year for the CPI did not change to 1993–1995 although early plans by BLS called for this change in 1999. Another major milestone in this revision is the introduction of a new housing sample, also introduced with January 1999 data.

With the 1998 revision, new goods and new outlets are brought into the CPI. In turn, item categories have been redefined to take into account new goods that would not have fit neatly into old categories. Some detail items have been moved to aggregates that are more logical; for example, electronic audio and video equipment are now part of recreation rather than housing. The CPI item structure is now organized around eight major expenditure categories rather than the previous seven (see Box 5–1). New geographic areas were added to the CPI's coverage. Eighty-seven geographic areas, known as primary sampling units, were picked for the latest CPI revision based on the 1990 decennial census, replacing the prior primary sampling units based on the 1980 census. Sample rotation procedures have been redesigned to accelerate the introduction of new items and outlets in product markets showing rapid change. BLS begins a major improvement in the estimation of homeowner shelter costs. The medical care component was extensively revised in 1997 as part of the 1998 revision effort and made significant changes in the hospital services category. Finally, the BLS made numerous technological enhancements, including modernized processing systems and increased use of computer-assisted data collection.

INDEX WEIGHT VERSUS RELATIVE IMPORTANCE

Understanding the size of the components in the CPI is important in comprehending long-term changes in the behavior of the index. However, users of the data often confuse the meaning of a component's index weight with that of its relative importance.

Essentially, a component's *index weight* is equal to its share of expenditures in the Consumer Expenditure Survey for the base years. Remember, the base year *weights* remain unchanged for the various historical segments even though the weight levels have been rebased. However, components do not grow at the same rate. Therefore, the value of each component includes both its base-period index

BOX 5–1
Highlights of the 1998 CPI Revisions

FOOD AND BEVERAGES

There were no significant changes to the content of this major product group, but some components were restructured. Within the Food at Home component, many small item strata were collapsed and some were redefined to include consumption companions rather than their industry associates. For example, butter moved from Dairy Products to be with margarine in Fats and Oils.

Food away from Home was restructured into five new strata: Full-Service Restaurants, Limited-Service Restaurants, Food at Employee Sites and Schools, Food from Vending Machines and Snack Bars, and Other Food away from Home. These replaced the previous strata Lunch, Dinner, and Other Meals and Snacks.

HOUSING: SHELTER

The Maintenance and Repairs component previously included in the Shelter subgroup moved to Household Furnishings and Operations. This was not a significant change in the composition of Shelter because the Maintenance and Repairs expenditure weight was very small compared with the expenditure weight for Shelter. There were also structural changes in the Shelter component. Rent of Primary Residence and Lodging away from Home are now separate expenditure classes. A new item stratum, Tenants and Household Insurance, was created by collapsing two strata.

HOUSING: FUELS AND UTILITIES

Some components of the Fuels and Utilities subgroup moved to other major groups. The Telephone stratum moved to the new Education and Communication product group; Cable TV moved to the Recreation product group.

HOUSING: HOUSEHOLD FURNISHINGS AND OPERATIONS

Several components of the Household Furnishings and Operations subgroup moved to other major groups. Televisions and Sound Equipment moved to Recreation. Sewing Machines joined Sewing Items and also went to Recreation, along with the now-combined Household Sewing and Clothing Sewing. Maintenance and Repair moved into this Housing subgroup. Components that remained in the Household Furnishings and Operations subgroup were restructured.

BOX 5-1 (*continued*)
APPAREL

The composition of the prior Apparel and Upkeep major product group changed; the new major group, Apparel, excludes the components of apparel upkeep. Apparel Laundry and Dry Cleaning combined with Household Laundry and Dry Cleaning from the Household Furnishings and Operations subgroup and moved to Other Goods and Services. Luggage moved to Other Apparel Goods and Services. The small amount of restructuring within the remaining Apparel strata was confined to the Women's Apparel expenditure class.

TRANSPORTATION

The composition of Transportation did not change; the components were restructured. Cars and Trucks were combined into a single, very large item stratum. BLS continues to produce substratum indexes for New Cars and New Trucks. Automobile Finance Changes were dropped entirely from the scope of the CPI.

MEDICAL CARE

The composition of Medical Care did not change. Within this group the emphasis was on improving the pricing methods. Hence, the three current hospital strata were collapsed into one combined item stratum, Hospital Services.

RECREATION

The Entertainment group changed to Recreation to make it clearer that it includes the costs associated with active leisure activities. Recreation now includes video and audio equipment and services, including cable TV. Recreation now also includes sewing and other sewing items. Recreational Reading Materials was transferred from Other Goods and Services. There was a major restructuring of the expenditure classes and item strata within the Recreation group.

EDUCATION AND COMMUNICATION

This is a new major group. The education components were drawn from the old Other Goods and Services major group; the communication components, consisting of telephones, computers, and postage, were previously in Housing.

BOX 5-1 (*continued*)
OTHER GOODS AND SERVICES

The size of this major group was reduced. It continues to include Tobacco, Personal Care, and Miscellaneous Services and Miscellaneous Goods, although these expenditure classes were restructured. Schoolbooks and Supplies, as well as Daycare, Tuition, and Other School Fees, are now listed in Education and Communication.

Source: Excerpted from *Monthly Labor Review,* December 1996. Minor editing changes were made to put commentary on revisions into the perspective of a past event rather than one pending.

weight *and* its growth relative to other components. Essentially, the *relative importance* measures a component's share of the CPI in any given year. The *index weight* generally refers to its share of the CPI during the base period whereas relative importance is calculated by multiplying a component's index weight times its price change since the base period relative to the overall index.

Why are these changes in relative importance significant? First, sources of inflation have changed dramatically. Services inflation not only remains above average, but its higher share in the CPI makes inflation fighting more difficult. Services are much less interest-rate sensitive, and purchases of items such as medical care and housing are not as discretionary as many goods that are bought.

Second, the shift in relative importance affects how one should forecast the CPI. For example, a CPI figure for 1989 does not represent the same expenditure bundle as in 1997 in terms of dollars spent. While the index weights in the CPI are fixed (in physical quantities since the years use the same base period), the relative importance figures change every year and even every month. This is because some components have different rates of growth over long periods of time. Components with rapid inflation rates have a growing share of relative importance. This makes a component approach for academic studies or business forecasting very desirable.

The U.S. Department of Labor releases official relative importance figures for December of each year. Over the years, relative importance figures have changed dramatically (see Table 5–4). In particular, the sustained, rapid inflation for nonenergy services has led to an increase in this component's relative importance from 37.5 percent in 1979 to 53.6 percent in 1997.[11] In contrast, energy's share dropped from a high of 12.4 percent in 1982 to 7 percent in 1997, and the share for nonfood, nonenergy commodities fell a little over 10 percent, from 34.5 percent in 1979 to 24 percent in 1997.

These trends in relative shares would continue as long as relative inflation rates remain the same. However, when the CPI is rebased, component weights—starting in the new base period—are changed to reflect the latest information on consumer spending patterns. Typically, consumers purchase fewer goods that have strong price increases. This shows up in Consumer Expenditure Surveys,

TABLE 5–4

Relative Importance Figures for Selected CPI Components, 1979–1997

	Food	Energy	Commodities less Food and Energy	Services less Energy
1979	17.655	10.313	34.488	37.544
1980	17.322	10.834	33.739	38.104
1981	16.577	11.133	32.792	39.498
1982	18.963	12.405	26.201	42.431
1983	18.743	11.896	26.501	42.861
1984	18.711	11.466	26.276	44.544
1985	18.513	11.252	25.875	44.360
1986	16.246	7.360	26.052	50.342
1987	16.055	7.618	25.760	50.567
1988	16.171	7.330	25.650	50.849
1989	16.318	7.366	25.188	51.127
1990	16.188	8.191	24.528	51.093
1991	16.007	7.361	24.757	51.876
1992	15.777	7.294	24.656	52.273
1993	15.779	6.993	24.369	52.839
1994	15.838	6.965	24.082	53.115
1995	15.766	6.700	23.885	53.648
1996	15.913	7.049	23.364	53.674
1997	15.326	7.013	24.053	53.608

Source: U.S. Department of Labor, Bureau of Labor Statistics, *Relative Importance of Components in the Consumer Price Indexes,* various years. Data for 1979 through 1985 are based on consumer expenditures in 1972–1973; data for 1986 through 1997 are based on 1982–1984 expenditures.

which are use to determine base weights. For a new base period, the initial weights reflect both changes in quantities purchased relative to the old base and relative price changes. Therefore, after rebasing, goods or services with rapidly rising prices over long periods of time generally end up with lower weights relative to the period just before rebasing.

COMMODITY AND SERVICE GROUPS

CPI data are also broken down by commodity and service group. The reason for this focus is straightforward. Within the product groups, there is considerable mixing of subcomponents by type of behavioral factors, whereas the commodity and service groups are arranged such that they tend to have similar behavioral variables within a few major components. For purposes of forecasting and analysis, this commonality is important. Also, producer prices—a key factor often used to explain consumer price behavior—are not cleanly organized by expenditure type. They are instead arranged by industry and commodity. Between consumer and producer prices, data are more easily compared by commodity.

Food

The food commodity and service group is broken down into two major groups, Food at Home and Food away from Home.[12] The 1997 relative importance figures for these two groups are 9.646 percent and 5.680 percent, respectively. The Food at Home group reflects primarily items purchased at grocery stores and prepared at home. Almost all of these items are of the commodity type; that is, there may be numerous brand names (national and regional) but there are also readily available perfect substitutes. For example, there are brand names for eggs and carbonated beverages, but in both instances brand names are very close substitutes for each other.

Major subcategories within Food at Home include cereals and bakery products; meats, poultry, fish, and eggs; dairy products (fresh and processed); fruits and vegetables (fresh and processed); and "other food at home." In this last category are sugar and sweets, fats and oils, nonalcoholic beverages (including carbonated drinks and coffee), canned foods, frozen prepared food, seasonings and related items, and miscellaneous prepared food (including baby food).

Food away from Home is broken down into five categories, as previously discussed in Box 5–1.

For those who like to follow data on supply of food from the producer perspective, *Agricultural Outlook,* a monthly publication of the U.S. Department of Agriculture, provides a wide array of data and other information. The USDA Economic Research Service occasionally publish forecasts for the food component of the CPI and detailed subcomponents.

Energy

Energy is best understood by separating it into energy commodities and energy services. For December 1997, energy commodities made up 3.256 percent of the total CPI, while energy services were 3.757 percent.

Energy commodities include motor fuel (including gasoline), fuel oil (for heating), and "other household fuels." By expenditure group, motor fuel falls under Transportation, while fuel oil is a part of Housing. Motor fuel is about 90 percent of Energy Commodities. Energy services consist of two major subcomponents: electricity and utility (piped) gas. Both of these are in the expenditure category of Housing.

In terms of behavior, energy commodities are much more volatile than services. Of course, these commodities are rapidly and significantly affected by the price of crude oil (see Chart 5–1). Additionally, supply-and-demand shocks quickly lead to price changes. For example, refinery shutdowns (caused by fire, strike, or even hurricane) can cut supply. OPEC overproduction or underproduction relative to quotas can lead to sharp price swings. OPEC played key roles in price surges in 1974 and 1979–1980 and OPEC overproduction (primarily by Saudi Arabia) led to a dramatic decline in oil prices in 1986. More recently, supply problems created by Iraq's invasion of Kuwait and the subsequent Persian Gulf war in 1990–1991 caused large swings in oil prices and energy commodities in the CPI.

CHART 5–1

Consumer Price Indexes and Oil Prices

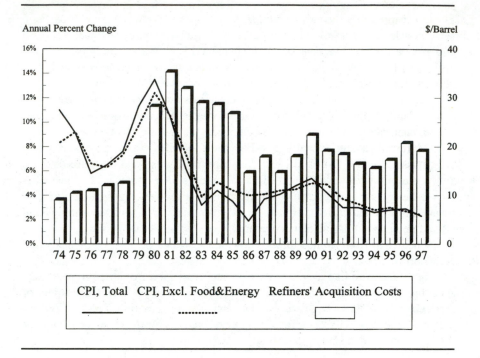

Annual Percent Change $/Barrel

CPI, Total   CPI, Excl. Food&Energy   Refiners' Acquisition Costs

Oil prices can also be affected by the supply of alternative energy commodities (e.g., natural gas, coal) for the consumer and industry and by energy demand worldwide. Demand generally is separated into trend growth based on strength in the economies of the industrial world and temporary-demand factors such as unseasonable weather.

Within energy services, electricity made up 2.649 percent of the total CPI in December 1997, while utility material gas services was 1.108 percent. These subcomponent prices are less volatile than the energy commodities. Electricity and utility gas prices are regulated by government agencies; hence, changes in producer costs are smoother and lag in reaching consumers. Also, for electricity, coal prices are an important cost factor and are relatively slow to change. The many electric utilities in New England that use oil to power the electricity-generating turbines are the exception. Regulations in the construction and operation of nuclear power plants and also changes in clean-air emission standards also affect electricity rates.

Commodities Excluding Food and Energy

Commodities excluding food and energy include, as a group, many items that are both discretionary and subject to significant import competition. Therefore, many items are inordinately affected by the strength of consumer demand in the economy or by the value of the dollar in foreign exchange markets. On a cyclical basis, many consumer durables goods are particularly sensitive; these items include furniture, appliances, and autos. Dollar-sensitive goods cover a variety of items, such as video and audio products, apparel, and autos.

While the relative importance of this broad commodity group was 24.053 percent in 1997, a few subcomponents account for more than half this figure. The largest is apparel (4.944), with numerous entry-level items for men, women, and children. From the transportation product group, the subcomponent for new vehicles accounts for 5.063 percent, and used cars and trucks for 1.880 percent. Under the product group of housing, there are a variety of relevant subcomponents, including furniture, appliances, and other goods. Many of these detail items carry much less weight than might be expected. Their small weight largely reflects the *average* expenditure per year rather than the much higher total cost.

Other major subcomponents are relatively small. For recreation commodities, examples are video and audio equipment and others such as newspapers, magazines, sporting equipment, toys, and photographic supplies and equipment.

The really significant components in this group are new vehicles and apparel. Both series are very seasonal and are difficult to seasonally adjust. Additionally, pricing for these items tends to occur with very large changes. Early in the season price increases may be very large; significant discounting may or may not occur, depending on sales strength.

Services Excluding Energy

Services excluding energy, as a group, is the largest major component of the CPI by commodity and services categories. At the end of 1997, its relative importance in the all-urban index was over 53 percent. This component is also important because longer-run inflation rates for these services subcomponents are slow to change.[13] They basically set the trend around which other components, especially food and energy, oscillate.

The largest grouping of these services components are housing-related and include various types of rental components (combined, they account for over one-fourth of the CPI) and also other household services.

Rent of Shelter

Under the current BLS philosophy for measuring housing costs, it is important to understand that the CPI seeks to measure the cost of services currently being consumed rather than the cost of obtaining an asset (buying a house). For shelter, the CPI measures the cost of housing services, that is, the use of shelter.

For rent of shelter, the two largest subcomponents are owners' equivalent rent of primary residence (OER) and rent of primary residence or residential rent for short. The relative importance of these two categories is 20.199 percent and 6.885 percent, respectively, for December 1997. Owners' equivalent rent was introduced into the CPI-U in 1983 and the CPI-W in 1985 and replaced the home ownership component. The "asset price" approach did not exclude the investment portion of these transactions from the consumption portion. The now-deleted home ownership series was composed of five elements: house prices, mortgage interest rates, property taxes, home owner insurance charges, and maintenance and repair costs. The old home ownership series was replaced by owners' equivalent rent and household insurance, for that portion of home owners' insurance not covering the structure.

Owners' equivalent rent and residential rent are a lot more closely related than one would initially suspect, since each measures a very different expenditure concept. OER is designed to measure the cost of renting the same type and quality housing as owner-occupied housing excluding utilities but including maintenance. Such housing is largely single-family houses but also condominiums and town houses. Residential rent measures the cost of housing in a broad rental market and includes rents for suburban apartment complexes, town house rentals, central-city flats and efficiencies, and of course single-family rental houses, among others.

While there is considerable variety and range in the types of housing represented in costs for owners' equivalent rent, the residential rent series covers a far broader spectrum of types of housing, with owner-occupied housing by type making up only a small subset of housing units in the residential rent component. As is discussed further below, this overlap provides a key link between the estimation of residential rent and OER.

Data for both rent series come from the BLS's housing survey which in its current form started in 1983.[14] The housing unit sample is stratified and consists of approximately 26,000 owner units and 36,000 rental units in 1998, with a planned increase to 50,000 rental units in 1999. Units are surveyed either in person or by telephone, with individual rental units surveyed every six months. Beginning in 1997, owner-occupied units were no longer recontacted, but previously they had been recontacted once every two years. The BLS actually tracks rents for individual units as separate time series. Of course, each month a portion of the sample is surveyed.

Field agents for the BLS gather from rental units information for the rent and services provided for the current month and the previous month. From owner-occupied units, they obtain an estimated or implicit initial rent. This implicit rent is the rent the owner says the unit would rent for on the market. However, because of the unreliability of owners' responses for implicit rent, field agents enter their own estimates. The field agents' figures are used by the BLS for actual computations for the OER index. Also, field agents collect information on the characteristics of the housing units, including structure type, number of rooms, and the age of the home.

After the initial implicit rent is established for a given unit, subsequent values of implicit rent are moved by matching units from the rental sample to owners' units. The rental units are matched to owners by location, structural type, and other characteristics. The BLS first tries to match owners with rental units that fit for all variables, but, if necessary, constraints are relaxed one at a time until a satisfactory set of renters is found for all owners.

After the initial interview, owners' responses on housing characteristics are more important than their implicit rent estimate because it is the match of housing characteristics to corresponding rental units that determines the change in OER. This is especially true since field agents' figures are used for the initial implicit rent number. In essence, a small subset of the rental sample is used to estimate the owners' equivalent rent index, which is about 20 percent of the overall CPI. Following this matching process, OER is estimated in the same technical manner as residential rent. Even though owner-occupied units are contacted only once every two years to check for quality and tenure changes, the characteristics of these units are used in the matching process and index calculations every six months.

For residential rent, the housing survey data are directly used (after adjustments for changes in quality) to estimate changes in the residential rent and owners' equivalent indexes by calculating six-month-ago percent changes for units surveyed in the latest month. These indexes are moved by changes based on the six-month change raised exponentially to the one-sixth power. Of course, percentage changes are applied by stratified components. Also, rents are quality-adjusted for each month's aging of units surveyed.

Rent figures collected in the housing survey are on a contract basis for residential rent and on a pure rent basis for owners' equivalent rent. The collected rents for residential rent include any labor provided as part of payment and also covers all services and facilities provided on a contract basis, such as furniture or utilities. Owners' equivalent rent excludes payment for these extra services. Both rental components are adjusted for changes in quality. These factors cover changes in services and facilities provided by the landlord. Examples include the elimination of the inclusion of utilities in the rent or might include the addition of a room to an apartment. Beginning in 1988, the BLS also began to adjust rent for aging; this is viewed as reducing the quality of housing units.

Other shelter services include lodging while out of town, lodging while at school, tenants' insurance and household insurance, and maintenance and repair services. These components are small, the largest being lodging away from home (1997 relative importance, 23 percent), followed by household insurance (1997 relative importance, 0.4 percent). However, in 1987, the lodging away from home component had a significant change in the sample. Previously, hotels and motels in the sample were in or near urban areas covered by the CPI. With the revision, the sampled hotels and motels could be anywhere in the United States that households from those urban areas went on vacation. Essentially, there was a switch from sampling hotels and motels in the central business district to sampling outlets primarily in tourist and vacation areas.

Other Services

Other nonenergy services are found in all of the other expenditure categories except for food. Relative importance figures for 1997 are in parentheses. Within transportation services (6.984) some of the components are motor vehicle maintenance and repair (1.603), automobile insurance (2.551), and airline fares (0.814). Medical care services (4.392) include professional medical services—for physicians' services, dental, eye care, and other (2.808), hospital and other medical care services (1.334), and health insurance (0.250). Various medical tests, x-rays, imaging, and the like are counted as services. Medical care commodities include "prescription drugs and medical equipment and supplies" and "nonprescription drugs and medical equipment and supplies."

Recreation covers some services such as club memberships, fees for participant sports, admission fees to movies, theater, etc., fees for lesson or instructions, and types of entertainment. Education and communication includes services such as tuition, other school fees, and childcare (combined 2.421), and telephone services (2.357). Finally, under the expenditure group "other goods and services," the services categories are for personal care, such as haircuts (0.963) and miscellaneous personal services (1.465). These latter include legal and personal financial services, and funeral expenses.

KEYS TO ANALYZING THE MONTHLY REPORT AND NEAR-TERM INFLATION TRENDS

Technical factors affecting the CPI are relatively few and include seasonal adjustment problems, unseasonal weather that affects demand, temporary supply problems, and sampling problems that create monthly volatility. Once technical factors are discounted, near-term inflation trends are generally analyzed by summing trends. The pace of near-term inflation is judged by a several-month average since some components are volatile. These issues are discussed below, primarily as they relate to separate commodity and services categories.

Within *food,* meat is a significant subcomponent because of its relative importance. Meats such as cattle and pork can be affected by adverse conditions (drought or flood) in the grain belt since grain is a major cost in production. Interestingly, shortages of feed can lead to near-term declines in meat prices as cattle are slaughtered early, increasing retail meat supplies. But because there are lags in meat production, this year's increased slaughter reduces next year's supply, thereby raising meat prices for next year. The full impact of grain losses are not felt for at least a year.

Vegetables and fruits are also affected by temporary supply problems. Freezes can damage crops and lead to a run-up in prices for fresh fruits and vegetables when affected. However, these price changes are usually temporary because over a year different regions in the United States and across the world supply various fresh fruits and vegetables. For analysis of food price trends, one should track not only the U.S. agricultural outlook but also agricultural trends worldwide.

Energy analysis is divided into three main components: refined oil products, electricity, and natural gas. Obviously, the key motor fuel and heating oil components are affected by changes in crude oil prices as well as by any taxes on these commodities. There are various market reports on spot and contract prices for crude oil, as well as the U.S. Department of Energy publication *Short-Term Energy Outlook.*

For electricity, prices are actually rates charged by utilities. Rates generally are determined on some form of cost-plus profit basis, although regulators are beginning to require competitive pricing. Nonetheless, costs are based primarily on fuel expense. The fuel used most by electric utilities is coal, although environmental legislation is causing switching not only from high-sulfur coal to cleaner low-sulfur coal but also to natural gas. Analysis of electric utility trends, therefore, is dependent on trends in coal prices, natural gas prices, and changes in environmental regulations. Utilities factor in the costs of pollution abatement equipment in their rate schedules. A small but significant share of electricity output is from nuclear power plants, but they have their own unique cost structure.

The natural gas industry is also heavily regulated. Rate changes are irregular, but general industry trends can be followed in industry publications such as *Oil and Gas Journal.* Spot and futures prices of natural gas are published daily in *The Wall Street Journal.*

Projecting *commodities excluding food and energy* requires tracking consumer demand trends, pricing strategies for various industries, the exchange value of the dollar, and changes in sourcing of various items by retailers. Demand affects prices of all goods and services, but some goods have demand that is relatively price-sensitive. Apparel goods is the largest subcomponent of these commodities, and demand clearly affects the amount of discounting over clothing seasons. The next largest subcomponent is new passenger cars; demand can have a significant impact on manufacturers' suggested retail prices, rebates, and dealer-price concessions. Industry perceptions of demand also affect pricing strategies. Additionally, both apparel and autos generally either have significant import competition or are primarily imported. Hence, tracking the exchange value of the dollar is important. Other factors being equal, a higher dollar leads to lower import prices, thereby constraining prices for domestically produced goods.

Finally, newly industrialized countries (NICs) are becoming increasingly important sources of imported goods. Latin America and Asia are growing in importance as U.S. trading partners. Owing to direct investment in these regions by the United States and other industrialized countries and to internal investment in manufacturing facilities, these areas are providing low-cost goods at quality often comparable to the goods produced in the United States. Therefore, to project inflation for these goods, an analyst must be aware of shifts in sources of imported goods. For example, sources of imports of some consumer electronics and power tools have shifted over time from Japan to South Korea and Taiwan and even to China and other NICs in Asia.

Services are difficult to forecast in terms of evaluating underlying fundamentals because these underlying factors are usually very broad. Services prices generally track overall inflation pressures. Also, services differ substantially in character from subcomponent to subcomponent. Housing rent is very different from medical care services. Fortunately, services inflation changes slowly and usually with a lag relative to goods inflation. Changes in direction of goods inflation is a good indicator of changes in direction of services inflation.

However, since housing rental series are the largest subcomponents in this services group, it is appropriate to track indicators that affect housing rents. First, demographic factors are important. Is there a rising or declining segment of the population in the rental market (baby boomers or baby busters)? Job availability also affects whether household formation is strong or not. Vacancy rate data also indicate whether there is an excessive supply or shortage of apartments. Finally, mortgage rates and housing prices can suggest whether apartment dwellers may be interested in leaving in order to purchase a house. When housing markets are attractive, apartment rents are less likely to rise significantly. However, when using variables such as multifamily vacancy rates and housing prices to project rent inflation, one should pay close attention to the lags involved.[15]

Problems with Seasonality

Financial markets usually focus on the seasonally adjusted CPI data for analysis of current inflation pressures. Even though the CPI data are seasonally adjusted using sophisticated statistical procedures,[16] problems with seasonality can create distortions in the data. The problems are not with the seasonal adjustment procedure but with the data: they do not have perfectly stable seasonal patterns. However, market analysts should be aware that the impact of seasonal irregularities can be either insustainable, with offsets later in the season, or significant, with a lasting impact on inflation for the year.

Seasonality can have significant effects on price changes if (1) the magnitude of seasonal discounting diverges from previous patterns only because of changes in marketing strategy (pricing) by stores or (2) there is a significant change in demand relative to supply that leaves end-of-season inventories atypically lean or overstocked. In the first instance, distortions early in the season are usually offset later in the season; in the second, the effect on inflation data remains intact with no offset.

First, one needs to be aware that not seasonally adjusted data are put into seasonally adjusted form with seasonal factors.[17] These numerical adjustments raise or lower unadjusted data to a moving average. For example, unadjusted heating oil prices are normally high in the winter and low in the summer. Seasonal factors raise unadjusted summer prices and lower winter prices to put into seasonally adjusted form. In turn, there are monthly seasonally adjusted increases or decreases in prices when unadjusted changes exceed or fall short of the changes anticipated by the seasonal factors.

However, seasonal factors, which are used to "inflate" or "deflate" unadjusted data, can exaggerate price movements when there are sharp changes in supply or demand for goods that have large seasonal swings in price and the distortion occurs during months with large seasonal factors. Such goods include motor fuel, heating oil, and fresh fruits and vegetables, among others. For example, during a warm winter, unadjusted heating oil prices might not rise as much as normal. Unadjusted prices would be up in midwinter, but not as much as usual because of relatively slack demand. This would push seasonally adjusted prices down because the rise was not as large as anticipated by the seasonal factor. Also, since the magnitude of the seasonal factor is very large in winter, the adjusted decline could also be very noticeable.

A change in marketing strategy (that is, initial pricing in the season) can affect early seasonally adjusted price changes in a clothing season. However, if demand and supply are little changed from the previous year, then the initial effects from higher- or lower-than-usual introductory prices are usually offset in subsequent months as discounting of the necessary magnitude takes place to clear inventories. If prices start out "too high," then discounting will likely be deeper later to move merchandise. If prices start out "too low," then inventories will move earlier than usual and less discounting will be needed later in the season. Generally, with no change in supply and demand conditions, these atypical starts in pricing early in the season "wash out" later in the season.

In contrast, if Christmas sales are strong and there is little inventory for after-Christmas sales, then there is less than typical discounting. This pushes seasonally adjusted prices up since the seasonal factor expects a specific amount of discounting that did not occur. In this situation, there are no offsetting subsequent "technical" movements in the seasonally adjusted price data. In summary, the amount of discounting is dependent upon inventories and demand. In turn, the degree of discounting compared to the past affects seasonally adjusted price movement. Less than typical discounting leads to seasonally adjusted price increases.

Occasionally one reads an analysis stating that early introduction of clothing in a season led to a price increase. However, this change in timing truly only affected the apparel data over the late 1980s when such a change did occur and was permanent. But a shift in timing of the clothing season distorts the seasonally adjusted data only as long as it takes for new seasonal factors to be incorporated into the data. This is for a time period of five to seven years, depending on the particular series. Since the introductions of clothing seasons are no longer being moved earlier, sharp increases in prices at the start of the season now reflect retailers attempting to pass on higher prices, which may or may not be sustainable.

Indexing Social Security

For indexing government Social Security payments, the CPI-W index is used instead of the CPI-U index. Generally, these cost-of-living adjustments (COLAs) take place on January 1 and are based on the year-over-year percent changes for the not seasonally adjusted average level for the third quarter in the previous year. The size of the COLA is not necessarily the same as the year-over-year percentage, but is typically a preset percentage of the CPI rise. The CPI-W is also usually used for collective bargaining contracts.

The Boskin Report

In recent academic and policy studies, an increasingly important issue has been and continues to be whether the CPI overstates inflation as a measure of the cost of living. Currently, the CPI tracks the changes in the cost of a fixed basket of goods and services, whereas a cost of living index would track the cost of a fixed level of well-being. This is an important issue because the CPI is used as a measure of inflation that is tracked by policy makers, including the Federal Reserve. Additionally, the CPI is used to index tax brackets for federal personal income taxes, Social Security benefits, veterans' pensions, national school lunch and breakfast programs, among others. A significant reduction in the growth rate of the CPI would go a long way toward helping to balance the Federal budget deficit.

The Congressional Budget Office has estimated that a hypothetical reduction in CPI growth of 0.5 percent over fiscal years 1996–2000 would cut federal outlays by $13.3 billion in fiscal year 2000, while revenues would be $9.6 billion higher.

On December 4, 1996, the Advisory Commission to Study the Consumer Price Index presented its final report to the Senate Finance Committee, which created the commission.[18] This report—commonly known as the Boskin Report, after the commission chair, Michael Boskin—concluded that the CPI would overstate inflation in coming years by a plausible range of 0.8 to 1.6 percent with 1.1 percent as the committee's best estimate. The commission listed three sources of bias and the impact of each on overall CPI bias.

Substitution bias	0.4
New-outlet vias	0.1
New-product, quality-change bias	0.6

Substitution bias is when consumers substitute relatively low-priced goods for higher-priced items in order to maintain the highest level of well-being. New-outlet bias occurs when consumers shift to discount outlets to make purchases. The commission claims that this shift is "not properly handled" by the BLS. The BLS does rotate outlets to reflect changes in consumer outlet preferences, but it generally treats the switch as a start of a new item being priced. The assumption is that the environment or "atmosphere" of the outlet or store is part of the good or service purchased.

New-product bias is the result of the long lag in incorporating new products into the CPI basket. Since new products are generally introduced to the public with high prices that typically fall after a year or two as average production costs decline and distribution is more widespread, the lagged introduction into the CPI misses this initial decline in price. However, new products are a very small portion of consumer expenditures.

Quality-change bias occurs when improvements in the quality of products are inadequately measured or discounted from the change in the price of the good. For example, automobile prices have risen sharply over the past decade but quality has also risen, notably in terms of safety, reduced lifetime repair costs, and lifetime. Medical services costs have also risen rapidly but many procedures are now on an outpatient basis with significantly reduced time needed for recovery, thereby lowering income losses.

The Boskin commission recommended that the BLS establish cost of living as the primary objective of measuring consumer prices, and that the BLS develop and publish two indexes: a monthly index designed in the spirit of COL, but timely, and an annual index revised historically to incorporate new information and research results.

The BLS response was mixed. First, the BLS noted that certain technical improvements phased in from 1996 to 1998 were already effectively reducing an upward bias by about 0.3 percent. It further noted that switching completely to a cost-of-living methodology would reduce the official inflation rate by only 0.15 percent. Importantly, a COL index would not be timely since information on consumer expenditure patterns is available only with lags of about one and a half to two years.

TABLE 5–5
Recent CPI Methodology Changes and Impact on Growth Rates

Date	Change	Impact on Growth Rate
January 1995	Food at home seasoning	−0.04% (annualized)
	Owners equivalent rent formula	−0.10
	Rent composite estimator	+0.03
June–July 1996	General seasoning	−0.10
January 1997	Hospital services index	−0.03 (CBO)
January 1998	Computer hedonic pricing	−0.06 (CBO)
	New basket weights	−0.1 to −0.2
January 1999	Geometric mean	−0.0 to −0.25
1999	Rotation by item	−0.08 (CBO)*
1995–1999	Cumulative	−0.48 to −0.83

Estimates of the impact of these methodology changes are from BLS except for items indicated from the Congressional Budget Office.[1] *Estimate of effect of four-year phase-in period.

The BLS was very critical of the Boskin commission's highly subjective estimates of quality adjustments, calling them "squishy" and ad hoc. The BLS agreed that quality adjustment is a serious issue needing further research, some of which has been underway for years. The BLS specifically challenged the validity of the commission's estimate that two-thirds (0.6 percent per year) of the overall bias in the CPI came from deficiencies in quality adjustments, leaving the impression that the BLS makes no adjustments for quality changes in deriving the CPI. In fact, the BLS stated, in routine calculations during 1995, more than half of the price change reported for goods and services was adjusted out: 4.7 percent year-over-year versus 2.2 percent after quality adjustments to the 70 percent of the index with quality adjustments. Shelter is the primary exclusion.

Recent Improvements in the CPI

The BLS continually strives to improve the methodology underlying the CPI, as shown in Table 5–5. (See also Tables 5–7 and 5–8 at the end of this chapter summarizing various CPI revisions since 1940.) With recent and planned changes during 1998 and 1999, CPI growth rates will differ from those of prior years. This is important in terms of forecasting post-1998–1999 growth rates based on prior data, especially prior to 1995. The cumulative effect of these methodological changes is to lower growth rates by 0.51 to 0.71 percent, compared to the pre-1995 data.

KEY ROLES IN THE ECONOMY AND UNDERLYING FUNDAMENTALS

The CPI is the primary measure of inflation in the United States. (See Summary Table 5–8 at the end of the chapter for inflation figures from 1970 to 1997.) To understand the uses of the CPI, it is important to understand some basics about the causes and dynamics of inflation.

BOX 5–2
Calculating the Monthly Percentage Changes

The financial press and electronic media report a given month's consumer price index primarily in terms of a simple monthly percentage change and an annualized monthly percentage change. For example, for the May 1990 CPI, released on June 15, 1990, the index was reported as rising a seasonally adjusted 0.2 percent or an annualized 1.9 percent. The April and May seasonally adjusted index levels were 129.1 and 129.3, respectively.

The simple monthly percentage change for May 1989 is calculated as follows:

$$[(129.3/129.1) - 1] \times 100 = [(1.0015492) - 1] \times 100$$
$$= 0.0015492 \times 100$$
$$= 0.15492\%, \text{ or } 0.2\%, \text{ rounded}$$

The annualized (compounded) monthly percentage change for May 1989 is calculated as follows:

$$[(129.3/129.1)^{12}] - 1 \times 100 = [(1.0015492)^{12}) - 1] \times 100$$
$$= [(1.0187495) - 1] \times 100$$
$$= 0.0187495 \times 100$$
$$= 1.87495\%, \text{ or } 1.9\%, \text{ rounded}$$

This compounded percentage change is referred to as a seasonally adjusted annual rate (SAAR). The 12 is an exponent and represents the number of periods required to obtain an annual rate. In this case, with a single-period change in the data (one month's span), 12 is the appropriate amount of compounding. For quarterly data, the compounding would be for four periods. For data spanning five months (e.g., May over the previous December), the exponential figure would be 12 divided by 5.

A cumulative-to-date annualized percentage change for May 1989 (with December 1989 being 126.3) is calculated as follows:

$$[(129.3/126.3)^{(12/5)}] - 1 \times 100 = [(1.023753)^{2.4}] - 1 \times 100$$
$$= (1.057958) - 1 \times 100$$
$$= 0.057958 \times 100$$
$$= 5.7958\%, \text{ or } 5.8\% \text{ annualized,}$$
$$\text{rounded.}$$

TABLE 5–6

Improvements to the Consumer Price Index, 1966–1995

Change	Date Implemented	Description
New construction	1966	Rent samples augmented with units built after 1960
Quality adjustment of new automobile prices	1967	New automobile prices adjusted for quality differences after model changeovers
Sample rotation	1981	Introduced a systematic replacement of outlets between major revisions
Rental equivalence	1983	Changed homeowners' component from cost of purchase to value of rental services for CPI-U
Return from sale price imputation	1984	Introduced procedure to eliminate downward bias for items discontinued by outlets that went out of index with discounted prices
Rental equivalence	1985	Changed CPI-W homeowners' component to value of services
Enhanced seasonal products methodology	1985	Enhanced methodology used for seasonal items by expanding the number of price quotations to select products from alternate seasons and eliminate under-representation of such items.
Quality adjustment of used car prices	1987	Prices of used cars adjusted for differences in quality after model changeovers.
Aging bias correction	1988	Rental values adjusted for aging of the housing stock.
Imputation procedures for new cars and trucks	1989	Price changes for non-comparable new models are imputed using only the constant-quality price changes for comparable model changeovers.
Quality adjustment of apparel prices	1991	Regression models used to adjust apparel prices for changes in quality when new clothing lines are introduced, and eliminate bias due to linking product substitutions into the CPI.
Discount air fares	1991	Substitution rules modified to expand pricing of discount airline fares.
Hotel and motels	1992	Samples for hotels and motels quadrupled to reduce variances related to seasonal pricing
Seasonal adjustment	1994	Procedures for seasonal adjustment revised to eliminate residual seasonality effects

TABLE 5–6 (*continued*)

Change	Date Implemented	Description
Quality adjustment for gasoline	1994	"Reformulated" gasoline treated as a quality change and the price adjusted to reflect quality difference; impact of the change estimated
Generic drugs	1995	Introduced new procedures that allow generic drugs to be priced when a brand drug loses its patent
Food-at-home base-period prices	1995	Introduced seasoning procedures to eliminate upward bias in setting of base-period prices of newly initiated items
Rental equivalence	1995	Modified imputation of homeowners' implicit rent to eliminate the upward drift property of the current estimator.
Composite estimator used in housing.	1995	Replaced current composite estimator with a 6-month chain estimator. Underreporting of 1-month rent changes had resulted in missing price change in residential rent and homeowners' equivalent rent. Old estimator also produced higher variances.
Commodities and services period prices	1996	Extended food-at-home seasoning procedures to remainder of commodities and services series. Based period prices left unchanged in most noncomparable substitutions.

Source: *Monthly Labor Review,* December 1996, p. 5.

Monetarist economists explain inflation in terms of growth in the money supply relative to the output of goods and services: when monetary growth is excessive, inflation rises, and when monetary growth slows relative to output, then inflation declines. Based on monetarist views of inflation, growth in monetary aggregates and growth in real output will largely determine inflation trends. Indeed, markets do compare these trends for long-term inflation projections.

However, there are two major limitations to the monetarist view of inflation. First, the demand for money is neither stable or very predictable. Consumers and businesses do not always have the same desire to hold money as they may have had in the past. Additionally, the definitions of money supply have not been constant from a practical perspective since changes in financial regulations have af-

TABLE 5–7
Previous CPI Revisions

Release of Revised CPI	Expenditure Base Period	Notable Innovations
1940	1934–1936	Introduced the concept of a sample of cities and items and the principle of imputation
1953	1950	Expanded population coverage to represent all urban wage earner and clerical worker families
1964	1960–1961	Expanded population coverage to represent individuals as well as families; introduced computer processing
1978	1973–1973	Expanded population coverage to represent all urban consumers; improved methodology for construction of outlet sample frame; introduced probability sampling techniques into the selection of the item and outlet samples techniques into the selection of the item and outlet samples.
1987	1982–84	Expanded scope of systematic outlet rotation; introduced advanced sample allocation model.

Source: *Monthly Labor Review*, December 1996, p. 6.

fected money growth. Therefore, the relationship between money growth and inflation is not as tight as theorists would like. Nonetheless, tracking growth in money supply is useful for projecting long-term changes in inflation trends.

Keynesian theory generally explains inflation in terms of aggregate demand relative to aggregate supply. Shortages of goods caused by heavy demand drive up prices and inflation. For this type of analysis, attention usually focuses on the strength of consumer and business demand and on indicators of supply bottlenecks. A few such indicators include the unemployment rate for labor markets, the capacity utilization rate for both manufacturing and vendor performance, and sensitive raw materials prices for both manufacturing and construction.

Inflation can also be temporarily affected by supply shocks, such as for crude oil. Hence, crude oil prices are an important indicator for tracking cost-push inflation.

Price levels can be affected directly by government policy changes. For example, government price supports for farmers affect a number of food items, including peanuts, sugar, and milk. Changes in import tariffs and export subsidies by foreign countries can lead to significant shifts in U.S. prices for various goods and services. Along this same line, international exchange rates clearly have an impact on inflation. A rise in the value of the dollar makes imports cheaper, thereby lowering the cost of imported goods and constraining prices of similar domestically produced goods. Inflation rates are affected by changes in exchange rates until trade patterns fully adjust to the change in relative costs for domestic versus foreign-produced goods.

Over the business cycle, inflation rates are affected by changes in supply and demand. Following a recession trough, demand rises but resources are not strained since there is substantial unused production capacity and unemployed or

TABLE 5–8

Consumer Price Inflation by Expenditure Group, 1970–1997

Annual Average Percentage Changes

	Total	Food and Beverages	Housing	Apparel	Transportation	Medical Care	Education and Communication	Other Goods and Services
1970	5.8	5.5	7.1	4.1	5.1	6.3	na	5.8
1971	4.3	3.1	4.3	3.2	5.2	6.5	na	4.7
1972	3.3	4.1	3.9	2.1	1.2	3.2	na	4.3
1973	6.2	13.3	4.3	3.7	3.2	3.9	na	3.9
1974	11.1	13.8	11.3	7.4	11.2	9.3	na	7.2
1975	9.1	8.4	10.5	4.5	9.4	12.1	na	8.3
1976	5.7	3.1	6.2	3.7	9.9	9.5	na	5.8
1977	6.5	6.0	6.8	4.5	7.0	9.6	na	5.9
1978	7.6	9.8	8.8	3.5	4.7	8.4	na	6.4
1979	11.3	10.7	12.2	4.4	14.3	9.3	na	7.3
1980	13.5	8.6	15.7	7.1	17.8	11.0	na	9.0
1981	10.3	7.8	11.5	4.8	12.1	10.8	na	9.9
1982	6.1	4.1	7.2	2.6	4.1	11.6	na	10.3
1983	3.2	2.2	2.7	2.5	2.4	8.7	na	10.9
1984	4.3	3.8	4.2	1.8	4.4	6.2	na	6.7
1985	3.5	2.3	4.0	2.9	2.6	6.2	na	6.2
1986	1.9	3.3	3.0	0.8	-3.9	7.5	na	6.1
1987	3.7	4.1	3.0	4.4	3.0	6.6	na	5.8
1988	4.1	4.1	3.7	4.3	3.1	6.5	na	6.7
1989	4.8	5.7	3.8	2.8	5.0	7.7	na	7.8
1990	5.4	5.8	4.5	4.6	5.6	9.1	na	7.6
1991	4.2	3.6	3.9	3.7	2.8	8.7	na	7.9
1992	3.0	1.4	2.9	2.5	2.2	7.4	na	6.8
1993	3.0	2.1	2.7	1.4	3.0	6.0	na	5.3
1994	2.6	2.3	2.5	-0.2	3.0	4.8	3.9	2.9
1995	2.8	2.8	2.5	-1.1	3.6	4.5	3.8	4.2
1996	2.9	3.3	2.9	-0.2	2.8	3.5	3.4	4.1
1997	2.3	2.6	2.9	0.9	0.9	2.8	3.3	4.4

Note: Annual data are not yet available for the newly created "recreation" expenditure group.

Source: U.S. Department of Labor, Bureau of Labor Statistics. Data are not seasonally adjusted.

underemployed labor. Eventually, resource prices (including wages) rise because of scarcity, growth in final goods is outstripped by demand, and inflation picks up. Generally, goods prices inflation accelerates before services inflation does. Services CPI is classified as a lagging indicator.

In summary, long-run inflation is caused by excessive growth in money supply or by the alternative explanation of demand rising faster than output. Analysts therefore watch growth in money supply aggregates as well as variables such as the unemployment rate, capacity utilization, and the exchange value of the dollar.

KEY QUESTIONS IN ANALYZING THE NEWS RELEASE

- What did the CPI excluding food and energy do?
- Are changes in food and energy diverging from the rest of the CPI? Is the CPI excluding food and energy really a trend series for the overall CPI?
- Are changes in crude oil prices still expected to impact the CPI in coming months?
- Did a freeze or another type of agricultural problem boost food prices? Will other food-growing regions or countries be able to replenish these supplies once their growing season reaches harvest or is the shortage for that crop going to continue all year?
- Are strong increases in feed costs likely to lead to near-term weakness in meat prices as stocks are taken to market but then lead to higher prices later owing to lower supply?
- Did passenger car prices have an unsustainably large increase? Did manufacturers' rebates affect the latest data or the previous month's data?
- Is underlying demand strong enough to support apparel prices existing at the start of the season?
- Did housing components for owners' equivalent rent and for residential rent diverge from recent trends? Monthly changes in these two series are volatile but year-over-year changes move slowly. Large one-month deviations from the several-month average generally should be discounted.
- Were there any special factors affecting seasonal demand for hotels and motels in resort areas? Lodging while out of town has very large seasonals for winter months.
- Are medical care services being affected either by new medical care plans or by expectations about passage of health care legislation?

NOTES FOR CHAPTER 5

1. U.S. Department of Labor, Bureau of Labor Statistics, *BLS Handbook of Methods,* Bulletin 2414, September 1992, p. 176.

2. For definition of a consumer unit, see Charles Mason and Clifford Butler, "New Basket of Goods and Services Being Priced in Revised CPI," *Monthly Labor Review,* January 1987, pp. 3–4.
3. Metropolitan areas are defined by the Office of Management and Budget. The BLS defines a few additional metropolitan areas.
4. See Mason and Butler, op. cit., p. 6.
5. Data are for the all-urban index (CPI-U).
6. Aizcorbe, Ana M., Robert A. Cage, and Patrick C. Jackman, "Commodity Substitution Bias in Laspeyres Indexes: Analysis Using CPI Source Data for 1982–1994," Working Paper, July 1996, p. 2.
7. *BLS Handbook of Methods,* op. cit., p.178.
8. This survey is also more formally called the Continuing Point-of-Purchase Survey (CPOPS).
9. For a detailed list of expenditure classes, item strata, and entry level items, *BLS Handbook of Methods,* op. cit., pp. 221–225.
10. See Greenlees, John S., and Charles Mason, "Overview of the 1998 Revision of the Consumer Price Index," *Monthly Labor Review,* December 1996, p. 9.
11. The period 1979–1993 reflects not only the impact of inflation, but also a potentially significant impact resulting from the 1979 data being based on 1972–1973 expenditures and the 1993 data being based on 1982–1984 expenditures.
12. The Food and Beverages group includes alcoholic beverages. Nonalcoholic beverages are included in the Food group. By commodities and services groupings, alcoholic beverages fall under Commodities Excluding Food and Energy.
13. In fact, the slightly broader component for overall services (which includes utility gas and electricity) is one of the components in the Conference Board's index of lagging indicators.
14. From 1953 to 1982, the shelter component was based on the cost of purchasing housing and included a mortgage rate component. The shelter component—and it can even be argued that the overall CPI—is a new series starting in 1983 because of the changes in definition.
15. See R. Mark Rogers, Steven W. Henderson, and Daniel H. Ginsburg, "Consumer Prices: Examining Housing Rental Components," *Economic Review,* Federal Reserve Bank of Atlanta, May-June 1993, pp. 32–51.
16. The procedure used is ARIMA X-12.
17. However, seasonally adjusted higher levels of aggregation often reflect the sum of independently adjusted series.
18. See Advisory Commission to Study the Consumer Price Index, Senate Finance Committee, "Toward a More Accurate Measure of the Cost of Living," *Final Report to the Senate Finance Committee,* December 4, 1996, p. 9.

BIBLIOGRAPHY

Advisory Commission to Study the Consumer Price Index. "Toward a More Accurate Measure of the Cost of Living," *Final Report to the Senate Finance Committee,* December 4, 1996.

Aizcorbe, Ana M., Robert A. Cage, and Patrick C. Jackman. "Commodity Substitution Bias in Laspeyres Indexes: Analysis Using CPI Source Data for 1982–1994," Working Paper, July 1996.

———— and Patrick C. Jackman. "The Commodity Substitution Effect in CPI Data, 1982–91," *Monthly Labor Review,* December 1993, pp. 25–33.

U.S. Department of Labor, Bureau of Labor Statistics. *BLS Handbook of Methods,* September 1992, Bulletin 2414.

"Measurement Issues in the Consumer Price Index," paper, June 1997.

Cage, Robert. "New Methodology for Selecting CPI Outlet Samples," *Monthly Labor Review,* December 1996, pp. 49–69.

Cardenas, Elaine M. "Revision of the CPI Hospital Services Component," *Monthly Labor Review,* December 1996, pp. 40–48.

Fixler, Dennis. "Anatomy of Price Change: The Consumer Price Index: Underlying Concepts and Caveats," *Monthly Labor Review,* December 1993, pp. 3–12.

Greenlees, John S., and Charles C. Mason. "Overview of the 1998 Revision of the Consumer Price Index," *Monthly Labor Review,* December 1996, pp. 3–9.

Henderson, Steven. "Measuring Homeownership in the CPI: The Flow of Services Using Rental Equivalence Has Replaced the Asset Approach," Paper delivered at the 65th Annual Western Economic Association International Conference, San Diego, California, July 1990.

Lane, Walter F. "Owners' Equivalent Rent in the American Consumer Price Index (CPI)," Prices Seminar Series Working Papers, U.S. Department of Labor, Bureau of Labor Statistics, Office of Prices and Living Conditions, Working Paper 8801–1, January 1988.

Lane, Walter. "Changing the Item Structure of the Consumer Price Index," *Monthly Labor Review,* December 1996, pp. 18–25.

Mason, Charles, and Clifford Butler. "New Basket of Goods and Services Being Priced in Revised CPI," *Monthly Labor Review,* U.S. Department of Labor, January 1987, pp. 3–22.

McKenzie, Chester V. Technical Note: Relative Importance of CPI Components," *Monthly Labor Review,* November 1961, pp. 1233–1236.

Moulton, Brent R. "Basic Components of the CPI: Estimation of Price Changes," *Monthly Labor Review,* December 1993, pp. 13–24.

Ptacek, Frank, and Robert M. Baskin. "Revision of the CPI Housing Sample and Estimators," *Monthly Labor Review,* December 1996, pp. 31–39.

Rogers, R. Mark. "Improving Monthly Models for Economic Indicators: The Example of an Improved CPI Model," *Economic Review,* September-October 1988, pp. 34–50.

Rogers, R. Mark, Steven W. Henderson, and Daniel H. Ginsburg. "Consumer Prices: Examining Housing Rental Components," *Economic Review,* May-June 1993, pp. 32–46.

William, Janet. "The Redesign of the CPI Geographic Sample," *Monthly Labor Review,* December 1996, pp. 10–17.

CHAPTER 6

THE PRODUCER PRICE INDEX

OVERVIEW

Probably the second most important price measure for the United States is the producer price index (PPI). It measures average changes in selling prices received by domestic producers for their output.[1] The PPI covers the mining and manufacturing sectors with some representation also in agriculture, fishing, forestry, services, and gas and electricity. The PPI is used in price escalation clauses; it is also used by government statistical agencies for deflating various goods into constant-dollar series. The PPI often provides some early warning for price pressures building or receding in the consumer sector. From the financial market's perspective, this release is important because it precedes the CPI release typically by several days and provides information on likely changes in that month's CPI. From a policy perspective, the PPI is also closely monitored by the Federal Reserve Board as it cover a variety of goods and services not tracked by the CPI series. In addition to pricing finished goods at the producer level, there are producer price indexes for crude materials and also for intermediate materials. These indexes provide early-warning signals for changes in inflation for finished goods at the producer level.

The PPI is produced by the U.S. Department of Labor, the Bureau of Labor Statistics. The monthly news release usually comes out during the second week in the month following the reference month. More extensive data are available in the *PPI Detailed Report.* Currently, the standard base year for the producer price index is 1982, which is set equal to 100. Individual PPI series beginning after the base year use a later base. Some PPIs are available in seasonally adjusted form (if a series passes statistical tests for seasonality), but all are available as not seasonally adjusted data. Annual revisions to seasonal factors may lead to revisions to data covering the preceding five years. Monthly revisions to the data occur only once, four months after the initial release. The not seasonally adjusted data are derived from a mail-in survey, and the BLS waits for late reports and corrections for this one monthly revision to unadjusted index levels.

By definition, the PPI actually measures changes in net unit revenues received by U.S. producers for the first significant commercial transaction within the United States. Taxes received by the government are not included. Rebates and other promotions by manufacturers affect the PPI. For example, low-interest financing plans paid by the manufacturer affect the PPI price for a car. A rebate by the manufacturer is also included since it affects net revenues, but a rebate by a dealer to a customer does not affect the PPI if no portion of the cost of the rebate is borne by the manufacturer. The PPI systematically attempts to capture actual transaction prices, not list prices.

Prices in the PPI are neither order prices nor "futures" prices. The PPI tries to measure prices for goods actually shipped in the reference month. Generally, prices are based on data for the Tuesday of the week containing the 13th of the month. There are exceptions for some farm products, some refined petroleum products, natural gas, and some industrial chemicals. Most prices are reported on a free on board (f.o.b.) basis.[2]

The producer price index used to be called the wholesale price index (WPI). The BLS changed the term in 1978 because of public misconceptions about the meaning of "wholesale." When the WPI began in 1902, *wholesale prices* referred to prices for goods sold in large quantities.[3] By the mid-1970s, the general public associated the term with wholesalers or distributors. There has never been a BLS price measure for goods sold at the distributor level. By force of habit, the media often use the phrase "wholesale prices" when referring to the PPI.

Data for the various producer price indexes are collected by mail-in surveys. The reporting companies are chosen by means of industry-specific probability sampling procedures. The universe for choosing the sample is the unemployment insurance (UI) system. The BLS updates the sample of each industry's producers every few years to take into account changes in production technology or industry structure. Usually, many of the same companies end up in the updated sample. Each month, over 100,000 price quotations are used in PPI calculations. The PPI system has several major classification systems, but the indexes in all are based on data from the same pool of company reporters. The BLS does attempt to adjust reported prices for any changes in quality.

As of 1998, the PPI program contained price indexes for approximately 500 mining and manufacturing industries, including over 10,000 indexes for specific products and product categories. There are also over 3,200 commodity price indexes and nearly 1,000 indexes for specific output of service industries.

DATA ORGANIZATION

The three most important classification structures are: (1) industry, (2) commodity, and (1) stage of processing (SOP). By far, the stage-of-processing classification is emphasized the most by the BLS and by financial analysts.

Industry Indexes

Industry PPIs measure an industry's net output; that is, the changes in prices received for that industry's output sold outside the industry. References to a "net output" index are basically references to industry indexes. *Net output* refers to the use of net output to derive component weights (see "Weighting of Components," below). Series are generally calculated at the four-digit standard industrial classification (SIC) industry level and often aggregated at three- and two-digit SIC levels.

Total mining and manufacturing PPIs are also calculated. Net output indexes are not available on a seasonally adjusted basis at this time.

There is no overall services index, but a number of service industries are covered by net output PPIs. These include railroads, the U.S. Postal Service, deep-sea transportation, water transportation of freight, air transportation, auto rentals, pipelines (except natural gas), petroleum pipelines, tour operators and travel agencies, radio broadcasting, electric power, natural gas utilities, scrap and waste materials, truck rentals, and hospitals.

The PPI Detailed Report tables for each industry include the overall industry index as well as indexes for primary products, some subcomponents of primary products, secondary products, and, sometimes, subcomponents of secondary products and "miscellaneous receipts."

Primary product indexes show changes in prices received by firms classified to be in the industry for products made primarily by that industry.[4] Such production of that product is not necessarily exclusive to that industry. Secondary products are those primarily producing in another industry. Miscellaneous receipts indexes show changes in prices of other sources of revenue (neither primary nor secondary products) received by firms in the industry. An example of this might be parking lot revenues if a firm operates a parking lot as an incidental business for the use of employees or the public. Consulting services for a manufacturer would also fit into this category. All physical product series fall under either the primary or secondary product components.

Commodity Indexes

The commodity indexes are the traditional PPI series—those closely followed before the emphasis on stage-of-processing by BLS. The commodity PPIs are organized by end use or material composition, regardless of the industry of origin (primary or secondary) for these products. This PPI commodity system is unique and does not directly correspond to any other standard system such as SIC or the standard international trade classification (SITC). It is based on the historical availability of various PPI series and has evolved because of specific needs of various users (such as other government statistical or regulatory agencies).

There are 15 major commodity groups in the all-commodities PPIs. The all-commodities index is the index that had been the overall measure of producer price inflation most closely followed prior to the introduction of the index for finished goods. For historical comparisons (especially for early in this century), the all-commodities index is often the only aggregate producer price series available.

The 15 major components are:

1. Farm products
2. Processed foods and feeds
3. Textile products and apparel
4. Hides, skins, leather, and related products
5. Fuels and related products and power

6. Chemicals and allied products

7. Rubber and plastic products

8. Lumber and wood products

9. Pulp, paper, and allied products

10. Metals and metal products

11. Machinery and equipment

12. Furniture and household durables

13. Nonmetallic mineral products

14. Transportation equipment

15. Miscellaneous products

The first two of the components for all commodities make up the index for farm products and processed foods and feeds, while the remaining major components form the industrial commodities PPI. There also are a variety of other commodity groups.

The key importance of the commodity classification PPIs is that (1) they are historically based and provide some continuity with early PPI data, and (2) with further regrouping at a finer level of detail, they provide the basis for the most closely followed PPI classification, namely, commodity-based stage-of-processing indexes.

Stage-of-Processing Indexes

The commodity-based stage-of-processing price indexes are those most emphasized by BLS. These indexes regroup commodities at the six-digit SIC level based on the class of the buyer and the amount of physical processing or assembling the products have undergone. The three stage-of-processing levels are finished goods, intermediate materials, supplies, and components; and crude materials for further processing (see Table 6–1). There also are industry-based stage-of-processing indexes, but they are little followed at this time. Subsequent discussion is for the commodity-based SOP indexes only.

Finished Goods

Finished goods for PPI purposes are goods for sale to the final-demand user—either consumers or businesses. The two primary components for the finished goods PPI are finished consumer goods and capital equipment. These categories roughly measure price changes at the producer level for the national income and product account (NIPA) categories for personal consumption expenditures on durables and nondurables plus utilities consumption and the producers' durable equipment component. For the consumer components, commonly followed subcomponents are finished consumer foods, finished energy goods, and finished consumer goods excluding food and energy. Finished energy goods are those sold to households; they include gasoline and heating oil and also what are technically services, residential electric power and residential gas. Both finished consumer goods and capital equipment are aggregated from individual commodity series, which are available separately.

TABLE 6–1

Producer Price Indexes by Stage of Processing

Stage of Processing	Relative Importance, December 1997
Finished goods	100.000
Finished consumer goods	74.733
Finished consumer foods	23.171
Finished energy goods	13.575
Finished consumer goods excluding food and energy	37.988
Capital equipment	25.267
Manufacturing industries	6.590
Nonmanufacturing industries	18.677
Intermediate materials, supplies, and components	100.000
Materials and components for manufacturing	47.581
Materials for food manufacturing	3.493
Materials for nondurable manufacturing	16.163
Materials for durable manufacturing	10.580
Components for manufacturing	17.345
Materials and components for construction	13.538
Processed fuels and lubricants	13.022
Containers	3.775
Supplies	22.084
Manufacturing industries	4.940
Nonmanufacting industries	17.144
Crude materials for further processing	100.000
Foodstuffs and feedstuffs	42.215
Nonfood materials	57.785
Nonfood materials except fuel	33.354
Manufacturing	32.018
Construction	1.336
Crude fuel	24.431
Manufacturing industries	2.029
Nonmanufacturing industries	22.402

Source: U.S. Department of Labor, Bureau of Labor Statistics, "Producer Price Indexes: January 1998," News Release,

For capital equipment, the typical breakdown in the monthly releases give the aggregates for manufacturing and nonmanufacturing industries. As of December 1997, nonmanufacturing industries made up about 19 percent of the finished goods index, while the manufacturing subcomponent was roughly 7 percent. Capital equipment PPIs include agricultural machinery, construction machinery; metal cutting machine tools; metal forming machine tools; tools, dies, jigs, fixtures, and industrial molds; pumps et al.; industrial material handling equipment; electronic computers; textile machinery; paper industries machinery; paper trades machinery; transformers et al.; communications equipment; x-ray and electromedical equipment; oil field and gas field machinery; mining machinery; office and store machines; commercial furniture; light motor trucks; heavy motor trucks; truck trailers; civilian aircraft; ships; railroad equipment; and photographic and photocopy equipment. Cars are included in both capital equipment and consumer goods.

Capital equipment indexes are strictly limited to the civilian sector; military capital items are not included.

Intermediate Materials, Supplies, and Components

The stage-of-processing PPI for intermediate materials, supplies, and components consists of partially processed commodities (for example, lumber and steel) as well as some nondurables that are physically complete but are used as inputs for business operations (for example, diesel fuel and corrugated boxes). The three major subcomponents are intermediate foods and feeds, intermediate energy materials, and intermediate materials less foods and energy. One should note that these broad components do not correspond directly with the broad components of the finished goods categories.

The intermediate materials less foods and feeds series includes flour, refined sugar, confectionery materials, crude vegetable oils, and prepared animal feeds. Examples of intermediate energy materials are commercial electric power, natural gas to electric utilities, jet fuel, and number 2 diesel fuel. Intermediate materials less foods and energy cover a wide array of goods such as synthetic fibers, industrial chemicals, agricultural chemicals, plywood, miscellaneous metal products, electronic components, cement, and motor vehicle parts.

Crude Materials for Further Processing

Crude materials for further processing are unprocessed commodities not sold to consumers directly. The major subcomponents are crude foodstuffs and feedstuffs, crude energy materials, and crude nonfood materials less energy.

TABLE 6–2

A Comparison between the PPI for Finished Goods and the CPI

PPI, Finished Goods	CPI
Covers consumer goods and capital equipment, but no services*	Covers consumer goods and services, but no capital equipment
Net unit revenues received by producers from first purchaser	Prices paid by consumers
Does not include taxes	Includes taxes paid by the consumer
Does not include imports	Includes imports
Prices generally refer to, Tuesday of the containing 13th of month	Prices taken over most of the month
Mail-in survey primarily	In-store survey of retailers and a housing survey
Includes the effects of rebates, etc., by producers but not retailers	Includes effect of rebates, etc., by producers or retailers as long as it shows up in the price paid by the consumer
Controls for quality changes	Controls for quality changes

*Natural gas and electric utilities for residences are included and technically are services. While not included in the PPI for finished goods, there are a number of services industries covered by producer price indexes for the net output of selected industries.

CHART 6–1
Producer Price Index versus Consumer Price Index

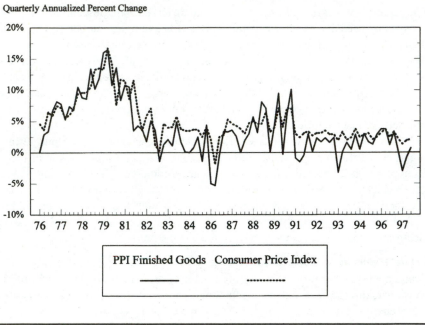

Quarterly Annualized Percent Change

PPI Finished Goods   Consumer Price Index

Crude foodstuffs and feedstuffs make up a little more than one-third of the crude materials index and are almost entirely farm products. Examples are citrus fruits, bulk dried vegetables, wheat, barley, cows, turkeys, fluid-use milk, oilseeds, and raw cane sugar. Crude energy materials are about one-half of crude materials and crude petroleum is about one-half of crude energy materials. Natural gas (to pipelines) is only a slightly smaller subcomponent. The remainder of crude energy materials consists of various specified types of coal. Crude nonfood materials other than energy span a wide variety of basic industrial and construction materials. A few representative series are cotton, leaf tobacco, pulpwood, carbon steel scrap, and various specified ores.

WEIGHTING OF COMPONENTS

Weighting methodologies differ according to the classification system of the PPIs. For industry series, the weights for each component are based on industry net output values of shipments. Net output values are the value of shipments from establishments classified in a particular industry to establishments classified in other industries. Because shipments within the industry are excluded, net output differs from gross shipment values. Owing to this exclusion, net output values are dependent upon the level of aggregation. As one moves from four-digit to three-digit industry levels and higher, there are greater opportunities for intra-industry shipments. One cannot simply add up disaggregated industry net output values to get higher levels. Net output values are based on data from the Census of Manufactures, BEA input-output tables, and other sources.

Weights for net output price indexes are constructed from input-output tables compiled by the Bureau of Economic Analysis. These PPIs are derived using 1992 net output weights and 1987 input-output relationships.

For the traditional individual and aggregated commodity price indexes, weights are based on gross value of shipments from Census Bureau data and other sources. Beginning with the reference month for January 1996, weights are based on 1992 shipment values from the Census of Manufactures (and other sources), although the index base period remains 1982. From January 1992 to December 1995, weights were based on 1987 shipment values. From January 1987 to December 1991, weights were based on 1982 shipment values. With PPI methodologies, previous weights for historical data are unchanged with updates on weights (as is also the case for the CPI).

Weights do not change over the period for which they define the mix of goods going into the index. However, the effective importance for a given good does vary over the period and even on a month-to-month basis as differing growth rates in components affect the relative standings. The weight of each component multiplied by its price increase relative to the base period and relative to the other components' price increase since the base period is that component's relative importance in the index.[5] Basically, components with higher rates of inflation have rising relative importance figures compared to those with low or negative inflation rates. BLS does not publish shipment values but does publish relative importance figures for December of each year.

KEYS TO ANALYZING THE MONTHLY REPORT

Each month market analysts usually focus on two primary numbers from the PPI report: total finished goods and finished goods excluding food and energy. Data generally are discussed in terms of simple monthly percentage changes or annualized rates. The primary use of PPI releases by financial markets is to project the upcoming CPI release for the same reference month and to add one more piece of information to corroborate their view of interest rates and potential changes in monetary policy by the Federal Reserve.

The PPI (in this section, for finished goods unless otherwise noted), is more volatile than the CPI. In particular the food and energy components are more erratic in monthly movements than their CPI counterparts. Therefore, analysts are generally predisposed to focus on the PPI less food and energy. This is often misleadingly called the "core" rate of inflation and is based on the assumption that the food and energy components are simply randomly oscillating each month and do not have trend growth rates separate from the rest of the PPI. Of course, if food or energy have trends that are different from the trend rate for the rest of the PPI, then the trend rate for the overall PPI will be different from the PPI excluding food and energy. Key questions for monthly analysis are shown in Table 6–3.

TABLE 6–3
Producer Prices by Stage of Processing, 1970–1997

	Annual Percentage Changes		
	Finished Goods	Intermediate Materials, Supplies and Components	Crude Materials for Further Processing
1970	3.4	3.8	3.5
1971	3.1	3.8	2.6
1972	3.1	4.1	10.8
1973	9.1	10.8	36.5
1974	15.3	23.8	12.7
1975	10.8	10.5	0.5
1976	4.4	5.0	2.9
1977	6.5	6.6	3.2
1978	7.9	6.9	12.0
1979	11.1	12.8	17.1
1980	13.5	15.3	11.1
1981	9.3	9.2	8.0
1982	4.0	1.4	−2.9
1983	1.6	0.6	1.3
1984	2.1	2.5	2.2
1985	0.9	−0.4	−7.5
1986	−1.4	−3.5	−8.4
1987	2.1	2.4	6.7
1988	2.5	5.5	2.5
1989	5.1	4.6	7.4
1990	4.9	2.2	5.7
1991	2.1	0.0	−7.0
1992	1.2	0.2	−0.8
1993	1.2	1.4	2.0
1994	0.6	2.0	−0.7
1995	1.9	5.4	1.0
1996	2.6	0.7	10.8
1997	0.4	−0.1	−2.4

Source: U.S. Department of Labor, Bureau of Labor Statistics.

For analysts interested in forecasting the CPI from the PPI, the most important factor is to use only the consumer component of the PPI.[6] The PPI has a capital equipment component that is not relevant for a CPI forecast. Also, the PPI should only be used to project durables, nondurables, and utility services for the CPI. The CPI has services comprising a little over half of its components by weight for which there are no PPI components. Also, the PPI has little lead time in predicting movement in the CPI. Studies indicate that most of the impact of changes in the PPI are seen in the same month's data for the CPI.[7] See Table 6–2 and Chart 6–1 for a comparison of PPI and CPI.

Other than food and energy, the components that often play the largest role in affecting the PPI are for passenger cars and light trucks ($\leq$ 10,000 lbs.). These components are volatile owing to the use of rebate programs and special incentives and to the difficulty in seasonally adjusting prices for motor vehicles. The

CHART 6–2
Producer Price Indexes by Stage of Processing

Quarterly Annualized Percent Change

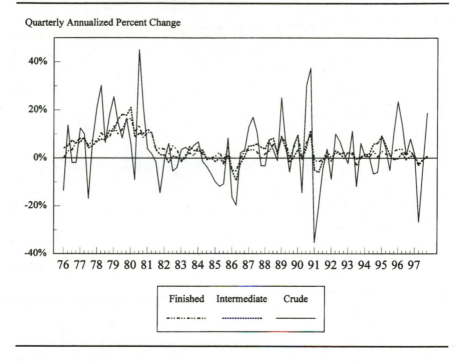

| Finished | Intermediate | Crude |
| .... | .... | ——— |

timing of the introduction of new models varies from year to year. Tobacco and prescription drugs components can also cause erratic movement in the PPI.

One of the broader problems with using the stage-of-processing indexes to track costs is that there is often no uniform, one-directional flow in the production process. For various goods, and even specific industries, there is not a perfect flow of materials from crude to intermediate to finished goods. Sometimes the intermediate level is skipped; this is often the case with farm products or energy materials. There are even examples of intermediate goods or finished products being used in the production of crude materials. The use of stage-of-processing indexes is best for specific commodities or industries rather than in terms of using the broad indexes to predict changes in the next stage. In particular, one should understand the direction of the production flow for specific goods and industries in order to best utilize the more detailed stage-of-processing PPIs (Chart 6–2).

KEY ROLES IN THE ECONOMY AND UNDERLYING FUNDAMENTALS

Producer price indexes—all three stage of production indexes—are early warning signals for consumer price inflation. The finished goods index also provides information on producer prices for capital equipment. The underlying fundamentals

TABLE 6-4

Producer Prices for Finished Goods, 1970–1997

		Annual Percentage Changes						
	Total Finished Goods	Total, Excluding Food and Energy	Consumer Goods	Capital Equipment	Total Consumer Goods	Consumer Goods Excluding Food and Energy	Consumer Foods	Finished Energy
1970	3.4	—	3.0	4.7	3.0	—	3.2	—
1971	3.1	—	2.7	4.1	2.7	—	1.5	—
1972	3.1	—	3.3	2.4	3.3	—	5.6	—
1973	9.1	—	10.8	3.4	10.8	—	20.2	—
1974	15.3	11.5	15.6	14.1	15.6	10.0	14.0	—
1975	10.8	11.4	9.6	15.3	9.6	9.2	8.5	17.2
1976	4.4	5.7	3.7	6.7	3.7	5.1	-0.3	11.9
1977	6.5	6.0	6.5	6.5	6.5	5.7	5.2	15.7
1978	7.9	7.5	7.8	7.9	7.8	7.3	9.1	6.5
1979	11.1	8.9	11.8	8.7	11.8	9.1	9.2	35.1
1980	13.5	11.2	14.2	10.7	14.2	11.4	5.9	49.2
1981	9.3	8.6	9.0	10.2	9.0	7.8	5.9	19.1
1982	4.0	5.7	3.6	5.7	3.6	5.7	2.2	-1.5
1983	1.6	3.0	1.3	2.8	1.3	3.2	1.0	-4.8
1984	2.1	2.5	2.0	2.4	2.0	2.5	4.4	-4.3
1985	0.9	2.4	0.5	2.2	0.5	2.5	-0.8	-3.9
1986	-1.4	2.3	-2.4	2.0	-2.4	2.5	2.6	-28.1
1987	2.1	2.4	2.1	1.8	2.1	2.8	2.1	-1.9
1988	2.5	3.2	2.5	2.4	2.5	3.8	2.8	-3.2
1989	5.1	4.4	5.6	3.9	5.6	4.6	5.5	9.8
1990	4.9	3.7	5.5	3.4	5.5	3.8	4.8	14.1
1991	2.1	3.5	1.9	3.1	1.9	3.8	-0.2	4.2
1992	1.2	2.4	1.0	1.9	1.0	2.7	-0.7	-0.4
1993	1.2	1.2	1.1	1.7	1.1	0.9	1.9	0.3
1994	0.6	1.0	0.2	2.1	0.2	0.3	0.9	-1.2
1995	1.9	2.1	1.9	2.0	1.9	2.1	1.8	1.4
1996	2.6	1.5	3.1	1.1	3.1	1.7	3.5	6.5
1997	0.4	0.3	0.5	0.0	0.5	0.5	0.7	0.2

Source: U.S. Department of Labor, Bureau of Labor Statistics.

for PPIs are similar to those discussed in Chapter 5 for consumer prices. However, producer price indexes are closely tied to manufacturing (although there are utilities components), and indicators of resource usage in manufacturing are useful for tracking and anticipating changes in PPI inflation trends. In particular, capacity utilization rates, vendor performance, and spot (cash) and futures prices for various commodities are readily available data series for detecting changes in price pressure at the producer level.

Because of their ready availability and timeliness, many market analysts like to track spot and futures prices for commodities to project changes in producer prices. A number of spot and futures prices are published daily in *The Wall Street Journal* and other financial publications.

However, a favorite series of many analysts is the Commodity Research Bureau's futures price index. The CRB index is calculated daily with ongoing updates during a trading day. This index currently is based on 21 commodities futures markets. The CRB publishes its index daily along with component groups for imports, industrials, grains, oilseeds, livestock and meats, energy, precious metals, and miscellaneous. The CRB index is not directly related to PPIs but contains many components similar to those in the PPI for crude materials for further processing (as well as some not include in this PPI).

When looking at these indicators, it is important to remember that these spot and futures data are a lot more volatile than PPI series. Both short-run supply and demand for these commodities are usually inelastic. Small shifts in either cause dramatic changes in prices. Only extended changes in these prices should be seen as portending a change in inflation. There are frequent false signals from these series owing to very temporary changes in supply or demand. Series such as capacity utilization rates and vendor performance are not as timely but are more reliable indicators of changing inflation pressures.

KEY QUESTIONS IN ANALYZING THE NEWS RELEASE

- What did the PPI excluding food and energy do?
- For anticipating the CPI release, what were the changes in the PPI for finished consumer goods and finished consumer goods excluding food and energy?
- Are trends in food and energy diverging from the rest of the PPI? Is the PPI excluding food and energy really a trend series for the overall PPI?
- Are changes in crude oil prices still expected to impact the PPI in coming months?
- Did a freeze or other type of agricultural problem boost food prices? Will other food-growing regions or countries be able to replenish these supplies once their growing season reaches harvest, leading to lower prices, or is the shortage for that crop going to continue all year?
- Did passenger car prices have an unsustainably large increase? Did manufacturers' rebates affect the latest data or the previous month's data?

- Were there any one-time, irregular changes such as for ship prices or aircraft prices, which have very lumpy changes?
- Were there any seasonal adjustment oddities (such as for passenger cars or tobacco)?

NOTES FOR CHAPTER 6

1. Since 1986, the PPI no longer includes imports. While imports have never had a significant role, the PPI survey currently actively filters out priced imports.
2. U.S. Department of Labor, Bureau of Labor Statistics, *BLS Handbook of Methods,* September 1992, p. 142.
3. Ibid., April 1988, p. 125.
4. Ibid., September, 1992 p. 143.
5. The concept of relative importance is discussed in greater detail in the CPI chapter.
6. Rogers, R. Mark. "Improving Monthly Models for Economic Indicators: The Example of an Improved CPI Model," *Economic Review,* September-October 1988, pp. 34–50.
7. Ibid., p. 39.

BIBLIOGRAPHY

Bechter, Dan M., and Margaret S. Pickett. "The Wholesale and Consumer Price Indexes: What's the Connection?" Federal Reserve Bank of Kansas City, *Monthly Review,* June 1973, pp. 3–9.

U.S. Department of Labor, Bureau of Labor Statistics. *BLS Handbook of Methods,* for April 1988; September 1992, and August 28, 1997.

———. *Producer Price Indexes, Data for June 1997.*

Rogers, R. Mark. "Improving Monthly Models for Economic Indicators: The Example of an Improved CPI Model," Federal Reserve Bank of Atlanta, *Economic Review,* September-October 1988, pp. 34–50.

CHAPTER 7

INDUSTRIAL PRODUCTION AND CAPACITY UTILIZATION RATES

The index of industrial production (IP) is compiled by the Federal Reserve Board of Governors and reflects levels of output for manufacturing, mining, and public utilities (gas and electricity). Capacity utilization rates are also estimated by the Federal Reserve and reflect the level of output relative to potential production, that is, capacity. IP and capacity utilization data are released together around the 15th of each month for activity of the previous month. With each release, revisions are also made for the prior three months. The initial estimate and early revisions reflect the differing times of availability for very different types of data used to estimate production levels. This is discussed in more detail later.

Both IP and capacity utilization are important in business cycle analysis since manufacturing, the largest component of IP, is one of the more cyclical sectors of the economy. In fact, overall IP is one of four components in the Conference Board's index of coincident indicators, which plays a key role in defining turning points in the business cycle. Since industrial production leads employment in the high-wage manufacturing sector, it is also a significant factor in cyclical changes in personal income growth. Capacity utilization rates are important as a measure of inflationary pressures and as a leading indicator for investment in the manufacturing sector.

INDUSTRIAL PRODUCTION

The industrial production index is based on 264 components—the individual series—which are weighted together with a base year currently of 1992 being set to 100.[1] Index components are weighted by value-added shares primarily reflecting the 1992 Census of Manufactures and subsequent Annual Survey of Manufactures. This is in contrast to gross value. Each component's share discounts the cost of materials and reflects only the value added during the production process. Each industry's production represents only its contribution to a product's value. This means that as production is summed across the various stages of production, there is no double-counting.

When the IP index is rebased, the base year is determined by the most recently available Census of Manufactures and Census of Mineral Industries, which occur every five years. Annual data are benchmarked against data from these censuses.

For each component and for aggregated indexes, the index value reflects changes in physical production relative to the base year. An index value of 130 means that output is 30 percent higher than for the average level of output in the base year of 1992.

Importantly, with the January 1997 historical revisions, the Board of Governors of the Federal Reserve began updating component weights with each annual revision. Previously they had been updated on only with each benchmarking. This methodology change was intended to eliminate or reduce substitution bias; this was also the underlying rationale for the BEA's change from constant-dollar GDP to chain-weighted GDP (see Chapter 13). Industrial production is now chained together annually from the year 1977 forward. The Board of Governors chose to apply appropriate annual weights to data for most current periods. Previously, component weights were updated only every five years.

IP data are organized from two different perspectives: from the supplier side, with data categorized by industry; and from the demand side, with data grouped separately by market category. The major industry sectors are, of course, manufacturing, mining, and public utilities. Public utilities include piped natural gas and electric utilities. Further divisions for industry groups are based on standard industrial classification (SIC) codes. The most familiar industry subcomponents are generally known by two- or three-digit SIC categories. Note that the U.S. index of industrial production differs in one significant respect from IP indexes devised by a number of other developed countries: the U.S. index does not include construction activity.

Industrial production data (and capacity utilization data) are published in *Industrial Production and Capacity Utilization,* also known as the Federal Reserve Board's G17 report. Other published sources include the monthly *Federal Reserve Bulletin.* Data are subject to preliminary revisions for three additional months following the initial release. More extensive revisions are made periodically. These revisions usually incorporate only late data for monthly estimates, updated seasonal factors, and corrected errors.

IP BY INDUSTRY STRUCTURE

Industrial production data for the industry groupings are based on the standard industrial classification (SIC) system, which is used by U.S. federal agencies for many economic statistics. This allows for comparisons of various statistics from differing agencies; it also enables the statistical agencies to use each others' data in many of their own estimates. For example, the Federal Reserve Board is able to use data by industry from the Bureau of Labor Statistics on the number of hours worked in estimates for industrial output. The Census Bureau uses SIC codes for new factory orders, for example, and the Bureau of Economic Analysis uses SIC codes for personal income. However, the Federal Reserve Board does not cover all industries at the four-digit SIC level (a fine level of detail). Some industries are reported with a higher level of aggregation only. The latest version of SIC codes were set in their basic form in 1972, with only minor revisions in 1977 and in 1987.[2]

Table 7–1 shows industrial production according to industry shares and SIC code. Chart 7–1 maps durable and nondurable manufacturing.

TABLE 7–1

Major Industry Groups of Industrial Production, 1997

Group	SIC Code	Value-Added Proportion
MANUFACTURING		**85.97**
Durable manufactures		**46.43**
Lumber and products	24	2.08
Furniture and fixtures	25	1.40
Clay, glass, and stone products	32	2.24
Primary metals	33	3.47
Iron and steel	331,2	1.86
Fabricated metal products	34	5.25
Industrial machinery & equip.	35	8.66
Computer & office equip.	357	1.48
Electrical machinery	36	8.33
Transportation equipment	37	8.94
Motor vehicles and parts	371	5.15
Autos and light trucks		2.59
Aerospace and miscellaneous transportation equipment	372–6,9	3.79
Instruments	38	4.69
Miscellaneous manufactures	39	1.37
Nondurable manufactures		**39.54**
Foods	20	9.30
Tobacco products	21	1.31
Textile mill products	22	1.52
Apparel products	23	1.77
Paper and products	26	3.42
Printing and publishing	27	6.58
Chemicals and products	28	10.00
Petroleum products	29	1.82
Rubber and plastics products	30	3.65
Leather and products	31	
Mining		**6.40**
Utilities		**7.62**

Source: Federal Reserve Board, *G17 Report,* March 17, 1998.

CHART 7–1
Industrial Production: Durable versus Nondurable Manufacturing

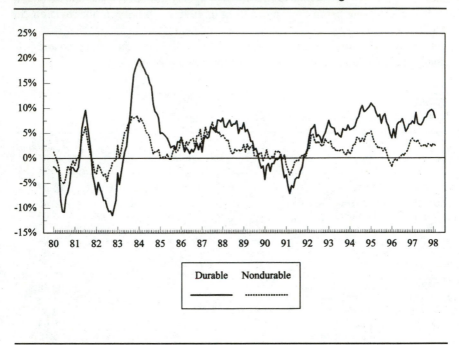

Durable   Nondurable

IP BY MARKET STRUCTURE

The market structure indexes for IP are based on the same 264 individual series as for the industry-based indexes. However, the market components are put together in different combinations. For example, canned and frozen foods are nondurables under industry classification, as is the aviation fuel and kerosene series. By market group, canned and frozen food are nondurable consumer goods, while the aviation fuel and kerosene component is an intermediate product under business supplies for commercial energy products.

Market groups are demand-oriented, with the two major groups being products and materials. Products are further divided into "final products" for consumer goods and equipment and into "intermediate products." This gives a stage-of-processing or input-output approach to the data. Final products are defined as products that undergo no further processing either in the industrial or other sectors and are consumed by the consumer or government sectors or purchased as investment goods by the business sector. Intermediate products and materials require further processing. However, intermediate products are used in production outside the industrial sector—such as construction, agriculture, and services—while materials remain in the industrial sector. Intermediate products are broken down into categories for construction and business supplies. Materials are subdivided into durable and nondurable materials and energy materials. Table 7–2 shows a breakdown of components by market categories.

Market groups are useful for analyzing imbalances among sectors of demand. Flows can be followed from producer to user and analyses can even take into account import-export flows by incorporating end-use merchandise trade data from the Census Bureau.

TABLE 7–2

Major Market Groups of Industrial Production, 1997

Group	Value-Added Proportion
Total Index	**100.00**
Products, total	59.89
Final products	45.08
Consumer goods	28.09
Equipment, total	17.00
Intermediate products	14.81
Materials	40.11
Consumer goods	**28.09**
Durable	5.82
Automotive products	2.56
Autos and trucks	1.57
Auto parts and allied goods	0.99
Other durable goods	3.26
Appliances and electronics	0.85
Carpeting and furniture	0.82
Miscellaneous	1.60
Nondurable	22.27
Nonenergy	18.99
Foods and tobacco	9.75
Clothing	1.81
Chemical products	4.53
Paper products	2.90
Energy products	3.28
Fuels	1.07
Utilities	2.21
Equipment total	**17.00**
Business equipment	13.91
Information processing and related	5.28
Computer and office	0.96
Industrial	4.51
Transit	2.68
Autos and trucks	1.32
Other	1.44
Defense and space equipment	2.02
Oil and gas well drilling	0.86
Manufactured homes	0.21
Intermediate products	**14.81**
Construction supplies	5.74
Business supplies	9.07
Materials	**40.11**
Durable	22.62
Consumer parts	4.25
Equipment parts	8.29

TABLE 7–2. (*continued*)
Major Market Groups of Industrial Production, 1997

Group	Value-Added Proportion
Other	10.08
Basic metals	3.30
Nondurable	8.87
Textile	0.91
Paper	1.85
Chemical	4.27
Other	1.84
Energy	8.62
Primary	5.59
Converted fuel	3.03

Source: Federal Reserve Board, *G17 Report*, March 17, 1998.

ESTIMATION METHODOLOGIES

The estimation methodology varies significantly from initial estimates to much later benchmark revisions. Not all actual counts of production are immediately available for each series. Various measures of inputs—notably labor hours and electricity usage—are available sooner than output measures for many IP components. In general, less reliable input data are available sooner than output measures for many IP components. But economy watchers want estimates for IP much sooner than is possible for more accurate final estimates of production. Hence, there is a tradeoff between timeliness and accuracy of the data.

The methodology used at each of the various stages of revision is heavily dependent upon the type of data that can be obtained. For estimating the IP index, there are three basic types of data series: physical product, production-worker hours, and electric power use by industry. Electric power use data are often referred to as "kilowatt-hours data." Various combinations of these are used for initial estimates through benchmark revisions. The physical product series is the least available initially, but grows in importance through the revision process.

Physical product series reflect an actual count or estimates of counts of production. Output is measured in quantity, not value. Physical product is the ideal in which IP is measured. Actual counts are preferred to dollar estimates of production in calculating production since price factors are often difficult to discount. These data frequently come from industry trade sources and from government agencies such as the Department of Energy, Bureau of the Census, and others.

Data for production-worker hours for each industry come from the Bureau of Labor Statistics and are the product of the number of production workers in a given industry and its average manufacturing workweek. Data are estimated by industry components and are used when other, more reliable physical product data are not yet available or when physical product counts are not desirable. For example, production-worker data are used even for late revisions for industries such as defense and space, where counting output may not be meaningful, especially over short time spans. Production-worker data are released by the BLS for public use the first week of the month following the reference month. Therefore, these series are available for the initial estimates for IP, which are released about 10 days to 2 weeks after the employment report.

The kilowatt-hours data—that is, electric utilities output—are collected by the district Federal Reserve banks. This is generally done with mail-in surveys and the results are forwarded to the Board of Governors. Almost all of the kilowatt hours data are available for use in estimates of industrial production about six weeks after the fact. Hence, the electric power data are not used in initial estimates for IP, but they are available for the first revision.

Initial monthly estimates of industrial production are heavily based on production-worker hours from the Bureau of Labor Statistics and on judgment by the Federal Reserve staff. This judgment is largely based on incomplete industry reports and other anecdotal sources. Actual counts of production for use in the initial industrial production report are limited to a small percentage of the industries covered. Some of the key series for which hard data are usually available for the initial news release include motor vehicles, steel and other metals, lumber, and paper. By the third monthly revision, physical product data accounts for about 37 percent of the IP index estimate by value added. Table 7–3 shows that initial IP estimates are heavily dependent on production-worker hours directly and indirectly (for Federal Reserve Board estimates). The indirect impact becomes less important with each revision as physical product and kilowatt-hours data become available.

For the manufacturing component, annual revisions are derived from the Census Bureau's Annual Survey of Manufactures (ASM), with the quinquennial Census of Manufactures being used for census years. The census is a nearly complete tally of the manufacturing sector in the United States. The ASM is less comprehensive, but it still has a panel of over 55,000 manufacturing establishments, with the reported value of shipments covering about 65 percent of manufacturing.[3]

TABLE 7–3

Estimated Availability of Industrial Production Data by Successive Months*

Type of Data	Percent of Value Added in 1994			
	1st Month	2nd Month	3rd Month	4th Month
Physical product	17.8	29.5	38.0	40.1
Kilowatt-hours (KWH)	0.0	28.3	28.3	28.3
Production-worker hour (PWH)	29.1	29.1	29.1	29.1
Federal Reserve estimates	53.1	13.1	4.5	2.5
Total industrial production	100.0	100.0	100.0	100.0

*Unpublished estimates by Federal Reserve staff, October 1997.

Annual revisions in almost all of the mining components are based on data from the U.S. Geological Survey. For utilities components, annual revisions are derived from data from the Department of Energy and other sources.

KEYS TO ANALYZING THE MONTHLY REPORT

Industry Series

Industrial production is a key indicator of the current strength of the economy. Financial markets place heavy emphasis on watching this indicator. However, analysts definitely need to sort through some of the components to see the underlying strengths and weaknesses.

Manufacturing

First, manufacturing is the key component. Its weight averages around 85 percent of the total index. Analysts generally look at trends in the manufacturing component and view utilities output as tracking overall economic growth, with deviations being weather-related. Mining has a larger share than utilities, but markets usually pay less attention to it because output is more affected by relative prices of energy materials than by changes in strength of the economy. Perhaps more importantly, there is very little employment in this sector, and there are limited spillover effects from employment and income.

When looking at the manufacturing component, one should try to discount any unsustainable fluctuations in output. This usually involves looking at the all-important auto industry. Often, auto output changes significantly over the course of a year owing to the need to bring production in line with sales. The auto industry is notorious for not quickly adjusting output to changes in sales trends. However, the Federal Reserve Board makes it easy to take into account the oscillations of auto and light truck production. There is a special index, Manufacturing Excluding Motor Vehicles, that is published each month.

To determine whether or not motor vehicle production is sustainable, one can look at production rates for autos and for light trucks as published in the IP release. These are easily comparable to unit sales figures put out by the BEA and by motor vehicle manufacturers. Production data for motor vehicles are in index form but are also published in millions of units, annualized and seasonally adjusted. This is the usual basis for comparisons between production and sales and inventories. Also auto makers generally announce planned production rates one quarter ahead, and these rates are usually in millions of units annualized.

Mining

The mining component was 6.4 percent of the overall IP index in 1997. The primary subcomponents are metal mining, coal, oil and gas extraction, and stone and earth minerals. Typically, over half of the mining component is oil and gas extraction. Extraction accounts for actual output of crude oil and natural gas and also of natural gas liquids. Changes in the extraction of these energy goods produces most of the monthly volatility in the mining component. Oil and gas well *drilling* is a subcomponent separate from extraction and is a market group series, not an industry group series. This series is also volatile but has a share under 1 percent of total IP. Data come from the Hughes Tool Company.[4]

Metal mining contains iron ores and copper ores, with breakdowns also available for lead and zinc ores, gold and silver ores, ferroalloy ores, and miscellaneous metal ores. The stone and earth minerals subcomponent includes series for stone, sand, and gravel; chemical and fertilizer materials; and "miscellaneous."

Public Utilities

The two biggest factors affecting utility output are economic activity in general and the weather. Since electricity is an input in manufacturing, utility output is indicative of industrial activity. This is the rationale behind some of the Federal Reserve's estimation methodology. Of course, weather affects utility output and, on a month-to-month basis, is this component's chief source of volatility. The impact of weather is usually discussed in terms of residential usage, but commercial usage is also affected.

Certainly, utility output is seasonally adjusted, but this adjustment only discounts "normal" weather patterns. Unseasonal weather leads to atypical monthly utility output; these changes in production frequently cause the overall IP index to swing sharply. When unseasonal weather returns to normal, output returns to trend and there is a technical reversal in the monthly percentage change in this IP component. For example, an abnormally severe January snow storm would cause the utility IP to jump. Return to a normal winter level the next month would cause a drop in output from the abnormally high level.

However, the utilities component should not be ignored by market watchers. Changes in residential utility usage is one of the key variables behind volatility in services personal consumption—a major component of GDP.

Among IP components, the computer equipment series (or more specifically, office and computing machines) is unique in that its growth rate over extended periods of time has been maintained by technological advances. Essentially, producers probably do view their production as being not as strong in real terms as indicated by the production index. While output may be up in terms of processing capability, the number of "boxes" has been down at times. Likewise, industry revenues have experienced declines even as real production rises after adjustments for technological change.

Market Group Series

Some of the "goods" in consumer goods are not really goods that the public generally thinks of in terms for consumer products. In particular, energy products are a subcomponent of nondurable consumer goods and are further broken down into fuel and utilities. While fuel, including gasoline, is a product, it is not what one generally conceives as a good in which production is following underlying consumer demand, as might be the case for apparel or consumer electronics. This is also the case for utilities. Changes in this component may simply be weather-related rather than being indicative of production trends for general type of consumer goods. Since much of the volatility in consumer goods production for nondurables is caused by swings in energy products, one should look at subcomponent detail before making assertions about trends for the broader component. Industry series for petroleum refining and residential electric utilities often move in tandem with the market group of nondurable consumer goods or at least the energy products series.

From the market perspective, interpreting the data is more demand-oriented. A key factor in production is demand for motor vehicles. Estimation methods and allocation between various sectors of demand can affect one's interpretation of the sustainability of production in this sector. Other IP market group series may not match up with various popular concepts of demand. This is the case for some market groups containing utilities and other energy goods.

Business equipment includes autos and trucks, computers, aircraft, industrial machinery, as well as others. The motor vehicle components are important because of their relative size and monthly volatility.

Motor vehicle data for market categories begin with industry data. Auto and truck production estimates are based on figures from *Ward's Automotive News*. Physical product data for the entire month is available for the first estimate for IP. Auto and truck production by industry go into market categories of both consumer durables and business equipment. Allocation of production between these two market categories is based on the BEA's division of unit sales between durables personal consumption and investment in producers' durable equipment. The BEA's allocation is based on *Polk* registration data. Since *Polk* registration data are not available for two months after the fact, initial allocation by market categories reflects rough estimates based on trends and anecdotal industry information on sales trends—particularly in reference to fleet sales to car rental agencies. Auto makers have developed ownership interests in many rental firms, and this does provide good information on sales to the business sector. Importantly, the roughness of the estimation of shares of production to these two market components does not change the strong reliability of the data on actual production of motor vehicles.

Defense and space production is based on production-worker hours and reflects the monthly employment data.

Intermediate products consists of construction supplies and business supplies. Intermediate products for construction closely follow building activity and indicators such as housing starts and nonresidential construction contracts. Examples of this group are lumber, flooring, plywood, and paint. Business supplies cover a wide range of goods going into business activity. Some items in this group are job printing, replacement tires for business vehicles, aviation fuel, and commercial gas.

Materials is the last major market group. Traditionally, materials production tracked product output. However, starting in the late 1970s, more materials were imported as foreign producers significantly increased capacity and became price-competitive. To track materials production, international commodity markets must be followed along with changes in exchange rates, subsidy policies, and even currency needs of foreign governments.

By components, durable goods materials include parts for consumer durables and for equipment as well as basic metal materials. Nondurable goods materials cover textile, paper, and chemical materials and various miscellaneous non-durables materials. Finally, energy materials comprise primary energy materials and converted fuel materials. Coal, crude oil, natural gas, and hydronuclear-generated electricity are included in primary energy materials, while converted energy materials are industrial electricity, industrial gas, nuclear materials, coke, LPG, gasline transmission, and residual materials.

KEY ROLES IN THE ECONOMY AND UNDERLYING FUNDAMENTALS

The index of industrial production is the primary measure of output in manufacturing, mining, and public utilities. While mining has declined in importance over the years, and public utilities output has tracked overall economic growth, manufacturing remains a very important segment of the economy. Even though employment in manufacturing has been on the decline, manufacturing's share of the economy's overall output has remained relatively constant. Importantly, manufacturing, particularly durables, is far more cyclical than the economy overall. Typically, manufacturing output growth must be noticeably stronger than overall economic growth during periods of expansion. Manufacturing also helps drive the consumer sector by providing high-wage jobs and also by supporting secondary service sector and even construction sector jobs.

Industrial production is driven by demand and inventory cycle adjustments. Changes in demand relative to output show up in unplanned changes in inventories. Unexpected declines in inventories (strong demand) lead to increased production. Unexpected increases in inventories (weak demand) result in decreased industrial production. Changes in demand (up or down) for manufacturing ouput are seen in changes in new factory orders. Basically, industrial production is demand-driven, with imbalances between supply (production) and demand being corrected by inventory movement and resulting changes in orders to factories.

To track underlying fundamentals, one should closely watch production by market categories and corresponding demand by similar categories for personal consumption, business investment, and exports and imports. If production appears to diverge from domestic and foreign consumption of output, then one should try to corroborate these imbalances in inventory data and in orders numbers. For durables, unfilled orders data provide significant information on potential imbalances between supply and demand. For nondurables, unfilled orders data are not as strong a signal for pending production changes because few nondurables industries provide data on unfilled orders.

CAPACITY UTILIZATION RATES

Capacity utilization rates are measures of actual production relative to capacity. These series are produced by the Federal Reserve Board of Governors and are useful indicators of overall availability of manufacturing resources and of pending or actual supply bottlenecks in the U.S. industrial sector. In turn, these series are useful in tracking changes in inflation pressures caused by supply conditions. Furthermore, these series provide information on which industries need to expand capacity and may boost planned investment. Also, for policy makers the data are useful in helping to determine if the economy is fully employed, at least from the perspective of physical capital.

Capacity utilization rates are also available by individual industry groups. Manufacturers can track industries providing materials to their plants to see if bottlenecks and higher prices are developing. Following these series allows for better planning within the manufacturing sector.

There are several different concepts of capacity upon which capacity utilization rates depend. Engineering capacity reflects the idea of maximum output, but it is not a realistic concept from a business or economic perspective. Maximum engineering capacity is not practical. The Federal Reserve concept takes into account various practical operating factors:

> The capacity indexes attempt to capture the concept of sustainable practical capacity, which is defined as the greatest level of output that a plant can maintain within the framework of a realistic work schedule, taking account of normal downtime, and assuming sufficient availability of inputs to operate the machinery and equipment in place.[5]

The Federal Reserve Board's concept of capacity utilization is that changes in utilization rates should primarily reflect changes in production—not monthly changes in capacity. The Federal Reserve assumes that growth in capacity is smooth. In fact, "current" estimates for capacity are based on projections from survey data of the previous year. Plant closings and openings rarely enter capacity figures and utilization rates until they show up in annual surveys for either capacity utilization rates or for capacity. To better understand these concepts, one should first get a brief idea of how capacity figures are derived.

ESTIMATING CAPACITY AND CAPACITY UTILIZATION

In overview, annual figures and "current" monthly estimates are derived with somewhat different methodologies. For annual end-of-year data, capacity utilization rates are based on data from surveys and various industry sources. Meanwhile, output is measured independently, as discussed in the industrial production section. Capacity then is derived as an identity from the other two series. These are preliminary estimates, however, and adjustments are made so that implied capacity figures are in line with capacity and capital stock data from various industry sources.

Official capacity utilization rates are then derived as an identity of these adjusted capacity figures and independently estimated production data. Capacity utilization is the ratio of production to capacity. One should note that capacity and capacity utilization rates are derived on an industry basis, as is the case for industrial production. Current-year monthly figures are dependent upon projections of capacity data, while annual figures for capacity are based on hard data either for capacity or for capacity utilization.

The Federal Reserve Board's methodology for estimating capacity and capacity utilization is a multistep process. Most of the process involves the estimation of capacity.

Step 1: Obtain preliminary estimates for capacity utilization rates.

The Federal Reserve's estimates for annual capacity utilization numbers begin with capacity utilization surveys of the Census Bureau, the Department of Energy, and various industry trade associations. Since surveys that had been conducted by the BEA and McGraw-Hill/DRI (and were key providers of capacity utilization data) are no longer produced,[6] the primary source of survey data is the Survey of Plant Capacity conducted by the Census Bureau. Owing to budget constraints, in 1989 the Census Bureau switched from an annual survey to one that takes place every two years. Surveys are conducted in the fourth quarter of even-numbered years, with data obtained for both the current and previous years. In 1996, about 17,000 industry plants participated. These surveys provide survey-based capacity utilization figures for the Federal Reserve to use as input in its estimates.

Step 2: Derive preliminary implied capacity estimates.

Once industrial production (already estimated by the Board of Governors) and survey-based capacity utilization rates are known, an implied figure for capacity can be derived for the year just ended. The identity or formula is:

Preliminary capacity = output ÷ the survey-based capacity utilization rate

This gives an implied capacity figure, which is an estimate of maximum sustainable output expressed as a percent of *actual output* in 1992. One should note that the ratio is not relative to capacity in 1987. Note that these capacity figures are preliminary in the sense that they are still inputs in the Federal Reserve Board's estimation procedure. These preliminary capacity figures—implied from the survey-based capacity utilization data—are never published as official data and then subsequently revised. They are merely part of the estimation process.

However, the preliminary capacity figures—based on survey capacity utilization rates—are unacceptably cyclical. They tend to rise sharply in expansion after declining in recession. Capacity tended to be "found" by survey respondents during expansion and "lost" during recovery. Apparently, plant managers can "find" capacity when they need it during periods of heavy demand. However, these extreme cyclical tendencies are not consistent with other measures of capacity growth, such as capacity in physical units, capital stock data, and capacity data from surveys in which capacity is reported directly.

Step 3: Adjust preliminary capacity estimates.

Adjust preliminary capacity estimates so that their cyclical movements are in line with those of capital stock and other data but have trend growth that tracks implied capacity figures from survey capacity utilization rates. Preliminary capacity estimates are therefore adjusted to be consistent with later reported and more reliable series on capacity and related capital stock data.

> These main types of data are used to refine the year-to-year changes in preliminary capacity indexes: (1) industry capacity estimates in tons, barrels, or other physical units when available; (2) capital stock estimates; and (3) direct estimates of capacity growth provided by surveys.[7]

Of these data, the capital stock series are the primary data used for refining the preliminary capacity figures. They are used in regression procedures on an industry-by-industry basis. Ratios for capacity (preliminary) to capital stock are regressed against time and an error term.[8] This regression retrends capital stock data to the growth path of preliminary implied capacity figures. The Federal Reserve then uses the fitted values from the regression as the refined capacity estimates. The survey-based capacity and capacity utilization figures "disappear" at this stage in terms of deriving official data.

Nonetheless, the result of this adjustment is that refined capacity figures are still generally procyclical, following investment cycles. Refined capacity estimates broadly follow the long-term growth trends of the preliminary capacity data but have less cyclical movement based on the capital stock data (or other series if capital stock figures are not available for a given industry).

This methodology covers most industries. However, the Federal Reserve does get direct estimates of annual capacity figures from a number of industry trade sources. Industries with capacity estimated in this manner include raw steel, oil and gas well drilling, and textiles.

Step 4: Create monthly capacity figures from end-of-year data.

Monthly capacity figures are derived using straightline interpolation between end-of-year refined capacity estimates. Interpolation is done for individual industries. Current-year monthly figures are derived as discussed in the following section.

Step 5: Adjust data to economic capacity concept to series where needed.

Adjustments are made to some directly reported capacity estimates to make the estimates consistent with the Federal Reserve Board's concept of economic capacity. Some data are based on engineering concepts of capacity. For example, some capacity figures from small establishments focus on maximum possible output without taking into account bottlenecks that occur within the overall economy when demand is heavy. Some of the engineering capacity is not available on an economic basis. Also, utility companies have "extra" capacity built in for heavy seasonal demand. While this extra capacity is available in an engineering sense, sustained output is not possible at levels of production seen during peak periods. Such capacity is not in use most of the time and in fact is not available for use all the time. From an economic sense, the capacity for peak loads is not excess capacity.

Step 6: Aggregate and calculate capacity utilization.

Monthly capacity indexes are aggregated into appropriate market and industry groups, using the same value-added weights as are used in the aggregation of industrial production indexes.

Step 7: Calculate capacity utilization rates.

An industry capacity utilization rate is defined as its individual output index divided by its capacity index. Aggregate capacity utilization rates are based on measures of aggregate output divided by aggregate capacity.

CURRENT-YEAR ESTIMATES

At the end of each year, an estimate is made for capacity growth in the upcoming year. This estimate includes implicit assumptions for plant closings and openings during the upcoming year. There are no specific inputs for plant closings and openings. Growth in capacity is based on projected cyclical growth in investment net of depreciation and other factors. These estimates are made on a statistical, probabilistic basis. Monthly capacity figures are interpolated from the yearly figures. In other words, capacity is assumed to grow at this smooth annualized rate throughout the year, regardless of actual plant openings and closings during the year. Implied capacity growth at levels of aggregation higher than for individual industries can vary from month to month because of shifts in relative importance of industries in industrial production caused by differences in production growth rates. Also, yearly growth rates can be revised and the smooth growth rates will change somewhat.

For the previous year and earlier, the Federal Reserve Board has hard data for output and capacity utilization rates. For each month of the current year, it assumes a growth rate (and levels) for capacity based on various inputs and compiles hard data on output:

Current-year capacity utilization rate = actual output
÷ capacity (FRB projection)

The inputs to the estimates include recent capital stock data, recent investment trends, and announced planned plant and equipment expenditures. Capacity projections are made on an individual industry basis.

While historic annual data use actual figures for production and utilization rates to derive capacity, "current" monthly series use actual production data together with smooth projections for capacity levels to derive current monthly figures for capacity utilization rates. Although the Federal Reserve Board projects capacity figures from previous annual survey data, it makes smooth monthly estimates of capacity growth so that monthly utilization rates are oriented to reflect changes in production. The capacity utilization rate is the ratio of an output index and a capacity index. The numerator for this ratio, industrial production, grows at varying rates during the year, while the denominator, capacity, grows at a constant rate. Hence, whenever industrial production grows at a rate greater (or lesser) than the assumed growth rate for capacity, the capacity utilization rate rises (or falls). (See Charts 7–2 and 7–3.)

CHART 7–2
Manufacturing Capacity and Production
(1992=100)

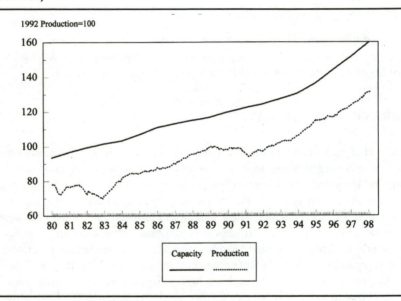

CHART 7–3
Manufacturing Capacity Utilization
(Percent of capacity)

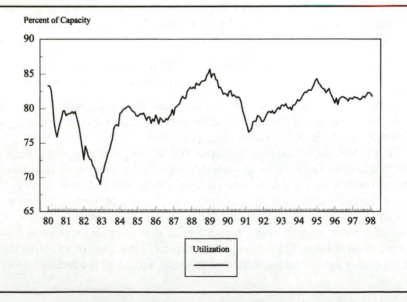

The above discussion has several implications for how plant closings enter capacity utilization figures. First, unexpected plant closings rarely enter monthly data directly for the current year. In fact, actual closing are not taken into account until data are revised at the end of the year and projections for the new year are made for capacity. Also, expected plant closings are not discretely discernable in the data. Furthermore, one cannot differentiate changes in utilization rates to either changes in operating rates at existing facilities (including plant closings) or to capacity expanded by new investment. As another aside, specific plants are removed from capacity (for purposes of annual data from survey questionnaires) only when equipment is removed from the inside of closed plants.

THE ROLE OF CAPACITY UTILIZATION RATES AS AN INFLATION GAUGE

For policy makers, these series indicate whether or not the economy has room to grow at faster rates or not. They help answer the question, Does the economy need more stimulus, less, or the same? These series provide similar information for physical capital as unemployment rates provide for the workforce. What the "optimal" capacity utilization rate is usually depends on perceived inflation tradeoffs. If capacity utilization rates can be boosted only through stimulus that also raises inflation rates beyond an acceptable pace, then capacity utilization rates are generally considered to be at a nonaccelerating inflation maximum. While policy makers may be interested in maintaining high capacity utilization rates, financial markets usually focus on what capacity utilization rate will lead to accelerating inflation.

Until the mid-1980s, the rule of thumb was that rates exceeding 80 percent for overall manufacturing capacity utilization would lead to an increase in inflation. However, this rule of thumb became less reliable owing to the greater internationalization of the U.S. economy. As imports played a larger role in the U.S. economy, U.S. capacity utilization rates have become less important relative to world capacity utilization rates. It is still an important inflation barometer (although more so for specific industries than for the overall economy), but the focus must be spread to world capacity utilization rates and changes in the exchange value of the dollar.

While the aggregated capacity utilization rates are useful in evaluating potential price pressures in manufacturing, disaggregated data are even more informative. In particular, studies indicate that industries producing materials and supplies—such as textiles; paper; chemicals; stone, clay, and glass; and primary metals—have capacity utilization rates that are closely associated with changes in producer prices for those commodities.[9] These differing peak rates for various industries are shown in Table 7–4.

TABLE 7–4

Capacity Utilization: Manufacturing, Mining, and Utilities

Item	SIC Code	1997 Proportion	Seasonally Adjusted Percent of Capacity					
			1967–1997 Average	1973 High	1978–1980 High	1982 Low	1988–1989 High	1990–1991 Low
Total industry		100.0	82.1	89.2	87.3	71.1	85.4	78.1
Manufacturing		87.20	81.1	88.5	86.9	69.0	85.7	76.6
Primary processing		26.38	82.4	91.2	88.1	66.2	88.9	77.7
Advanced processing		60.83	80.5	87.2	86.7	70.4	84.2	76.1
Durable		47.85	79.4	89.2	87.7	63.9	84.6	73.1
Lumber and products	24	2.10	82.6	88.7	87.9	60.8	93.6	75.5
Furniture and fixtures	25	1.43	81.5	96.8	85.5	68.9	86.6	72.5
Stone, clay, & glass products	32	2.24	78.3	88.8	88.0	64.3	83.5	69.7
Primary metals	33	3.11	81.2	100.2	94.2	45.1	92.7	73.7
Iron and steel	331,2	1.70	81.0	105.8	95.8	37.0	95.2	71.8
Nonferrous	333–6,9	1.41	81.5	90.8	91.1	60.1	89.3	74.2
Fabricated metal products	34	5.42	77.9	87.8	83.9	63.7	82.0	71.9
Industrial machinery & equip.	35	8.64	81.4	96.0	93.2	64.0	85.4	72.3
Electrical machinery	36	8.89	81.0	89.2	89.4	71.6	84.0	75.0
Transportation equipment	37	9.78	75.8	86.1	84.8	57.2	85.8	68.5
Motor vehicles and parts	371	5.67	76.6	93.4	95.0	45.5	89.1	55.9
Autos and light trucks*		2.66	n.a.	n.a.	94.6	40.6	92.3	53.3
Aerospace and miscellaneous transportation equipment	372–6,9	4.11	75.2	78.4	81.9	66.6	87.3	79.2
Instruments	38	4.84	81.7	89.9	92.7	78.4	81.4	77.2
Miscellaneous	39	1.40	75.4	82.9	79.4	65.4	79.0	71.7

	Code							
Nondurable		39.36	83.4	87.8	87.5	76.4	87.3	80.7
Foods	20	9.50	82.9	86.0	84.6	79.1	85.4	82.7
Textile mill products	22	1.51	85.5	91.4	91.2	72.3	90.4	77.7
Apparel products	23	1.93	81.0	84.2	87.5	77.5	85.1	75.5
Paper and products	26	3.13	89.3	97.1	96.1	80.6	93.5	85.0
Pulp and paper	261–3	1.37	92.4	97.2	98.3	82.0	98.0	89.9
Printing and publishing	27	6.49	85.7	89.7	93.9	82.0	91.7	79.6
Chemicals and products	28	10.40	79.5	87.6	84.6	69.9	86.2	79.3
Petroleum products	29	1.57	86.6	96.7	90.0	66.8	88.5	85.1
Rubber and plastics products	30	3.44	84.8	95.5	91.2	72.7	89.6	77.4
Leather and products	31	0.21	81.2	81.3	92.1	75.8	83.3	76.1
Mining		5.84	87.5	94.3	96.0	80.3	88.0	87.0
Metal mining	10	0.38	79.0	89.6	87.9	44.4	89.4	79.9
Coal mining	12	0.82	86.9	91.0	99.4	76.6	91.5	83.4
Oil and gas extraction	13	4.07	88.6	96.9	97.3	82.3	88.2	88.7
Stone and earth minerals	14	0.57	85.8	95.0	92.7	63.3	89.0	79.4
Utilities		6.96	87.3	96.2	89.1	75.9	92.6	83.4
Electric	491,3pt	5.43	89.1	99.0	88.2	78.9	95.0	87.1
Gas	492,3pt	1.52	82.4	94.1	93.7	69.1	85.0	67.1

*Series begins in 1977.

Source: Federal Reserve Board, *G17 Report*, March 17, 1998. Table 3.

KEY QUESTIONS IN ANALYZING THE NEWS RELEASE

Industrial Production

- How strong was the manufacturing component—separate from the overall index?

- Was manufacturing affected by strikes or severe weather?

- Was there a sharp change in motor vehicle assembly rates? Can this pace be maintained? In other words, are production rates too optimistic relative to sales of domestics or are sales outstripping production?

- How strong was the special index, manufacturing excluding motor vehicles?

- Are recent overall production figures in line with growth in demand or will production return to a more sustainable level? Are there any apparent unplanned inventory changes that must be met with changes in production?

- For utilities, did atypical weather affect production (unseasonably hot or unseasonably cold)?

- For durables manufacturing, how do changes in production compare with changes in order backlogs?

KEY QUESTIONS IN ANALYZING THE NEW RELEASE

Capacity Utilization Rates

- Has production growth been trending above or below implied capacity?

- How does the latest figure for capacity utilization compare with previous periods of rising inflation?

- How does the latest figure compare to long-term averages or recent peaks or troughs?

- How do various industry capacity utilization rates compare to their own industry historical averages? Various industries have very different tendencies for standard utilization rates.

- Has capacity increased abroad as a viable substitute for capacity in the United States? Relative to the past, are foreign suppliers able to fill U.S. demand if shortages were to occur or if prices were to rise noticeably?

TABLE 7–5

Industrial Production: Annual Average Percentage Changes for Major Industries, 1960–1997

	Total IP	Mining	Manufacturing			Public Utilities
			Total	Durables	Nondurables	
1960	2.2	1.8	2.2	2.0	2.3	7.0
1961	0.7	0.7	0.3	−1.7	3.2	5.6
1962	8.3	2.9	8.8	10.8	6.0	7.6
1963	6.1	4.1	6.3	6.8	5.6	6.9
1964	6.7	4.1	6.8	7.2	6.5	8.6
1965	9.9	3.6	10.7	13.6	6.7	6.1
1966	8.8	5.4	9.2	11.2	6.4	7.7
1967	2.2	1.9	1.9	1.0	3.1	5.1
1968	5.6	3.8	5.6	4.9	6.4	8.1
1969	4.7	4.0	4.4	4.0	5.3	8.7
1970	−3.3	2.6	−4.5	−7.6	0.0	6.2
1971	1.4	−2.5	1.5	−0.5	4.0	4.8
1972	9.6	2.1	10.5	11.7	9.0	6.4
1973	8.2	0.9	8.8	11.6	4.9	3.9
1974	−1.5	−0.5	−1.5	−2.1	−0.7	−1.2
1975	−8.8	−2.2	−9.9	−12.3	−6.2	0.9
1976	9.2	0.8	10.2	10.3	10.1	4.0
1977	8.1	3.1	8.9	10.1	7.0	2.6
1978	5.9	3.0	6.4	8.0	4.2	3.0
1979	3.3	1.7	3.6	5.3	1.2	2.9
1980	−2.8	3.0	−3.8	−5.2	−2.0	0.6
1981	1.6	3.6	1.6	1.6	1.5	−2.7
1982	−5.4	−3.7	−5.9	−8.6	−2.3	−3.1
1983	3.7	−4.2	5.7	5.9	5.5	1.7
1984	8.9	6.8	9.9	14.5	4.2	3.6
1985	1.6	−2.6	2.3	3.5	0.8	2.4
1986	1.1	−7.5	2.8	2.1	3.6	−2.7
1987	4.6	−0.5	5.3	5.3	5.3	3.4
1988	4.5	2.6	4.7	6.6	2.3	5.0
1989	1.8	−1.4	1.9	2.4	1.4	3.5
1990	−0.2	1.6	−0.5	−1.5	0.6	1.2
1991	−2.0	−2.1	−2.3	−3.6	−1.0	2.2
1992	3.2	−2.5	4.0	4.7	3.1	−0.4
1993	3.5	0.2	3.8	5.7	1.8	3.9
1994	5.4	2.5	6.0	8.3	3.4	1.3
1995	4.9	−0.3	5.4	8.3	2.0	3.6
1996	3.5	1.6	3.6	6.2	0.6	3.2
1997	5.0	1.8	5.6	8.0	2.9	0.5

Source: Federal Reserve Board of Governors. Based on averages of monthly seasonally adjusted indexes.

TABLE 7–6

Industrial Production: Annual Average Percentage Changes for Major Market Categories, 1960–1997

	Total IP	Final Products	Consumer Goods			Equipment				Intermediate Products	Materials Products
			Total	Durable	Nondurables	Total	Business Equipment	Defense and Space	Oil and Gas Drilling		
1960	2.2	3.3	3.8	5.6	3.1	2.8	2.7	2.8	−6.3	0.7	1.4
1961	0.7	0.9	2.0	−1.4	3.3	−1.4	−3.0	1.6	3.2	1.9	0.1
1962	8.3	8.4	6.8	13.1	4.7	11.3	8.8	15.9	6.1	6.2	8.9
1963	6.1	6.0	5.7	8.7	4.7	6.1	4.9	7.9	0.2	5.6	6.5
1964	6.7	5.7	5.6	7.5	4.9	5.7	12.0	−3.2	6.3	6.6	8.2
1965	9.9	9.7	7.8	16.8	4.4	13.1	14.5	10.7	3.4	6.4	11.4
1966	8.8	9.5	5.0	5.7	4.7	16.5	15.9	17.6	−1.0	6.2	9.0
1967	2.2	4.1	2.6	−3.6	5.2	6.3	1.9	14.1	−8.5	4.1	−1.0
1968	5.6	4.7	5.9	11.3	3.8	2.8	4.4	0.2	4.3	5.8	6.6
1969	4.7	3.2	3.8	4.4	3.4	2.6	6.4	−4.8	3.4	5.4	6.0
1970	−3.3	−3.6	−1.2	−7.7	1.6	−7.1	−3.5	−15.3	−13.0	−1.5	−3.6
1971	1.4	0.9	5.8	13.2	2.9	−6.4	−5.0	−10.2	−4.0	3.0	1.5
1972	9.6	8.5	8.1	12.0	6.4	9.4	14.0	−2.8	14.8	11.6	10.3
1973	8.2	7.5	4.4	7.7	3.0	11.7	17.0	−2.3	8.5	6.5	9.5
1974	−1.5	−0.3	−3.1	−10.3	0.0	3.2	4.5	−1.4	24.1	−3.5	−2.1
1975	−8.8	−5.8	−3.8	−8.9	−1.9	−8.4	−10.7	−1.9	13.4	−9.7	−12.2

1976	9.2	7.0	9.8	17.2	7.3	3.4	3.7	1.6	0.5	10.1	11.8
1977	8.1	8.2	7.1	13.2	4.7	9.4	11.7	0.0	21.4	8.9	7.9
1978	5.9	6.5	3.9	3.6	3.9	10.4	11.7	2.8	12.2	5.6	5.2
1979	3.3	3.2	-1.3	-5.0	-0.1	9.4	11.5	3.3	-2.9	2.6	3.7
1980	-2.8	-0.4	-2.3	-12.8	1.1	1.9	-0.8	9.4	24.2	-5.2	-4.3
1981	1.6	2.4	0.5	0.5	0.5	4.6	1.7	2.0	33.3	-0.1	1.4
1982	-5.4	-3.7	-1.6	-7.1	0.0	-6.1	-9.5	12.6	-6.2	-2.3	-7.8
1983	3.7	2.3	5.5	18.1	2.3	-1.8	-3.2	10.8	-13.0	6.9	4.3
1984	8.9	8.6	4.3	13.9	1.6	14.7	15.9	11.3	15.0	7.3	9.7
1985	1.6	2.7	1.0	0.8	1.1	4.9	4.2	16.0	-12.2	2.4	0.4
1986	1.1	1.2	3.6	4.8	3.2	-2.0	-0.6	8.9	-44.8	4.1	0.1
1987	4.6	3.3	3.3	5.9	2.5	3.3	3.8	3.9	-8.8	8.6	4.7
1988	4.5	4.9	3.2	6.2	2.4	7.5	9.9	-0.4	14.8	1.8	5.2
1989	1.8	2.1	1.0	1.6	0.8	3.8	5.7	0.3	-6.8	0.3	2.0
1990	-0.2	-0.4	-0.4	-3.3	0.5	-0.5	-0.7	-1.2	8.0	-0.9	0.2
1991	-2.0	-1.8	-0.3	-5.1	1.0	-4.3	-2.5	-8.0	-14.9	-4.3	-1.4
1992	3.2	2.4	3.0	7.5	1.9	1.3	4.4	-6.2	-22.2	2.6	4.3
1993	3.5	3.4	3.0	9.2	1.5	4.1	5.8	-6.2	22.6	2.5	4.1
1994	5.4	3.9	4.0	9.4	2.5	3.8	6.3	-7.3	3.6	3.7	7.9
1995	4.9	3.6	2.6	1.7	2.8	5.3	8.0	-6.4	-0.4	1.9	7.6
1996	3.5	3.0	1.7	3.5	1.3	5.1	6.8	-5.5	9.1	2.3	4.4
1997	5.0	4.2	2.3	3.9	1.9	7.4	9.1	-2.2	8.3	4.0	6.2

Source: Federal Reserve Board of Governors. Based on averages of monthly seasonally adjusted indexes.

NOTES FOR CHAPTER 7

1. With the release for the initial December 1996 industrial production and capacity utilization report, which included annual revisions, the number of individual industrial production series rose to 264 (for the period since 1992) from 255, netting both series added and dropped.
2. Data are currently classified in accordance with the 1987 Office Management and Budget, *Standard Industrial Classification Manual.*
3. Board of Governors of the Federal Reserve System, *Industrial Production, 1986 Edition, with a Description of the Methodology,* p. 46.
4. Ibid., p.132.
5. Board of Governors of the Federal Reserve System, "Explanatory Note," *Industrial Production and Capacity Utilization,* February 18, 1993, p. 18.
6. McGraw-Hill/DRI discontinued its survey after 1988, while the BEA provided data only for the 1965–1983 period.
7. Richard D. Raddock, "Revised Federal Reserve Rates of Capacity Utilization," *Federal Reserve Bulletin,* October 1985, p. 762.
8. Ibid., p. 763. Raddock provides a detailed discussion of the regression specification.
9. Richard D. Raddock, "Recent Developments in Industrial Capacity and Utilization," *Federal Reserve Bulletin,* June 1990, p. 412.

BIBLIOGRAPHY

Armitage, Kenneth, and Dixon A. Tranum. "Industrial Production: 1989 Developments and Historical Revision," *Federal Reserve Bulletin,* April 1990, pp. 187–204.

Board of Governors of the Federal Reserve System. *Industrial Production, 1986 Edition, with a Description of the Methodology,* December 1986.

———. *Industrial Production and Capacity Utilization: a Revision,* December 9, 1997.

———. *Industrial Production and Capacity Utilization,* October 17, 1997.

———. *Industrial Production and Capacity Utilization, Historical Revision,* January 27, 1997.

Raddock, Richard D. "Revised Federal Reserve Rates of Capacity Utilization," *Federal Reserve Bulletin,* October 1985, pp. 754–766.

———. "Recent Developments in Industrial Capacity and Utilization," *Federal Reserve Bulletin,* June 1990, pp. 411–435.

———. "Industrial Production, Capacity, and Capacity Utilization since 1987," *Federal Reserve Bulletin,* June 1993, pp. 590–605.

CHAPTER 8

MANUFACTURERS' ORDERS AND OTHER RELATED SERIES

OVERVIEW

While industrial production is the key measure for gauging the current strength of the manufacturing sector, the factory orders series are the primary indicators of the future health of this sector. The series that gets the most media attention is new factory orders but it is only one of several related indicators that are compiled and released by the Census Bureau in its publication *Manufacturers' Shipments, Inventories, and Orders*. This publication, which is often referred to informally as the M3 report, is part of the *Current Industrial Reports* put out by the Census Bureau.

These indicators also provide key data for estimating some of the components in other important economic indicators, primarily the gross domestic product (GDP) and the Commerce Department's composite indexes. For example, M3 data are inputs for GDP figures on producers' durable equipment and inventory investment at the manufacturing level. M3 data also contribute to estimates for two components in the composite index of leading indicators, namely, the sales component in the coincident index and the inventory-to-sales component in the lagging index.

There are two release dates associated with M3. The full set of data is released near the end of the month following the reference month or sometimes the following week if holidays affect the compilation schedule. An earlier report containing only data on durables is released about three weeks after the end of the report month. The publication containing the early release is the *Advance Report on Durable Goods Manufacturers' Shipments and Orders*. The full report usually contains minor revisions in the durables data, based on later-arriving survey data. Tables 8–1 and 8–2 at the end of this chapter summarize data from 1970 to 1996.

Definitions

For the M3 survey, the Census Bureau provides respondents with definitions of each indicator, and these are used as a basis for reported dollar values. For M3 survey purposes, manufacturers' new orders reflect commitments to purchase factory goods and are defined to include only those supported by binding legal documents, such as signed contracts, letters of award, or letters of intent. However, orders in some industries do not strictly adhere to this definition. Published data for new orders differ in definition; they are based on both earlier benchmark figures and current survey responses, as explained in the section "Monthly Estimates." Orders at the end of the reporting period "are equal to unfilled orders at the beginning of the period plus net new orders less net shipments."[1]

Shipments data are based on definitions used in the Annual Survey of Manufactures (ASM). The value of these shipments are "net selling values, f.o.b. plant, after discounts and allowances and excluding freight charges and excise taxes. . . . Where the products of an industry (four-digit SIC) are customarily delivered by the manufacturing establishment (such as in certain food industries—fluid milk, bakery products, soft drinks), the value is based on delivered price rather than the f.o.b. plant price."[2] In the case of shipbuilding, and also aircraft produced under a cost-plus contract, shipments are based on the value of work done during the year. For aircraft produced on a fixed-price contract, shipments are reported when products are shipped.

For the ASM, shipments are collected at the four-digit SIC level.[3] For major groups (two-digit SIC level and higher), the shipments data contain some duplication since the products of some four-digit SIC industries are used as inputs by other four-digit SIC industries under the same industry aggregate. This problem is most pronounced in a few highly integrated industries, for example, in primary metals and motor vehicles and parts.

Inventories have been based on three different definitions over the course of the 1980s. Prior to 1982, respondents were asked to report inventories at book values. Firms would report according to the method used for tax purposes and different respondents would use different accounting techniques. This, of course, created difficulties in aggregating inventory data. With the 1982 Census of Manufactures, last in, first out (LIFO) users were asked to report inventories prior to the LIFO adjustment, the LIFO reserve, and the LIFO value after adjustment for the reserve.[4] Beginning with January 1987, inventory data have been collected on a current-cost or pre-LIFO basis. Data for 1982 to 1987 have been redefined to a current-cost basis.

Inventory data by stage of fabrication should be used cautiously. Response rates are low, since not all companies keep this level of detail for monthly data. Also, there is some double counting because what is a finished good in one industry may be an input in another.

The Survey

Data for the M3 reports are collected by mail-in survey, with telephone follow-up. Dollar values for seven data items are collected in each survey for sales, new orders, order backlog, total inventory, materials and supplies inventory, work-in-process inventory, and finished-goods inventory.[5] However, for about three-fourths of the nondurables manufacturers, only sales and inventory figures are collected—not data for new and unfilled orders.

Census mails the M3 report form to 3,500 reporting units. The survey covers most manufacturers with $500 million or more in annual shipments and includes selected smaller companies for additional coverage. Each company or reporting unit of a company is classified according to 1 of 80 industry categories, based on the primary activity of the reporting unit. By value, the reporting units represent about 50 percent of the published dollar values. The monthly survey data are historically benchmarked against data from the quinquennial Census of Manufactures and, between census years, to data from the Annual Survey of Manufactures. Typically each year, the benchmark to the ASM is released just before the May report. However, the benchmark is made to ASM data of two calendar years prior. The annual benchmark released on June 18, 1997, was based on data from the 1994–1995 Annual Survey of Manufactures. Benchmarking to the quinquennial census usually takes longer than with ASM data.

Response rates do vary by industry. For shipments, about 50 percent of the estimates are based on reported data. However, at the industry category level, coverage rates vary from 20 to 99 percent.

Because of consolidated reporting by some large companies, the 80 industry categories are combined into 45 publication levels for shipments and total inventories. Low response rates lead to the need for further aggregation for published series for new and unfilled orders and for inventories by stage of fabrication.

Monthly Estimates

Following the latest census, industry levels for shipments, unfilled orders, and inventories are moved forward based on percentage changes derived from the monthly surveys. This is done by "multiplying the industry estimate for the previous month by the percentage change from the previous month for companies reporting in the current month."[6] If a particular reporting unit's data exhibit unusual movement relative to the rest of the industry, that unit's contributions are removed from the computation of the rest of the industry's percentage change and the atypical unit's impact of the level is factored in separately.

New orders are not calculated by this ratio method. Not all companies report new orders and some only report on new orders for specific products with long lead times in the production cycle. In the latter case, these companies exclude new orders for products shipped from inventory. To get around these problems, new orders are defined as "current month shipments plus current month unfilled orders minus prior month unfilled orders."[7] New orders are net of order cancellations. Orders data are affected by contract changes in the value of unfilled orders.

ORGANIZATION OF THE DATA

Industry Data

Data are organized by industry and also by less publicized topical series. Industry data are divided into categories that are similar to components for industrial production for manufacturing. As with IP indexes, durables data are readily available at the two-digit SIC level for shipments, inventories, and new and unfilled orders. For general trends in durables, analysts often use broader, more comprehensive special topical series.

Within durables, the industrial machinery and equipment component deserves a little extra explanation.[8] This component includes computers and other types of information-processing equipment. These subcomponents have become more important in recent years as the use of computers and other electronic equipment has become more widespread in businesses—both manufacturing and nonmanufacturing. By tradition, information-processing equipment is included in industrial machinery and equipment rather than in electrical machinery. Originally, computers were a very minor subcomponent and functionally fit in the category for adding and accounting machines when they were mechanical rather than electronic in nature.

For nondurables, only shipments and inventories are published at the two-digit industry level. Only a small percentage of nondurables industries report unfilled orders. These industries include textile mill products, paper and paper products, printing and publishing, and leather and leather products. For nondurable industries that do not report unfilled orders, new orders are defined as shipments. These major industry groups new orders are foods, tobacco, apparel, petroleum, rubber and plastics, and chemicals. These industries account for about three-fourths of nondurables shipments by value.

Topical Series

Topical series are regroupings of the separate industry categories into market groups and specially aggregated series. Market groups are similar to those for industrial production. Data for shipments, new orders, unfilled orders, and inventories are arranged in topical format.

Market categories are automotive equipment, home goods and apparel, consumer staples, machinery and equipment, business supplies, construction materials and supplies, defense products, and "other materials, supplies, and intermediate products."[9] However, the market categories are aggregated more broadly than market groups for industrial production. For example, the shipments series for "home goods and apparel" roughly corresponds to the combined IP series of "home goods" and "apparel." Also, the M3 market groupings are not always segregated between the consumer and business sectors. Two examples of this are "automotive equipment" and "other materials, supplies, and intermediate products."

Topical series also include special series. The most familiar topical series are for groupings of durables goods industries. Durables data are completely recategorized into nondefense capital goods, defense capital goods, and durables excluding capital goods.[10] Nondefense capital goods are further separated to exclude aircraft and parts.

Miscellaneous topical series include producers' durable equipment, household durable goods, information technology industries, and health care equipment and products. Except for some of the health care items, these fall under durables but do not subsume all of the durables component series. Also, some of the miscellaneous series contain components that overlap.

In the advance report for durable goods, the only topical series available are for capital goods industries and the breakdowns between defense and nondefense subcomponents and, within nondefense, for excluding aircraft and parts.

KEYS TO ANALYZING THE MONTHLY REPORTS

Technical Factors

New orders for durables are naturally very volatile. Contracts for items such as aircraft or various types of military goods tend to be very large and do not recur every month. This makes the new orders for durables series very "lumpy": a large increase is often followed by a decline since very large contracts do not get placed every month. Tracking unfilled orders for durables helps eliminate some of the lumpiness problem. Also, tracking unfilled orders eliminates the problem of some new orders data being derived from shipments data (such as with the motor vehicle industry).

Additionally, many analysts look at series that exclude defense capital goods or the transportation component. This is because of the volatility in these series, which also tend to have sharp swings. However, one should remember that the transportation component and the defense capital goods components overlap. Transportation includes military aircraft as well as ships and tanks. Transportation is an industry series, while defense capital goods is a special topical series.

Within transportation, motor vehicles and parts account for over half of the new orders for this subcomponent. Therefore, it usually accounts for some of the monthly volatility in the transportation. However, the widest swings in transportation are generally caused by aircraft orders, which are usually made in very large dollar volumes—but not every month.

New Orders as Leading Indicators: Intuition versus Statistics

Despite the often-held belief that new orders are a leading indicator of manufacturing activity, in actual practice such is not always the case—or at least not to the degree assumed. Much depends on how the data are defined and on the timing of data availability.

First, new orders can be filled out of inventory instead of out of future production. Orders met with inventory primarily reflect current demand. Unfilled orders are better used for an indication of future production, and unfilled orders—capital goods in particular—are found primarily in the durables sector.

For both durables and nondurables aggregates, the Census Bureau publishes data on shipments, new orders, and inventories for the industries that report unfilled orders. For the nondurables aggregate, the unfilled orders data are not as meaningful simply because for most nondurables industries, unfilled orders are not reported. Over the business cycle, industries reporting shipments and not reporting unfilled (or new) orders may strengthen faster than those reporting unfilled orders. In this situation, the ratio of unfilled orders to shipments falls. At first glance, one might interpret this decline as a sign of nondurables weakness, but if it results from certain industries having rapid gains in shipments and new orders but no reported unfilled orders, then the decline in this ratio is actually a indication of improvement in nondurables manufacturing.

Motor vehicles provide a good example of an instance in which the new orders data provide little leading information. New orders are basically derived from shipments data reported to the Census Bureau by motor vehicle manufacturers. For any given month, the impact of this orders information has already shown up in the Federal Reserve's production figures for that industry, since its production and shipments are closely tied.

Because much of the new orders data is based on shipments data, many goods are precluded from being produced after the order is recorded statistically. Also, the Census Bureau's M3 reports for a given month are released to the public about two weeks after the release of industrial production data for the same month. These data are still useful for tracking and projecting manufacturing trends, but the orders and production data do not follow the "intuitive" cycle of orders leading production. It should be remembered that although the monthly report of M3 data is late relative to industrial production, the M3 includes hard data from surveys of manufacturers. The initial IP data for most components are, to a large degree, rough estimates based on econometric models and various inputs, especially production worker data from the employment report.

Extracting useful information out of nondurables data is a little more difficult, primarily because most nondurables orders have no leading information. Nondurables new orders—that is, shipments—are indicators of current demand. As long as inventories are stable, nondurables orders are also a good measure of current production. On a monthly basis, much of the volatility in nondurables data is price-related. This is particularly true for petroleum products.

Shipments' Role in Investment Estimates

For estimating investment in producers' durable equipment (PDE) in GDP, the BEA uses Census M3 data on shipments from capital goods industries. The BEA also incorporates figures on business purchases of motor vehicles and capital equipment exports and imports. In the past, most private analysts used shipments for nondefense capital goods as a close estimate for the series used by the BEA; the monthly data provided early estimates for that component in the GDP release. They also used new and unfilled orders for nondefense capital goods as an indicator of future investment in business equipment or PDEs in the national income and product accounts. Until 1991, this was the best series to follow for PDEs, but then Census calculated a broader topical measure specifically for PDEs, using the same components that the BEA uses from the M3 report as inputs into its calculations for PDE expenditures in GDP. However, the BEA uses different weights for the M3 PDE components.

TABLE 8–1

M3 Shipments, Orders, and Inventories, 1970–1996 (In Billions of Current Dollars)

	Durables				Nondurables			
	Shipments	New Orders	Unfilled Orders	Inventories	Shipments	New Orders	Unfilled Orders	Inventories
1970	338	328	100	67	296	296	5	35
1971	359	359	100	66	312	312	5	36
1972	408	420	113	70	348	350	6	38
1973	475	512	149	81	400	401	7	43
1974	530	562	182	101	487	486	6	56
1975	524	504	162	103	516	518	8	57
1976	608	616	170	112	578	579	8	63
1977	710	734	193	121	648	649	9	68
1978	813	868	248	138	710	712	11	74
1979	911	954	291	161	817	818	12	81
1980	929	953	315	175	924	924	12	90
1981	1004	1003	315	186	1013	1013	12	97
1982	950	936	301	200	1009	1009	11	111
1983	1026	1059	333	200	1045	1048	14	113
1984	1175	1201	360	221	1113	1113	14	118
1985	1214	1227	372	218	1118	1119	15	117
1986	1238	1242	377	212	1097	1098	17	111
1987	1296	1328	409	221	1178	1183	22	117
1988	1420	1464	452	242	1274	1274	22	127
1989	1476	1511	487	258	1362	1362	22	134
1990	1483	1505	509	263	1426	1426	22	142
1991	1453	1440	496	250	1426	1427	23	141
1992	1542	1516	470	238	1462	1462	24	144
1993	1629	1596	436	239	1497	1495	22	145
1994	1789	1795	442	254	1558	1562	26	151
1995	1920	1937	459	266	1668	1666	24	163
1996	2005	2038	492	271	1729	1731	26	163
1997	2160	2183	515	284	1787	1788	26	170

Shipments and new orders are annual sums of monthly data, seasonally adjusted. Others are December data seasonally adjusted.

Source: U.S. Department of Commerce, Bureau of the Census.

TABLE 8–2
M3 Shipments, Orders, and Inventories, 1970–1996 (Year-Over-Year Percent Changes)

	Durables				Nondurables			
	Shipments	New Orders	Unfilled Orders	Inventories	Shipments	New Orders	Unfilled Orders	Inventories
1970	-4.2	-8.5	-8.8	3.2	2.3	2.3	10.0	4.2
1971	6.2	9.3	-0.2	-0.8	5.5	5.5	9.3	4.2
1972	13.6	17.2	12.8	5.9	11.7	11.9	25.7	4.5
1973	16.6	21.7	32.0	15.9	14.7	14.6	16.5	13.8
1974	11.5	9.9	21.7	25.0	22.0	21.2	-24.9	29.6
1975	-1.2	-10.4	-10.9	1.1	5.9	6.8	42.7	1.8
1976	16.1	22.3	5.1	9.2	12.1	11.6	4.9	9.7
1977	16.8	19.1	13.8	7.9	12.1	12.1	5.2	7.7
1978	14.4	18.3	28.4	14.3	9.5	9.8	25.1	8.9
1979	12.0	9.9	17.3	16.3	15.0	14.9	12.7	10.8
1980	2.1	0.0	8.2	8.7	13.1	12.9	-0.5	11.1
1981	8.0	5.3	-0.2	6.7	9.6	9.6	-3.1	7.2
1982	-5.4	-6.7	-4.4	7.5	-0.4	-0.4	-6.3	14.9
1983	8.1	13.1	10.7	-0.3	3.5	3.9	27.7	1.0
1984	14.4	13.5	8.0	10.7	6.6	6.2	-2.0	5.0
1985	3.4	2.1	3.5	-1.4	0.4	0.6	8.8	-1.4
1986	1.9	1.3	1.2	-2.8	-1.9	-1.9	11.4	-5.1
1987	4.7	6.9	8.5	4.2	7.4	7.7	29.3	6.0
1988	9.6	10.2	10.6	9.8	8.1	7.7	1.2	8.2
1989	3.9	3.2	7.7	6.2	6.9	6.9	-1.1	5.4
1990	0.5	-0.4	4.5	2.2	4.7	4.7	1.2	6.1
1991	-2.0	-4.3	-2.6	-5.0	0.0	0.1	6.3	-0.7
1992	6.1	5.3	-5.3	-4.7	2.5	2.5	0.6	2.4
1993	5.7	5.3	-7.1	0.5	2.4	2.3	-7.3	0.2
1994	9.8	12.4	1.2	6.0	4.1	4.5	17.8	4.6
1995	7.3	7.9	3.8	4.8	7.1	6.7	-6.3	7.8
1996	4.4	5.2	7.3	2.0	3.6	3.8	6.9	0.0
1997	7.7	7.1	4.7	4.7	3.4	3.3	2.4	4.1

Source: U.S. Bureau of the Census.

KEY QUESTIONS IN ANALYZING THE NEWS RELEASE

- Since the data are so volatile for new orders, what has been the trend over the last three months?
- How much were data for the previous two months revised?
- Excluding the very volatile aircraft series (or the broader transportation component, which includes aircraft), how strong were new orders?
- Within nonelectrical machinery, was much of the movement for computers?
- Excluding the volatile defense capital goods component, which overlaps with aircraft, how strong were new orders?
- For a longer run perspective, are unfilled orders rising or declining?
- If unfilled orders are little changed, are shipments and new orders trending upward or downward together, thereby portraying changes in underlying strength for manufacturing that unfilled orders miss?
- For nondurables orders, did changes in oil prices appear to have an impact?
- For helping to estimate the producers' durable equipment component in *current* quarter GDP, how strong were *shipments* of nondefense capital goods orders (or more specifically, the topical series for PDEs)?
- To get an idea of future spending on business equipment investment, how strong were new and unfilled orders for nondefense capital equipment?

NOTES FOR CHAPTER 8

1. U.S. Department of Commerce, Bureau of the Census, "Description of Survey," *Manufacturers' Shipments, Inventories, and Orders (M3): 1982–1990,* p. xi.
2. *M3: 1982–1988,* Chapter 2, p. xix.
3. In the SIC manual, a four-digit SIC is an industry, a three-digit SIC is an industry group, and a two-digit SIC is a major industry group or major group.
4. *M3: 1982–1990,* op. cit.
5. *M3: 1982–1990.* One should note that the 1982–1990 version inadvertently includes an old report form that still requests inventories on a LIFO basis. The M3 report now requests inventories on a current-cost basis.
6. *M3: 1982–1988,* Chapter 2, p. xvii.
7. Ibid., p. xviii.
8. Prior to the 1987 revision to SIC classifications, the industrial machinery and equipment component was known as "nonelectrical machinery." Both are the equivalent of SIC major group 35.
9. In more detail, consumer staples include meat products, dairy products, fats and oils, beverages, other food, cigars and cigarettes; chewing and smoking tobacco and snuff; miscellaneous converted paper products; newspapers, periodicals, and books; other publishing and printing products; drugs, soaps, and toiletries; and petroleum refining products. Home goods and apparel include knitting mills, carpets, and rugs; apparel and other finished textile products, household furniture, rubber and plastic footwear; hose, belting, gaskets, and other rubber products; leather products, kitchen articles and pottery;

stone, clay, and glass products; cutlery and hand tools; refrigeration, heating, and service industry machinery; household appliances, household audio and video equipment; ophthalmic goods, watches and clocks, jewelry, silverware, toys and games, miscellaneous goods, and caskets.

10. Nondefense capital goods industries include ordnance and accessories; steam, gas, and hydraulic turbines; internal combustion engines; construction, mining, and material handling equipment; metalworking machinery; special industry machinery; general industrial machinery; computer and office equipment; refrigeration, heating and service industry machinery; electrical transmission and distribution equipment; electrical industrial apparatus; communications equipment; aircraft, missiles, space vehicles, and engines and parts; ships and tank components; railroad equipment; and search and navigation equipment. Defense capital goods industries include ordnance and accessories; communications equipment; aircraft, missiles, space vehicles, and engines and parts; ships, tanks and tank components; and search and navigation equipment. See footnotes to topical series tables in monthly M3 report.

BIBLIOGRAPHY

U.S. Department of Commerce, Bureau of the Census. *Current Industrial Reports, Manufacturers' Shipments, Inventories, and Orders: 1982–1988.*

————. *Current Industrial Reports, Manufacturers' Shipments, Inventories, and Orders: 1982–1990.*

————. "Census Bureau Releases Benchmark Report for Monthly Manufacturers' Shipments, Inventories, and Orders Survey," News Release, June 18, 1997, CB97–103.

CHAPTER 9

BUSINESS INVENTORIES AND SALES

The business inventories and sales series are the last major monthly indicators to be released for a given month. Even though data are released two months after the fact, financial markets do not give these indicators the attention they deserve. In terms of the business cycle, it is inventories that keep sales and production in line with each other. Unplanned declines in inventories lead to higher production while unplanned increases lead to cutbacks in output. Inventory change is the tail that wags the dog in manufacturing.

Similarly, inventories play a key role in the GDP accounts. The monthly inventory data are used as input for the inventory investment component in GDP. This series has the greatest quarterly volatility of any GDP component. Analysts use this GDP component to assess the sustainability of GDP growth. Ironically, financial analysts pay more attention to the less timely inventory investment component in GDP than to the monthly inventories data, even though the monthly figures are inputs into the GDP figures.

Monthly business inventories and sales figures are produced by the Census Bureau and are part of the release entitled *Manufacturing and Trade Inventories and Sales.* This report is largely a compilation of data from three earlier reports for retail sales, manufacturers' sales and inventories, and wholesale trade. However, the retail inventories numbers for the most recent reference month are not released until the Census publication on overall inventories comes out. The business inventories release date is generally midmonth, two months after the reference month. Revisions are directly incorporated from series prepared separately for retail trade, manufacturing, and wholesale trade. For summary data from 1960 to 1997, see Table 9–1 at the end of this chapter.

THE WHOLESALE TRADE REPORT

Retail trade and manufacturers' orders, inventories, and sales were discussed in Chapters 3 and 8. Most analysts consider the wholesale trade report to be a minor report, because wholesale sales are driven by retail sales and also because wholesale inventories are the smallest of the three levels. The monthly wholesale trade report covers only a specific portion of the wholesale trade sector. As defined by the 1987 economic census, wholesale trade includes establishments "selling merchandise to retailers; to industrial, commercial, institutional, farm, or professional business users to other wholesalers; or acting as agents or brokers in buying merchandise for or selling merchandise to such persons or companies."[1] These establishments can be merchant wholesalers, sales branches of manufacturers, or various agents, brokers, and commission merchants. However, the scope of the monthly wholesale trade survey and report is narrowed to only merchant wholesalers owing to budgetary constraints and the greater difficulties involved in obtaining a survey sample of properly defined nonmerchant wholesalers.[2]

The primary defining characteristic of merchant wholesalers is their ownership of inventories. Merchant wholesalers take title to goods they sell. They include "wholesale merchants or jobbers, industrial distributors, voluntary groups wholesalers, exporters, importers, cash-and-carry wholesalers, drop shippers, major distributors, retailer cooperative warehouses, terminal elevators, and cooperative buying associations."[3]

To get some perspective on the size of merchant wholesale activity, at the end of 1997, merchant wholesale inventories stood at $274.3 billion in current dollars, compared to $44.4 billion for nonmerchant wholesalers (based on data in the GDP accounts). There are small accounting differences between NIPA and Census figures for merchant wholesale inventories; the Census estimate for December 1997 was $272.5 billion.

The wholesale data for initial estimates are based on a monthly sample of establishments drawn by the Census Bureau from all employer identification numbers issued by the Internal Revenue Service for merchant wholesalers and from a list of all establishments of known (from Social Security and other agencies) multiestablishment firms. Rotating panels of wholesalers are used, except for very large businesses which report each month. As with the retail sales procedure, there are three rotating panels, with each month's panel providing data for the current month and the previous month. Each month's first estimate is a composite of: (1) the current month's change in the reporting panel's sales and inventories (35 percent weight) and (2) a ratio estimate based on the previous month's estimate (from a separate panel) multiplied by the current month's ratio to the previous month (65 percent weight).[4]

The final estimate, which is also the first revision, is released the next month. It is a weighted average of the preliminary composite estimate (70 percent weight) for the given reference month and the unbiased estimate (30 percent weight) for the reference obtained from the following month's panel, which reports the next month's preliminary estimate and figures for the month being revised.

Annual revisions are usually released with the March report and sales and inventory data are adjusted to reflect estimates from the Census Bureau's Annual Trade Survey for the calendar year of two years prior. Benchmark revisions are based on and follow quinquennial Census of Wholesale Trade.

Data are classified by kind-of-business categories. Durables subcomponents are motor vehicles and automotive parts and supplies; furniture and home furnishings; lumber and other construction materials; professional and commercial equipment and supplies; metals and minerals, except petroleum; electrical goods; hardware, plumbing, and heating equipment, and supplies; machinery, equipment, and supplies; and miscellaneous durable goods. Nondurables include paper and paper products; drugs, drug proprietaries, and druggists' sundries; apparel, piece goods, and notions; groceries and related products; farm-product raw materials; chemicals and allied products; petroleum and petroleum products; beer, wine, and distilled alcoholic beverages; and miscellaneous nondurable goods.

KEYS TO ANALYZING THE MONTHLY REPORT

The primary uses of monthly inventory data are to anticipate inventory effects on industrial production and to project the nonfarm inventory investment component in real GDP.

Evaluating the Status of the Production Cycle

A key question in business cycle analysis is whether inventory movement is planned or unplanned. Essentially, production responds to undesired or unplanned changes in inventories. If inventories fall below desired levels, then firms respond by raising production levels. If inventories exceed desired levels, then production is reduced. Subsequently, employment and income, as well as aggregate demand, are affected. Unplanned changes in inventories lead to oscillations in business activity or, if large enough, create changes in the business cycle.

Sometimes one comes across an analysis of inventory data that implies that production will have to be cut back simply because inventories rose sharply during a given month or quarter. Similarly, some assume that if inventories decline, then production will rise to rebuild inventories. This type of analysis is erroneous to the extent that there has been no determination of whether desired inventory levels have changed. Inventories may be rising, but desired levels may also be rising. In fact, if desired inventory-to-sales ratios remain constant, then an expanding economy requires an uptrend in desired inventory levels.

However, the monthly inventory data measure "actual" inventories (taking into account that these actual inventory figures include both sampling and nonsampling errors). They are not broken down between planned and unplanned inventory changes. Properly analyzing inventory movements relative to their impact on the business cycle requires making some assumptions about how much of the changes are desired or not.

Over the business cycle, desired inventories change with businesses' view of the economy. As the end of recession nears and a rise in demand appears to be imminent, then businesses typically add to inventories. This rise does not portend a later decline in production. In fact, moderate inventory stocking normally helps fuel economic growth during the early stages of recovery. Often, it is when the economy is sluggish—late in expansion—that a sharp rise in inventories leads to a slowdown in production.

Similarly, if firms accurately anticipate a drop in demand, inventories can be drawn down, and if demand remains weak, then the drop in inventories may not be followed by a near-term increase in production.

Over the 1980s and 1990s, the United States has become more of an open economy. Increasingly, consumers and businesses have purchased goods and equipment from abroad. While analysts easily remember that consumers are buying more imports, and are starting to understand the importance of imports in capital equipment, they often overlook the fact that significant portions of inventory needs are met with imports.

Importantly, if imports meet a noticeable share of inventory needs, then as inventory adjustments are made in the overall economy, domestic production is generally less affected than if there were no imports. For example, when auto demand falls (for both domestics and imports) and inventories are "too high," auto dealers cut back on orders to manufacturers. Since some inventories are imports, the order reductions affect foreign as well as domestic producers. In turn, domestic production declines by less than the overall inventory adjustment. The reverse is also true when demand rises. Inventory stocking is met partially by imports and domestic production does not receive all of the benefit of higher demand. Essentially, the foreign content of inventories has moderated the inventory cycle for domestic producers.

How does one determine the impact of imports on domestic production through inventory adjustments? That is, if an inventory adjustment is under way, how much of inventories is imported and how will this impact changes in orders to domestic and foreign producers?

The answers to these questions do not come easily or precisely. Just as inventory data are not designated as planned or unplanned, inventories are not classified as imported or domestic. Only inferences can be made from various data series. For a complete analysis (which is heavily subjective), one must track the flow of demand, production, and inventories. Essentially, one must compare data series by market categories for consumer spending, business investment for equipment, industrial production, and merchandise trade. The industrial production data indicate where domestic strengths and weaknesses likely occur in inventories, while merchandise trade data suggest what inventories are likely to be imported. After becoming familiar with production and trade data, one can examine more detailed inventory figures and ask the basic question: Are the various goods in the inventory change more likely domestically produced or imported? For example, if inventories of consumer electronics rise, there is a high probability that much of the inventories were imported. On the other hand, if aircraft inventories are up, it is almost certain that these are domestically produced.

Assessing Nonfarm Inventory Investment in Real GDP

To estimate current-quarter inventory investment, one needs to look at business inventory data that have been deflated into constant-dollar terms and then put into quarterly averages to evaluate quarter-to-quarter absolute changes. Of course, when the initial quarterly GDP estimate is released, only two months of business inventory data are available. The missing month must be projected. However, since unit auto inventories are available for the missing month, this information can be used in making the projection. Nonetheless, because of the missing month of data and because of the complexities of deflating nominal inventory figures— using both CPIs and PPIs—it is difficult to project the nonfarm inventory component in current-quarter real GDP. Also, the BEA makes various accounting adjustments to the monthly data, as well as independent estimates for nonmerchant wholesale inventories, because the monthly report does not provide data for nonmerchant wholesale inventories.

TABLE 9–1
Business Inventories, 1960–1997*

	Total	Manufacturing	Retail	Merchant Wholesale
1960	NA	53.786	NA	NA
1961	NA	54.871	NA	NA
1962	NA	58.172	NA	NA
1963	NA	60.029	NA	NA
1964	NA	63.410	NA	NA
1965	NA	68.207	NA	NA
1966	NA	77.986	NA	NA
1967	NA	84.646	35.249	NA
1968	NA	90.560	38.885	NA
1969	NA	98.145	42.455	NA
1970	NA	101.599	43.641	NA
1971	NA	102.567	49.856	NA
1972	NA	108.121	54.809	NA
1973	NA	124.499	62.989	NA
1974	NA	157.625	70.852	NA
1975	NA	159.708	71.510	NA
1976	NA	174.636	79.087	NA
1977	NA	188.378	89.149	NA
1978	NA	211.691	102.306	NA
1979	NA	242.157	110.804	NA
1980	508.924	265.215	121.078	122.631
1981	545.786	283.413	132.719	129.654
1982	573.908	311.852	134.628	127.428
1983	590.287	312.379	147.833	130.075
1984	649.780	339.516	167.812	142.452
1985	664.039	334.749	181.881	147.409
1986	662.738	322.654	186.510	153.574
1987	709.848	338.109	207.836	163.903
1988	767.222	369.374	219.047	178.801
1989	815.455	391.212	237.234	187.009
1990	840.396	405.073	239.773	195.550
1991	834.287	390.950	243.275	200.062
1992	842.204	382.547	251.994	207.663
1993	867.513	384.138	267.497	215.878
1994	930.049	405.028	290.128	234.893
1995	985.905	429.089	303.750	253.066
1996	1,004.708	434.434	314.096	256.178
1997	1,047.574	453.591	321.454	272.529

*End-of-Period, Monthly SA, in Billions of Dollars.

Source: U.S. Department of Commerce.

KEY QUESTIONS IN ANALYZING THE NEWS RELEASE

- Are inventories rising (or declining) faster than demand (or sales)?
- Are inventory-to-sales ratios changing? Are firms implementing tighter inventory controls?
- Are auto manufacturers running special incentives to move inventories?
- Do inventory changes (increases or decreases) appear to be planned?
- If accumulation or rundown appears to be unplanned, are the goods produced primarily domestically or are they generally imported? (*Note:* Inferences can be made only through comparisons with production and import detail.)
- Are auto sales noticeably above or below expectations, causing sharp inventory changes?

NOTES FOR CHAPTER 9

1. U.S. Department of Commerce, Bureau of the Census, *Revised Monthly Wholesale Trade, Sales and Inventories January 1986 Through March 1992,* p. 4.
2. There are a few minor exceptions, the most significant being the inclusion of sales and inventories of manufacturers sales branches of ferrous metals service centers with inventories, as part of SIC 505 (metals and minerals, except petroleum).
3. U.S. Department of Commerce, op. cit.
4. Ibid., p. 3.

BIBLIOGRAPHY

U.S. Department of Commerce, Bureau of the Census. *Revised Monthly Wholesale Trade, Sales and Inventories, January 1986 Through March 1992.*

CHAPTER 10

THE PURCHASING
MANAGERS' INDEX

The purchasing managers' index contains an overall purchasing managers' composite index as well as other series not in the composite index. The purchasing managers' index is a composite index based on data from the monthly *Report on Business,* compiled and released by the National Association of Purchasing Management (NAPM), which is based in Tempe, Arizona. The importance of this index is its broad coverage of the U.S. manufacturing sector and its timeliness. The NAPM report is released the first business day following the reference month and is used by financial analysts to help project government-produced economic indicators related to manufacturing—industrial production in particular.

METHODOLOGY

The purchasing managers' index is based on data from a survey mailed to about 350 NAPM members. The survey is mailed by midmonth of the reference month and responses are tallied around the 21st day of the month. The questionnaires are distributed by the industry according to value-added shares in U.S. production. However, response rates vary each month by industry, and this affects how well the index sample is stratified. (The variance in response rate is not published.)

Survey members are asked to provide information on various facets of their firm's manufacturing activity. Questions cover five key categories: production, new orders, inventories of purchased materials, employment, and vendor deliveries.[1] For most categories, the possible answers are essentially "increase," "same," or "decrease." For vendor performance, replies are in terms of "faster," "same," and "slower." For supplier deliveries, "decrease" indicates slower, which is a positive for this component.

For each category, the NAPM tallies the number of positive, negative, and no-change responses and publishes them in terms of percentages of total responses per category. From this information, the NAPM computes a diffusion index, indicating the broadness of worsening or improving conditions among surveyed members. This approach is in contrast to other surveys (such as those conducted by the U.S. Commerce Department's Bureau of the Census), which measure actual levels by components for series like new orders, inventories, and shipments.

By the NAPM's own definition, an overall index above 50 indicates an expanding manufacturing sector, and a number below 50 suggests a generalized contraction. These conclusions are based on the component indexes being equal to the percent responding "increase" plus one-half of the percent indicating no change.

$$\text{Index} = \% \text{ increase} + 1/2 \text{ of } \% \text{ same}$$

The NAPM index is thus ordinal, not cardinal: the index does not report precise levels of activity but instead indicates whether a given month is better or worse than the preceding one. Diffusion indexes such as the NAPM series have the merit of being highly correlated with growth rates, but they are not as precise as surveys that measure actual production levels from period to period. This is not to say that the NAPM survey is wrong in any sense by design but simply that a diffusion index does not measure growth rates based on precise levels of activity. Because the NAPM index is designed to gauge whether manufacturing is expanding or contracting in industries represented in the survey, forecasters believe that it reasonably reflects current conditions in manufacturing. That is, respondents' views are seen as similar to actual production as measured in the Federal Reserve Board's index of industrial production—in technical terms, the two are correlated.

THE NAPM COMPOSITE INDEX

The overall NAPM composite index is derived from five component diffusions indexes. Published data originally were limited to percentages for each answer category. The data were first put into composite form in February 1982, based on the work of Theodore Torda, an economist at the Department of Commerce.

Component diffusion indexes are derived from not "seasonally"-adjusted percents. They are then seasonally adjusted before being combined into a composite index. The Commerce Department seasonally adjusts the indexes and provides the seasonal factors to the NAPM. The composite index components and their respective weights (out of 100 percent) are as follows: new orders, 30; production, 25; supplier deliveries, 15; inventories, 10; and employment, 20. Table 10–1 shows how each month's data are combined into a composite index.

TABLE 10–1

Putting Together the NAPM Composite Index, December 1992

Component	Diffusion Index, SA		Weight in Index		Component Contribution
New orders	64.4	×	.30	=	19.32
Production	59.4	×	.25	=	14.85
Supplier deliveries	52.1	×	.15	=	7.82
Inventories	44.8	×	.10	=	4.48
Employment	47.1	×	.20	=	9.42
Composite index (rounded to one decimal place)				=	55.9

Source: "December U.S. Purchasing Managers' Index Summary Data," *Market New,* December 31, 1992.

The supplier deliveries component requires a little elaboration. It is also known as vendor performance. This series reflects how quickly manufacturers' suppliers deliver factory inputs. Slower deliveries suggest shortages of supplies, possibly due to heavy demand. Quicker deliveries suggest the opposite. Therefore, this component is the sum of the percent of companies reporting *slower* deliveries and half of the percent reporting the same delivery speed. A decline in vendor performance—reflecting slower deliveries—is a positive for the index.

THE PRICE SERIES

Apart from the series in the composite index, the most notable series is that of prices paid by manufacturers. Financial analysts use the price series as an indicator of early price pressures. However, this series is very volatile because it contains a high percentage of series for crude and intermediate materials. While a sharp rise in this series generally precedes an acceleration in overall inflation, the series also has many false signals of inflation.

REVISIONS

The NAPM does not revise monthly data on an ongoing basis. Late reports are not carried over for revisions with the next month's release. The only revisions are for new seasonal factors for both individual components and the composite index based on these components. Annual revisions usually cover the previous three calendar years and are released with each year's report for January. The NAPM first began seasonally adjusting the data in late 1988. The Commerce Department derives the seasonal factors; this is their only contribution to the data.

PROBLEMS WITH THE DATA

Two of the key problems with NAPM data are closely tied to its primary benefit. The data are diffusion indexes that are based on questions that can be answered, compiled, and published quickly. However, the data are not as precise as data published by the Federal Reserve Board or the Census Bureau. No NAPM component explains more than half of the variation in the corresponding government data series for the month. Timeliness creates another problem. The surveys are mailed out early in the reference month and are tabulated around the 21st of the reference month. In effect, survey respondents must base answers partly on information from weeks prior to the reference month. Studies show that industrial production in month t is as closely related to NAPM data in month $t + 1$ as in month t.[2] In other words, January industrial production is as statistically related to the later February NAPM as to the concurrent January NAPM index.

KEYS TO ANALYZING THE MONTHLY REPORT

How the Monthly Report Is Used by the Markets

The purchasing managers' index is used as a direct gauge of the strength of the manufacturing sector. Analysts look to see if the composite index suggests any change in the perceived strength or weakness in the manufacturing sector. Because of the construction of the composite from its component diffusion indexes, the index level of 50 is said by NAPM to be the break-even point between expansion and contraction in manufacturing. The component diffusion indexes are supposed to represent the percentage of firms reporting increases, even though they are really the sum of positive responses plus one-half of those reporting no change. Nonetheless, if the percentage of positive responses equals that of negative responses (regardless of the share of those answering "no change"), then the diffusion indexes produce a value of 50. A diffusion index value above 50 indicates that more firms are reporting increases than those with decreases; hence, above 50 indicates expansion.

However, this index level of 50 as a neutral point is strictly definitional. An index level of over 50 in a given month does not necessarily mean that actual U.S. manufacturing activity is in expansion. Statistical analysis of NAPM data and more definitive government data are necessary to determine what NAPM index level is related to a break-even point for all of manufacturing. In fact, econmetric studies indicate that 50 is not the exact break-even point for industrial production, or even for the manufacturing component within industrial production.

Standard Regression Models Using NAPM Data

Analysts usually use NAPM data to forecast the industrial production release produced by the Federal Reserve Board of Governors. Modelers want to project the change in industrial production, specifically the monthly percent change. Since the NAPM index is a diffusion index, its *level* is associated with the *rate of growth* in manufacturing. A low index level (near but still above 50) is associated with low growth rates and a high index level is associated with high growth rates. There are similar relationships between NAPM index levels below the break-even point and the strength of declines in manufacturing. Therefore, in simple regression models, the NAPM composite index in levels is used as an explanatory variable for predicting the percent change in industrial production:

$$\% \text{ IP} = \beta \times \text{NAPM} + \text{constant} + \text{error term}$$

There are a number of variations on this model. Some forecasters choose to use initial estimates of the data for one or both dependent and independent variables, while others use revised data. Also, some analysts prefer to predict only the manufacturing component of industrial production—and exclude mining and utilities—since the NAPM data cover only manufacturing.

TABLE 10–2

An NAPM-Based Model for Monthly Industrial Production* (Regression period: January 1982–November 1992)

Independent Variables	Coefficient	Standard Error	t Statistic
NAPM index, initial	0.06	0.0075	8.03
Constant	−2.87	0.39	−7.44

Number of observations	119	R^2	0.36
Mean absolute percent change		Adjusted R^2	0.35
of dependent variable	0.55	Durbin-Watson	1.87
Standard error of regression	0.58	Standard deviation	
		of MAE	0.41
Mean absolute error (MAE)	0.40		
Root mean square error	0.57		

Dependent variable: Monthly percent change in industrial production for manufacturing, initial release.

Source: R. Mark Rogers, "Forecasting Industrial Production: Purchasing Managers' versus Production-Worker Hours Data," *Economic Review*, January-February 1992, p. 28.

Table 10–2 presents the output of one NAPM-based model. The monthly percent change for manufacturing IP is regressed against the level for the purchasing managers' composite index and a constant. Data for both the dependent and independent variables are from initial releases. The model has only modest predictive power, with an adjusted R^2 of 0.36 and a mean absolute error of the regression of 0.40 percentage points, compared with the mean of the absolute value of the dependent variable of 0.55 percentage points.

However, the model does have the expected signs for the coefficients. For each index point change in the index, the initial manufacturing IP changes by 0.006 percentage points minus the constant of 2.87. The purchasing managers' composite index is positively correlated with manufacturing IP, as expected, and with notable statistical significance for the regression coefficients.

The degree of confidence one can place in the reliability of the estimate for the coefficients is indicated by *t* statistics. The *t* statistic is the ratio of the coefficient value to its standard error. The greater the coefficient to its standard error (ignoring the sign of the coefficient), the greater the confidence that the coefficient is significantly different from zero. If the coefficient is not significantly different from zero, then that variable does not "explain" changes in the dependent variable.

This model might best be interpreted by setting the model solution equal to zero and solving for the index for the "no change" value. Values for the NAPM greater than this solution value would tend to be associated with increases in industrial production (as measured by the Federal Reserve Board's index), while lower index levels would suggest declines in industrial production:

$$\% \ IP_{mfg} = \beta \times NAPM + constant$$
$$0 = 0.06 \times NAPM - 2.87$$
$$47.83 = NAPM$$

This model shows that "no change" in manufacturing IP is statistically associated with a value of 47.83 for the purchasing managers' index over the 1982–1990 period. Thus zero is the point estimate (forecast) for IP manufacturing when the NAPM equals 47.83. The constant is negative because index numbers below 47.83 are associated with declines in production. This figure is somewhat below the level of 50 identified by the NAPM as associated with a generalized decline in the manufacturing sector. Although the difference is not statistically significant, regressions using different periods consistently estimated break-even values of below 50.

Importantly, the NAPM data do not forecast industrial production as well as a model using aggregate production hours data from the BLS. However, adding the NAPM index as a variable to production hours models improves its accuracy to a noticeable degree. Also, NAPM data are available earlier than the hours data.

The other primary modeling use of the NAPM data is to project payroll employment (or just the manufacturing portion) for the same month's employment report. The structure of these models is similar to that for industrial production. The level of the NAPM diffusion index for employment is used as an explanatory variable to predict the percent change in employment. To a lesser degree, component series are used in regression models for new orders and for inventories.

Break-even Points for Monthly Analysis

A study by Ethan S. Harris of the Federal Reserve Bank of New York confirms that break-even points for NAPM component diffusion indexes relative to their government statistical counterparts are not exactly 50, as implied by the NAPM methodology.[3] There are better, statistically derived rules of thumb for evaluating the monthly NAPM data. This study used revised data for dependent and independent variables. The Census Bureau's new orders data were deflated with implicit deflators for shipments. The statistically derived break-even points are shown in Table 10–3. Using these statistically derived break-even points should provide a clearer idea of what each month's report suggests for pending economic releases.

These break-even points suggest that there are biases in the data due to either a sample bias or certain tendencies by the respondents. Except for the price series, all break-even points are below 50. This general tendency may be a result of the NAPM survey being sent to older, larger, and more established firms. These firms remain in the sample even during stages of decline and into bankruptcy. Firms are replaced when closed (or they drop out from lack of interest) and the replacement firm is usually a mature firm. New, smaller, and faster-growing firms do not make it into the survey, although the government industrial production, orders, and employment data are more likely to be inclusive of these or use adjustment factors to account for them.

TABLE 10–3
Statistically Derived Break-even Points

	Using Data Covering	
	1959–1991	*1980–1991*
Series explained with NAPM components		
Industrial production	51.5	49.3
Payroll employment	49.1	47.4
New orders	51.4	49.3
Materials inventories	44.7	47.0
Crude producer prices	56.3	56.1
Series explained with NAPM composite index		
Industrial production	49.0	46.9
Real GNP	44.4	44.5

For inventories and prices, special biases appear to be built in. The inventory series' break-even point is the lowest of all components, and this may be the result of firms partly reporting desired inventories instead of actual inventories. The purchasing managers filling out the survey may not always check actual inventory levels before answering the qualitative response deemed appropriate. For materials prices, manufacturers may be influenced by the fact that they almost always have more types of materials inputs than goods produced. Purchasing managers may focus on a tendency for more input prices to be rising than output prices. Also, manufacturers' tendency to see input prices rising is consistent with their ongoing worries about cost.

While the intent of a diffusion index survey with qualitative responses is to reduce the reporting burden and to speed up processing, an unintended consequence is that respondents may not be compelled to check precise levels of indicator activity. Qualitative surveys have the flaw of more easily allowing respondents' biases into the data, as is suggested by the statistically derived break-even points for inventories and materials prices.

NAPM Data as Leading Indicators

While the NAPM index is helpful in interpreting changes in the business cycle, it is not definitive. The composite index leads the business cycle, but the lead prior to peaks and troughs varies significantly from cycle to cycle. The index also tends to send numerous false signals. Because the NAPM index is a diffusion index that correlates with growth rates, the composite index will peak as economic growth decelerates but still remains in the positive growth range for some time before turning negative. Essentially, a diffusion index peak represents a peak in growth rates. The NAPM lead is quite long because slower growth in a business cycle occurs well before the level of activity peaks and then declines. Any moderate rebound in growth rates will then cause the index to rise to another peak. Hence, prior to official business cycle peaks and troughs, the NAPM index typically will peak several times. One cannot know which NAPM peak is correctly predicting a business cycle downturn and which is a false signal of recession—portending only slower growth instead.

If NAPM data are examined in terms of the timing of crossing the break-even points shown in Table 10–3, the data generally still lead government statistics. However, the false-signal problem remains; during periods of sluggish activity the NAPM data tend to cross break-even points several times before an official turning point occurs. Over the business cycle, the NAPM data are best used to confirm cyclical movements rather than to anticipate them.

THE NAPM COMPOSITE INDEX: A MIXED INDEX OF CURRENT AND FUTURE ACTIVITY

The NAPM's composite index is advertised as an indicator of the current strength of manufacturing. And it also is touted as a leading index. There is some truth to both of these claims since the composite index includes some components that are measures of current activity and some that are indicative of future activity. Additionally, the inventory component can be interpreted in two ways: at times it is a measure of current strength and at others it portends pending changes in output. How does the composite index do all this?

First, of the five components, two—production and employment—are generally considered to reflect current conditions. The corresponding government statistics are part of the Commerce Department's composite index of coincident indicators. A third component, new orders, generally leads production, while the supplier deliveries component—also known as vendor performance—is one of the components of the Commerce Department's index of leading indicators. However, the coincident and predictive nature of these components relative to government statistics is somewhat hampered by the survey's early compilation deadlines, which force respondents to partially rely on previous month's data.

The inclusion of the inventory component in the composite index also creates a special problem for evaluating the manufacturing sector's strength with this index. Inventory changes can be either planned or unplanned. Importantly, it is the unplanned changes—when actual levels differ from desired levels—that lead to changes in planned production. Yet this NAPM component does not indicate whether inventory changes are desired or not for the current month (this is also the case with government data on inventories). The implication is that if the inventory component rises to meet *anticipated* demand, it should be construed as a positive for that month. In contrast, if inventories rise because of a drop in demand (orders and shipments), then the accumulation of unwanted stocks is a negative in terms of the impact on pending production. Therefore, the movement of the inventory component should be carefully interpreted in terms of whether it is a plus or minus for gauging strength in manufacturing through the use of the current month NAPM composite index.

RELATED SURVEYS

There are other surveys covering the manufacturing sector similar to the NAPM survey which are useful for complementing the NAPM data or even in some instances for predicting the NAPM release. First, the Chicago purchasing managers' index, published by the Purchasing Management Association of Chicago, is released at the end of the reference month, thereby preceding the national index's release. Additionally, four regional Federal Reserve banks—Philadelphia, Richmond, Atlanta, and Kansas City—produce manufacturing surveys. However, the reference period definitions and release dates vary. Each of these surveys is produced independently.

The longest running of these, the Philadelphia Fed's Business Outlook Survey, is generally released during the third week of the reference month. The historical series goes back to early 1969. Answers by respondents are essentially based on about three weeks of data from the prior month plus one week's worth of information from the reference month. The Philadelphia Fed's release does provide some prior information before the NAPM release, which is 10 days to two weeks later. The NAPM index is processed in the third week of the reference month and is based on about two weeks of information from the reference month.

The Richmond Fed's survey of business conditions originally was timed to be released just prior to each of the Federal Open Market Committee (FOMC) meetings and originally was published eight times a year. Historical data go back to mid-1986. Starting in January 1994, the Richmond Fed's survey switched to a monthly periodicity.

The Atlanta Fed's Survey of Southeastern Manufacturing Conditions is the newcomer, with official data starting with January 1992. Their survey is mailed out late in the reference month (around the 25th) and is not tallied until early the following month. The Atlanta survey is published the second business day after the 10th of the month immediately following the reference month. Respondents' answers are based on a little more than three weeks' worth of information on actual data and planned activity for the reference month. Hence, data for the Atlanta reference month more closely corresponds to the calendar month than do the NAPM survey.

The Kansas City Fed's manufacturing survey comes out quarterly. This survey dates back to the fourth quarter of 1994. The questionnaire is similar to those used by the other Federal Reserve regional banks.

KEY QUESTIONS IN ANALYZING THE NEWS RELEASE

- To get an indication of whether manufacturing growth is positive or negative, is the composite index above or below the break-even point? (Index levels are associated with growth rates for corresponding government indicators.)
- To get an indication of whether growth is accelerating or decelerating, is the composite index rising or falling?

- How does the latest month's composite index compare to statistically derived break-even points rather than to the definitional break-even point of 50?
- Is one component in particular causing most of the movement in the latest month's composite index?
- How is the production trend relative to the employment trend? (This will give an idea of changes in productivity.)
- Do the components paint a different picture of future production relative to current production? Are new orders healthy even though production may have been weak for the same month?
- Is the inventory component playing a large role in moving the composite index for the month? Is the inventory movement "perverse"? Does a decline in inventories portend a rise in production even though it is a negative in the composite index?

NOTES FOR CHAPTER 10

1. There are also questions on commodity prices, quantity of purchased materials, buying policy, and, in recent years, new export orders. However, these components do not enter into the composite index.
2. Ethan S. Harris, "Tracking the Economy with the Purchasing Managers' Index," *Quarterly Review,* Autumn 1991, pp. 61–69; Mark R. Rogers, "Tracking Manufacturing: The *Survey of Southeastern Manufacturing Conditions,*" *Economic Review,* September-October 1992, pp. 26–33.
3. Ethan S. Harris, ibid., p. 63.

BIBLIOGRAPHY

Bell, John, and Theodore Crone. "Charting the Course of the Economy: What Can Local Manufacturers Tell Us?" *Business Review,* July-August 1986, pp. 3–16.

Chmura, Christine. "New Survey Monitors District Manufacturing Activity." *Cross Sections,* Winter 1987–88, pp. 9–11.

Harris, Ethan. Tracking the Economy with the Purchasing Managers' Index." *Quarterly Review,* Autumn 1991, pp. 61–69.

The Report on Business: Information Kit. National Association of Purchasing Management, Tempe, Ariz., 1990.

Rogers, R. Mark. "Forecasting Industrial Production: Purchasing Managers' versus Production-Worker Hours Data," *Economic Review,* January-February 1992, pp. 25– 35.

———. "Tracking Manufacturing: The *Survey of Southeastern Manufacturing Conditions.*" *Economic Review,* September-October 1992, pp. 26–33.

———. "Tracking Manufacturing: An Update on the *Survey of Southeastern Manufacturing Conditions,*" *Economic Review,* March-April 1996, pp. 37–44.

Smith, Tim R. "Tenth District Survey of Manufacturers," *Economic Review,* Fourth Quarter 1995, pp. 61–72.

CHAPTER 11

U.S. INTERNATIONAL TRADE
IN GOODS AND SERVICES

OVERVIEW

The monthly report on international trade, published as the *U.S. International Trade in Goods and Services*, is important because it is the most timely publicly available data on the U.S. foreign trade sector. The data are viewed as important by the financial markets because they reflect the strength of domestic demand for imports to the U.S. relative to foreign demand for exports of U.S. goods and services. In turn, perceptions of the strength of these trade flows affect the value of the dollar and other currencies in foreign exchange markets.

The flow of goods through the foreign sector also helps to determine how much changes in domestic demand impact changes in domestic production. In other words, if domestic demand is rising but a greater share than in the past is being met with imports, then gains in domestic production will lag import growth. Similarly, if foreign demand for U.S. products is rising faster than domestic demand, then U.S. production would likely rise more rapidly. In a world economy that is becoming more integrated, these considerations are of growing importance.

Financial effects are also more complex. As foreign exchange markets react to changes in the international flow of goods and services, money and credit markets move also. For example, if the dollar depreciates owing to a rapid buildup in imports, then (assuming no other factors change) U.S. interest rates are bid higher by foreign holders of U.S. currencies. This is to offset their losses in asset values from dollar depreciation. Dollar depreciation is also generally associated with a near-term rise in price levels due to higher import costs and less competitive price pressure on domestic producers.

In contrast, if there is a strong upward trend in export growth for the United States, then one would likely see the opposite effects. Over time, the dollar would appreciate, and eventually imports would become cheaper, inflation pressures would ease, and U.S. interest rates would decline—at least relative to foreign rates. These scenarios are generalized, but in sum, changes in international trade trends can have significant effects on domestic production and employment. Changes can also occur in exchange rates, interest rates, and even long-run inflation rates, although international financial flows generally overwhelm the effects of real trade flows.

From a political perspective, these trade data are significant because they are used in international trade negotiations such as the General Agreement on Tariffs and Trade (GATT). The data are also used to meet a number of legal and regulatory requirements, including import duties and quotas and export restrictions.

Finally, in terms of statistically measuring the strength of the economy, the monthly goods and services trade data are the key inputs for the foreign accounts in both GDP and the balance-of-payments accounts. The international trade report is the first of the various monthly releases on U.S. trade flows.

Publication, New Format, and Timing of Releases

The monthly trade report has seen notable changes in recent years. Prior to 1994, monthly international trade data were published only for merchandise components. Monthly merchandise trade data were compiled and published by the U.S. Bureau of the Census in a publication officially entitled *U.S. Merchandise Trade,* but commonly referred to as the FT-900 report. The Commerce Department discontinued its quarterly merchandise trade report on a balance-of-payments basis following the fourth-quarter 1993 report, released March 3, 1994. Beginning with the March 22, 1994, release of trade data for January, the Census Bureau combined its FT-900 report with the BEA's report of balance-of-payments data, renaming the publication *U.S. International Trade in Goods and Services,* but retaining its shorthand title of FT-900. Its release date is the third week of the second month following the reference month. This report combines two of the three major types of trade data for the United States, the third being NIPA net exports (in GDP). The Census, balance-of-payments, and NIPA data are produced for different purposes. The Census data are primarily taken from U.S. Customs tabulations, with data collected for Customs' needs. Balance-of-payments data are estimated to track international financial flows. The NIPA data are oriented toward estimating domestic output. These differences are discussed in greater detail further below.

The change in format of monthly international trade data is very useful to economists and financial analysts trying to gauge the strength of the economy. The data on a balance of payments basis puts the figures into a format that is closer to the GDP data. Also, the addition of services in the monthly report provides an earlier glimpse of the strength in services exports and imports than was the case when the first estimate of balance-of-payments services data were released after the advance release of real GDP for a given quarter.

The full-scale balance-of-payments report, entitled, *U.S. International Transactions,* also includes components for income transactions and unilateral transfers (see Table 11–1). However, the monthly balance-of-payments components for goods and services provide coverage similar to the goods and services components within GDP exports and imports.

Census Data within the FT-900 Report

The published Census data in the joint Census-BEA release are the same series as in the earlier FT-900 report. For merchandise trade, the primary components are for major end-use categories. Discussion of major end-use categories for Census

TABLE 11–1

U.S. International Transactions Balance-of-Payments Basis for 1997 (Millions of Dollars)

Exports of goods, services, and income (credits)	1,167,619
Goods, adjusted, excluding military*	678,348
Net adjustments	10,549
Goods exports, Census basis	688,896
Services#	253,220
Transfers under U.S. military agency sales contracts	15,175
Travel	74,407
Passenger fares	21,710
Other transportation	28,194
Royalties and license fees	30,269
Other private services	82,681
U.S. government miscellaneous services	784
Income receipts on U.S. assets abroad	236,043
Direct investment receipts	109,227
Other private receipts	123,278
U.S. Government receipts	3,538
Imports of goods, services, and income (debits)	− 1,295,530
Goods, adjusted, excluding military*	− 877,282
Net Adjustments	6,559
Goods imports, Census basis	− 870,723
Services†	**− 167,929**
Direct defense expenditures	− 11,345
Travel	− 52,029
Passenger fares	− 16,927
Other transportation	− 29,771
Royalties and license fees	− 7,512
Other private services	− 47,548
U.S. government miscellaneous services	− 2,796
Income payments on foreign assets in the United States	**− 250,320**
Direct investment payments	− 41,527
Other private payments	− 117,712
U.S. government payments	− 91,081
Unilateral transfers, net	**− 38,526**

* Adjusted for timing, valuation, and coverage to balance of payments basis; excludes exports under U.S. military agency sales contracts and imports of U.S. military agencies.
† Includes some goods that cannot be separately identified from services.

Source: U.S. Department of Commerce, *U.S. International Transactions,* March 12, 1998. This table is partial excerpt of current account flows; capital inflows and outflows are not shown.

data carry over to the new format for balance-of-payments figures, since they are also categorized by major end-use categories.

The new FT-900 includes both seasonally adjusted and not seasonally adjusted series for major end-use commodity categories. For the seasonally adjusted end-use categories, data are provided in current dollars and constant dollars. Tables are also included for some not seasonally adjusted detail by selected countries and geographic areas and by principal standard industrial trade classification (SITC) commodity groupings. Finally, special tables are presented for imports of energy-related petroleum products and for exports and imports of advanced technology products. For the energy-related petroleum products table, imports are tracked in value, quantity (barrels), and unit price (dollars per barrel).

The FT-900 supplement provides detail for SIC-based product codes that differ from SITC codes. Also included are general imports of crude petroleum by country, SITC export and import data by broad commodity sections, and greater detail (than in the FT-900) for exports and imports by country and area. Figures are also tabulated for the origin of movement of U.S. exports by state and by SIC-based product code groupings. All of these series in the supplement are in not seasonally adjusted form. Finally, historical data are given for the overall trade balance, exports, and imports in both adjusted and not seasonally adjusted form. The Census Bureau also publishes a number of other detailed reports on foreign trade.

For Census basis data, revisions are made only for the previous month's data to incorporate statistics arriving too late to be included in the transaction month. Therefore, each month's recorded data do not exactly reflect the actual transactions that occurred, although the difference between the two are small. Not all published data series are revised—only those for seasonally adjusted aggregates (nominal and constant-dollar); unadjusted aggregates for exports, imports, and trade balance; and end-use totals. SITC and country detail are not revised monthly, but the timing adjustments in the relevant tables reflect the difference between originally reported and revised data.

Annual revisions are usually published in June and include information received after the monthly revisions. These revisions are available in the FT-900 final report (informally referred to as the 13th month report). However, these revisions are usually only applied to totals, end-use, SITC, and country summary data. Annual revisions also incorporate updates for seasonal factors where applicable and go back as far as 1979 for some series. New seasonal factors that are published generally go back two calendar years. Seasonal adjustment for series adjusted is done at the five-digit end-use level.

Methodology

In contrast with other economic statistics compiled by the Census Bureau, the Census basis merchandise trade figures are not derived from surveys. Data on exports from the United States to countries other than Canada come from shipper's export declarations (SEDs). Filing an SED is mandatory under federal law and these are collected by the U.S. Customs Service at the port of export. In turn, the U.S. Customs Service electronically transmits SED data directly to the Census Bureau. For exports to Canada (as a final destination), the United States substitutes Canadian figures for imports from the United States. Similarly, Canada uses U.S. data on Canadian imports for estimates of its exports. Finally, for exports some specific grants-in-aid from the Defense Department are reported directly to the Census Bureau.

The Census Bureau's U.S. import data are compiled primarily through the U.S. Customs Automated Commercial System. Other data come from various documents filed with the U.S. Customs Service as required by law.

In summary, the Census basis U.S. merchandise export and import data are obtained from three basic sources, in descending order of importance: the U.S. Customs Service, Canadian Customs via Statistics Canada, and the U.S. Department of Defense.

Coverage and Definitions

The Census basis monthly merchandise trade data reflect movement into and out of U.S. customs jurisdictions. This means that the data not only reflect goods to and from foreign countries into and out of the 50 states and the District of Columbia but also into and out of Puerto Rico, the U.S. Virgin Islands, and U.S. foreign trade zones. Essentially, the monthly trade data are not defined by U.S. national boundaries but by U.S. Customs' geographic authority. Shipments by both nongovernment and government entities are included. However, shipments that do not represent a shift in use of merchandise between U.S. Customs area residents or government and those of foreign countries are generally excluded from the data.

The Census Bureau's *Guide to Foreign Trade Statistics* lists nine types of transactions that are excluded from the statistics used to compile the Census basis merchandise trade balance.

1. United States trade with U.S. possessions, trade between U.S. possessions, and trade between U.S. possessions and foreign countries (except Puerto Rico and the U.S. Virgin Islands)

2. Merchandise shipped in transit through the United States from one foreign country to another

3. Shipments to the U.S. Armed Forces, including post exchanges, for their own use, as well as U.S. merchandise returned by the U.S. Armed Forces for their own use

4. Monetary gold and silver

5. Issued monetary coins (in current circulation) of all component metals

6. Bunker fuels and other supplies and equipment for use on departing vessels, planes, or other carriers engaged in foreign trade

7. Shipment of furniture, equipment, and supplies to U.S. government agencies, as well as such merchandise when returned to the United States

8. Imports of articles repaired under warranty

9. Some other transactions not considered to be of statistical importance, such as shipments of personal and household effects of travelers and certain temporary exports and imports

Exports and imports are defined as follows:

Exports measure the total physical movement of merchandise out of the United States to foreign countries whether such merchandise is exported from within the U.S. Customs territory or from a U.S. Customs bonded warehouse or a U.S. Foreign Trade Zone.

Imports of merchandise include commodities of foreign origin as well as goods of domestic origin returned to the United States with no change in condition or after having been processed and/or assembled in other countries.[1]

The Census basis monthly merchandise trade balance is simply U.S. merchandise exports based on free alongside ship (f.a.s.) values less U.S. general imports based on Customs values.

For exports, the f.a.s. value includes all inland costs incurred to get the merchandise placed alongside the carrier at the port of exportation. This includes inland freight, insurance, and other charges but does not cover the cost of loading the merchandise on the carrier or transporting it beyond the port of exportation.

General imports include the total physical arrivals of merchandise from abroad regardless of whether the imports are for immediate consumption or not. Merchandise imports are classified as for immediate consumption if the goods are duty-free merchandise or if duty is paid on arrival.[2] Merchandise imports that are not classified as for immediate consumption either go into bonded warehouses or foreign trade zones under Customs custody.

Customs import value is based on Customs appraisal standards and is generally the price actually paid or payable for merchandise ready for export from the exporting country. It includes the cost of getting the merchandise to (not on) the carrier but excludes U.S. import duties, freight, insurance, and other costs of transporting the goods to the United States. While not currently used to derive the merchandise trade balance, Census also reports imports on a cost, insurance, and freight (c.i.f.) basis. Basically, this is the landed value of imported goods at the first port of arrival in the United States and does not include U.S. import duties.

RECENT TRENDS IN INTERNATIONAL TRADE

Over the last few decades, the foreign trade sector has grown dramatically in importance worldwide. In 1960, as a percentage of nominal GDP, goods exports and imports were 3.9 percent and 2.9 percent, respectively.[3] By 1997, goods exports and import shares had risen to 8.5 percent and 11.0 percent, respectively. Domestic demand has increasingly been met by imports, while exports have become a more significant factor underlying growth in manufacturing output.

What does the United States export and import? In 1997, by principal end-use categories, exports were led by capital goods excluding autos, with second place held by industrial supplies and materials.[4] Most imports were for industrial supplies and materials, followed by automotive vehicles, parts, and engines. Table 11–2 gives export and import shares by principal end-use categories. End-use categories are the primary classification of Census trade data.

Export and import flows between various trading partners have changed significantly since the end of World War II. Though still important, western Europe no longer dominates as the United States' primary trading region. For exports, Canada is by far the most important buyer of U.S. goods. In 1996, Canada also was the number one supplier of goods to the United States. In recent years, however, Japan, China, and Mexico have become increasingly important. While the United States' largest unilateral trade deficit for goods is with Japan, China's goods trade surplus with the United States has grown rapidly in recent years. Table 11–3 shows the top 10 trading partners of the United States for goods exports, imports, and balance.

TABLE 11-2

Export and Import Shares for Census Goods Trade By Principle End-Use Categories, 1997 Data

	Exports	Imports
Foods, feeds, and beverages	7.5	4.6
Industrial supplies and materials	22.9	24.6
Capital goods, except automotive	42.7	29.2
Automotive vehicles, parts, and engines	10.7	20.4
Consumer goods (nonfood), except automotive	11.2	22.2
Other merchandise	5.0	3.4

Source: Census Bureau, *U.S. International Trade in Goods and Services,* March 19, 1998

TABLE 11-3

Top 10 U.S. Goods Export-Import Trading Partners in 1996 (Millions of Current Dollars)

Exports to	Rank	Value	Percent of Total	Imports from	Rank	Value*	Percent of Total
Canada	1	$134,210.3	21.5	Canada	1	$155,892.6	19.6
Japan	2	67,606.8	10.8	Japan	2	115,187.0	14.5
Mexico	3	56,791.5	9.1	Mexico	3	74,297.3	9.3
United Kingdom	4	30,962.5	5.0	China	4	51,512.6	6.5
South Korea	5	26,621.1	4.3	Germany	5	38,945.1	4.9
Germany	6	23,495.0	3.8	Taiwan	6	29,907.3	3.8
Taiwan	7	18,460.2	3.0	United Kingdom	7	28,978.8	3.6
Singapore	8	16,720.0	2.7	South Korea	8	22,655.1	2.8
Netherlands	9	16,662.6	2.7	Singapore	9	20,343.1	2.6
France	10	14,455.5	2.3	France	10	18,645.8	2.3
Total goods exports		$625,075.0		Total goods imports		$795,289.3	

Trade Surplus	Rank	Value		Trade Deficit	Rank	Value
Netherlands	1	$10,079.4		Japan	1	−$47,580.2
Australia	2	8,139.6		China	2	−39,520.0
Belgium	3	5,756.6		Canada	3	−21,682.3
Hong Kong	4	4,101.8		Mexico	4	−17,505.8
South Korea	5	3,966.0		Germany	5	−15,450.1
Brazil	6	3,944.2		Taiwan	6	−11,447.1
Egypt	7	2,472.9		Italy	7	−9,527.8
Argentina	8	2,237.6		Malaysia	8	9,282.6
United Arab Emirates	9	2,034.4		Venezuela	9	−8,423.7
United Kingdom	10	1,983.7		Nigeria	10	−5,159.9

*Exports are Census basis, f.a.s. Imports are on a customs value basis.

Source: U.S. Bureau of the Census, Foreign Trade Division, FT-900 *Final Report, 1996.*

Over the 1990s, international trade has grown worldwide. For the United States, Latin America has begun to resume its importance as a trading block due to the implementation of the North American Free Trade Agreement (NAFTA) with Canada and Mexico. Many foreign trade analysts expect that this agreement will be expanded to include most of South America and the Caribbean. During the 1970s, Latin America was a significant buyer of U.S. exports, but trade dwindled owing to the debt problems of many of these countries in the mid-1980s and early 1990s: many Latin American nations were constrained in their ability to pay for foreign-produced goods. In the mid- to late-1990s, Latin America became a big purchaser of U.S. capital equipment and consumer goods. Similarly, eastern Europe will likely be heavily dependent on capital from abroad, including the United States.

Newly industrialized countries will likely specialize in producing goods that are not capital-intensive and require a workforce that is not as technologically advanced as in the developed nations. These nations will increasingly export more consumer goods such as apparel to the United States and worldwide.

KEYS TO ANALYZING THE MONTHLY CENSUS TRADE DATA

End-Use Categories

Understanding the key subcomponents in each major end-use category is important to making sense of the trends in trade. Table 11–4 shows export, import, and balance levels for the major end-use categories, which are food, feeds, and beverages; industrial supplies and materials; capital goods except autos; consumer goods except autos; automotive vehicles, parts, and engines; and other merchandise.

The *foods, feeds, and beverages* end-use category is usually in surplus owing to the large U.S. volume of agricultural exports. Large swings can be caused by drought in agricultural areas abroad or in the United States. In recent years, the surplus has been eroded by greater U.S. dependence on imports for vegetables and some meats. Grain is still the primary source of export strength. The United States primarily exports foods and feeds that use economies of scale—for example, wheat and corn—which are made possible by wide expanses of arable land and by the ability to use farm equipment extensively. Food imports are generally for crops that are labor-intensive or simply those imported during the United States off season. Many off-season crops come from Latin America.

Foods, feeds, and beverages are primarily categorized between agricultural and nonagricultural components. For exports, listed agricultural components are grains and preparations (largely wheat and corn), soybeans, meat products and poultry; vegetables, fruits, nuts, and preparations; and other agricultural foods, feeds, and beverages. For imports, the listed agricultural components are the same except for the deletions of grains and preparations and soybeans and the additions of coffee, cocoa, and sugar; and wine and related products. Of course, there are minor quantities of many of these goods in both exports and imports, but these are not specifically listed categories. Exported or imported goods that do not fall into listed categories go under "other agricultural." For both exports and imports,

TABLE 11–4
Merchandise Trade: Principal End-Use Categories, Census Basis (Millions of Current Dollars)

	Total	Foods, Feeds and Beverages	Industrial Supplies and Materials	Capital Goods, except Automotive	Automotive Vehicles, Parts, and Engines	Consumer Goods (Nonfood), except Automotive	Other goods
Exports							
1994	512,626	41,956	121,396	205,022	57,775	59,981	26,495
1995	584,742	50,473	146,247	233,046	61,828	64,425	28,723
1996	625,075	55,534	147,652	252,895	65,021	70,138	33,836
1997	688,896	51,372	158,025	294,117	73,390	77,418	34,573
Imports							
1994	580,659	27,867	145,606	152,365	102,420	134,015	18,386
1995	743,543	33,176	180,849	221,431	123,795	159,905	23,387
1996	795,289	35,710	204,482	229,050	128,938	171,007	26,102
1997	870,723	39,704	213,788	254,168	140,720	192,946	29,398
Balance							
1994	−68,033	14,089	−24,210	52,657	−44,645	−74,034	8,109
1995	−158,801	17,297	−34,602	11,615	−62,967	−95,480	5,336
1996	−170,214	19,824	−56,830	23,845	−63,917	−100,869	7,734
1997	−181,827	11,668	−55,763	39,949	−67,330	−115,528	5,175

Source: U.S. Bureau of the Census, Foreign Trade Division.

nonagricultural goods are primarily fish and shellfish, along with distilled beverages and other miscellaneous categories.

The import component for *industrial supplies and materials* often swings sharply owing to the inclusion of oil imports. Oil exports, of course, are negligible. Usually, this also causes this end-use component to be in a sharp deficit. On the import side, industrial supplies and materials are largely petroleum and products, metals, and metallic products. For exports, this component is led by chemicals, nonferrous metals, paper, petroleum and products, and coal. A critical factor in analyzing this end-use category is being able to take into account both price and volume changes in oil imports. It can be difficult to translate nominal data into estimates of real net exports for real GDP. This component also includes nonmonetary gold and occasionally reflects large shipments for numismatic reasons, even though the gold is still in bullion form.

Petroleum imports do get special attention in the merchandise trade reports. Petroleum imports are listed in the monthly publications in tables by dollar value and by volume of barrels imported. Also published is the average price per barrel of imported oil.

The *capital goods except autos* component is generally in surplus, since the production of capital goods is one of the United States' significant comparative advantages. In contrast, the *consumer goods except autos* component and the *automotive vehicles, parts, and engines* components are usually in deficit, as newly industrialized countries have tended to specialize in consumer goods, including autos.

Exports of civilian aircraft, computers, semiconductors, industrial machinery, and oil drilling, mining, and construction machinery lead capital goods except autos. Because aircraft shipments can be very large when they take place, this end-use category for exports is often volatile. Very large swings in this end-use export component are usually attributable to this subcomponent. For imports, this end-use category is led by nonelectrical machinery, especially computers and semiconductors.

The *other merchandise* component primarily includes military goods and low-value shipments. Exports valued under $2,501 per commodity classification per shipment do not have to be documented; Census makes estimates for this component. For exports to Canada, the Canadian import exemption level is used. For imports to the United States, only shipments valued at $1,251 and higher generally require formal reports. An exception is textile imports under certain textile programs. Otherwise, imports under $1,251 per shipment are low value and are estimated by Census. The dollar value definition of what is low value has changed over time.

On the export side, the other merchandise end-use category also includes an adjustment for exports to Canada as documented by Canadian Customs. Import data are usually better documented than export information. The difference between U.S. estimates for exports to Canada and Canadian estimates for U.S. imports to Canada is entered as a subcomponent in this end-use export category. This is done with the first monthly revision to merchandise trade data. In the initial report, the adjustment is assumed to have a zero value. There is no equivalent adjustment on the import side for the other merchandise component.

End-use components are very useful in analyzing the supply and demand flow for U.S. goods production and consumption. Data are available on a similar basis for production and consumption as for end-use exports and imports. Imports are now an important factor in meeting demand for consumer goods and business equipment as well as for playing a key role in keeping inventories at desired levels. Exports are now a growing source of demand for industrial production.

The impact of changes in export or import flows cannot be determined by simply looking at aggregate values. There must be an understanding of flows by end-use categories and even finer detail. For example, does a monthly surge in imports mean that domestic production will falter? It might if these imports directly compete with goods also produced in the United States, such as automobiles or apparel. However, a jump in imports of consumer electronics probably would not since most such goods purchased in the United States are no longer produced domestically.

Somewhat detailed analysis of end-use trade categories also helps to explain events in other demand sectors. If inventories rise unexpectedly, does this imply a downturn in domestic production? Production cutbacks are not likely if inventory accumulation is fueled by imports, foreign production will slip instead. However, inventory data are not maintained by domestic or import status, and import shares can only be inferred by analysis of U.S. production by types of goods and by trends in consumer and business consumption and in exports and imports by types of goods.

Other Insights into the Monthly Data

For the trade data, the levels are as important to focus on as the percent changes in exports and imports by components. The levels define the surplus or deficit, and for some components there are significant or even dramatic differences between the export and import levels where the United States has a large comparative advantage or disadvantage. Additionally, it is whether the trade balance is improving or growing worse that affects growth rates in the economy in the near term—not whether the trade balance is in surplus or deficit. However, the size of the surplus or deficit does affect the economy in the medium and longer run through delayed effects on the dollar and other financial markets.

On a monthly basis, financial analysts use the Census data to project the current quarter net exports component of real GDP since the Census data are published before the GDP data. This process has been made easier since Census began publishing monthly constant-dollar seasonally adjusted export, import, and balance data beginning with January 1990 statistics and with data going back to January 1989. Even though Census figures are already seasonally adjusted at highly aggregated levels, the monthly data must be summed and then annualized for estimates of GDP trade components. When estimating NIPA net exports and components, Census data should only be used to project the merchandise trade portion of GDP net exports. Services data in the NIPA trade figures should be estimated separately. Nonetheless, there are definitional differences between NIPA trade data and Census data, and these lead to differences in dollar levels. However, the changes in the Census data from quarter to quarter give a good estimate of the changes in the NIPA data. The definitional differences are discussed in a following section. The balance-of-payments data can also be used for estimating net exports, but these series are not in constant-dollar terms

Broader Perspectives

It is hard to say what level of statistics actually indicate when a nation's trade flow is in balance. First, services surpluses can balance deficits in merchandise. Also, even though theoretically the sum of all nation's merchandise trade balances should equal zero (an import by one nation should be claimed as an export by another), this does not work out in practice. Statistically, there is a worldwide merchandise trade deficit. This is largely due to the fact that every nation has more incentive to closely monitor imports than exports. Generally, governments tend to tax imports while exports are taxed little or not at all. Domestic producers for each nation want to keep track of import competitors and lobby their politicians to maintain various restrictions. Finally, trade statistics are used in trade negotiations, and each nation finds it to be advantageous to understate exports but not imports.

Each month, the monthly international trade figures provide one of the last pieces of the GDP puzzle for the current quarter (inventories are last). Certainly, the strength for the current quarter is partially determined by whether or not the deficit is widening or narrowing. However, for the longer run—or even for the next quarter—a broader perspective is needed. For example, a surge (or sharp drop) in imports in the last month of a quarter does not necessarily mean that it is part of a change in trend. Basic questions must be asked about the data: Can domestic demand continue to absorb imports at current growth rates or even at current levels or will imports sit in inventories and cause a slowdown in the coming months? Are foreign economies capable of absorbing or demanding U.S. exports at current rates; are they strong enough or is the latest data merely a blip caused by due to the timing of shipments?

One of the keys to interpreting international trade trends is to remember that trade patterns change slowly owing to long lags caused by the time between contracts being signed and shipments being made. True changes in trend are caused by long-term factors, such as significant exchange rate movements, changes in tariffs or export subsidies, changes in income domestically or abroad, changes in relative costs separate from exchange rates (financial capital and labor), and changes in availability of products abroad (capacity). Trade data are not significantly changed by these factors on a month-to-month basis.

On a final note, it should be apparent that many factors affect trade trends, but the value of the dollar is often the focus of attention and analysis of its impact is frequently misunderstood. A focus on bilateral exchange rates or certain composite dollar indexes does not take into account the impact of changes in trade patterns on the overall level of exports and imports. Even though the dollar depreciated sharply against a number of traditional trading partners in the early

1990s, U.S. retailers and manufacturers imported goods and materials increasingly from newly industrialized countries that had currencies which showed little or no appreciation against the dollar. Traditional dollar indexes often missed this facet of emerging trade patterns and many forecasts underestimated the strength of imports over the period when the dollar fell according to these traditional measures.

CENSUS DATA INPUT IN OTHER FOREIGN TRADE REPORTS

The monthly Census-BEA merchandise trade report provides data that are key inputs into other reports on foreign trade published by U.S. statistical agencies. There are two other major reports in which the monthly data play significant roles. These are the summary of U.S. international transactions, or current account report, and the net export portion of the national income and product accounts, or real GDP report. Both reports are produced by the Bureau of Economic Analysis, first under the direction of the Balance-of-Payments Division and the second by the National Income and Wealth Division.

Both of these reports are part of what is known as the balance-of-payments accounts. These accounts are designed to be a comprehensive measure of the financial position of the United States with other nations in the world, and they have similar accounts. While the emphasis is on financial flows, the flow of physical goods is an important part of international financial transactions because merchandise trade balances affect financial standings. That is, exports and imports of goods are exchanged for either a monetary payment or a promise to pay.

The Current Account Report

The monthly Census data are used as direct inputs into monthly figures for monthly exports and imports on a balance-of-payments basis. There are three basic categories of adjustments made to Census foreign trade data for the figures to conform with other international transactions in the balance of payments data: timing, coverage, and valuation.[5]

First, *timing adjustments* are made to correct for documentation lags that result in exports and imports not being reported in the month of actual transactions.

Next, *coverage adjustments* reflect a variety of changes to incorporate a broader sphere of financial transactions, to substitute more reliable sources of data for the later published balance-of-payments data (relative to Census data), to fill in minor gaps in coverage, and to eliminate known sources of double-counting in the data.

There is a coverage adjustment for nonmonetary gold transactions made by the Federal Reserve Bank of New York on behalf of foreign governments and the International Monetary Fund (IMF). This adjustment is necessary because these transactions do not show up in Census documents, as there is no movement across borders. Next, the Balance of Payments Division substitutes data on Department of Defense exports and imports from a special comprehensive report it receives. The data the Census Bureau receives is not as detailed, and the Census-based data on DOD exports and imports are excluded to prevent double-counting. These transfers under U.S. military agency sales contracts are excluded from the Census merchandise trade data and are not part of the merchandise portion of the trade data on a balance-of-payments basis. The more detailed DOD data enter the balance-of-payments accounts under services.

Until January 1989, an adjustment was made for electrical energy exports and imports to and from Canada, with historical data coming from Statistics Canada. Beginning in January 1989, Census began including this data for electrical energy transactions with Canada. There is also a continuing adjustment for electrical energy trade with Mexico, with the source of the data being the U.S. Department of Energy. This adjustment is small.

A variety of other coverage adjustments are made for:

- Shipping vessels purchased or transferred by U.S. persons, including any change of flag
- Excluding exposed movie film as an offset to the inclusion of royalties and fees
- Some double-counting in the repair of U.S. vessels and aircraft
- Repairs and alterations of equipment exported from and imported into the United States
- Grain shipped by the United States to other countries through Canada
- Private gift parcel post exports
- Canadian reconciliation of trade statistics
- Sales of fish caught in U.S. territorial waters by both U.S. and foreign vessels and exported directly without landing in the United States
- Imports of petroleum into Guam.[6]

The *valuation adjustment* is made only for trade with Canada and is made to correct for inland freight charges not included in Customs estimates. Some estimates for exports to Canada and for imports to the United States are shipments valued at f.o.b. plant rather than including the cost of bringing the merchandise to the border.

Table 11–5 compares the dollar values of Census basis merchandise trade figures and the data on a balance-of-payments basis and NIPA basis. The levels differ somewhat but the changes from year to year are close. The exclusion of military transfers is the largest adjustment to Census exports, and this is why balance of payments data are lower for exports than Census data. On the import side, the biggest adjustment is for inland freight to Canada; this raises the value of imports on a balance of payments basis relative to the Census basis. The only significant offset is the exclusion of merchandise imports of U.S. military agencies, but the value of this adjustment is usually less than half of the addition of the inland freight adjustment. The only other sizable (but still minor) adjustments are for private gift remittances and nonmonetary gold exports and imports.

TABLE 11–5

Foreign Trade Data: Census, Balance-of-Payments Accounts, and NIPA Basis (Billions of Current Dollars)

	Exports				
	Census Goods	BPA Goods	NIPA Goods	BPA GSI*	NIPA Total
1994	512.6	502.4	509.6	854.2	721.2
1995	584.7	575.9	583.9	991.5	818.4
1996	625.1	612.1	617.6	1,055.2	870.9
1997	688.9	678.1	686.5	1,167.6	958.0
	Imports				
	Census Goods	BPA Goods	NIPA Goods	BPA GSI*	NIPA Total
1994	−663.3	−668.6	−676.8	−948.8	−812.1
1995	−743.5	−749.4	−757.6	−1,086.5	−904.5
1996	−795.3	−803.2	−809.0	−1,163.5	−965.7
1997	−870.7	−877.1	−888.8	−1,295.5	−1,058.8
	Balance					
	Census Goods	BPA Goods	NIPA Merchandise	BPA GSI*	BPA Current Account	NIPA Total
1994	−150.6	−166.2	−167.2	−94.7	−133.5	−90.9
1995	−158.8	−173.6	−173.6	−95.0	−129.1	−86.1
1996	−170.2	−191.2	−191.4	−108.2	−148.2	−94.8
1997	−181.8	−199.0	−202.3	−127.9	−166.4	−100.8

* GSI = goods, services, and income.

Notes: The current-account balance differs from that for balance-of-payments goods, services, and income owing to the inclusion of unilateral transfers. Other than "goods" alone, the components in the BPAs include both services and income receipts and payments on income. The lower overall export and import levels for GDP relative to the BPAs are primarily due to the BPA's inclusion of income receipts and payments.

Sources: U.S. Department of Commerce: Bureau of the Census and Bureau of Economic Analysis.

The current account report incorporates information not just on merchandise trade but also on transfer payments by individuals and by governments, travel expenditures, royalties and license fees, various private and government services, and income to and from abroad, such as income on direct investment and income on financial investments (government and private securities). The monthly merchandise trade data on a balance-of-payments basis are combined with similar figures for services, income, and unilateral transfers to get a complete current account report. Table 11–5 also shows the dollar values of merchandise trade to overall trade in the balance of payments data.

The Real GDP Report

The monthly balance-of-payments data are inputs into the international trade components of exports and imports in gross domestic product (GDP). However, the National Income and Wealth Division of the BEA does not use the Balance-of-Payment Division's trade data directly. This division of the BEA receives both merchandise and services trade data as adjusted for the balance-of-payments accounts (BPAs), and the data in this form provide the basis for the foreign transactions series in the national income and product accounts (NIPAs). Still, there are a few definitional and statistical differences between the BPA and NIPA data.

> The differences between the NIPA and BPA entries, called reconciliation items, . . . reflect different publication and revision schedules, different definitions of the United States, and—most importantly—different treatment of certain transactions. The first source of difference arises because the NIPA estimates incorporate BPA revisions with lags. The second arises because the NIPAs exclude Puerto Rico and U.S. territories from the definition of the United States, while the BPAs include them. The third arises because the two sets of accounts serve different purposes and, therefore, treat certain types of transactions differently.[7]

In more detail, BPA data are typically revised in a number of ways prior to when the revisions are made to NIPA data. Each year, annual revisions are made first to BPA series and then to NIPA figures. Additionally, BPAs may be benchmarked earlier or incorporate a new methodology prior to NIPA data (or be based on new source data for some services components).

For balance-of-payments data, Puerto Rico and U.S. territories and possessions are included in the definition of the United States. For NIPA data, they are not included. Therefore, territorial adjustments are made to merchandise series. Exports to other countries from U.S. territories and Puerto Rico are subtracted from the BPA data, and exports from the 50 states and the District of Columbia to U.S. territories and Puerto Rico are added. Similar adjustments are made for imports.

Limiting discussion to merchandise components, the only difference in the treatment of transactions between BPAs and NIPAs is for gold. Census data ignore monetary gold transfers. BPA data make a distinction between monetary and nonmonetary gold, and adjustments are made to incorporate monetary gold transactions for BPAs. Industrial-use gold enters BPA accounts through standard Census data for exports and imports. However, official transactions between monetary authorities and governments take place in capital accounts in BPAs. Beginning in 1975, gold sold to private foreigners by the U.S. Treasury is recorded as exports and gold purchased by private U.S. residents from the International Monetary Fund and foreign official agencies is counted as imports. This background helps explain the focus in the GDP account for gold in terms of production of industrial-use gold and changes in holdings of industrial-use gold: other uses are generally extraterritorial.

> In the NIPAs, U.S. gold production is included in GNP, and transactions in nonmonetary gold held for industrial use are recorded as any other commodity in the expen-

diture components of GNP. Nonmonetary gold held for nonindustrial use, however, is treated as if it were in the foreign sector in the same manner as monetary gold owned by the U.S. Treasury, because purchases on nonindustrial gold have an investment aspect that would make their inclusion in the domestic expenditure components problematic for many types of analysis.[8]

Essentially, the gold subcomponents in the BPA exports and imports are removed. Then an entry is made in imports for gold on a NIPA basis. The replacement entry for gold in NIPA net exports is the difference between domestic gold production and the change in holdings of industrial gold. This entry incorporates movement of industrial-use gold between U.S. residents and foreigners and also shifts between industrial and nonindustrial use by U.S. residents. Because of inadequacies in the data, exports and imports of gold are not measured separately. NIPA exports of gold are set equal to zero and net exports of gold are defined as imports (with the sign reversed). There is no NIPA gold component in exports.

The biggest adjustments to BPA exports and imports to get corresponding NIPA merchandise series are the adjustments for U.S. territories and Puerto Rico. As shown in Table 11–5, these adjustments raise the levels of exports and imports relative to BPA levels since in the GDP data, shipments to and from the states to these territories are counted as U.S. imports and exports. The adjustments for gold are a distant second in magnitude, and the exclusion has a lowering effect, but not enough to offset the territorial adjustments.

For services exports and imports, the only major adjustment to BPA data to get NIPA series is a bottom-line adjustment each for exports and imports to take into account territorial differences. The adjustment is "bottom line" in that adjustments are not made to individual components. There are other minor adjustments in these adjustment line items but the dollar values are very small.

THE SERVICES COMPONENTS IN THE MONTHLY REPORT

Table 11–1 shows the balance-of-payments services components. The importance of these series is that they give a direct indication of the BEA's view for trends in these services exports and imports—which are major inputs in GDP services exports and imports. However, estimates for current-year services exports and imports are very preliminary. Estimates are based on annual trends plus partial information on prices and quantities from sources such as travel agencies, trade sources, Customs data, and the Treasury reporting system. Annual data are based on more complete sources.

Annual data are for balance-of-payments services from a variety of voluntary and mandatory surveys, U.S. Treasury Department data, data from other U.S. government agencies, and private trade sources. Voluntary surveys include the Survey of U.S. Travelers Visiting Canada and also Expenditures of U.S. Travelers in Mexico. These BEA surveys are distributed continuously at border points. Mandatory surveys cover ocean freight revenues and foreign expenses of U.S. carriers,

U.S. airline operators' foreign revenues and expenses, foreign ocean carriers' expenses in the United States, foreign airline operators' revenues and expenses in the United States, and other private services, royalties, and license fees.

Services exports and imports have seven broad categories. These types of services are the same for six of the components. For the seventh, on the export side, the category is "Transfers Under U.S. Military Sales Contracts," while on the import side, the category is "Direct Defense Expenditures." The following brief descriptions of the categories are from the appendix of the July 1997 *U.S. International Trade in Goods and Services.*

Travel. Purchases of services and goods by U.S. travelers abroad and by foreign visitors to the United States. A traveler is defined as a person who stays for a period of less than 1 year in a country of which the person is not a resident. Includes expenditures for food, lodging, recreation, gifts, and other items incidental to a foreign visit.

Passenger Fares. Fares paid by residents of one country to residents in other countries. Receipts consist of fares received by U.S. carriers from foreign residents for travel between the United States and foreign residents for travel between the United States and foreign countries and between two foreign points. Payments consist of fares paid by U.S. residents to foreign carriers for travel between the United States and foreign countries.

Other Transportation. Charges for the transportation of goods by ocean, air, waterway, pipeline, and rail carriers to and from the United States. Includes freight charges, operating expenses that transportation companies incur in foreign ports, and payments for vessel charter and aircraft and freight car rentals.

Royalties and License Fees. Transactions with foreign residents involving intangible assets and proprietary rights, such as the use of patents, techniques, processes, formulas, designs, know-how, trademarks, copyrights, franchises, and manufacturing rights. The term "royalties" generally refers to payments for the utilization of copyrights or trademarks, and the term "license fees" generally refers to payments for the use of patents or industrial processes.

Other Private Services. Transactions with affiliated foreigners, for which no identification by type is available, and of transactions with unaffiliated foreigners. (The term "affiliated" refers to a direct investment relationship, which exists when a U.S. person has ownership or control, directly or indirectly, of 10 percent or more of a foreign business enterprises's voting securities or the equivalent, or when a foreign person has a similar interest in a U.S. enterprise.) Transactions with unaffiliated foreigners consist of education services; financial services (includes commissions and other transactions fees associated with the purchase and sale of securities and noninterest income of banks, and excludes investment income); insurance premiums and losses; telecommunications services (includes transmission services and value-added services); and business, professional, and technical services. Included in the last group are advertising services; computer and data processing services; database and other information services; research, development, and testing services; management, consulting, and public relations services; legal services; construction, engineering, architectural, and mining services; industrial engineering services; installation, maintenance, repair of equipment; and other services, including medical services and film and tape rental.

Transfers under U.S. Military Sales Contracts (Exports only). Exports of goods and services in which U.S. Government military agencies participate. Includes both goods, such as equipment, and services, such as repair services and training, that cannot be separately identified.

Direct Defense Expenditures (Imports only). Expenditures incurred by U.S. military agencies abroad, including expenditures by U.S. personnel, payments of wages to foreign residents, construction expenditures, payments for foreign contractual services, and procurement of foreign goods. Includes both goods and services that cannot be separately identified.

U.S. Government Miscellaneous Services. Transactions of U.S. Government nonmilitary agencies with foreign residents. Most of these transactions involve the provision of services to, or purchases of services from, foreigners; transfers of some goods are also included.

KEY QUESTIONS IN ANALYZING THE NEWS RELEASE

- To determine the impact on real GDP—that is, real net exports for merchandise regardless of the level of the balance, is the constant-dollar monthly merchandise trade deficit improving or worsening?
- Does a surge in imports represent a sustainable rise in domestic demand or merely special timing factors?
- Are imports up in late summer owing to earlier-than-usual shipments for Christmas inventory needs?
- Is an increase in imports due to pending import restrictions, and therefore only temporary? Similarly, is a drop in imports the result of reaching import restrictions such as voluntary import restrictions on motor vehicles?
- Were imports up as a result of replenishing needs for oil inventories through increased oil imports?
- Are capital goods exports unusually high because of the timing of shipments of aircraft out of inventories?

NOTES FOR CHAPTER 11

1. U.S. Department of Commerce, Bureau of the Census, *Guide to Foreign Trade Statistics, 1991 Edition,* Section 2, pp. 3–4.
2. The term *consumption* is unrelated to the term in NIPA categories. These imports can be used for purchases by consumers, businesses, and government; for inventory accumulation; or for inputs as crude or intermediate products.
3. Exports and imports are on a NIPA basis. Census data are not consistent series back to 1960.
4. For both exports and imports, this category includes petroleum products.
5. The following discussion on adjustments to Census data to put into balance-of-payments form is based on *Balance of Payments of the United States: Concepts, Data Sources, and*

Estimating Procedures, U.S. Department of Commerce, Bureau of the Census, May 1990, pp. 31–35.

6. The full list appears in Ibid.
7. U.S. Department of Commerce, Bureau of Economic Analysis, *Foreign Transactions, Methodology Papers: U.S. National Income and Product Accounts,* May 1987, p. 7.
8. Ibid.

BIBLIOGRAPHY

Bach, Christopher L. "U.S. International Transactions, Revised Estimates for 1974–96," *Survey of Current Business*, July 1997, pp. 43–64.

U.S. Department of Commerce, Bureau of Economic Analysis. *Balance of Payments of the United States: Concepts, Data Sources, and Estimating Procedures,* May 1990.

————. *Foreign Transactions, Methodology Papers: U.S. National Income and Product Accounts*, May 1987.

U.S. Department of Commerce, Bureau of the Census. *Guide to Foreign Trade Statistics, 1991 Edition.*

————. *U.S. International Trade in Goods and Services,* July 1997.

————. *U.S. Merchandise Trade: 1991 Final Report.*

————. *U.S. Merchandise Trade: 1992 Final Report.*

CHAPTER 12

MONTHLY CONSTRUCTION
INDICATORS

OVERVIEW

Construction tends to be a very cyclical activity that can have a significant impact on the national economy and even more so on various local economies. Construction activity has a significant impact on local employment owing to secondary effects on construction supply and services industries. While the federal government releases many construction statistics each month, the two most watched are housing starts and housing permits. They are followed for two key reasons: (1) starts and permits are key indicators of the near-term health of the housing industry, and (2) these data series tend to be leading indicators for the overall economy.

Of lesser notoriety are the new single-family homes sales and the monthly construction outlays series. The sales series, of course, is a closely watched indicator of housing demand, while outlay data are broader in scope. They cover not only residential activity but also nonresidential and public sector construction spending. These data are important for monitoring the level of current, as opposed to future, construction activity and because they are key inputs in the GDP accounts.

In short, permits and starts reflect plans for construction activity, sales reflect demand, and outlays are a measure of actual production in the construction sector.

The source for each of these series is the Census Bureau of the U.S. Department of Commerce. They are part of the Census Bureau's eight *Current Construction Reports*. This chapter focuses on four of the reports, referred to here by their publication number, as follows:

C20   *Housing Starts*

C25   *New One-Family Houses Sold and for Sale*

C30   *Value of New Construction Put in Place*

C40   *Housing Units Authorized by Building Permits*

HOUSING PERMITS

The C40 construction report is the housing permit series, officially known as the new privately owned housing units authorized series. The Commerce Department discontinued the printed publication for permits after the December 1995 release.

For historical reference, it was known as the C40 report, and the electronic version available on the Internet is known by the same name. Preliminary permit data are released to the public at the same time as housing starts, in print and electronic form, generally the third week of the month following the reference month. The housing permit series is an indicator of planned construction activity in the residential sector. Permit authorization is one of the first steps in the construction process taken by builders, with later steps including the start, continuing outlays, and completion. The permit data are important because it is the only construction indicator in the Conference Board's index of leading indicators (see Chart 12–1).

Permit authorization is granted by local governments such as cities and counties. Housing permit data no longer incorporate publicly owned housing. This component was last published at the national level in 1986 owing to the difficulty in getting the data from the U.S. Department of Housing and Urban Development and to the declining significance of publicly owned housing.

The housing permit series represents only new housing units intended for occupants on a housekeeping basis. Hotels, motels, nursing homes, and dormitories are excluded. So are mobile homes.

Statistics for these series are derived from reports by local building permit officials in response to a mail-in survey by Census. For reports that are not returned, Census replaces the missing data with information from its Survey of Use of Permits (SUP), which is used to collect data for estimates of housing starts, or uses an indirect estimate. The SUP is much more limited in sample coverage for permit-issuing places than the mail-in survey. Where the SUP cannot substitute for missing data, the estimate is based on the assumption that the ratio of current month authorizations to those of a year ago is the same for both reporting and nonreporting places. That is, nonreporting places have the same year-ago change in permits as reporting places, and this ratio is applied to known year-ago data for nonreporting places.

With each month's initial release, only the prior month is revised. Annual revisions to seasonal factors are made for the release of data for the reference month of April and cover the previous two calendar years. However, monthly permit data are not benchmarked to annual survey levels. Therefore, pure annual figures do not equal the sum of monthly permit data.

The Sample

The current version of the housing permit series is based on data from a sample of about 8,500 permit-issuing places, which were chosen from a universe of approximately 19,000 places. These 19,000 permit-issuing places account for over 94 percent of all new private residential construction in the United States. Estimation of the permit data from a sampling technique applies only to the statistics at relatively high levels of aggregation: the United States, the Census regions, and the individual states. Lower-level statistics (such as for MSAs) are based not on samples but on actual, reported data. There is complete enumeration of all permit-issuing places in selected metropolitan areas and certain states with a small number of permit-issuing places. The rest of the sample is stratified by state, with large

CHART 12–1
Housing Permits

Millions of Units Annualized   Millions of Permits Annualized

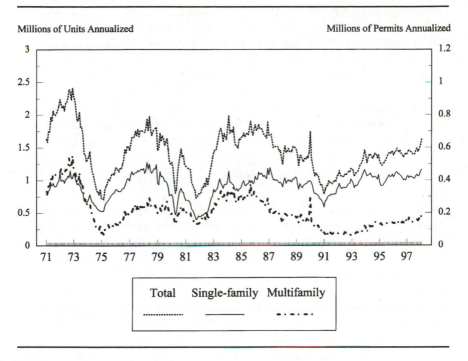

Total	Single-family	Multifamily

permit-issuing places chosen with certainty and other places selected at a rate of 1 in 10. The definition of "large" varies by state and was set to ensure a minimum reliability for each state. Estimates for the United States, the Census regions, and most states are based on techniques applicable to samples.

Because of the constantly changing number in actual permit-issuing places, Census chooses a fixed universe for the data series. Changes include adding new permit-issuing places and deleting places no longer issuing permits. A chosen, fixed universe keeps the data consistent. The universe is used only for the annual data, while a sample of this universe is used for the monthly estimates. As already mentioned, the monthly sample for the current 19,000 universe is roughly 8,500 places.

Monthly permit levels are estimated from the 8,500 sample. First, about 7,500 places are selected with certainty; these are the places issuing greater numbers of permits—essentially metropolitan areas. Permit levels from these places are entered directly into monthly estimates. These 7,500 are not just representative in the 19,000 sample but are themselves in terms of actual numbers used. The remaining 1,000 reporting places in the monthly sample are representative of the places that are not selected with certainty in the monthly sample. To obtain the appropriate level of permits in the monthly sample, the data for the remaining 1,000 places are weighted by a factor of 10.

For the places selected with certainty, the criteria differ somewhat from state to state owing to the need to maintain a sufficiently large sample for each state in order to publish state data that are statistically meaningful.

The number of permit-issuing places that define the permit series has changed over time. This has changed the size of the sample and essentially changed the definition of permit data at specific times. Permit data from the Census Bureau originally were based on 13,000 permit-issuing places, with the data starting in 1967 and going through December 1972. In January 1973, data were reported that were based on 14,000 permit-issuing places, with data starting in 1973 and ending in December 1977. The sample size was increased to 16,000 in April 1979 and then to 17,000 in 1985. Data based on the 16,000 sample runs from 1978 through 1984. Overlap data are available for the first year of each series. The latest change occurred for 1994, when a 19,000 sample was first used. The 17,000 place series continued through 1994 for overlap comparisons.

Keys to Analyzing Monthly Permits Data

The housing permit series is a leading indicator of the economy because permit issuance is the initial stage of housing activity and because the housing sector is itself a leading indicator. Housing typically leads the economy because of its interest rate sensitivity. Also, decisions to make housing purchases are highly dependent on consumer confidence, including expectations of income. Changes in housing activity also lead to significant secondary effects in other industries. Housing demand also affects demand for goods such as appliances, furniture, and carpeting. Analysts of these industries closely watch housing data. Interestingly, booms in new housing later lead to booms for replacement appliances, as much original equipment wears out over a common time span. That is, air-conditioning and heating units and carpeting each need replacing a certain number of years after being installed in new housing. The new housing boom in the 1970s later led to a rise in demand for replacement goods in the late 1980s and early 1990s.

Permits represent planned construction: they are potential activity rather than actual outlays. They do not represent starts or the amount of construction that has taken place. Also, permit data differ from starts in another aspect: permits reflect coverage in permit-issuing places, whereas starts include activity in both permit-issuing and nonpermit-issuing areas. Of course, the issuance of a permit does not necessarily mean that a start or further construction must occur.

Housing permit data—like other housing statistics—are very seasonal and volatile on a monthly basis even after seasonal influences have been accounted for statistically. Housing data for winter months are heavily influenced by seasonal factors; reports of unusually large increases or declines (after seasonal adjustment) should be viewed with caution until a several-month trend is established. The Census Bureau acknowledges this by charting the data in the construction report series typically with a four-month moving average as well as with one-month actual data.

Seasonal factors for permit data for the U.S. are derived indirectly:

> The seasonally adjusted building permits estimates are computed using a procedure similar to that used for housing starts. . . . The seasonally adjusted U.S. total is the sum of six seasonally adjusted components: single-family structures in each of the four regions, U.S total for two-to-four unit structures, and U.S. total for structures with five

units or more. Also, the unadjusted data for the four regions are seasonally adjusted and subsequently modified so that the seasonally adjusted U.S. total derived from the regions equals the seasonally adjusted U.S.total derived from the structures.[1]

Therefore, for total permits (and starts) there are only implied seasonal factors at the national level—no directly derived seasonal factors.

Permits can also be heavily influenced by changes in regulations. For example, California passed legislation in the fall of 1985 that changed building codes for handicap access. Multifamily permits for that state surged prior to the new codes' effective date and even led to a large increase in U.S. totals.

For use in the index of leading indicators, the data in the index typically do not quite match the levels in the most recent advance release for permit data. This is because the Conference Board, when compiling its composite indexes, uses data from a Census release subsequent to the initial report which incorporates late-received data. These data do end up in the revised numbers in the next C40 initial release.

HOUSING STARTS

The C20 construction report is the housing starts series, formally, the new privately owned housing units started series. It measures when construction activity begins. For privately owned housing, the start of construction is "when excavation begins for the footings or foundation of a building."[2] Beginning with the September 1992 release, the estimates for both starts and permits also include units in structures being totally rebuilt on an existing foundation.[3] This definition of starts covers buildings intended for "housekeeping purposes." It excludes group homes such as dormitories and nursing homes and residential structures such as hotels. For multifamily buildings such as apartments and condominiums, all housing units in the building are counted as being started when the excavation has begun. As with permit data, starts no longer include publicly owned housing units.

Housing units are defined to exclude mobile homes. Data for mobile home shipments are published in the C20 report but represent an entirely different data series. However, the starts data do include prefabricated, panelized, componentized, sectional, and modular housing units in addition to the conventional "stick-built" units.[4]

With each month's initial release, the two prior months are revised. Three-year seasonal adjustment revisions are published with the release of data for the reference month of January.

Derivation of Starts Estimates

Housing starts estimates are based on permit data for permit-covered areas and on separate on-site surveys for other areas.

For the 19,000 permit-issuing places, a mail-in survey is sent to a sample of 8,500 to estimate the number of permits issued. Next, Census sends interviewers on-site to an 840 representative subset of the 8,500 sample to determine which units were started for a particular month. This survey of 840 is the Survey of Use of Permits (SUP). Follow-up interviews are made if a unit is not started by the end of the month.

From the data gathered with the interview process, ratios are calculated (by type of structure—single-family, etc.) of the number of units started to units covered by permits. These ratios are called starts rates and are calculated for each month following (and including) the month of permit issuance. For units with permit authorization, starts estimates are derived by applying the starts rates to permits authorized over the appropriate number of months and by structure type.

The above methodology only covers starts for units that received permit authorization. In permit-issuing places, some starts take place without permit autho-

TABLE 12–1

Housing Data: Permits and Starts (Levels in Thousands)

Year	Permits Total	Permits Single-Family	Permits Multi-Family	Starts Total	Starts Single-Family	Starts Multi-Family
1970	1,351.5	646.8	704.8	1,433.6	812.9	620.7
1971	1,924.6	906.1	1,018.6	2,052.2	1,151.0	901.2
1972	2,218.9	1,033.1	1,185.8	2,356.6	1,309.2	1,047.5
1973	1,819.5	882.1	937.5	2,045.3	1,132.0	913.3
1974	1,074.4	643.8	430.5	1,337.7	888.1	449.7
1975	939.2	675.5	263.7	1,160.4	892.2	268.3
1976	1,296.2	893.6	402.6	1,537.5	1,162.4	375.1
1977	1,690.0	1,126.1	564.0	1,987.1	1,450.9	536.1
1978	1,800.5	1,182.6	617.9	2,020.3	1,433.3	587.0
1979	1,551.8	981.5	570.2	1,745.1	1,194.1	551.0
1980	1,190.6	710.4	480.2	1,292.2	852.2	440.0
1981	985.5	564.3	421.2	1,084.2	705.4	378.8
1982	1,000.5	546.4	454.1	1,062.2	662.6	399.6
1983	1,605.2	901.5	703.7	1,703.0	1,067.6	635.5
1984	1,681.8	922.4	759.4	1,749.5	1,084.2	665.4
1985	1,733.3	956.6	776.7	1,741.8	1,072.4	669.5
1986	1,769.4	1,077.6	691.9	1,805.4	1,179.4	626.0
1987	1,534.8	1,024.4	510.4	1,620.5	1,146.4	474.0
1988	1,455.6	993.8	461.8	1,488.1	1,081.3	406.8
1989	1,338.4	931.7	406.8	1,376.1	1,003.3	372.8
1990	1,110.8	793.9	316.9	1,192.7	894.8	297.9
1991	948.8	753.5	195.2	1,013.9	840.4	173.5
1992	1,094.9	910.7	184.2	1,199.7	1,029.9	169.8
1993	1,199.1	986.5	212.6	1,287.6	1,125.7	161.9
1994	1,371.6	1,068.5	303.1	1,457.0	1,198.4	258.6
1995	1,332.5	997.3	335.2	1,354.1	1,076.2	277.9
1996	1,425.6	1,069.5	356.1	1,476.8	1,160.9	315.9
1997	1,442.3	1,055.6	386.7	1,474.0	1,133.7	340.3

Source: U.S. Department of Commerce, Bureau of the Census. Annual figures are not seasonally adjusted totals.

rization. To take this into account, Census makes an upward adjustment of 3.3 percent to the number of single-family structures started with permits. This figure is based on a study during the 1970s on the number of starts covered by permits in permit-issuing places. Adjustments are also made to account for units started before permit authorization in permit-issuing places and for late reports.

Given the sample design, approximately 95 percent of start activity typically occurs within permit-issuing places. In nonpermit-issuing places, a small sample of the land area is surveyed to provide an estimate of starts. This small sample data is then used to derive starts for the total area not covered by permits. Finally, this estimate of starts in nonpermit-covered areas is added to the estimate of starts in the 19,000 permit-issuing places to get an estimate of total private housing starts.

Keys to Analyzing Monthly Starts Data

Housing starts data generally closely track housing permit data in terms of changes in levels (see Table 12–1). It is normal for starts levels to exceed permit levels because not all areas require permits for a start. While not all permits are started, the percentage not started is very small owing to the expense of obtaining a permit.

The primary factors causing temporary divergent movement between permits and starts include weather (delaying or accelerating starts), expected changes in permit regulations, and perceived changes in housing demand by builders—particularly in reference to whether home buyers anticipate changes in mortgage rates (see Charts 12–2 and 12–3).

CHART 12–2
Housing Starts versus Fixed-Rate Mortgage Rates

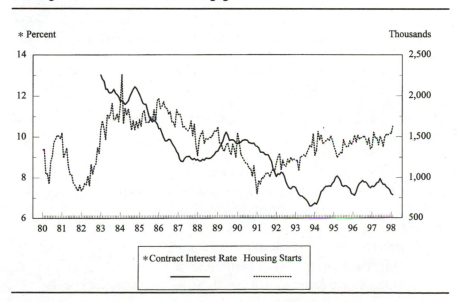

* Percent   Thousands

14		2,500
12		2,000
10		1,500
8		1,000
6		500

80 81 82 83 84 85 86 87 88 89 90 91 92 93 94 95 96 97 98

*Contract Interest Rate   Housing Starts

CHART 12–3
Single-Family Starts versus Demographic Trends

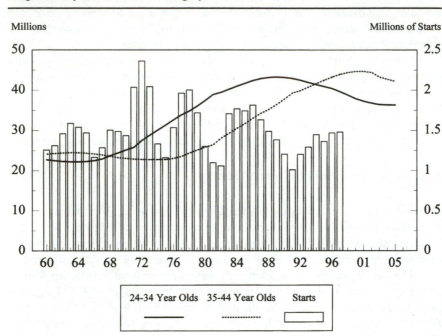

CONSTRUCTION EXPENDITURES

Construction outlays data are published in the C30 construction report and are more formally known as the value of new construction put in place series. In contrast to permit and start information, construction outlay expenditures refer to actual construction rather than planned or just initiated activity. In essence, construction outlays are a measure of current production in the construction sector. Importantly, these data series cover nonresidential and public sectors as well as residential construction (see Table 12–2).

This "value of new construction put in place" is a measure of the value of construction installed or erected at the site during a given period. For an individual project, this includes:

- Cost of materials installed or erected
- Cost of labor (both by contractors and force account) and a proportionate share of construction equipment rental
- Contractor's profit
- Project owner's overhead and office costs
- Cost of architectural and engineering work
- Miscellaneous costs chargeable to the project on the owner's books
- Interest and taxes paid during construction[5]

Expenses do not include the cost of land.

For public construction, there are two main components: building and nonbuilding. In nominal terms, over the 1990s, the buildings component has been about 40 to 45 percent of public expenditures, with educational buildings the largest subcomponent. The nonbuilding subcomponent overwhelmingly consists of highways and streets, with sewer systems and water supply facilities being distant second and third largest components.

Private construction includes two major components—residential buildings and nonresidential buildings—plus a number of minor series. Residential construction includes new private housing and improvements. For new housing units, included are new houses, apartments, condominiums, and townhouses. Other types of residential construction that are generally for nonhousekeeping or institutional purposes (hospitals, dormitories, hotels, etc.) are included in nonresidential construction. New private housing units are classified as "one unit" or "two or more units."

Private nonresidential construction put in place includes a variety of familiar components as well as a number of components not typically assumed to be in a series defined as nonresidential. As might be expected, nonresidential buildings include industrial, office buildings, and "other commercial," such as shopping centers, banks, service stations, warehouses, and other categories. Also falling under the nonresidential heading are hotels, motels, religious, educational, hospital and institutional, and "miscellaneous nonresidential" building.[6] These subcomponents are only for private construction.

Rounding out the private construction component are telecommunications and "all other private." These are generally of a nonresidential nature, but are not part of nonresidential buildings. Although included in totals, the Census Bureau no longer publishes components for railroads, electric light and power, gas, petroleum pipelines, and farm nonresidential. Farm nonresidential construction is a relatively minor series and includes structures such as barns, storage houses, and fences. Land improvements such as leveling, terracing, ponds, and roads are also a part of this subcomponent. Data for farm nonresidential construction reflect activity only for establishments having annual agricultural sales of $1,000 or more.

"All other private" includes privately owned streets and bridges, parking areas, sewer and water facilities, parks and playgrounds, golf courses, airfields, and similar construction.

Some series aggregates are available in constant 1992 dollar series. In turn, fixed weighted price indexes and implicit price indexes are also available.

Estimating Construction Outlays

Residential Expenditures

Residential expenditures for one-unit houses are based on estimated final construction costs and a predetermined pattern for the distribution of the total cost over the construction period. The construction cost is estimated using data from the Census Bureau's Housing Starts Survey, and Housing Sales Survey, while the distribution pattern is based on historical data on typical monthly distributions of construction progress from start to finish. Census publishes a table showing the assumed progress by percent completed each month. There is a separate distribution pattern for each month that new units are started.

For units built to be sold or rented and units built by the owner, construction cost is estimated separately. For units to be sold or rented, estimates are based on the average sales price at the time of the start and then discounted to take into account the cost of nonconstruction items such as raw land, marketing costs, closing costs, and movable appliances. For units built for the owner, the cost is based on the contract value at the time of the start, with a minor net upward adjustment to eliminate nonconstruction items but also to add the value of land development done by the developer.

For multifamily units, a subsample of the Census Bureau's Housing Starts Survey is used to estimate construction progress. There are about 1,800 projects in the survey. Owners report construction progress until the project is completed.

Estimates of value put in place are derived from the sum of the adjusted reported value for all projects. Upward adjustments are made for architectural, engineering, and miscellaneous costs (which are not reported monthly in the survey).

Residential improvements are derived from Census surveys using household interviews in a representative sample for owner-occupied units and a mail-in survey of owners of rental or vacant properties. Data from these surveys are oriented for quarterly estimates and substantially lag the monthly estimates of expenditures on new construction. As a result, monthly figures for total residential improvements are usually forecasted from incomplete data. Estimates based on complete data are first used in the May publication for revisions to the previous year.[7]

Private Nonresidential Expenditures

Private nonresidential expenditures are based on a monthly Construction Progress Reporting Survey. The sample is primarily based on reports from the F. W. Dodge Division of the McGraw-Hill Information Systems Company for projects valued at $50,000 or more in the United States except Hawaii. Census uses building permit notifications for sample projects in portions of Hawaii. Census also seeks sample projects in areas not covered by building permit systems or reported by Dodge. Monthly progress reports are requested from the owners of selected projects until the project is completed. About 4,600 projects are in the survey.

Estimates for value put in place are derived by the summed weighted reported values of the projects, with upward adjustments for architectural, engineering, and miscellaneous costs. An upward adjustment is also made for undercoverage of projects not reported by F. W. Dodge.

Other Private Construction Categories

Farm nonresidential construction expenditure estimates are extrapolations from the annual U.S. Department of Agriculture report, *Income and Balance Sheet Statistics.* These expenditures are not reported separately on a monthly or quarterly basis.

For utility construction, a variety of sources are used. Data are derived and organized by industry. Actual monthly construction progress reports are available for telephone and telegraph components of telecommunication construction. Annual reports from federal regulatory agencies and various private organizations are used for annual construction put-in-place estimates for TV cable, electric light and power, gas, railroad, and petroleum components. Monthly estimates for railroads are derived from quarterly estimates by the Interstate Commerce Commission. Other monthly figures are based on forecasts primarily from industry sources.[8]

Public Construction

State and local public construction expenditures are based on progress reports from a stratified survey. The survey is created from information from F. W. Dodge. Federal construction expenditures are reported almost entirely by each federal agency. For the few agencies not reporting, information is obtained from the federal budget, with annual expenditures prorated to derive monthly figures.

Keys to Analyzing Monthly Construction Outlays

Broad Cyclical Trends

The construction outlays data basically reflect the value of construction that has taken place over a given time period. Data are for current production, however. Over the business cycle, different components of outlays exhibit differences in cyclical timing. First, residential outlays is a leading series. Housing outlays are interest-rate sensitive and track housing starts and permits with a short lag. Most new houses are completed within three or four months of a start.

Over the business cycle, the nonresidential outlays series is a lagging indicator. Business investment in structures are interest-rate sensitive, but nonresidential outlays lag investment in producers' durable equipment. Businesses expand equipment investment first because it is quicker to boost production capacity with purchases of machinery than with new plant construction. Also, structures investment is more costly in absolute dollar size, and it is riskier in terms of demand remaining strong long enough to pay off the cost of the structures investment.

Public construction is primarily state and local outlays. State and local construction is dependent on revenue growth (or decline) and therefore sometimes lags behind peaks and troughs in the business cycle. Perhaps more importantly, secular trends are also largely affected by changes in federal funding for various types of infrastructure improvement programs. Federal grants-in-aid show up in state and local outlays and at times counterbalance the cyclical changes in other state and local revenues. Over the long run, public construction outlays are largely affected by population growth—which affects highway, sewer, and water line types of construction—and by the size of the school age population—which affects construction of education buildings.

Use as Source Data for GDP

Construction outlays series are measures of output and are primary inputs in several key expenditure series in GDP, for nominal and chained 1992 dollars. For nonresidential fixed investment in GDP, construction outlays are the main

TABLE 12–2

Construction Outlays, 1970–1997 (In Billions of Current Dollars)

	Total	Private Residential Buildings	Private Nonresidential Buildings	Public Constr.
1970	105.890	35.863	28.171	27.908
1971	122.414	48.514	29.307	29.699
1972	153.781	65.085	37.639	32.348
1973	155.170	55.967	39.889	38.132
1975	152.635	51.581	35.409	43.293
1976	172.132	68.273	34.628	43.980
1977	200.501	92.004	38.245	43.083
1978	239.867	109.838	48.824	50.146
1979	272.873	116.444	64.765	56.656
1980	273.936	100.381	72.480	63.646
1981	289.070	99.241	85.569	64.691
1982	279.332	84.676	92.690	63.064
1983	311.576	125.521	87.069	63.450
1984	369.025	153.849	107.680	70.238
1985	401.370	158.474	127.466	77.815
1986	429.924	187.148	120.917	84.582
1987	441.647	194.656	123.247	90.648
1988	455.618	198.101	130.854	94.735
1989	469.797	196.551	139.953	98.174
1990	468.532	182.856	143.506	107.478
1991	424.176	157.835	116.570	110.109
1992	452.086	187.819	105.646	115.847
1993	478.648	210.455	110.635	115.960
1994	519.896	238.874	120.285	120.530
1995	534.068	230.688	135.022	127.292
1996	568.585	247.177	149.376	131.506
1997	600.873	260.076	161.517	138.745

Source: Bureau of the Census.

inputs for nonfarm buildings, utilities, and "other nonfarm structures." GDP estimates for residential investment rely heavily on C30 data for permanent-site single-family and multifamily housing. However, quarterly changes in broad categories of residential and nonresidential outlays do not precisely match movement in corresponding GDP components because not all of the GDP subcomponents are based on C30 data. For nonresidential structures investment, other sources are used to estimate: oil and gas well drilling and exploration, construction of mine shafts and exploration, and broker commissions. For residential investment, subcomponents not based on Census outlays figures include mobile homes, brokers' commissions, and the producers' durable equipment component of residential investment.[9]

For the public sector, value put in place figures are used for estimates for the state and local structures subcomponent of government purchases within GDP data.

NEW SINGLE-FAMILY HOME SALES

The new single-family home sales series, officially the new one-family houses sold and for sale series, is commonly known as C25. The Housing Sales Survey is conducted by the Bureau of the Census under contract with the U.S. Department of Housing and Urban Development. Data are published for sales, inventory, median and average prices for houses sold, and months on the market for houses sold and for sale. Data are organized by Census region and are generally seasonally adjusted at that level of detail and higher. This report is usually released to the public near the end of the month following or the first week of the second month following the reference month. With each initial release, monthly revisions cover the previous three months. Seasonal adjustment revisions normally occur with the release for data for the reference month of January (usually released in early March) and affect data for the previous three calendar years (see Chart 12–4).

The Sample

A sale takes place when a home buyer signs a contract or makes a deposit. Land must be included in the sale or the house is assumed to be for the landowner's use. The monthly sample used for this housing survey excludes owner-built houses,

CHART 12–4
New Single-Family Home Sales

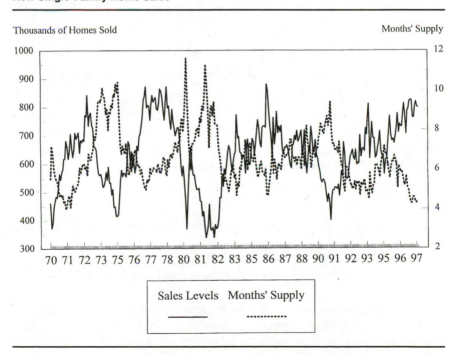

contractor-built houses, houses built to be rented, nonresidential buildings, and mobile homes. The reason for these exclusions is to keep the permits selected by Census to a common cost basis for residential, single-family housing. Census basically seeks a sample of speculatively built single-family housing, which includes both land and structure costs in the transaction. If land is not included—as with owner-built and contractor-built houses—then there is typically a 20 percent discrepancy in the sales price.[10] This difference is around 25 percent in the northeast and west Census regions. The above exclusions are the primary reason that the level of Census new one-family houses sold is lower than that of one-family starts or permits.

The housing sales survey sample is a subset of the sample used for building permit and housing starts data. About 840 permit-issuing places are selected, based on proportions of permit activity, and used for selecting sample permits for determining if the unit is for sale. Interviewers call to check on whether a chosen permit meets the criteria for this survey. Nonpermit areas are taken into account, with Census interviewers canvassing selected areas for one-family houses started. For 1989, the Housing Sales Survey's average monthly sample size was 12,000 sample cases.[11]

The sales sample consists of one-family houses either sold or for sale. Even though the basic sample used is permit-based, overall estimates of new houses sold include estimates for new houses sold before issuance of building permits in permit-issuing places and new houses sold prior to start in nonpermit places.[12] There is no follow-up to see if sales are actually completed. If a buyer makes a deposit on a house but later backs out, it is still counted as a sale for this report.

The C25 sales series does include a small number of houses not actively being marketed, for example, model or sample houses being used as temporary offices by builders, houses involved in bankruptcy procedures, and houses in estate settlements.[13]

The C25 report includes a number of tables, such as:

Table 1: Houses for sales and months' supply at current sales rate

Table 2: Houses sold and for sale, by region

Table 3: Houses sold and for sale, by stage of construction. The stages of construction are completed under construction, and not started.

Table 4: Houses sold, by sales price. This table includes median and average sales prices.

Table 5: Median number of months on sales market. This is for houses sold and for sale.

There also are tables listing seasonal factors and detailing the monthly variability of the series.

Keys to Analyzing Monthly New Home Sales and Price Data

As with other construction data, deviations from seasonal norms for weather can cause significant month-to-month volatility. This is particularly true for winter months, when seasonal factors are very large. The very seasonal nature of housing sales—and other monthly housing data—is seen in the data shown in Table 12–4.

TABLE 12–4

Comparison of Monthly Housing Data: Not Seasonally Adjusted to Seasonally Adjusted Data (Thousands of Single-Family Units)

1992	Permits		Starts		New Houses Sold	
	NSA*	SAAR†	NSA*	SAAR†	NSA*	SAAR†
January	55.4	913	58.4	989	48	667
February	60.8	946	69.2	1,109	55	627
March	82.1	907	90.9	1,068	56	555
April	88.9	873	93.5	933	53	546
May	82.9	879	100.2	1,019	52	554
June	91.4	872	102.7	999	53	583
July	83.6	879	93.2	956	52	616
August	76.7	877	91.8	1,042	56	627
September	80.4	913	91.4	1,051	51	671
October	80.8	959	96.1	1,077	48	618
November	63.5	955	74.1	1,090	42	617
December	66.1	1,045	68.2	1,130	41	656

*Not seasonally adjusted.
†Seasonally adjusted at an annual rate.

Sources: U.S. Department of Commerce, Bureau of the Census, "Housing Starts and Building Permits in December 1992," News Release, January 22, 1993; Bureau of the Census, C25 report, February 2, 1993.

Changes in mortgage rates are certainly another factor affecting sales, as lower rates generally lead to higher sales and higher rates to lower sales. However, expectations can lead to the opposite effect in the short run. Sales can jump if mortgage rates rise and further increases are expected. The reverse may hold for declining mortgage rates if buyers wait for lower rates.

The months' supply concept is analogous to an inventory-to-sales ratio. On a not seasonally adjusted basis, it is the ratio of houses for sale divided by the number of houses sold. However, sales are usually annualized, and for monthly figures on months' supply, annualized sales data must be divided by 12 to get the correct number. For seasonally adjusted figures, the series is not calculated as the seasonally for sale divided by seasonally adjusted sold. Instead, actual unadjusted months supply data are seasonally in this form directly. Therefore, published adjusted numbers for months' supply differ slightly from numbers calculated with published adjusted sales and inventories data.

Months' supply is a cyclically volatile series. A slowdown in sales can lead to a sharp rise in "overhang." However, at the start of recovery in the business cycle, months' supply should not be interpreted in terms of ratios based on very weak actual sales. Instead, "true" overhang might better be based on a ratio assuming a reasonable, improved sales pace that would be reflective of lower mortgage rates once the recovery is under way. In other words, once sales have picked up, how long will the supply of houses for sale last?

For the home price data, one must use caution in interpreting price trends because the prices are not for a constant set of features for homes sold. Changes in the median and average prices reflect changes in costs as well as changes in the types of homes sold. For example, if during distressed economic times, the "low end" of the market has weak demand owing to layoffs and fears of layoffs, then sales prices will, more than on average, be influenced by buyers of more expensive houses, regardless of what is happening to the costs of building these houses. Also, recessions and expansions are not even throughout the United States. For example, in 1993 California and Hawaii were roughly 40 percent of the west, not 60 percent as was

TABLE 12–5

Housing Data: New Single-Family Houses Sold and for Sale, 1963–1997

	Houses Sold (000s)	Houses for Sale (000s)	Months Supply	Average Sales Price	Median Sales Price
1963	560	265	8.5	$19,300	$18,000
1964	565	250	7.6	20,500	18,900
1965	575	228	6.1	21,500	20,000
1966	461	196	8.5	23,300	21,400
1967	487	190	6.2	24,600	22,700
1968	490	218	6.9	26,600	24,700
1969	448	228	8.1	27,900	25,600
1970	485	227	6.2	26,600	23,400
1971	656	294	6.7	28,300	25,200
1972	718	416	8.9	30,500	27,600
1973	634	422	14.1	35,500	32,500
1974	519	350	14.4	38,900	35,900
1975	549	316	8.1	42,600	39,300
1976	646	358	7.7	48,000	44,200
1977	819	408	8.0	54,200	48,800
1978	817	419	8.3	62,500	55,700
1979	709	402	11.6	71,800	62,900
1980	545	342	10.3	76,400	64,600
1981	436	278	9.5	83,000	68,900
1982	412	255	7.8	83,900	69,300
1983	623	304	6.3	89,800	75,300
1984	639	358	9.4	97,600	79,900
1985	688	350	7.5	100,800	84,300
1986	750	361	7.4	111,900	92,000
1987	671	370	10.0	127,200	104,500
1988	676	371	8.8	138,300	112,500
1989	650	366	9.2	148,800	120,000
1990	534	321	10.9	149,800	122,900
1991	509	284	7.9	147,200	120,000
1992	610	267	6.4	144,100	121,500
1993	666	295	5.8	147,700	126,500
1994	670	340	8.5	154,500	130,000
1995	667	374	6.4	158,700	133,900
1996	757	326	5.0	166,400	140,000
1997	803	286	4.4	175,800	145,900

Sales are annual totals. Houses for sale and months supply are December data. All data are not seasonally adjusted.

Source: Bureau of the Census.

the case in 1987. This 20 percent difference has the impact of lowering the west average and median prices over what they would have been with a constant share.

KEY QUESTIONS IN ANALYZING THE NEWS RELEASES

Construction Data in General

- Did atypical weather (more or less favorable) affect activity?
- What are general expectations for interest rates in order to take into account their impact on current and future demand?
- Are there pending regulatory or tax changes that will affect the industry?
- How are demographic trends impacting activity?

Housing Starts and Permits

- How is strength or weakness divided between single-family and multifamily components?
- How are vacancy rates affecting multifamily construction?
- Did an expected change in government regulations affect permits?

Construction Outlays

- How were changes in outlays allocated between the public and private sectors?
- After making assumptions for any missing months in the current quarter, what do current quarter growth rates imply for real residential and nonresidential investment in real GDP?
- After making assumptions for any missing months in the current quarter, what do current quarter growth rates for real public outlays imply for the structures component of state and local government purchases in the GDP accounts?
- Has there been a shift in residential expenditure growth relative to recent start and permit activity that suggests concern over a possible change in demand? For example, builders may slow construction if sales are below expectations and inventories are higher than desired.
- For analysts with access to Dodge construction data, what does recent contract activity suggest for near-term outlays?

New Single-Family Home Sales

- Are expectations of a change in interest rates leading to an acceleration or delay in sales (for expected higher or lower rates, respectively)?
- Are inventories low or high, thereby likely encouraging or discouraging further starts in the near term?

NOTES FOR CHAPTER 12

1. U.S. Department of Commerce, Bureau of the Census, *Current Construction Reports,* C20-93-4, April 1993, p. 14.
2. *Construction Reports,* C20-86-1, January 1986, p. 13.
3. This change in definition was due to the extensive rebuilding in south Florida following Hurricane Andrew in late August 1992. The impact on the data was negligible at the national level. See U.S. Department of Commerce, Bureau of the Census, "Housing Starts and Building Permits in September 1992," News Release, October 20, 1992.
4. *Current Construction Reports,* C20-86-1, January 1986, p. 13.
5. *Current Construction Reports,* C30-93-6, June 1993, p. 2.
6. For greater detail of component definitions, see the May issue of each year's C30 report, which includes annual revisions.
7. *Current Construction Reports,* C30-93-5, May 1993, p. B2.
8. Ibid., p. B3.
9. This subcomponent of residential investment is purchased by landlords of movable appliances. These are purchases for structures intended for rental purposes only. Similar purchases made by home owners are classified as durables personal consumption.
10. "Contractor-built" primarily refers to custom-built houses where the owner of land arranges for a general contractor to build the house.
11. *Current Construction Reports,* C25-93-1, "Appendix A: Description of Monthly Housing Sales Survey Report," January 1993, p. 11.
12. The methodology for estimating these "presales" changed with the initial estimate for December 1992 data. Previously a historical ratio of presales to sales after permit issuance (or after start) was used for the initial estimate. This ratio generally was constant over the business cycle. This changed with the release of the initial December 1992 estimate. Over the 1992 recovery, Census estimates were regularly low owing to a cyclical increase in presales—a phenomenon that also occurred in 1983. Initial estimates were regularly revised up as permits were eventually taken out on presales. These upward revisions would show up one to three months after the initial estimate. Currently, Census uses a moving average of this ratio for initial estimates, with judgment determining the length of the moving average (generally four to six months).
13. *Current Construction Reports,* C25-90-1, "Appendix A: Description of Monthly Housing Sales Survey Report," January 1990, p. 9.

BIBLIOGRAPHY

U.S. Department of Commerce, Bureau of the Census, *Current Construction Reports,* C20-86-1, January 1986.

———. "Appendix A: Description of Survey and Supplementary Information," *Housing Units Authorized by Building Permits,* December 1995.

———. "Appendix A: Description of Monthly Housing Sales Survey," *New One-Family Houses, Sold and For Sale,* January 1993.

———. *New One-Family Houses, Sold and For Sale,* February 1997.

———. *Value of New Construction Put in Place,* May and June 1993.

CHAPTER 13

GROSS DOMESTIC PRODUCT

OVERVIEW

Gross domestic product (GDP) is the broadest measure of the health of the U.S. economy. Real GDP is defined as the output of goods and services produced by labor and property located in the United States.[1] This series generally lags behind other indicators' release dates. As such, other indicators "build up" to the market's anticipation of how the GDP numbers describe the state of the economy.

Real GDP is an important indicator to track because it provides the greatest and broadest sectoral detail of all other series. Data reflect income as well as expenditure flows. Sectoral coverage includes durable and nondurable goods, structures, and services. Also, price data by sector are available for detailed sub-components. Because of the detail available in the GDP reports, this series provides comprehensive information on supply and demand conditions, including various types of developing imbalances over the business cycle.

Real GDP is a quarterly figure, but it is released on a monthly basis with an initial estimate—referred to as the "advance estimate"—and two subsequent revisions over the following two months. The BEA produces the GDP figures and generally releases the advance estimate during the fourth week of the first month following the reference quarter. That is, the first quarter advance estimate is published in late April and subsequent first estimates are released in July, October, and January. The first revised estimate for a given quarter is known as the "preliminary estimate" and the third estimate for a given quarter is called the "revised" or "final estimate." Annual revisions are usually released in July with the first figures for the second quarter. They cover the three prior calendar years plus the quarter(s) already published in the current year. Benchmark revisions occur about every five years, with the base year tied to a recent quinquennial economic census, such as the Census Survey of Manufactures.

Gross Domestic Product versus Gross National Product

In December 1991, the BEA switched its emphasis from GNP to GDP as the key measure of aggregate economic activity in the NIPA accounts. The move was part of a long-time objective to make the U.S. accounts more consistent with those of most other countries, which use the United Nations System of National Accounts (UNSNA, or SNA for short).[2] The SNA emphasizes GDP instead of GNP. As a practical matter, when the BEA prepares initial estimates for GDP, there is little or no reliable data on net income from the rest of the world (factor income) which is used to derive GNP from GDP. With the switch in emphasis to GDP, the BEA no longer provides an initial estimate of GNP at the same time as the initial release of GDP. The first release of GNP is now with the first revision of GDP for a given quarter. Finally, GDP is more of a measure of domestic production than is GNP. Therefore, it more closely tracks other measures of domestic economic activity, such as industrial production or employment. GNP is more of a measure of income, since it reflects income from domestic production (GDP) plus net income from abroad:

> Domestic measures relate to the physical location of the factors of production; they refer to production attributable to all labor and property located in a country. The national measures differ from the domestic measures by the net inflow—that is, inflow less outflow—of labor and property incomes from abroad.[3]

Essentially, gross domestic product includes production within national borders regardless of whether the labor and property inputs are domestically or foreign owned. In contrast, gross national product is the output of labor and property of U.S. nationals regardless of the location of the labor and property. Gross national product includes income earned by the factors of production (assets and labor) owned by a country's residents but excludes income produced within the country's borders by factors of production owned by nonresidents.

The estimates for GDP and GNP are derived from the same expenditure measures, the difference being income (net) from foreign sources. Gross national product is equal to gross domestic product plus receipts of factor income from the rest of the world less payments of factor income to the rest of the world. As is the case for the United States, GNP exceeds GDP when a nation is earning more from its businesses, financial investments, and labor that are overseas than U.S. nonresidents are earning on businesses in the United States that they own plus returns on U.S. financial investments plus labor income for nonresidents in the United States. Receipts of this factor income consist largely of receipts by U.S. residents of interest and dividends and reinvested earnings of foreign affiliates of U.S. corporations. The payments are largely those to foreign residents of interest and dividends and reinvested earnings of U.S. affiliates of foreign corporations.

For the United States, the dollar difference between GDP and GNP is very small—about 0.1 percent of nominal GDP and also chain-dollar GDP for 1996. Hence, growth rates for these aggregates in the United States typically are very similar.

Chain-Weighted Real GDP versus Constant-Dollar Real GDP

In January 1996, the BEA released in first estimates of newly benchmarked real GDP (largely reflecting 1992 data from the Census of Manufactures along with other sources) with the primary focus of aggregate output being the Census Bureau's measure, known as chain-weighted GDP. Census had been publishing chain GDP estimates for the three prior years but with a small lag (generally one day) after the initial GDP release. In early 1996, the BEA and Commerce Department began emphasizing the use of chain GDP and deemphasizing the use of constant-dollar GDP. What is chain GDP and why did the BEA make the switch? The answers to these questions lie with problems with the old constant-dollar real GDP methodology, succinctly stated by J. Steven Landefeld:

> Within the index number literature, it has been long recognized that output measures that use fixed price weights tend to overstate current-period growth as one moves further from the base period. This tendency, often called "substitution bias," reflects the fact that the commodities for which output grows rapidly tend to be those that register declines, or the smallest increases, in prices. Thus, when real GDP is recalculated using more recent prices, the commodities with strong output growth generally receive less weight, and growth in the aggregate measure is reduced.[4]

Essentially, chain-weighted GDP differs from constant-dollar GDP in terms of the price index methodology used to deflate nominal series in GDP to real components. Chain-type GDP uses chain-type price, or Fisher ideal, indexes to deflate nominal components of GDP, while constant-dollar GDP used fixed-weight, or Laspeyres, price indexes for deflating.[5] The Fisher price indexes hold utility constant, while Laspeyres indexes hold a basket of goods and services constant. Fisher indexes allow consumers to substitute relatively lower priced goods for relatively higher priced goods when relative prices change. Fisher indexes compare the ratio of expenditures needed to maintain constant utility rather than expenditures needed to purchase a constant market basket. The well-known problem with deflating with Laspeyres indexes is that the substitution problem in the long run leads to an overstatement of real growth subsequent to the base period and an understatement of growth prior to the base period. In turn, when base years are changed, economic history is rewritten in terms of real GDP changes.

How significant was the problem of substitution bias? Note that the old fixed-weighted (1987 base) data were available only through the third quarter of 1995:

> The old fixed-weighted (1987) index understated real GDP growth during post–World War II era expansions prior to 1987 by an average of 0.4 percentage point and overstated growth during the current expansion [1991:1–1995:3] by 0.5 percentage point. . . . As a result, comparisons of the relative strength of the current expansion may have been overstated by roughly a full percentage point.
>
> The fixed-weighted (1987) index understated real GDP annual growth for 1929–87 by 0.4 percentage point; use of the chain index raises the long term growth rate from 3.0 percent to 3.4 percent. The growth rate from 1987 to 1994—the last full year for which BEA prepared fixed (1987) weighted estimates—was reduced from 2.4 percent to 2.3 percent.[6]

Why is the measure called "chain-weighted" GDP? As mentioned above, a chain-type price index is used to deflate nominal GDP components. These price indexes have expenditure weights that are updated annually. In turn, the deflated GDP series using chain-type price indexes do not have a single base year, as do constant-dollar real GDP series. The BEA essentially chains together deflated GDP data in index form with annually updated weights. The conversion of the chain-type output indexes to chained 1992 dollars is merely done to facilitate certain traditional comparisons of real GDP and components in circumstances when adding dollar values is convenient. In fact, because of the weighting scheme underlying chain-type GDP data, dollar-denominated data do not precisely sum to the aggregate using traditional addition of components. Chain data are "added" together using indexing method-ologies. It is only when using indexing methodologies—and the exact same series and detail that the BEA uses—that the components index-sum to the aggregate. The traditional dollar-added sum of chain components leaves a "residual" value relative to the aggregate chain-dollar values. This and related complications of using chain-type GDP data are discussed in more detail in a later section of this chapter.

GDP BY PRODUCT OR EXPENDITURE CATEGORIES

Gross domestic product is a measure of production within the national income and product accounts. There are three alternative ways for deriving GDP: sum of expendi-tures, sum of incomes, and sum of value added (either by industry, by firm, or by es-tablishment, depending on what data are available). In theory, GDP as measured by all three methods should be the same. This would be the case if perfect data were avail-able. In actual practice, of the two methods primarily followed by the financial markets, it is easier to obtain reliable estimates for expenditures than for income components. Basically, expenditures are measured more directly than income.[7] (For summaries of GDP and components, 1960–1996, see Table 13–6 at the end of the chapter.)

This chapter focuses on the expenditure components for GDP, since the ex-penditure approach is most closely followed by markets. This is partly because most expenditure data are more readily available than some of the income data. While quarterly personal income data are released with the advance GDP release, corporate profits are not available until the following month.[8] The expenditure ap-proach to estimating GDP clearly is the method most closely followed by the fi-nancial markets. The major expenditure components are personal consumption (C), gross private domestic investment (I), government purchases (G), and net ex-ports ($X - M$) and they form the familiar identity of:

$$GDP = C + I + G + (X - M)$$

This holds exactly true in current dollars but in chain dollars it only holds true in "index addition," as explained above. As already mentioned, the export and im-port components no longer include income from abroad (in the old identity for GNP, X and M included factor income from abroad.) See Table 13–1.

The following sections discuss key series in each expenditure component, data sources, unusual methodological factors, and various cyclical and secular trends.

Personal Consumption Expenditures

The components for personal consumption—durables, nondurables, and services—have already been discussed in detail in Chapter 2. The monthly personal income data and personal consumption figures are part of the NIPA framework, and the quarterly personal consumption numbers in GDP are merely quarterly averages of the monthly data. Monthly personal consumption levels are already seasonally adjusted and are on an annualized basis. The sources for personal consumption es-timates are also discussed in Chapter 2.

TABLE 13–1

Gross Domestic Product (Billions of Chained 1992 Dollars)

	1996	1997	Share in 1997* (%)
Gross domestic product	**$6,928.4**	**$7,188.8**	**100.0%**
Personal consumption expenditures	4,714.1	4,867.5	67.7
Durable goods	611.1	645.5	9.0
Nondurable goods	1,432.3	1,458.5	20.3
Services	2,671.0	2,764.1	38.5
Gross private domestic investment	**1,069.1**	**1,197.0**	**16.7**
Fixed investment	1,041.7	1,123.6	15.6
Nonresidential fixed	771.7	848.3	11.8
Structures	188.7	195.4	2.7
Producers' durable equipment	586.0	659.0	9.2
Residential	272.1	279.5	3.9
Change in business inventories	25.0	65.7	0.9
Net exports of goods and services	**−114.4**	**−146.5**	**−2.0**
Exports	857.0	962.7	13.4
Goods	628.4	725.0	10.1
Services	229.9	241.7	3.4
Imports	971.5	1,109.2	−15.4
Goods	823.1	947.5	−13.2
Services	149.0	163.0	−2.3
Government consumption expenditures and gross investment	**1,257.9**	**1,269.6**	**17.7**
Federal	464.2	457.0	6.4
National defense	317.8	308.6	4.3
Nondefense	146.1	147.9	2.1
State and local	793.7	812.7	11.3
Residual	−44.3	−80.5	−1.1
Gross domestic product	$6,928.4	$7,188.8	
Plus: Receipts of factor income from the rest of the world	214.2	236.3	
Less: Payments of factor income to the rest of the world	210.2	250.1	
Equals: Gross national product	$6,932.0	$7,174.4	

*Chained real components are not directly additive.

Source: U.S. Department of Commerce, "Gross Domestic Product: Fourth Quarter 1997 (Final)," News Release, March 26, 1998.

Without going into the same detail as in the earlier chapter, durables are the most volatile and services are the most stable. Durables are dependent on interest rates, which are cyclical, while both nondurables and services are more dependent on population trends. Overall personal consumption expenditures (PCEs) make up about two-thirds of GDP. However, this is a somewhat awkward comparison, since some GDP components, such as net exports and inventory investment, are negative on an occasional basis.

Gross Private Domestic Investment

The broad category of gross private domestic investment covers several categories, both nonresidential and residential. Also, most of the investment is fixed investment although a portion is not. These definitions and overlapping classifications may create some confusion. By definition, these series are limited to the private sector; government purchases of structures and equipment are under the government purchases component. While the data are for domestic investment in the United States, equipment purchased by U.S. businesses from abroad are included. However, capital goods produced in the United States but shipped as exports are not part of gross private domestic investment. They are entered in the GDP accounts as exports; counting them as investment would be double-counting. By definition, all investment subcomponents in the broad category are for purchases of physical capital: that is, actual buildings, machinery, and inventories.[9]

There are a number of major components in gross private domestic investment. The first level of disaggregation is between private fixed investment and business inventory investment. Inventory investment is not considered fixed in the obvious sense that inventories are quite movable; they do not remain with a facility producing either goods or services as would structures or equipment. Private fixed investment is further divided between nonresidential and residential investment. Nonresidential investment has two major components—structures and producers' durable equipment—while the residential investment component is residential structures. Next, what are the basic concepts covered by each major component and what are the key sources of data for estimates?

Nonresidential Structures

The nonresidential structures series is the first major component of business fixed investment. This component represents expenditures made by business on structures, both farm and nonfarm. Structures covered include commercial buildings (such as office buildings); retail store structures; hotels and motels; private hospitals and educational facilities; industrial plants, warehouses, and public utilities; mining exploration, shafts, and wells; and farm buildings.

Nonresidential structures investment is cyclical because it is sensitive to interest rates and because expansion is dependent upon capacity utilization. Typically, nonresidential structures investment rises relatively late in expansion, following a rise in investment in producers' durable equipment. Structures investment is costlier than equipment; if demand were to fall, it would significantly raise a firm's average costs. These factors help explain why structures investment usually lags behind that for equipment. Also, oil and natural gas prices play key roles in changes in nonresidential structures. Investment in the oil industry surged over the first half of the 1980s owing to the strong run-up in oil prices but then collapsed after the OPEC oil price cuts in 1986. Similarly, natural gas exploration was depressed in the early 1990s owing to the natural gas "bubble" (oversupply).

The basic source for nonresidential structures is the Census Bureau's value put in place data. These are used for nonfarm buildings, telecommunications utilities, and "other nonfarm structures." For "other public utilities," preliminary and annual estimates are derived from regulatory agency and trade source data. Except for benchmark years, data for mining, exploration, shafts, and wells are calculated as follows: for petroleum and natural gas, physical quantity times average price; for footage drilled, cost per foot comes from industry sources; other mining expenditures are derived from the Census Bureau plant and equipment survey. Finally, farm building investment is initially an extrapolation from Census value put in place data and is then later revised with annual data from Department of Agriculture surveys.

Producers' Durable Equipment

Producers' durable equipment (PDEs) is the second of the two major components of nonresidential fixed investment. This series covers purchases of equipment by private businesses and nonprofit institutions for their use in the production of goods and services. The primary subcomponents are information processing and related equipment, industrial equipment, transportation and related equipment, and "other."

In recent years, the largest subcomponent has come to be information processing and related equipment. In 1997, this subcomponent was 34 percent of nominal PDEs and 46 percent of real PDEs. The best-known category under information-processing equipment probably is computers and peripheral equipment. However, it also includes diverse series such as photocopying equipment, communications equipment (telephones and facsimile machines), and scientific instruments.

Industrial equipment primarily includes equipment purchased for use by manufacturers. The transportation equipment component is led by automobiles, trucks, and aircraft.

PDEs are very cyclical owing to the durability factor (purchases can be deferred during times of economic weakness) and to their sensitivity to interest costs. Certainly, the primary factors affecting equipment investment are the cost of financial capital—interest rates—and the expected rate of return. The capacity utilization rate is generally a good indicator of the trend in expected returns. However, other significant factors affect investment, especially in equipment. Increased foreign competition leads to the need for productivity-enhancing (cost-cutting) investment. Over the 1980s, a strong dollar and increased foreign capacity spurred this type of investment in the United States in addition to investment for expansion of capacity. Over the 1970s, strong increases in labor costs encouraged capital substitution for labor. Finally, changes in pollution control regulations and standards affect equipment investment. The amended Clean Air Act spurred significant amounts of spending on pollution-control technology in the early 1990s.

Movement in particular series in PDEs can be very interesting from a technical view. The industrial equipment component is particularly cyclical and responds to changes in manufacturing capacity utilization. For aircraft, production rates change relatively smoothly because of the long lags between order and delivery (usually four to five years), but quarterly purchases are volatile because the

BEA figures are based on actual shipments of aircraft. Interestingly, transportation includes not only automobiles and light trucks purchased by businesses for their own traditional uses (such as "company cars" and delivery vehicles), but also includes motor vehicles leased to consumers. This means motor vehicles purchased by rental companies for their fleets and vehicles leased on a long-term basis by individuals as an alternative to a purchase. However, for consumers the value of the service of the leased vehicle is included in services PCEs, in contrast to durables PCEs when consumers make an outright purchase.

Occasionally, for the most recent quarterly revisions to GDP, PDEs and durables PCEs move in opposite directions due to the BEA's receiving more up-to-date *Polk* data on motor vehicle registrations. Unit estimates for motor vehicle sales are already in for all three months in the quarter for the initial GDP release but registration data are not. As more current registration data become available, the BEA shifts motor vehicle sales between durables PCEs and PDEs (and to a far lesser degree also between government purchases of motor vehicles) when *Polk* data differ from their assumptions for missing months. Registration data lag figures on motor vehicle sales by two months.

Preliminary estimates and annual estimates are based primarily on several key sources. The most important source is the Census Bureau's monthly and annual surveys of manufactures for shipments of capital goods. Since the BEA's series for PDEs only covers business purchases for capital accounts, adjustments and deletions are made to the Census shipments data for current account purchases (e.g., parts) and for purchases by government and persons. Other adjustments then are made for exports and imports of capital equipment (nonautomotive) from Census' merchandise trade reports. Exports that are shipped from manufacturers are excluded from PDEs since this is a domestic purchases concept. Similarly, imports of capital equipment are added to the Census shipments figures. Finally, a share of motor vehicle sales (in units) is allocated to PDEs. Industry data—such as from the American Automobile Manufacturers Association, for example, are used. These are the same series the BEA carries as unit new auto sales and light truck sales. The PDEs portion is determined by *Polk* registration data and are converted into dollar values using the appropriate producer price indexes.

Residential Investment

Residential investment covers private investment in housing. Although the aggregate is often called "residential structures," formally "residential structures" is the larger of two higher-level components of residential investment, whereas the other component is the little-known producers' durable equipment. However, residential PDEs are very small in magnitude and have very different subcomponents from nonresidential PDEs. In 1997, residential investment was $279.5 billion in chained 1992 dollars; structures contributed $272.0 billion, and residential PDEs only $7.5 billion.

Residential structures are further broken down into components for single-family, multifamily, and "other structures." In 1997, these real components were $136.7 billion, $20.2 billion, and $115.7 billion, respectively. "Other structures" includes mobile homes, brokers' commissions, improvements, nonhousekeeping, and net purchases of existing structures.

For improvements, data are primarily based on estimates from BLS's Consumer Expenditure Survey (CES), which is conducted on a monthly basis by Census for BLS. Data are obtained from a rotating panel of households. The survey covers a broad range of topics and includes questions on expenditures for improvements. The CES also obtains information on which households do not make home improvements because they do not own their house. From these responses a landlord survey is constructed by Census and data on their expenditures are obtained by mail. However, the landlord survey is completed only after the initial quarterly data are closed out for GDP estimates and this survey first enters estimates with annual revisions. Prior estimates are based on a judgment of the trend.

Residential PDEs consist of certain items purchased by owners for use in tenant-occupied housing. These include furniture (mattresses and bedsprings), other durable house furnishings, and radio and TV receivers. These items are essentially movable in nature and are not a built-in part of the structure.

In business cycle analysis, residential investment is important not only because of its highly cyclical nature but because this component tends to lead other components in the business cycle. Residential investment has these properties because it is very interest rate–sensitive and also dependent upon consumer confidence (job security and anticipated income gains). Residential investment is also cyclical because households can postpone housing purchases during recessions or periods of high interest rates. During these periods, pent-up demand accumulates. When interest rates decline and expectations for economic improvement rise, pent-up demand can lead to a surge in housing activity.

While most analysts focus on short-run factors such as mortgage rates and personal income gains for predicting housing activity, long-run factors are equally important. Perhaps two of the most important long-run variables are demographics and taxes. Over the 1970s and 1980s, the baby-boom generation reached the critical household formation years when first-home purchases are made. This led to a surge in housing activity. By the recovery of 1991–1992, the baby-boom generation had been replaced by the baby-bust generation as first-time house buyers. Contrary to the expectations of many lending institutions, very sharp interest rate declines did not lead to a traditional housing boom in that recovery, primarily because the house-buyer market was much thinner than during the 1970s and 1980s because of demographics.

Changes in tax policy can also affect housing investment. Early in the 1980s, favorable depreciation schedules and other factors encouraged construction of multifamily housing. Apartment complexes were profitable even with relatively high vacancy rates. Tax reform measures passed in 1986 removed these investment incentives, and the previously profitable multifamily sector suddenly was riddled with oversupply. This overhang in multifamily buildings carried over long enough to leave this sector out of the initial phase of the overall economic recovery following the recession of 1990–1991.

The source data for permanent-site single-family and multifamily housing are Census value put in place data. Mobile home preliminary estimates are based on trade sources for physical quantity shipped, while the average retail price is obtained from the Census Bureau. For benchmark years, mobile home shipments are derived from the Census Bureau's quinquennial census. Brokers' commissions are estimated as the product of the number of houses sold, the mean sales price, and the average commission rate. Data come from the Census Bureau and trade sources. Producers' durable equipment is based on special surveys conducted by the Census Bureau.

Inventory Investment

Inventory investment is one of the key components for analyzing the strength of the economy. Its importance is likely second only to that of personal consumption expenditures. Inventory investment or changes in inventories help to keep goods production and demand in balance. Changes in inventories can portend either a weakening or a strengthening in the economy depending on the circumstances. These conditions and methods of analysis are discussed more in the chapter on monthly business inventories. But first, what is inventory investment?

The inventory investment concept is best understood in the context of measuring GDP—an estimate of *current* production. Economists want to measure the inventory component's contribution to current output through an accounting of expenditures without double-counting. Certainly, over any given period, the dollar value of goods placed in inventory by manufacturers, wholesalers, and retailers fluctuates because inventory is sold to consumers, businesses, or government or it is exported. But these inventories are counted as expenditures within PCEs, PDEs, government purchases, or exports. To avoid double-counting, inventories are measured on an end-of-period basis. Also, since GDP is a measure of current production, inventories already produced or existing in prior periods must be excluded. Therefore, only the change in inventories is included in the expenditure equation for adding up GDP. Inventory investment is the change in business inventories (CBI) from the previous period; it is not the level of inventories (see Chart 13–1).

Typically, inventories rise and investment is positive, but if sales outstrip inventory stocking, then inventories decline and inventory investment is negative. Negative inventory investment often occurs during recession as businesses cut operating expenses during periods of weak revenues. However, the relationships between inventory change and business cycle turning points is a little more complex and are discussed in greater detail in Chapter 9.

Inventory data are organized by farm and nonfarm sectors. Farm inventories are generally analyzed as a single aggregate for macroeconomic analysis, but the BEA has greater unpublished detail for crops and livestock. Because of the heavy seasonality of farm inventories and because inventories cannot be estimated until output is estimated, the BEA must make assumptions about current-year farm production to derive these figures. The BEA distributes estimated flows of crop and livestock output into consumption (as well as government purchases and exports) across the year. However, production estimates are very crude early in the calendar year for most crops and livestock. As the calendar year progresses and production estimates become more reliable (as crops and livestock mature), the BEA makes adjustments in its output assumptions (and others); these show up in farm inventory investment data.

CHART 13–1
Real GDP versus Inventory Change

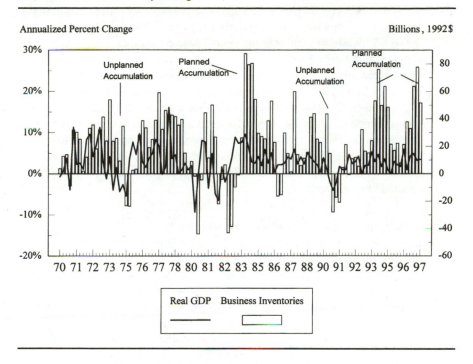

Annualized Percent Change   Billions, 1992$

Data for NIPA-based inventory levels are available for analysis, even though it is the change in inventories that represent inventory investment—the figures going into GDP estimates. Levels are useful for comparing various demand concepts, such as goods GDP, to inventories. However, the change in the published nominal levels differ from nominal CBI because nominal CBI is based on end-of-period physical quantities times the average price in the period.

Source Data for Farm Inventory Investment
Farm inventories are estimated by the BEA using a commodity flow approach for crop inventories and by using U.S. Department of Agriculture (USDA) data for livestock inventories. The constant-dollar crop inventory change is based on an annual forecast for production and sales. Estimates for these are largely dependent on data from the USDA for estimated acreage planted and expected yields. For the year, the BEA produces a smooth pattern for quarterly sales of crop commodities and takes known quarterly data on Commodity Credit Corporation forfeitures, subtracting these from production projections to get an estimate of farm inventories for crops. Sales are made to all sectors but mainly to business wholesalers. For livestock inventories, the BEA generally uses USDA data directly; these include livestock on the range and in feedlots.

As the calendar year progresses, changes in projections for crop production and sales are made to reflect the latest information. However, the USDA and BEA estimates for production become more reliable in the latter part of the year. Even though errors in early annual estimates for crop production and sales can be significant in some years (as during drought), quarterly inventory estimates late in the year are usually made without compensating for earlier errors in projection that are "locked in" the earlier quarter in the year. These are corrected with annual revisions made the following year.

Farm sector output for GDP is estimated in the process of deriving figures for farm inventory investment. The difference between GDP and farm output is, of course, nonfarm GDP. However, there is no allocation of farm output to various expenditure components in GDP except for farm inventories. In other words, there is no input from the farm sector in deriving expenditure components in GDP except for the farm inventory component. However, CCC purchases under federal nondefense do represent farm activity. But farm production and CCC purchases are estimated independently.

Source Data for Nonfarm Inventory Investment

Nonfarm inventory data are disaggregated into manufacturing, wholesale (merchant and nonmerchant), retail trade, and "other." Manufacturing and trade inventories are further divided into durables and nondurables, although the retail trade durables data also separate automotive from nonautomotive.

Estimates for nonfarm inventory change for manufacturing and trade are based on Census Bureau surveys, including quinquennial censuses for benchmark years, annual surveys for other annual revisions, and monthly manufacturing and trade surveys for estimates following the latest annual surveys and for quarterly movement between annual surveys. Adjustments are made for data reported using different accounting methods to put into NIPA valuation. Deflators to put inventories in constant-dollar format are mostly PPIs with only a few deflators being CPI-based.

Other nonfarm inventories primarily provide coverage for mining and also for various utilities such as electric and transportation. Data sources include the Internal Revenue Service, the Federal Reserve Board, the Census Bureau, and the Energy Information Administration.

The Inventory Contribution to GDP Growth

The concept of inventory contribution to GDP growth differs from inventory investment. The inventory contribution is merely the dollar value of the inventory component in dollar value growth in GDP—that is, the change in GDP. For the *level* of GDP, the inventory portion is the change in inventory levels. However, to determine the inventory contribution to GDP *growth,* one must look at the difference in inventory investment from period to period; one must subtract current-period inventory change from previous-period inventory change. Inventory levels are differenced two times to get this contribution. For inventory contribution to be positive, inventories must be rising at a faster rate each period or must be falling at a slower rate. A slower rate of decline in inventories is a positive in terms of inventories' contribution to GDP growth.

Where Δ equals current-period value less previous-period value

$$\text{GDP} = \text{PCEs} + \text{fixed investment} + \Delta \text{ inventories}$$
$$+ \text{ government purchases} + \text{net exports}$$

whereas

$$\Delta \text{ GDP} = \Delta \text{ PCEs} + \Delta \text{ fixed investment} + \Delta (\Delta \text{ inventories})$$
$$+ \text{ goverment purchases} + \Delta \text{ net exports}$$

One should note that these formulas hold precisely for nominal GDP but not precisely for chain-weighted GDP, owing to the problem of residuals in adding components. Using differences in dollar-denominated data provides a reasonable approximation only for recent years, as residuals grow larger in size going backward in time. The BEA does produce and publish separate series for component contributions to real GDP.[10]

Government Consumption Expenditures and Gross Investment

With the January 1996 benchmarking of real GDP, the BEA changed the treatment of government investment and, in turn, redefined the government component within GDP in terms of two categories, with the combined name of government consumption expenditures and gross investment (GCE & GI). To understand GCE & GI, it is useful to first explain the concept of government purchases. Prior to this benchmarking, the government component was known as government purchases.

Government purchases were not the same as broadly defined budget expenditures, and many of these differences apply to the GCE & GI concept. Purchases were expenditures for goods and services strictly for governments' current use, with investment included in the definition of current use. There are three primary reasons for the difference between government purchases and budget expenditures.

First, some budget expenditures may actually be transferred as income to other sectors for their use. Expenditures that are transfers are not part of purchases made by the government that originally raise the revenues funding the transactions. These budget expenditure categories include transfers to persons, transfers to foreign governments, and grants-in-aid to state and local government. Also included in this transfer concept are net interest, subsidies, and current surplus of government enterprises. Importantly, government purchases did not distinguish between purchases for current use and those for investment. Investment types of expenditures were treated as though entirely expended in the current period.

A second difference between the GDP government component and the federal budget concept of expenditures—applicable to both purchases and GCE & GI concepts—is that GDP government spending is required to stay within bounds of the current-use concept. This means that land purchases and financial transactions (net lending) are excluded. GDP government spending also excludes transactions involving U.S. territories. Finally, there are "netting and grossing" differences between expenditures and purchases.

How do these differences fit in current definitions of the government component of GDP? The switch to the government expenditures and gross investment concept was motivated by the desire to recognize that not all purchases were expended in the current period.[11] The establishment of a capital account for the government sector was also consistent with the BEA's long-term plan to bring the NIPAs into line with the UN System of National Accounts (SNA).[12] The new government component also was redefined to include the consumption of general government fixed capital. Government consumption expenditures exclude gross government investment but include general government consumption of fixed capital (CFC). This is analogous to the housing services component of PCEs such that consumers derive services from the use of housing stock. The switch in government sector definition raised the *level* of GDP by the amount of CFC relative to what it would have been under the old methodology. The new treatment of investment within the government sector acknowledges that the government sector's contribution to GDP is more than the past assumption of it being only equal to compensation of employees. Now this contribution is equal to compensation of employees plus the government sector's consumption of fixed capital. GDP growth rates are affected only negligibly by this new treatment in that the CFC contribution to overall GDP is small and deviations in its growth rate are not significant relative to overall GDP growth.

Currently, the government component within GDP is broadly divided into federal and also state and local government subcomponents. The federal sector is further divided into defense and nondefense components. Each of these has breakdowns for consumption expenditures and for gross investment. For consumption expenditures, subcomponents are classified as durable goods, nondurable goods, and services. Gross investment has components for structures and for equipment.

Consumption is the larger component of the government sector. For government overall, consumption was 84 percent of real consumption expenditures and gross investment in 1997. For the federal component and for the state and local government component, these figures were 88 and 82 percent, respectively, for 1997. The state and local government proportion for gross investment is higher, largely reflecting spending on highways and bridges and for educational structures.

For the federal government, durable goods include items such as spare parts (the biggest portion of federal government durables consumption) and complete systems purchased for "someone else" (basically transfers to other countries). Examples of nondurables are petroleum, office supplies, food, clothing, and ammunition. The services component is mostly compensation along with research and development, travel, transportation, consulting services, rents, and utilities among others. Federal government equipment investment includes airplanes, tanks, missiles, ships, trucks, and others. Federal structures include military construction, buildings, highways, and streets.

Within the federal nondefense component, significant quarterly volatility sometimes comes from the Commodity Credit Corporation (CCC) inventory change component—part of nondurables consumption. Expenditures are made for farm price support programs. However, when these expenditures swing sharply, there usually is an offsetting entry in the farm inventory component of private gross domestic investment. CCC purchases do not affect the level of current production; there is only a transfer of ownership of inventories between the public and private sectors.

In 1997, just over 70 percent of the state and local government component (nominal and real) was for services—almost entirely for compensation of employees. Key services include education and law enforcement. Structures—a part of gross investment—are still a large component of the state and local government aggregate and include expenditures on highways and bridges, educational facilities, corrections facilities, other public buildings, and waste treatment plants, among others.

Turning to sources of data for the government component, for preliminary estimates, federal government purchases are based on outlays data from Treasury Department, available in the *Monthly Treasury Statement of Receipts and Outlays of the U.S. Government,* and from monthly reports of selected agencies. State and local government wages and salaries are based on the product of employment from BLS's establishment survey and earnings from BLS's quarterly employment cost survey. The initial structures estimates at the state and local levels come from value put in place data from the Census Bureau. Other initial estimates for state and local government components are based on judgmental trend.

Annual estimates at the federal level are based on OMB outlays data (published in the *Budget of the United States*) and Treasury data (see the Appendix of the *United States Government Annual Report*), and on annual reports of selected federal agencies. Annual figures for state and local government purchases for employee compensation are derived from BLS data as well as from information from the Social Security Administration and the agencies administering social insurance programs. Census Bureau surveys of state and local governments for retirement funds also are used. For structures, annual estimates are derived from Census Bureau's construction put in place. For components other than compensation, the two most recent years are based on judgmental trend. Earlier years are based on expenditure data from the Census Bureau's quinquennial censuses and annual surveys of state and local governments.

Net Exports

The net export component of GDP is the difference between exports and imports of goods and services. However, the net exports component has been redefined to be on a GDP basis. Under the old GNP basis, exports and imports each included subcomponents for factor income (receipts from the rest of the world for exports and payments to the rest of the world for imports). On the GDP basis, net exports exclude factor income and the identity of $GDP = C + I + G + X - M$ is valid since factor income is no longer part of exports and imports.[13]

Markets tend to discuss the foreign trade component in GDP as the net export deficit. However, the United States historically had been a trade surplus nation—at least until the bill for imported oil rose dramatically over the 1970s as both oil prices and demand for imported oil rose. Currently, the United States is in a deficit position because of high levels of oil imports. Excluding imports of petroleum and petroleum products, the nominal net export position of the United States was actually in a surplus of $22 billion in 1992, compared to an overall net export deficit of $29.5 billion. However, this nonoil surplus was due to the United

States' strength in services as well as in merchandise components for foods, feeds, and beverages and for nonautomotive capital goods. Nominal services net exports were negative as recently as 1973 but have been in surplus since, widening to $80.9 billion in 1996 before slipping in 1997.

To understand what the key components of exports and imports are, it is best to examine each component separately. Exports and imports are each broadly divided between goods and services. While discussion of trade data usually involve traded goods, services components are quite large and deserve greater attention. Also, because of comparative advantages by the United States and its trading partners, the size of various components differ for exports versus imports. Essentially, exports and imports should be analyzed from very different perspectives for merchandise and for services. Both exports and imports have components for merchandise and for services. While goods make up the majority of exports and imports, services are still important. Services in 1997 made up 28 percent of nominal exports and 16 percent of nominal imports. While the United States has run a nominal net export deficit since 1976, the services component has remained in surplus through 1997, the most recently available year.

Merchandise and services export and import NIPA data are derived from balance-of-payments accounts data. As discussed in Chapter 11, the NIPA merchandise export and import data are primarily based on Census monthly merchandise trade data, which are put in balance-of-payments form before being adjusted to a NIPA basis. Elaboration on the individual end-use categories is also found in Chapter 11.

Exports and imports on a GDP basis cover only goods and services. These categories do not include net receipts of factor income, as was the case for exports and imports when the key NIPA aggregate was gross national product. Net receipts of factor income—which are divided into corporate profits, net interest, and compensation of employees—are now merely the accounting difference between GDP and GNP.

Merchandise exports and imports are divided into end-use categories, similar to the categories that form monthly merchandise trade. The principal end-use categories are foods, feeds,and beverages; industrial supplies and materials; capital goods, except automotive; automotive vehicles, parts, and engines; consumer goods (nonfood) except automotive; and other merchandise. However, for imports the industrial supplies and materials component is actually presented as industrial supplies and materials, except petroleum and products. Petroleum and products imports is a separate end-use category in the NIPA data.

As in the balance-of-payments data, services exports and imports are broken down into receipts (exports) and payments (imports) for travel, passenger fares, "other transportation," "other private services," and U.S military transfers and direct defense expenditures abroad.

"Other transportation" covers port expenditures and freight charges for international shipments as well as operating expenses that transportation companies incur in foreign ports. "Other private services," exported and imported, cover transactions not falling in categories for travel, passenger fares, other transportation, or royalties and license fees. Examples include service charges for management, professional or technical services, lease payments, rentals, education, financial services, insurance, telecommunications, and medical services. Transfers under U.S. military agency sales contracts cover goods transferred, not grants. U.S direct defense expenditures reflect expenses for maintaining armed forces abroad, including for permanent bases. U.S. military transfers are only an export component, while U.S. direct defense expenditures abroad are only an import component. Today, military transfers are mostly cash that foreigners use to make purchases in the United States. For direct expenditures abroad, there are offsetting entries in government purchases.

For services exports (in current dollars), the two largest subcomponents are travel and other private services, combining for over half of services exports. Next in importance are "other transportation," followed by royalties and license fees. Military transfers slipped to 5 percent of nominal services exports in 1997. On the import side, nominal services also is led by travel and, to a lesser degree, by "other private services" and "other transportation." Direct defense expenditures abroad recently peaked in 1990—an effect of the Gulf War—and fell to under 7 percent of services imports in 1997.

Within services net exports (nominal), the current largest surpluses are for "other private services," followed by royalties and license fees and by travel. The biggest drain is direct defense expenditures abroad. The most volatile component in services exports and imports is travel, which is very sensitive to exchange rate movement. The travel net surplus position swings sharply and tends to be in deficit when the dollar is strongly valued and in surplus when it is weak.

The primary difficulty in tracking services subcomponents is that the BEA does not publish detail below the totals for these exports and imports. However, the BEA does publish the balance-of-payments equivalent series. The main differences between the NIPA and balance-of-payments data are bottom-line adjustments. The BEA takes the balance-of-payments subcomponents, makes an adjustment for Puerto Rico and U.S. territories, and then makes other minor adjustments. The level of overall services exports and imports differs from the balance-of-payments data, but the primary subcomponents (excluding the adjustment line items) are basically the same for analytical purposes.

GDP Price Deflators and Price Indexes

GDP deflators measure inflation across all sectors of the economy, taking into account changes in prices for consumer goods and services, business fixed and inventory investment, housing investment, government purchases, and exports and imports. While there are a number of variations for GDP deflators using different weighting and base-year schemes, the most commonly used GDP deflators are the chain-type and implicit GDP deflators; the fixed-weighted GDP deflator is currently a distant third.

The implicit GDP deflator is merely the ratio of nominal GDP to real GDP. Official GDP deflator numbers are set so that the base-year deflator equals 100 rather than 1. The nature of the implicit price deflator has changed with the switch in real GDP to a chain GDP basis. Hence, the implicit GDP deflator is the ratio of nominal GDP to chain-type real GDP. The weights for the real components change each year as a result of the changes in weights for component price indexes. Except for very minor effects from methodological differences, the implicit deflator growth rates are essentially the same as for the chain-type price index.

TABLE 13–2

Component Contributions to Real GDP Growth over Decades, Calculated Using Chain-Type Annual Weighted Indexes

Decade	1930–1940	1940–1950	1950–1960	1960–1970	1970–1980	1980–1990
Gross domestic product	**100.0**	**100.0**	**100.0**	**100.0**	**100.0**	**100.0**
Personal consumption expenditures	**55.1**	**55.8**	**61.5**	**66.7**	**63.4**	**71.3**
Durable goods	7.0	13.9	5.7	12.0	10.5	15.5
Nondurable goods	40.9	21.7	24.7	22.6	18.0	16.5
Services	7.7	20.5	31.4	32.0	34.2	39.0
Gross private domestic product	**25.5**	**21.1**	**7.1**	**16.3**	**19.9**	**13.6**
Fixed investment	2.7	19.1	8.7	16.5	20.8	11.4
Nonresidential	−2.0	9.5	7.3	14.4	18.5	9.2
Structures	−6.3	3.2	4.2	3.9	4.7	0.6
Producers' durable equipment	4.1	6.3	3.1	10.5	13.6	8.6
Residential	4.3	9.5	1.5	2.1	3.0	2.3
Change in business inventories*	—	—	—	—	—	—
Exports of goods and services	**3.2**	**3.8**	**7.1**	**7.7**	**20.2**	**17.5**
Goods	2.8	2.9	5.6	5.8	16.6	12.4
Services	0.4	0.9	1.5	2.0	3.7	5.3
Imports of goods and services	**0.8**	**−3.4**	**−7.2**	**−9.0**	**−10.0**	**−22.0**
Goods	−0.4	−2.0	−3.5	−7.2	−10.0	−17.8
Services	1.1	−1.2	−3.6	−1.7	−0.3	−4.2
Government consumption expenditures and gross investment	**20.5**	**17.1**	**32.3**	**18.3**	**6.0**	**21.0**
Federal	17.0	12.4	20.7	5.8	−2.3	9.9
National defense	6.2	12.1	19.4	3.4	−5.5	8.4
Nondefense	11.1	−0.3	1.2	2.4	3.1	1.4
State and local	3.1	3.7	11.2	12.3	8.3	11.0
Residual	**−5.1**	**5.5**	**−0.8**	**−0.1**	**0.4**	**−1.3**

*Because change in business inventories can be positive or negative, chain-type indexes cannot be constructed for it, but it is within gross investment. The contribution is not available separately. Residual is GDP less the sum of aggregates for personal consumption expenditures, gross private domestic investment, exports of goods and services, and government consumption expenditures and gross investment.

Source: U.S. Department of Commerce, *Survey of Current Business*, May 1997, p. 65.

Prior to the July 1997 annual revisions to the NIPA data, the BEA had retained the use of fixed weights for the deflators for the quarters subsequent to the actual weights available from nominal GDP. This created what had been known as the Laspeyres tail for those last few quarters.[14] For these quarters, the implicit defla-tor's growth rate would diverge from that of the chain-type index. This Laspeyres tail arose because the annual weights for chain data are based on averages of the current- and adjacent-year quarters. For the current and prior year, these annual weights cannot be constructed. Prior to July 1997, the recent-quarter deflators were constructed by using the most recently available component weights and treating the subsequent deflators as fixed-weighted. With the July 1997 revision, the BEA changed methodology so that more recent quarterly data on component weights are incorporated into deflator estimates, thereby eliminating the Laspeyres tail.

Analysis of changes in growth rates in the implicit deflator has changed with the switch to chain GDP. Prior to this change, with the implicit deflator, there were no fixed weights for the components. Each quarter, each component's weight would depend on expenditure patterns for that quarter. Therefore, changes in the implicit GDP deflator did not solely reflect price changes but were a combination of the effects of shifts in the composition of GDP (between high- and low-priced sectors relative to the base year) and period-to-period price changes. This shift problem has mostly been eliminated owing to annual updates of weights.

There are some problems with comparability between the most recently available expenditure weights and historical data. An early explanatory article on the new chain data notes:

> The new IPD's [implicit price deflators] will be identical to the chain-type price in-dexes because the weights used to aggregate the detailed prices for the two measures will be the same.
>
> For the revised estimates beginning with the third quarter of 1994, the weights used for the chain-type output and price measures will be those for 1994 because weights for 1995 are not available. Thus, the weights used for the chain-type price indexes for each period will be fixed 1994 weights, and those used for the IPD's will be the chained-dollar weights for each period.[15]

The article predates the 1997 annual revision to GDP data. Essentially, prior to the elimination of the Laspeyres tail, the "recent" quarterly data for the chain-type implicit deflators still had some of the problems of the old constant-dollar basis implicit GDP deflators.

Because of recognition of the problems of substitution bias, the fixed-weighted GDP deflator has fallen into disfavor but is still available on a unpublished basis. The fixed-weighted GDP deflator has fixed weights for the components based on expenditure shares in the base year, currently 1992. As such, component weights (the "basket" of goods, services, and structures) are fixed but the relative importance of each component changes over time, depending on relative inflation rates for each component subsequent to the base year. Percentage changes in the fixed-weighted GDP deflator reflect only price changes. The drawback for this deflator is that it does not keep up with changes in expenditure patterns (the "basket") and may not be as relevant in the current year as in the base year.

Insights into the GDP Deflators

While GDP deflators measure prices for the domestic economy, it is not accurate to say that these price measures exclude the effects of import prices. Exports and imports—as well as all components of nominal and real GDP—enter the calculations for GDP deflators. Expenditures on imports technically are subtracted from both nominal and real GDP to derive deflator numbers, but imports also make their way into other expenditure measures, including PCEs, PDEs, inventories, and even government purchases. Also, import prices enter these other components with lags when the imported goods or services are inputs rather than for final consumption. It would be incorrect to say that GDP deflators are unaffected by import prices. First, imports—nominal and real—are part of the formula for calculating these deflators. Second, imports are significant portions of other goods and services components in GDP. Finally, imports provide competitive price pressure for domestically produced goods and thereby affect prices of domestically produced goods. Whether import prices show up more readily in the CPI goods component or the GDP goods deflator is an empirical question—not entirely one of definition. Table 13–3 compares the characteristics of GDP deflators to those of the CPI and PPI.

Sharp swings in quarterly GDP deflators are often caused by changes in prices for oil, apparel, and computers, as well as by annual wage increases for government employees, and occasionally by drought or other disaster affecting crops and Commodity Credit Corporation commodities. The latter two effects show up in farm inventories and federal government purchases, respectively.

As mentioned above, analysis of changes in growth rates of implicit deflators has changed with the switch to chain GDP. For historical perspective, it is important to know what types of analysis were used. Prior to the switch, growth in the implicit deflator could be due to either more rapid increases in prices for various components or to a shift in expenditures to higher cost sectors in the economy. The higher cost is relative to the base year. However, a shift in spending between GDP expenditure components could cause unusual quarterly movement in the implicit GDP deflator. This was not a shifting to or from components with higher or lower inflation rates but to or from components with higher or lower component deflator *levels*. Of course, the effects of component price increases and sectoral shifts in GDP expenditures could have a reinforcing impact on quarterly changes in the implicit deflator, or they could be offsetting.

Source Data for GDP Deflators

While the implicit, chain-type, and fixed-weighted GDP deflators are aggregate price indexes, they are derived on an individual series basis. Essentially, real GDP is derived by deflating individual nominal components and then summing to get the real GDP total. Nominal and real GDP are then available to calculate the implicit deflator. Given this process, there is no one source of data for the deflator estimates; there are many sources for the deflators for real GDP components.[16]

For deflating nominal personal consumption components, the primary deflators used are individual CPI series. Also used for PCEs are foreign consumer price

TABLE 13–3
Deflator and Price Index Comparisons

Producer Price Index for Finished Goods

- Covers consumer goods and capital equipment
- Includes prices only for domestically produced goods
- Fixed weights
- Monthly periodicity

Consumer Price Index

- Covers consumer goods and services based on Consumer Expenditure Survey
- Includes prices of imported goods as well as domestically produced goods
- Fixed weights
- Changes in methodology over the years; not a consistent series
- Monthly periodicity

Personal Consumption Deflator

- Covers consumer goods and services based on coverage in GDP
- Includes prices of imported goods as well as domestically produced goods
- Chain-weighted but also version using fixed weights
- Consistent methodology over the time series
- Monthly and quarterly periodicity

GDP Price Indexes and Deflators

- Covers finished goods, services, and structures across consumer, business, government, and foreign trade sectors
- Orientation is toward an aggregate for domestic production but imports enter calculations directly and indirectly; component deflators are available for imports as well as other expenditure series
- Implicit, fixed-weighted, and chain-weighted series are available
- Focus is on chain-weighted series to eliminate (reduce) substitution bias
- Quarterly periodicity

---

indexes (for expenditures abroad by U.S. residents), price indexes maintained by private trade groups and associations for many services, and various price indexes from the BEA (such as for computers). Brokerage charges and financial services furnished without payment are deflated using an index of paid employee hours of relevant financial institutions.

Under business fixed investment, the nonresidential structures deflator is based mainly on price indexes from trade sources. Producer price series are used for a few components (for gas and petroleum pipelines and for portions of mining). For deflating producers' durable equipment, most series used are producer price indexes. Also used are import price indexes from the BLS, a BEA price index for computers, the new autos CPI for new and used autos, and trade source data for telephone and telegraph installation.

For putting residential investment into real terms, the BEA uses a Census Bureau price deflator for new one-family houses under construction, a BEA price index for multifamily housing, and a PPI for mobile homes; for improvements, a CPI series is used along with Census Bureau price data. For the producers' durable equipment component of residential investment, deflation is based on PPIs.

To derive constant-dollar change in business inventories, nominal inventory levels are deflated and then real inventory levels are differenced to get the inventory change. Nominal nonfarm inventories are deflated primarily with PPI series. The BEA also incorporates data from the Energy Information Administration for petroleum stocks, BLS import price indexes for goods purchased by trade industries, a BLS price index for computers, and BEA indexes of unit labor costs for work-in-progress and finished goods in manufacturing. Farm inventories are valued in real terms directly for crops and livestock by type and are then put in current-dollar terms using current prices from Department of Agriculture surveys.

For the merchandise components of net exports, deflators are based on export and import price indexes from BLS, a BLS index and other information for computers and gold prices from trade sources; a PPI is used for transportation equipment. For services, a wide variety of indexes are used to put these components in constant-dollar form. These include selected implicit price deflators for national defense purchases, BLS export and import price indexes for passenger fares, and a BEA composite index of foreign consumer price indexes for travel payments and U.S. government payments for miscellaneous services. Also used are CPI series for travel receipts and student expenditures and a PPI for freight and port expenditures.

For federal defense purchases, deflators are based on Department of Defense price data, a BEA earnings index, a BEA price index for computers, cost indexes from trade sources for nonmilitary structures, a PPI series for selected goods, and CPI and PPI series for utilities and communications. For federal nondefense, key series are cost indexes from trade sources and government agencies for structures, a BEA rice index, a PPI for computers, and BEA earnings indexes for most services.

For state and local government, compensation deflators are derived indirectly. Constant-dollar figures for compensation are based on the change in full-time equivalent employment from the base year in hours worked with an adjustment for experience for education workers. The deflator for state and local compensation can then be derived as the ratio of nominal to real compensation. For state and local structures, the BEA uses cost indexes from trade sources and government agencies to convert nominal data into constant-dollar series. Deflators for brokerage charges and financial services received without payment are derived in the same manner as for PCEs. For remaining components, state and local purchases are deflated using miscellaneous CPI and PPI series and miscellaneous BEA price indexes.

Complications in Using Chain-Weighted GDP

The switch to chain-weighted GDP clearly has resulted in data that have the benefits of reduced substitution bias, and economic history does not get "rewritten" every time GDP is rebased. But there are costs involved in this switch. Chain-type

GDP presents a number of complications for "everyday" forecasting, modeling, and analysis (see Table 13–4).

As already mentioned, real series are not strictly additive; components do not exactly sum to a given aggregate except in indexing methodologies and only with levels of detail that the BEA uses. The implications are numerous. Users of the data cannot count on using accounting identities in models to "proof" various parts of econometric programs or spreadsheets. Another complication is that component contributions to GDP growth can only be approximated from component levels. For precision in component contributions, users must download or obtain separate series.

Forecasters must forecast components and component residuals if forecasts extend much into the future. Or forecasters must implicitly model component residuals within econometric models. Importantly, residuals vary according to the level of component detail used. Residuals are not additive, and as more component detail is added to an identity, the impact of the residual must be reevaluated for a given model or set of equations.

Chain-type data also affect how data users track quarterly data versus annual data in the GDP accounts. Averages of quarterly data are not the same as annual figures for chain-weighted series. For constant-dollar series, the average of quarterly annualized levels would equal the annual figure. To be precise, users of chain-weighted series should download or obtain annual series in addition to quarterly series.

Finally, the additive relationship of real GDP and price deflators differs for chain-type series from fixed-weighted series. The sum of the percent change in chain-weighted GDP and the percent change in the deflator equal the percent change in nominal GDP but only for the annual figures. This identity does not precisely hold for quarterly data since quarterly price indexes are interpolated from annual data.

TABLE 13–4
Fixed-Weighted GDP versus Chain-Weighted GDP

Fixed-Weighted	Chain-Weighted
Fixed weights for components in price indexes	Annual changes in weights for components in price indexes
Also called Laspeyres-type price index	Also called Fisher ideal–type price index
Price index measures cost of a fixed basket of goods and services	Price index measures nominal income necessary to obtain base-year level of satisfaction from purchases
Dollar-value components of real GDP sum to total real GDP	Components of real GDP are in index form, but if put in dollar form do not exactly equal total real GDP
Has substitution bias in real GDP measure	Significantly reduces or eliminates substitution bias
Changes in nominal GDP not easily divided into "price" and "quantity" (real) components owing to substitution bias	Fisher ideal–type real GDP and GDP price index have property that price times real GDP equals nominal GDP for annual data (this is in contrast to using constant-dollar implicit deflators)

EVALUATING BROAD TRENDS IN GDP

The GDP report is indeed very comprehensive and can be used for gauging the strength of many sectors. In fact, analysis of GDP trends is most productive when done at component levels. Questions regarding the sustainability of a component's contribution to overall growth and the possible development of imbalances can only be answered by looking at components.

First, for a given GDP report one needs to discount any special temporary factors. Most of these are discussed in the section on expenditure components. Next, one should ask whether underlying fundamentals support current trends or whether there are temporary aberrations in growth. One can get an idea of trends in current growth by looking at historical data over the business cycle, as shown in Chapter 1. Importantly, component growth should be consistent with other corroborating data. For example, for personal consumption, is rapid growth supported by income growth, lower interest rates (which increase consumer purchasing power), lower prices, or pent-up demand? For business fixed investment, are interest rates and the profits outlook favorable? Is investment supported by high-capacity utilization rates? For housing, are interest rates favorable and how are demographic factors affecting the size of the market? Is there pent-up demand and how long can it last? For government purchases, what is planned in the federal budget and what are the revenue projections for state and local governments?

Key imbalances often occur in the inventory component and in net exports. Particular attention should be given to these components. First, inventory investment is a by-product of production and demand trends. Inventories provide a cushion between sudden changes in demand and in production. As such, inventory investment, which is the change in inventory levels from period to period, has a planned component and an unplanned component. Businesses plan production and inventory levels to be in line with expected demand. When sales deviate from expectations, inventories change from desired levels and production is adjusted accordingly. Unexpected declines in inventories generally lead to increased output (GDP) in the near term, while unexpectedly high inventories lead to production cutbacks. These relationships are discussed in further detail in Chapter 9.

Also, inventories can be evaluated by using the little-watched NIPA data on inventory levels. The BEA does release data on actual inventory levels (remember, it's the *change in levels* that goes into GDP) as well as a few inventory-to-sales ratios. For those not having easy access to these inventory-to-sales series, crude inventory-to-sales ratios can be constructed by creating rough estimates for sales of goods and then creating a ratio of inventories to sales to see if this ratio is "getting out of line" with recent history. Of course, services and structures are not inventoried in the same sense as goods. Using expenditure categories, rough estimates of sales might be a combination of personal consumption of durables and nondurables added with investment for producers' durable equipment. However, GDP data are available by type of goods (durable, nondurable, services, and structures), and these series are broken down between inventory change and final sales. Hence, one can add together durable and nondurable final sales for use in creating an inventory-to-sales ratio. Inventories should focus on nonfarm components.

For analyzing trends in government consumption expenditures and gross investment, two subscriptions are highly recommended: *Monthly Treasury Statement of Receipts and Outlays of the U.S. Government,* put out by the U.S. Department of the Treasury, and *State Budget and Tax News,* published by State Policy Research, located in Birmingham, Alabama.

Net exports help balance domestic demand growth and domestic production. However, corrections between domestic demand and U.S. consumers' (and businesses') ability to pay take longer than inventory corrections. A surge in imports is usually caused by a strong dollar and strong income growth. In turn, the net export deficit widens. This is seen in growth in domestic demand (defined as GDP less net exports) exceeding GDP growth. Basically, U.S. demand exceeds growth in domestic production. Since income is closely tied to production, when domestic demand exceeds GDP growth, a nation is consuming more than it is producing—a situation that is not stable in the long run.

Of course, imports are paid with dollars (in exchange), and as foreign holding of dollars rises, the exchange value of the dollar declines. This pushes up import prices and also reduces income growth in the United States since dollars for imports go abroad. Eventually, imports are reduced owing to weaker income growth and higher import prices. In contrast, foreign growth generally picks up owing to earlier strong demand and begins to buy U.S. exports, which now cost less.

Basically, to judge the sustainability of export and import growth, one must look at growth in domestic demand relative to GDP growth over several quarters, trends in exchange rates, and income growth—both domestic and for major trading partners.

TRACKING REVISIONS TO GDP

For the initial GDP release each quarter, not all source data are available for all months in the quarter. For the missing data, the BEA must make assumptions. The BEA releases its major data assumptions on the Department of Commerce's economic bulletin board or by special request from the BEA. This table is entitled "Key Source Data and Assumptions for the Quarterly Current-Dollar Estimates of the Gross Domestic Product."

Since this table includes actual values assumed for various key monthly series, one can track subsequent economic releases to see if actual figures are higher or lower than assumed by the BEA. Of course, one needs to also compare revisions to previously released series to get a more comprehensive picture of the likely direction and magnitude of revisions to GDP. However, a comparison of dollar values for these series—actual to assumed—does not exactly correspond to GDP revisions because the BEA also makes assumptions for series that are dependent on data sources other than the key series listed. These other sources include private industry data as well as later received government data such as various quarterly surveys conducted by the Census Bureau. Also, many of the key series are in nominal terms and must be deflated in an often complex process or source data series may require accounting adjustments to be in NIPA format.

Nonetheless, for serious economy watchers, keeping up with the assumptions and tracking subsequent economic releases is a valuable exercise.

Additionally, the same monthly series used for tracking revisions to GDP are useful for producing one's own estimate of current-quarter GDP before the advance report is released. Of course, one would have to make one's own assumptions about the missing source data in the same manner as the BEA. Table 13–5 shows the availability of key source data at the time of the initial GDP release.

When analyzed as time series, overall GDP and components are typically expressed as series in percentage growth rate form. The BEA publishes them as compound growth rates, generally referred to as seasonally adjusted annualized rates, or SAAR. These calculations are properly done only by compounding. For example, the growth rate for real GDP in the first quarter of 1997 is calculated as:

$$PC_{SAAR} = (7092.1/6993.3)^4 - 1 \times 100$$
$$= 5.8$$

The shorthand method espoused by some analysts does not produce accurate calculations of the official growth rates but only rough approximations. The

TABLE 13–5

Principal Source Data for GDP: Availability for the Advance GDP Release

GDP Component and Monthly Series	Months Available
Personal consumption expenditures	
Retail sales	3
Unit auto and truck sales	3
Nonresidential fixed investment	
Unit auto and truck sales	3
Value of construction put in place	2
Manufacturers' shipments of machinery and equipment	2
Exports and imports of machinery and equipment	2
Residential Investment	
Value of construction put in place	2
Housing starts	3
Change in business inventories	
Manufacturing and trade inventories	2
Unit auto inventories	3
Net exports of goods and services	
Merchandise exports and imports	2
Government purchases	
Federal outlays	2
Value of construction put in place by state and local government	2
GDP prices	
Consumer price index	3
Producer price index	3
Nonpetroleum merchandise export and import price indexes	3
Values and quantities of petroleum imports	2

Source: Daniel Larkins, Larry R. Moran, and Ralph W. Morris, "The Business Situation," *Survey of Current Business,* U.S. Department of Commerce, July 1992, p. 2.

shorthand method of multiplying a simple quarterly percentage change by 4 produces the following:

$$PC_{S\text{-hand}} = (7092.1/6993.3) - 1 \times 100 \times 4$$
$$= 5.7$$

The shorthand method certainly is an approximation of the actual, but it does not necessarily give you the exact number that others might be discussing. (Table 13–7, at the end of the chapter, provides data on real GDP levels and percent changes for 1960–1997.

KEY QUESTIONS IN ANALYZING THE NEWS RELEASE

- For personal consumption, see Chapter 2 list of questions about monthly personal consumption expenditures, from which the quarterly data are averaged directly.

- For business fixed investment, how is growth or decline allocated between the two major components, producers' durable equipment (PDEs) and nonresidential structures?

- For PDEs, is investment spurring domestic production, or does a significant share appear to be imported?

- Was a rise in PDEs caused by a spike in motor vehicle purchases by leasing companies? Is it due to fleet building or to incentives for consumers to make long-term leases instead of for outright purchases?

- Are purchases of computers inflating real PDE figures more than usual, thereby overstating the impact on the economy?

- Was residential investment (construction) speeded up or hindered by unseasonable weather?

- Did residential investment get a boost from additions and alterations?

- If inventories rise sharply, how much appears to be planned for expected stronger domestic demand or for a near-term rise in export shipments?

- If inventories are drawn down, is it due to an unexpected surge in current demand or to weaker expected demand?

- If inventories rise significantly and appear to be unplanned, how much appears to be in goods that are generally imported?

- If inventories decline, will rebuilding be met with domestic production or imports?

- How much of the change in business inventories is in the nonfarm component and how much is in the farm component?

- Does the change in farm inventories reflect the yearly trend that is consistent with estimates for growth in farm output or was there a temporary aberration (e.g., a shift in inventory ownership between the private sector and the government Commodity Credit Corporation)?

- Are exports temporarily boosted by a surge in aircraft exports, which are discrete and volatile.

- Are overall imported goods raised by a temporary restocking of oil inventories?

- Were services exports and imports—travel components in particular—affected by personal safety issues caused by conflict abroad?

- Do changes in the exchange value of the dollar portend a change in the travel components of services net exports?

- Have services net exports been affected by a change in the level of U.S. military activity abroad?

NOTES FOR CHAPTER 13

1. U.S. Department of Commerce, "Gross Domestic Product: First Quarter 1993 (Final)," News Release, June 23, 1993, p. 1.
2. Carol S. Carson, "Replacing GNP: The Updated System of National Economic Accounts," *Business Economics,* July 1992, pp. 44–48.
3. Carol S. Carson, "GNP: An Overview of Source Data and Estimating Methods," *Survey of Current Business,* U.S. Department of Commerce, July 1987, p. 105.
4. J. Steven Landefeld, "BEA's Featured Measure of Output and Prices," *NABE News,* September 1995, p. 3.
5. The differences between Fisher and Laspeyres price indexes are discussed in more detail in Chapter 5.
6. J. Steven Landefeld and Robert P. Parker. "BEA's Chain Indexes, Time Series, and Measures of Long-Term Economic Growth," *Survey of Current Business,* U.S. Department of Commerce, May 1997, p. 60.
7. For U.S. accounts, the sum of expenditures GDP and the sum of incomes differ by a series known as the "statistical discrepancy." Also, there is the question of whether or not all income is properly reported even though expenditures from unreported income are often measured. A related question is whether there are significant (illegal) expenditures that are missed. The BEA's policy has been to not estimate such activity.
8. The BEA also provides GDP by industry, but these data are available only on an annual basis. Annually, GDP by industry in current dollars is equal to the sum of incomes. However, in constant dollars, GDP by industry is based on largely independent deflation and differs from constant-dollar GDP by the deflated statistical discrepancy and by the "residual." For further information on GDP by industry, see "Gross Product by Industry, 1977–90," *Survey of Current Business,* May 1993, pp. 33–54.
9. Asset transfers are generally not included in the GDP accounts, since GDP measures income and expenditure *flows*—not asset levels—as a basic objective. Exceptions include grants-in-aid (sometimes to foreign countries) when transfers are in kind and changes in ownership of Commodity Credit Corporation (CCC) inventories between the federal government and private corporations.
10. For discussion on how to derive approximations for contributions to GDP growth, see box in Landefeld and Parker, op. cit., p. 63.
11. For further elaboration on definitional detail of government consumption expenditures and gross investment and BEA's new treatment of government investment elsewhere in NIPAs, see "Preview of the Comprehensive Revision of the National Income and Product Accounts: New and Redesigned Tables," *Survey of Current Business,* October 1995, pp. 31–32.

12. The new NIPA treatment of military equipment does diverge from that of most other countries. U.S. NIPAs put purchases of military equipment into investment, while other countries generally place these under current consumption.

13. See earlier discussion on the switch in emphasis from GNP to GDP for further elaboration on factor income.

14. See Joel Prakken and Lisa T. Guirl, "Macro Modeling and Forecasting with Chain-Type Measures of GDP," *NABE News,* September 1995, pp. 7–13.

15. See "Preview of the Comprehensive Revision," op. cit., p. 31.

16. U.S. Department of Commerce, "Annual Revision of the U.S. National Income and Product Accounts," *Survey of Current Business,* July 1992, Table 8, pp. 37–42.

REFERENCES

Carson, Carol S. "GNP: An Overview of Source Data and Estimating Methods," *Survey of Current Business,* U.S. Department of Commerce, July 1987, pp. 103–126.

———. "Replacing GNP: The Updated System of National Economic Accounts," *Business Economics,* July 1992, pp. 44–48.

Landefeld, J. Steven. "BEA's Featured Measure of Output and Prices," *NABE News,* September 1995, pp. 3–6.

——— and Robert P. Parker. "BEA's Chain Indexes, Time Series, and Measures of Long-Term Economic Growth," *Survey of Current Business,* U.S. Department of Commerce, May 1997, pp. 58–68.

Parker, Robert P., and Eugene P. Seskin. "Annual Revision of the National Income and Product Accounts," *Survey of Current Business,* U.S. Department of Commerce, August 1997, pp. 6–32.

Prakken, Joel, and Lisa T. Guirl. "Macro Modeling and Forecasting with Chain-Type Measures of GDP," *NABE News,* September 1995, pp. 7–13.

U.S. Department of Commerce. "Gross Domestic Product as a Measure of U.S. Production," *Survey of Current Business,* August 1991, p. 8.

———. "Improved Estimates of the National Income and Product Accounts for 1959–95: Results of the Comprehensive Revision," *Survey of Current Business,* January-February 1996, pp. 1–31.

———. "Preview of the Comprehensive Revision of the National Income and Product Accounts: New and Redesigned Tables," *Survey of Current Business,* October 1995, pp. 30–39.

———. "Preview of the Comprehensive Revision of the National Income and Product Accounts: Recognition of a New Methodology for Calculating Depreciation," *Survey of Current Business,* September 1995, pp. 33–41.

———. "The Comprehensive Revision of the U.S. National Income and Product Accounts: A Review of Revisions and Major Statistical Changes," *Survey of Current Business,* December 1991, pp. 24–42.

———. "Annual Revision of U.S. National Income and Product Accounts," *Survey of Current Business,* July 1992, pp. 6–42.

Young, Allan H. "Alternative Measures of Change in Real Output and Prices, Quarterly Estimates for 1959–92," *Survey of Current Business,* March 1993, pp. 31–41.

TABLE 13–6a
Gross Domestic Product and Components, 1960–1997 (Annual Data)*

Year	Gross Domestic Product, %	Total PCEs, %	Durables PCEs, %	Nondurables PCEs, %	Services PCEs, %
1960	2.4	2.7	2.0	1.5	4.4
1961	2.3	2.0	-3.8	1.8	4.1
1962	6.1	4.9	11.7	3.2	4.9
1963	4.3	4.1	9.7	2.1	4.5
1964	5.8	6.0	9.3	4.9	6.1
1965	6.4	6.3	12.6	5.3	5.3
1966	6.5	5.7	8.5	5.5	5.1
1967	2.5	3.0	1.6	1.6	4.8
1968	4.7	5.7	11.0	4.5	5.2
1969	3.0	3.7	3.6	2.7	4.8
1970	0.1	2.3	-3.3	2.4	4.0
1971	3.3	3.7	10.0	1.8	3.7
1972	5.5	6.0	12.7	4.4	5.4
1973	5.8	4.8	10.3	3.3	4.5
1974	-0.6	-0.7	-6.9	-2.0	2.4
1975	-0.4	2.2	0.0	1.5	3.5
1976	5.4	5.6	12.8	5.0	4.2
1977	4.7	4.3	9.3	2.6	4.2
1978	5.4	4.3	5.2	3.5	4.7
1979	2.8	2.3	-0.5	2.3	3.2
1980	-0.3	-0.3	-8.0	-0.4	1.9
1981	2.3	1.2	1.1	0.9	1.5
1982	-2.1	1.2	-0.1	0.6	1.9
1983	4.0	5.2	14.7	2.9	4.7
1984	7.0	5.2	14.5	3.5	4.1
1985	3.6	4.7	9.7	2.3	5.0
1986	3.1	4.0	9.0	3.2	3.2
1987	2.9	3.1	1.4	1.9	4.2
1988	3.8	3.9	6.3	2.8	4.0
1989	3.4	2.3	2.6	2.3	2.3
1990	1.2	1.7	-0.6	1.0	2.6
1991	-0.9	-0.6	-6.3	-1.0	0.8
1992	2.7	2.8	5.7	1.5	2.9
1993	2.3	2.9	7.2	2.2	2.5
1994	3.5	3.3	7.1	2.9	2.7
1995	2.0	2.4	4.0	1.6	2.5
1996	2.8	2.6	4.7	1.4	2.7
1997	3.8	3.3	5.6	1.8	3.5

*Chained 1992 Dollars.

TABLE 13–6b

Gross Domestic Product and Components, 1960–1997 (Annual Data)

Gross Domestic Private Investment, %	Private Fixed Investment, %	Fixed Nonresidential Investment, %	Produc. Durable Equipment, %	Nonresidential Structures Investment, %	Inventory Change, (Billions, 92$)
−0.4	0.8	5.6	4.1	7.9	$10.5
−1.1	−0.5	−0.9	−2.4	1.4	8.6
12.9	9.0	8.7	11.7	4.5	19.5
6.5	7.4	5.0	7.5	1.1	17.8
8.3	9.6	11.7	12.6	10.4	15.6
14.0	10.1	17.4	18.1	15.9	30.3
8.4	5.4	12.1	15.4	6.9	42.4
−4.4	−2.0	−1.6	−1.0	−2.5	32.0
5.2	6.9	4.3	6.0	1.4	26.9
5.8	5.9	7.2	8.3	5.4	27.0
−7.0	−2.4	−1.0	−1.8	0.3	5.4
11.5	7.6	−0.1	0.8	−1.6	22.3
12.0	11.9	9.0	12.7	3.1	24.7
12.0	9.1	14.6	18.5	8.1	37.7
−8.2	−6.6	0.5	2.1	−2.1	23.4
−18.3	−11.2	−10.5	−10.5	−10.5	−10.2
20.3	9.9	4.8	6.1	2.5	29.8
15.8	14.7	11.8	15.6	4.9	38.8
11.5	11.3	13.7	15.1	10.9	43.3
2.4	5.3	9.6	8.1	12.6	23.4
−11.5	−6.8	−0.5	−4.5	6.7	−10.2
9.2	1.9	5.3	3.7	7.9	33.1
−14.4	−7.6	−4.4	−6.4	−1.5	−15.6
9.3	7.2	−1.7	4.6	−10.4	−5.7
29.8	16.5	17.3	19.2	14.3	75.3
−1.2	4.8	6.2	5.5	7.4	30.2
−1.5	0.7	−3.5	1.0	−10.8	11.1
1.2	−0.7	−1.1	0.3	−3.6	26.4
0.8	2.4	4.4	6.4	0.5	11.7
4.3	1.7	4.0	5.0	2.2	33.3
−5.6	−3.1	−0.6	−1.5	1.0	10.4
−9.4	−8.0	−6.4	−4.1	−10.7	−3.0
7.1	5.7	1.9	6.1	−6.8	7.0
9.3	7.6	7.6	10.5	0.9	22.1
13.0	8.6	8.0	11.0	1.0	60.6
1.6	5.1	9.0	10.8	4.3	27.3
7.8	8.3	9.2	10.9	4.9	25.0
12.0	7.9	9.9	12.5	3.6	65.7

TABLE 13–6c

Gross Domestic Product and Components, 1960–1997 (Annual Data)

Year	Residential Investment, %	Total GCE & GI, %	Federal GCE & GI, %	Defense GCE & GI, %	Nondefence GCE & GI, %	State and Local GCE & GI, %
1960	−7.1	−0.2	−3.1	−2.0	−8.0	4.0
1961	0.3	4.9	3.9	4.1	2.6	6.2
1962	9.6	6.0	8.3	5.9	20.4	2.9
1963	11.7	2.3	−0.4	−2.5	9.1	6.0
1964	5.8	2.0	−1.7	−4.4	8.6	6.8
1965	−2.9	3.0	0.0	−2.0	6.8	6.7
1966	−8.9	9.1	11.4	14.6	1.3	6.4
1967	−3.1	7.6	9.9	13.0	−1.2	4.9
1968	13.6	3.1	1.0	1.9	−2.6	5.7
1969	3.0	−0.5	−3.4	−4.8	2.2	2.8
1970	−6.0	−2.3	−7.1	−8.5	−1.5	2.8
1971	27.4	−1.8	−7.1	−10.1	4.0	3.3
1972	17.7	0.4	−1.7	−4.3	6.5	2.2
1973	−0.6	−0.7	−4.9	−6.4	−0.4	3.0
1974	−20.6	1.7	−0.6	−2.7	5.4	3.6
1975	−13.0	1.6	−0.2	−1.4	2.8	2.9
1976	23.6	0.1	−1.0	−1.9	1.3	0.8
1977	21.1	0.9	1.6	0.6	3.9	0.4
1978	6.6	2.9	2.1	0.1	6.8	3.5
1979	−3.7	1.6	1.5	1.6	1.2	1.6
1980	−21.1	1.8	4.2	3.6	5.6	0.0
1981	−8.0	0.7	4.2	5.5	1.2	−2.0
1982	−18.2	1.3	3.2	6.9	−5.9	−0.3
1983	41.0	2.8	5.4	5.7	4.6	0.7
1984	14.6	3.2	2.4	4.0	−2.2	3.8
1985	1.4	6.1	6.9	7.5	5.1	5.4
1986	12.0	5.1	4.6	5.2	2.8	5.5
1987	0.2	2.7	3.1	4.0	0.1	2.4
1988	−2.0	1.3	−1.8	−0.9	−4.9	3.9
1989	−3.7	2.8	1.3	−1.0	9.2	4.0
1990	−9.3	3.0	2.0	0.0	8.0	3.8
1991	−12.3	0.6	−0.5	−1.0	1.1	1.4
1992	16.6	0.5	−2.1	−5.5	7.2	2.4
1993	7.5	−0.9	−4.2	−5.7	−0.7	1.4
1994	10.1	0.0	−3.8	−4.9	−1.1	2.6
1995	−3.7	0.0	−3.3	−4.2	−1.3	2.1
1996	5.9	0.5	−1.3	−1.5	−0.9	1.5
1997	2.7	0.9	−1.6	−2.9	1.2	2.4

TABLE 13–6d

Gross Domestic Product and Components, 1960–1997 (Annual Data)

Net Exports, (Billions, 92$)	Total Exports, %	Goods Exports, %	Services Exports, %	Total Imports, %	Goods Imports, %	Services Imports, %
−21.3	20.7	23.4	10.8	1.4	−1.5	8.0
−19.1	1.7	0.6	6.8	−0.7	−0.1	−1.9
−26.5	5.3	4.4	9.1	11.4	14.7	4.9
−22.7	7.5	7.9	6.3	2.7	4.1	−0.3
−15.9	13.3	13.7	12.2	5.3	6.6	2.6
−27.4	2.0	0.5	7.7	10.7	14.2	3.0
−40.9	6.7	7.0	5.8	14.8	15.7	12.5
−50.1	2.2	0.5	8.9	7.3	5.3	12.4
−67.2	7.3	7.9	5.1	14.9	20.7	1.7
−71.3	5.5	5.2	6.2	5.7	5.4	6.3
−65.0	10.8	11.4	8.8	4.3	3.9	5.2
−75.8	0.7	−0.4	4.4	5.3	8.4	−2.7
−88.9	8.0	10.7	−0.7	11.1	13.6	3.3
−63.0	21.9	23.0	17.7	4.4	7.0	−4.1
−35.6	9.6	7.9	17.1	−2.7	−2.8	−2.3
−7.2	−0.7	−2.3	6.5	−11.3	−12.6	−5.2
−39.9	5.9	4.7	10.5	19.6	22.6	7.0
−64.2	2.4	1.3	6.5	10.7	12.2	3.9
−65.6	10.4	11.1	7.5	8.7	9.0	7.0
−45.3	9.5	11.8	1.1	1.7	1.7	1.4
10.1	10.8	11.9	6.3	−6.7	−7.4	−2.5
5.6	1.2	−1.1	10.4	2.6	2.0	5.8
−14.1	−7.1	−9.0	0.0	−1.3	−2.5	5.4
−63.3	−2.6	−2.9	−1.7	12.6	13.6	8.0
−127.3	8.3	7.9	9.4	24.3	24.2	24.9
−147.9	2.7	3.6	0.2	6.5	6.3	7.3
−163.9	7.4	5.1	13.4	8.4	10.3	0.5
−156.2	11.0	11.0	10.9	6.1	4.6	12.9
−114.4	15.9	18.8	8.7	3.9	4.0	3.5
−82.7	11.7	12.5	9.4	3.9	4.2	2.6
−61.9	8.5	8.3	9.1	3.9	3.0	7.7
−22.3	6.3	7.0	4.4	−0.7	0.0	−3.2
−29.5	6.6	7.0	5.5	7.5	9.6	−1.0
−70.2	2.9	3.3	2.0	8.9	10.5	1.9
−104.6	8.2	9.9	4.3	12.2	13.6	5.3
−98.8	11.1	12.6	7.4	8.9	9.5	6.0
−114.4	8.3	9.5	5.5	9.1	9.9	5.5
−146.5	12.3	15.4	5.1	14.2	15.1	9.4

TABLE 13–7

Real Gross Domestic Product, 1960–1997 (Levels and Percent Changes, SAAR)

		Billions, Chain-Type 1992 $	Percent Change			Billions, Chain-Type 1992 $	Percent Change
1960	Q1	2,279.2	8.9	1972	Q1	3,604.7	8.3
	Q2	2,265.5	−2.4		Q2	3,687.9	9.6
	Q3	2,268.3	−0.5		Q3	3,726.2	4.2
	Q4	2,238.6	−5.1		Q4	3,790.4	7.1
1961	Q1	2,251.7	2.4	1973	Q1	3,892.2	11.2
	Q2	2,292.0	7.4		Q2	3,919.0	2.8
	Q3	2,332.6	7.3		Q3	3,907.1	−1.2
	Q4	2,381.0	8.6		Q4	3,947.1	4.2
1962	Q1	2,422.6	7.2	1974	Q1	3,908.1	−3.9
	Q2	2,448.0	4.3		Q2	3,922.6	1.5
	Q3	2,471.9	4.0		Q3	3,880.0	−4.3
	Q4	2,476.7	0.8		Q4	3,854.1	−2.6
1963	Q1	2,508.7	5.3	1975	Q1	3,800.9	−5.4
	Q2	2,538.1	4.8		Q2	3,835.2	3.7
	Q3	2,586.3	7.8		Q3	3,907.0	7.7
	Q4	2,604.6	2.9		Q4	3,952.5	4.7
1964	Q1	2,666.7	9.9	1976	Q1	4,044.6	9.7
	Q2	2,697.5	4.7		Q2	4,072.2	2.8
	Q3	2,729.6	4.8		Q3	4,088.5	1.6
	Q4	2,739.7	1.5		Q4	4,126.4	3.8
1965	Q1	2,808.9	10.5	1977	Q1	4,176.3	4.9
	Q2	2,846.3	5.4		Q2	4,260.1	8.3
	Q3	2,898.8	7.6		Q3	4,329.5	6.7
	Q4	2,970.5	10.3		Q4	4,328.3	−0.1
1966	Q1	3,042.4	10.0	1978	Q1	4,345.5	1.6
	Q2	3,055.5	1.7		Q2	4,510.7	16.1
	Q3	3,076.5	2.8		Q3	4,552.1	3.7
	Q4	3,102.4	3.4		Q4	4,603.7	4.6
1967	Q1	3,127.2	3.2	1979	Q1	4,605.7	0.2
	Q2	3,129.5	0.3		Q2	4,615.6	0.9
	Q3	3,154.2	3.2		Q3	4,644.9	2.6
	Q4	3,178.0	3.1		Q4	4,656.2	1.0
1968	Q1	3,236.2	7.5	1980	Q1	4,679.0	2.0
	Q2	3,292.1	7.1		Q2	4,566.6	−9.3
	Q3	3,316.1	2.9		Q3	4,562.3	−0.4
	Q4	3,331.2	1.8		Q4	4,651.9	8.1
1969	Q1	3,381.9	6.2	1981	Q1	4,739.2	7.7
	Q2	3,390.2	1.0		Q2	4,696.8	−3.5
	Q3	3,409.7	2.3		Q3	4,753.0	4.9
	Q4	3,392.6	−2.0		Q4	4,693.8	−4.9
1970	Q1	3,386.5	−0.7	1982	Q1	4,615.9	−6.5
	Q2	3,391.6	0.6		Q2	4,634.9	1.7
	Q3	3,423.0	3.8		Q3	4,612.1	−2.0
	Q4	3,389.4	−3.9		Q4	4,618.3	0.5
1971	Q1	3,481.4	11.3	1983	Q1	4,663.0	3.9
	Q2	3,500.9	2.3		Q2	4,763.6	8.9
	Q3	3,523.8	2.6		Q3	4,849.0	7.4
	Q4	3,533.8	1.1		Q4	4,939.2	7.7

TABLE 13–7 (*continued*)

Real Gross Domestic Product, 1960–1997 (Levels and Percent Changes, SAAR)

		Billions, Chain-Type 1992 $	Percent Change			Billions, Chain-Type 1992 $	Percent Change
1984	Q1	5,053.6	9.6	1991	Q1	6,047.5	−2.1
	Q2	5,132.9	6.4		Q2	6,074.7	1.8
	Q3	5,170.3	2.9		Q3	6,090.1	1.0
	Q4	5,203.7	2.6		Q4	6,105.3	1.0
1985	Q1	5,257.3	4.2	1992	Q1	6,175.7	4.7
	Q2	5,283.7	2.0		Q2	6,214.2	2.5
	Q3	5,359.6	5.9		Q3	6,260.7	3.0
	Q4	5,393.6	2.6		Q4	6,327.1	4.3
1986	Q1	5,460.8	5.1	1993	Q1	6,327.9	0.1
	Q2	5,466.9	0.4		Q2	6,359.9	2.0
	Q3	5,496.3	2.2		Q3	6,393.5	2.1
	Q4	5,526.8	2.2		Q4	6,476.9	5.3
1987	Q1	5,561.8	2.6	1994	Q1	6,524.5	3.0
	Q2	5,618.0	4.1		Q2	6,600.3	4.7
	Q3	5,667.4	3.6		Q3	6,629.5	1.8
	Q4	5,750.6	6.0		Q4	6,688.6	3.6
1988	Q1	5,785.3	2.4	1995	Q1	6,703.7	0.9
	Q2	5,844.0	4.1		Q2	6,708.8	0.3
	Q3	5,878.7	2.4		Q3	6,759.2	3.0
	Q4	5,952.8	5.1		Q4	6,796.5	2.2
1989	Q1	6,011.0	4.0	1996	Q1	6,826.4	1.8
	Q2	6,055.6	3.0		Q2	6,926.0	6.0
	Q3	6,088.0	2.2		Q3	6,943.8	1.0
	Q4	6,093.5	0.4		Q4	7,017.4	4.3
1990	Q1	6,152.6	3.9	1997	Q1	7,101.6	4.9
	Q2	6,171.6	1.2		Q2	7,159.6	3.3
	Q3	6,142.1	−1.9		Q3	7,214.0	3.1
	Q4	6,079.0	−4.0		Q4	7,280.0	3.7

CHAPTER 14

THE INDEX OF LEADING INDICATORS AND OTHER COMPOSITE INDEXES

OVERVIEW

The index of leading indicators is important because it is considered a recognizable leading barometer of recession or recovery. Traditionally, this and other composite indicators were produced and published by the U.S. Department of Commerce. But in 1995, Commerce handed over responsibility for maintaining and publishing these composite indicators to the private not-for-profit Conference Board. The privatization deal, although involving no money directly, was intended to allow the Commerce Department to allocate tighter budget funds to statistical needs that could not be met by the private sector. The Conference Board, which is based in New York, defines itself as a worldwide research and business membership group, with more than 2,700 corporate and other members in 60 countries. It performs various public functions in a nonadvocacy manner, educating and informing rather than acting in an official lobbyist capacity.[1]

There are three composite indexes—leading, coincident, and lagging indicators—which are designed to track turning points in the economy:

> Each index measures the average behavior of a group of economic time series that show similar timing at business cycle turns but represent differing activities or sectors of the economy. The series that tend to lead at business cycle turns are combined into one index, those that tend to coincide into another, and those that tend to lag into a third.[2]

They use what is generally referred to as the cyclical indicators approach in identifying peaks and troughs. These historical relationships are then used to identify the turning points in a current business cycle.

The indexes are put into composite form and are considered to be superior to individual series because they represent a broad spectrum of the economy. Also, in different business cycles, some individual indicators may perform better than others. In particular, the components that perform best each cycle may vary and there would likely be little foreknowledge of which of these would be better for each turning point. Using a composite index reduces some of the risk of tracking the economy with the wrong component or components. Also, a composite index reduces some of the monthly measurement error normally associated with a given cyclical indicator.

The system of composite indicators originated with the work of Arthur F. Burns and Wesley C. Mitchell at the National Bureau of Economic Research (NBER).[3] Their first list of cyclical indicators was published in 1938. In 1961, the Department of Commerce began publishing monthly reports of the NBER's indicators; these were classified as leading, coincident, or lagging. In 1968, the Commerce Department first published the composite indexes of cyclical indicators. For many years, the NBER and Commerce Department consulted in evaluating and improving these composite indexes and in developing new cyclical indicators. This tradition continues with panels of economists selected by the Conference Board.

To be included in the composite indexes of the Conference Board, components are evaluated according to six major characteristics:

1. Conformity to the general business cycle

2. Consistent timing as a leading, coincident, or lagging indicator

3. Economic significance, based on generally accepted business cycle theories

4. Statistical adequacy by way of a reliable data collection process

5. Smoothness in month-to-month movements

6. Currency through a reasonably prompt publication schedule[4]

Traditionally, the magnitude (or lack of) revisions has also played a significant role in determining if a series is included in a composite index.

This means that cyclical indicators are grouped in terms of whether they lead, coincide with, or lag behind business cycle turning points; the leading, coincident, or lagging tendency of a given component must be generally consistent across business cycles. Indicators are judged on how well they quantify some aspect of the economy in a theoretically meaningful way: that is, the components in each index are chosen to represent various facets of the economy. The chosen indicators must be reasonably accurate statistically. They should not be volatile, giving conflicting signals from month to month. They should be available to the public soon after the occurrence of the actual economic activity. Finally, a component series should not be subject to large monthly revisions.

Traditionally, the Bureau of Economic Analysis under the Commerce Department has grouped cyclical indicators by economic process, and even published composites for each economic process. Over the years, however, the different categories have changed. Until the end of 1991, seven categories of economic processes were in use.[5] Originally, the economic processes were defined so as to have some commonality in terms of economic behavior or theory. Currently—and this was true even several years prior to the Conference Board taking over the composite indexes—the categories are no longer clearly defined as economic processes but do represent diverse facets of the economy. The Conference Board delineates 13 groups for individual cyclical indicators (domestic U.S.) and 1 group for composite indicators. Not all of the 13 groups are represented in the composite index of leading indicators.

The index of leading indicators is broadly representative of the economy, as its components are drawn from five separate groups of business cycle indicators: labor force, employment, and unemployment; sales, orders, and deliveries; fixed capital investment; personal income and consumer attitudes; and money, credit, interest rates, and stock prices. Groups that the leading index does *not* draw from are output, production, and capacity utilization; inventories and inventory investment; prices; profits and cash flow; wages, labor costs, and productivity; saving; national defense; and exports and imports.[6] These latter sectors do not have series that exhibit good leading characteristics; some have too many false signals (for example, the sensitive price series, which was part of the leading index prior to the 1996 revisions).

The Conference Board's composite indexes are generally released to the public in news release form the first week of the second month following the reference month; data are published in the Conference Board's *Business Cycle Indicators*. With each monthly release, the Conference Board provides an initial value to the latest month plus revisions for the previous six months. Most of the components of the three composite indexes are seasonally adjusted prior to inclusion in the indexes. (The stock price index and the index of consumer expectations are in not seasonally adjusted form.) Monthly revisions are not made to earlier periods even if data from original sources are revised further back historically; however, annual revisions pick up changes in seasonal factors and other minor changes missed earlier. As of late-1997, the Conference Board had not yet formalized the timing of planned annual revisions. Comprehensive revisions are irregular. All three composite indexes currently have a base year of 1992, which is set equal to 100. The latest comprehensive revision was released in December 1996, with the initial release of data for the statistical month of October 1996.

THE INDEX OF LEADING INDICATORS

The composite index of leading indicators is the most closely followed of the three indexes because it typically foreshadows changes in the direction of the economy. Policymakers, players in the financial markets, and businesspeople can use these data in making key decisions about the state of the economy. This chapter will discuss the importance of the leading index's 10 components, how well the leading index forecasts turning points, and how it should be used to predict these turning points. Finally, the methodology used to derive the leading index from its components is reviewed in moderate detail.

Components and Economic Content of the Leading Index

Based on the December 1996 revisions to the index of leading indicators, this series' 10 components are:

1. Average weekly hours of production or nonsupervisory workers in manufacturing
2. Average weekly initial claims for unemployment insurance, state programs (inverted)
3. Manufacturers' new orders in 1992 dollars for consumer goods and materials industries

4. Vendor performance, slower deliveries diffusion index

5. New orders for nondefense capital goods in 1992 dollars

6. New private housing units authorized by local building permits

7. Index of stock prices, 500 common stocks

8. Money supply, M2, in 1992 dollars

9. Interest rate spread

10. Index of consumer expectations

Average Weekly Hours of Production or Nonsupervisory Workers in Manufacturing

The average workweek in manufacturing usually changes direction before the economy, first, because the manufacturing sector itself is very cyclical, and second, businesses prefer to change the number of hours worked than to hire or lay off workers. Changing hours worked is less costly and faster in the short run than changing the size of the labor force. This component is originally released in BLS's monthly employment report.

Average Weekly Initial Claims for Unemployment Insurance, State Programs (Inverted)

This component measures the number of people filing for unemployment benefits. As the economy enters recession, the number of people asking for benefits rises because of layoffs. Prior to recovery the number of initial claims declines. Obviously, this component moves in the opposite direction of the economy; this component is inverted (multiplied by negative one) before entering the calculations of the overall index. The BLS tabulates the data from the state programs and releases the data on a weekly basis. This series is different from the U.S. Labor Department's civilian unemployment rate, which is derived from its national survey of households. While both the initial claims series and the civilian unemployment rate generally lead peaks in the business cycle, the unemployment rate is classified as lagging, following troughs, and the claims indicator is coincident, relative to troughs.[7] In late 1992, the initial claims series was redefined to include initial claims made under the July 1992 Emergency Unemployment Compensation amendments.[8] The emergency claims program was separate from the regular state programs, and there were often incentives for workers to file under the emergency program rather than the regular unemployment insurance program.

Manufacturers' New Orders in 1992 Dollars for Consumer Goods and Materials Industries

The placement of orders with manufacturers is the first step in the production process for consumer goods (as well as for other goods). Once there is an increase in orders, production rises, and, in turn, employment and income increase. The reverse is true for a decline in orders. Hence, the orders indicator tends to lead the economy. This component is derived from the Census Bureau's monthly report on new factory orders (the M3 report), and nominal dollar values are deflated using chain-weighted deflators based on manufacturing shipments data with a base year of 1992. Deflators had been based on producer price indexes.

Vendor Performance, Slower Deliveries Diffusion Index

This component is from a monthly survey of national manufacturers produced by the National Association of Purchasing Management, which covers many facets of manufacturing activity—such as production, orders, and employment—in addition to vendor performance. The data are from responses to a question pertaining to whether supplier (vendor) deliveries are slower, unchanged, or faster. The idea is that when business increases, supplier firms are not able to make deliveries as promptly as when orders are slack. Slower deliveries are generally viewed as a positive indicator of improving economic conditions. That is, more manufacturers report supplier deliveries as slower than the month before because of a pickup in economic activity. Data from the National Association of Purchasing Management are used only from 1976 to the present. Prior to 1976, the data came from a similar survey produced by the Purchasing Management Association of Chicago. The more recent data have broader national coverage but were not available prior to 1976.

New Orders for Nondefense Capital Goods in 1992 Dollars

In December 1996, this series replaced the prior series for contracts and new orders for plant and equipment. The contract portion for plant was deleted, as it was more volatile than the new orders component. This deletion also simplified the data collection process, as the series was proprietary, from F. W. Dodge. Plant was typically only 10 percent of the old component. This revised investment indicator acts as a leading indicator from at least two major perspectives. First, an increase (decrease) in business capital investment suggests that firms are more (less) optimistic about the economy. More importantly, as the actual investments are made (equipment being manufactured) at a later date, changes in employment and income (both of which are coincident indicators) occur. Changes in this component of the leading index suggest that businesses foresee turning points in their own business activity; the production that is related to the investment brings about further changes in other sectors. The new orders data in current dollars come from the Census Bureau's M3 report (*Manufacturers' Shipments, Inventories and Orders*). Chain-weighted deflators for the orders are derived by the BEA using manufacturing shipments data.

New Private Housing Units Authorized by Local Building Permits

Housing activity itself is very cyclical since consumers generally can postpone house purchases until the business cycle is in a period of relatively low mortgage rates and high consumer confidence. High interest rates lead to a buildup of housing demand. Lower interest rates unleash this pent-up demand. Low mortgage rates typically occur during later stages of a slowdown or the early stages of recovery, since total credit demands have not yet built back up to the point of putting pressure on rates. These lower rates enable more households to purchase housing, while rising consumer confidence makes them more willing to purchase. Builders, being aware of more favorable conditions, usually take out more building permits to build both speculative and nonspeculative housing stock. Housing construction generally leads a recovery, and the issuance of permits precedes construction. Also, permits generally decline during the latter stages of expansion (that is, just before the onset of recession) because, typically, rising interest rates and increasing consumer concern about the strength of the economy slow housing purchases, lead to a rise in housing inventory, and cause a decline in permits issued. This component in the leading index is based on standard Census data from the monthly housing permit release (the C40 report). This series incorporates late-received data not previously included in the initial housing permit release for a given month. Prior to the December 1996 revision of the composite indicators, this component was in index form. Currently, this series is number of permits issued.

Index of Stock Prices, 500 Common Stocks

This component is the well-known Standard and Poor's index of 500 common stocks and is a monthly average taken directly from S & P's publication, *The Outlook*. This index is a measure of expected profitability, since markets price stocks on profit potential rather than solely on past earnings. The competitive nature of the stock market forces traders to not wait on actual earnings reports but to bid for stocks based on knowledge of general economic conditions as well as factors affecting earnings potential for specific firms. If the stock market participants expect profits to improve as a result of an impending recovery, then stock prices are bid upward prior to a rise in actual earnings. If a recession is expected, profits are projected to weaken; bidding for stocks is less aggressive or participants begin to sell stocks to lock in profits and minimize losses.

Money Supply, M2, in 1992 Dollars

This financial indicator leads the economy for several reasons. In the short run, a rise in the real money stock will typically lower interest rates and stimulate demand for durables both for consumers and businesses. Lower interest rates also boost housing sales. For businesses, inventories are cheaper to finance, and this increases demand for goods. Eventually, production increases and income rises to give further support to the economy. If the money supply declines, interest rates typically increase and have effects to the opposite of the above. Nominal money supply data are produced by the Federal Reserve Board of Governors and are deflated by a chain-type PCE deflator from the BEA.

Interest Rate Spread

This component is defined as the 10-year Treasury bond rate less the federal funds rate. The rationale for its inclusion in the leading composite index is that it reflects changes in monetary policy generally viewed in terms of changes in short-term interest rates—more specifically, the federal funds rate. This short-term rate is the rate banks charge each other for use of overnight funds to cover reserve needs (reserve needs required by the Federal Reserve as a ratio to deposits). The federal funds rate is directly affected by reserves as supplied by the Federal Reserve (although there can be numerous temporary factors affecting the rate).

The impact of the changes in this interest rate spread on changes in the business cycle can be couched in terms of yield curve analysis, which is essentially the same as looking at the difference between short-term and long-term yields. Normally, interest rates rise with the maturity of the instrument (long-term rates generally are higher than short-term rates), reflecting higher risk and the need to compensate lenders more in order to defer consumption longer. As example of a change in monetary policy, a tightening in credit occurs when short-term interest rates are boosted enough to lead to an inverted yield curve. That is, very short-term rates become higher than notes of middle-term maturities such as five-year or seven-year notes and even possibly long-term yields. When short-term rates are higher than mid-maturity yields and possibly long-term yields, recessions generally follow. When the Federal Reserve engages in a loosening in monetary policy, short-term interest rates decline, in absolute terms and generally relative to long-term rates, and stronger economic activity ensues.

Index of Consumer Expectations

Changes in consumer attitudes often lead the economy. The theory behind the leading nature of a consumer confidence index is that consumers as workers are aware of economic conditions at the workplace. A general belief that conditions are improving—as reflected in new orders at work or increased production schedules—lead to higher consumer confidence. Similarly, consumer confidence declines as company or plant financial prospects appear to deteriorate. In turn, consumer willingness to spend or make financial commitments is affected. For example, consumers are more (less) willing to purchase a new car or buy a new house if work prospects are improving (worsening). Another theory behind the leading nature of this component is that the index reflects consumers' awareness of other indicators discussed in the news that affect the economy. These other indicators allegedly include interest rates, unemployment rates, layoff notices at major companies, and the stock market. The index of consumer expectations is compiled monthly by the University of Michigan's Survey Research Center. The base period is the first quarter of 1966, which equals 100.

Comprehensive Revisions in December 1996

The December 1996 revision is the primary basis for components currently included in the composite indexes. Table 14–1 summarizes the changes in the components of each of the composite indexes.[9] The *principal changes* are as follows:

- *The deletion of two series:* The price series was deleted because the series has many false signals and there is no reliable substitute. The unfilled orders series is largely duplicative of the information in two other orders series, namely, manufacturers' new orders in 1992 dollars for consumer goods and materials industries, and manufacturers' new orders in 1992 dollars, nondefense capital goods industries.

- *The addition of one series:* The interest rate spread—10-year Treasury bonds less federal funds—was added because it reflects changes in monetary policy.

TABLE 14–1

Revisions to the Components of the Composite Indexes, December 1996

Components	Prior to December 1996	1996 Revisions
Composite Index of Leading Indicators		
Average weekly hours of production or nonsupervisory workers, manufacturing		No change
Initial claims for unemployment insurance, state programs (inverted)	Monthly average based on prorated weekly series; Puerto Rico excluded	Four-week average centered on middle of month and based on weekly series; includes U.S. territories
Manufacturers' new orders, consumer goods and materials industries	Expressed in 1987 constant dollars	Same, but expressed in 1992 chained dollars
Vendor performance, slower deliveries diffusion index	Percent of companies receiving slower deliveries	No change
Contracts and orders for plant and equipment, expressed in 1987 dollars		Replaced by manufacturers' new orders, non-defense capital goods, expressed in 1992 chained dollars
New private housing units authorized by local building permits	Expressed in index form	Same, but expressed in thousands
Index of stock prices, 500 common stocks		No change
Money supply, M2	Expressed in 1987 constant dollars	Same, but expressed in 1992 chained dollars
Interest rate spread, 10-year Treasury bonds less federal funds		New
Index of consumer expectations		No change
Change in manufacturers' unfilled orders in 1982 dollars, durable goods industries, smoothed		Deleted
Change in sensitive materials prices, smoothed		Deleted
Composite Index of Coincident Indicators		
Employees on nonagricultural payrolls		No change
Personal income less transfer payments	1987 base expressed in constant dollars	Expressed in 1992 dollars, with adjustment for outliers in 1990s related to unusual timing of bonus payments
Index of industrial production		No change
Manufacturing and trade sales		Expressed in 1992 dollars

TABLE 14–1 (*continued*)
Revisions to the Components of the Composite Indexes, December 1996

Components	Prior to December 1996	1996 Revisions
Composite Index of Leading Indicators		
Average duration of unemployment in weeks (inverted)		No change
Ratio, manufacturing and trade inventories to sales	1987 base expressed in constant dollars	Expressed in 1992 dollars
Average prime rate charged by banks		No change
Commercial and industrial loans outstanding	1987 base expressed in constant dollars	Expressed in 1992 dollars
Ratio, consumer installment credit outstanding to personal income		No change
Change in index of labor cost per unit of output, manufacturing, smoothed		Same, except change in smoothing methodology
Change in consumer price index for services, smoothed		Same, except change in smoothing methodology

Note: The Commerce Department's composite indexes were first released in their current form for the January 1989 release. See Marie P. Hertzberg and Barry A. Beckman, "Business Cycle Indicators: Revised Composite Indexes," *Survey of Current Business,* U.S. Department of Commerce, January 1989, pp. 23–28.

- *The change in the base year for constant-dollar series:* This series was changed from 1987 to 1992, and all deflators are now on a chain-weighted basis. Some of the prior deflators had been based on CPIs or PPIs. Series with new chain-weighted deflators are manufacturers' new orders in 1992 dollars for consumer goods and materials industries, manufacturers' new orders for nondefense capital goods in 1992 dollars, and money supply, M2, in 1992 dollars.

Other changes to the leading index largely simplified the data collection process but without any notable impact on the behavior of the affected component and its contribution to the index.[10] These other changes are as follows:

- *Initial claims for unemployment insurance* are now based on a four-week average centered around the middle of each month. The current series is based on the weekly series reported by the Department of Labor without changes and is for the United States and U.S. territories. Previously, the claims series was adjusted to exclude Puerto Rico, was a monthly average of prorated weekly data, and had a special set of seasonal adjustment factors.

- *Building permits* are now expressed in millions of new private housing units—the same as reported by the U.S. Census Bureau except with revised data not available with the initial news release. Previously, this component was expressed as an index. Because the index form had fewer significant digits than the number of permits series, the change removed some imprecision due to rounding effects.

- *Manufacturers' new orders, nondefense capital goods industries* replaced contracts and orders for plant and equipment. This substitution both simplified the process of maintaining the composite index and made a marginal improvement in the index's leading properties. The new series is equivalent to about 90 percent of the old series, as the excluded component—contracts for commercial and industrial buildings—was only about 10 percent of the old series on average. The contract series as produced on a monthly basis was also very volatile because structures generally are a much larger budget item than are equipment purchases. The contract series is a private, proprietary data series of Dodge/McGraw-Hill, which also complicated the index maintenance process.

Table 14–1 also lists changes to the indexes of coincident and lagging indicators.

INDEX OF LEADING INDICATORS AS A FORECASTING TOOL

Before going into detail about some guidelines for using the index of leading indicators to forecast, one should look at one of the more popular techniques for predicting changes in the economy: the three-month rule of thumb. By analyzing the problems with this technique, one can better understand a more comprehensive approach in using this index.

The Three-Month Rule of Thumb

Many business analysts use a common rule of thumb to predict a turn in the economy: three consecutive declines (or increases) in the index of leading indicators indicates a coming recession (or recovery)—generally with the turning point occurring, within a year. Of course, there are rules for two or four consecutive months, but the three-month rule is the most commonly used. But how good is this rule in predicting turning points in the economy? Table 14–2 shows business cycle peaks and troughs since the end of World War II and the number of months of lead (or lag) time that the three-month rule precedes the turning point (based on current revisions to the index). Table 14–3 shows the dates that the three-month rule makes false predictions for turning points. As shown, the three-month rule suggests that some problems exist with this index being used as a forecasting tool: The index at times provides false signals. Leads prior to recovery are often negative (after-the-fact).[11] And leads prior to recession are variable and can be short at times. These shortcomings, however, are not as severe as one might first think.

First, were the false signals *really* misleading? According to the three-month rule, using the most recent data revisions, four recessions were predicted in which no recession occurred for at least two years thereafter. While there were no official recessions following these signals, real GDP growth did slow significantly within two quarters of the leading indicator's warnings in 1962, 1966, and 1984.

TABLE 14–2

Accuracy of Three-Month Rule of Thumb as Indicator of Business Cycle Recovery or Recession (Using 1989, 1993, and 1996 Revisions)

Peak	Number of Months Lead Time Using Revision of			Trough	Number of Months Lead Time Using Revision of		
	1/89	12/93	12/96		1/89	12/93	12/96
November 1948	+2	+2	NA	October 1949	+1	+1	NA
July 1953	+2	+2	NA	May 1954	+1	+1	NA
August 1957	+6	+6	NA	April 1958	−1	−1	NA
April 1960	+1	+8	+8	February 1961	+5	−1	−3
December 1969	+5	+5	+5	November 1970	−2	−2	−3
November 1973	+3	+6	+6	March 1975	−2	−2	−2
January 1980	+12	+12	+12	July 1980	−1	−1	0
July 1981	−4	+5	0	November 1982	0	0	0
July 1990	+12	+12	−2	March 1991	−1	−2	−1
Average lead for last 6 peaks	+4.8	+8.0	+4.8	Average lead for last 6 troughs	−0.2	−1.5	−1.5

Note: Peaks and troughs are dated as determined by the National Bureau of Economic Research (NBER). Pluses indicate number of months prior to turning point and minuses indicate months following the turning point.

TABLE 14–3
False Signals of Recession Sent Using Three-Month Rule of Thumb

	Using Revision of		
Period	1/89	12/93	12/96
February 1951–August 1951	✓	✓	NA
April 1962–June 1962	✓	✓	✓
April 1966–December 1966	✓	✓	✓
May 1984–October 1984	✓		
March 1984–October 1984		✓	
October 1987–December 1987	✓		
October 1987–January 1988		✓	✓
October 1991–December 1991		✓	
June 1992–September 1992		✓	
January 1995–May 1995			✓
February 1995–November 1995		✓	

Note: There were no false signals of recovery for the period 1948–1996.

Earlier versions of the leading index did have a greater incidence of false signals. See Gary Gorton, "Forecasting with the Index of Leading Indicators," *Business Review,* Federal Reserve Bank of Philadelphia, November-December 1982, p. 20. One should remember that the 1989 version of the leading index stopped in 1993 and the current version of the index only goes back to 1959.

Manufacturing output in particular declined and other sectors slowed. From a definitional point of view, the index signals were false on these occasions: from a practical perspective, the index was an accurate predictor of either a downturn in manufacturing or a growth slump overall. The index is a better forecaster for turning points in manufacturing than for the economy overall.

Posing another problem for the three-month rule is the fact that frequent data revisions may "overturn" what originally was a three-month change in trend. Table 14–2 is based on the December 1996 revised version of the leading index. Since the overall index is based on 10 components, most of which are revised for two or three months (and longer for some) following the original estimate of the leading index, revisions in the overall index is a fact to be lived with. Sometimes, a three-month rule may be invoked only for later revisions to turn into a two-month decline followed by a small rise. Hence, frequent data revisions make the indicator more difficult to interpret. For example, when the index for September 1984 was released (using an earlier version of the leading index), figures for June, July, and August were revised to show three consecutive declines.[12] Disagreement arose within the economic community over whether this meant that a recession was imminent. In hindsight, no recession developed in terms of an actual decline in economic activity. But were the revised data truly misleading? The indicator did presage a sharp deceleration in real GDP growth in the first half of 1985 from very rapid growth in the early stages of recovery. Specifically, the manufacturing sector was very weak.

As shown in Table 14–2, the leads of the leading index are highly variable, and sometimes even after the fact relative to official turning points. Also, data for a given month are released about four weeks after the reference month. That is, data are available for forecasting one month after the economic event and this further reduces the lead time of the index in terms of real-time availability to a user. Business decisions based on the information in the index are not as timely as one might prefer. So is the index really useful for forecasting?

On a qualified basis, the index is indeed very useful for forecasting. The index is not as timely in predicting recoveries as in predicting recessions. From a business perspective, being a little late recognizing a recovery is considerably more tolerable than not foreseeing a recession. In terms of lead times, the index has longer leads than other popular economic series, such as real GDP (which really helps to define the cycle), the unemployment rate, or retail sales. All of these series also have a one-month lag or greater in being reported and also do not have any "leading" information. While the index of leading indicators occasionally has a very short lead prior to recession, actually knowing—or at least being fairly confident—that a recession is underway is still very important information. Even if there is no lead in some recessions, this index is still the best indicator for confirming the onset of recession, or at least very weak economic growth. Recognizing that the economy has just peaked allows for better planning in anticipation of a further weak economy.

At first glance based on the simplistic three-month rule of thumb, the current version of the leading index does not appear to have done as good a job predicting the 1990–1991 recession as did the prior version. A closer review of the data indicates that the current version of the index portrays an economy in 1988–1989 that fits the definition of the proverbial soft landing. There were several instances of two negative months and then a marginally positive month. The current version of the leading index clearly showed (ex post) an economy that was very sluggish. Given that the "final straw" causing the 1990–1991 recession was an oil price shock and possibly consumer confidence related to the Gulf War, it is reasonable that a leading index would not anticipate a recession that was caused by exogenous factors. If one takes the view that the economy was not necessarily headed into recession prior to the Iraqi invasion of Kuwait, then the current index is more consistent with that view. Additionally, the current version of the index came very close to meeting the three-month rule in late 1988; not meeting it was really a "technicality." Had it done so, its track record on this basis would have equaled that of the 1993 version. Importantly, the 1996 version of the index had fewer false signals of recession than the prior version. Furthermore, the current version portrayed shallower false signals than the prior version during periods of economic weakness in 1984 and 1995.

The Three Ds

Apparently, the three-month rule can pose problems for a forecaster. Should one wait to see if data are revised before analyzing changes in the index? To do so would certainly reduce the predictive value of the index since lead times are already short for some business cycles. To predict turning points in the economy, economists at the NBER and BEA have long suggested that the focus should not be entirely on the duration facet of changes in the index; the Conference Board continues this emphasis. Three consecutive declines (or increases) just is not enough information on which to base a prediction of recession (or recovery). For example, what if three very shallow declines are followed by a sharp rebound? Or what if only two or three components are pulling down the overall index because of special, temporary factors? These questions lead to the "three Ds": depth, diffusion, and duration.

Simply put, the significance of changes in the index depends on how strong the percentage changes are (depth), how widespread the changes are among the various components (diffusion), and for how many months the reversal in trend has continued (duration). The three-month rule only focused on the duration facet. The three Ds approach helps to eliminate some of the uncertainty created by data revisions. For example, a decline in June through August 1984 (in the version released October 31, 1984) obviously met the three-month rule. Furthermore, later revisions could be interpreted to still forecast weakness in the economy—or at least in manufacturing. Current versions of the data (as of September 1992) indicate the index fell six consecutive months beginning in May 1984, with decreases ranging between 0.2 and 1.0 percent, yet no official recession occurred. Nonetheless, industrial production fell over the September-through-December 1984 period, thereby suggesting that the original data correctly predicted a weakening in the economy even though there was no official recession. By looking at the depth and diffusion of the original changes, one could see that pending temporary weakness was the correct way to interpret the original signal—even though the three-month rule was not met.

Another occasion in which looking at the three dimensions of the leading index would have helped to interpret the status of the economy was in late 1987. The October-through-December 1987 period was a false signal of recession using the simple three-month rule. This period included and immediately followed the October 1989 stock market crash. Importantly, the three declines in the composite index were led by sharp drops in financial variables—the S&P 500 component and real M2—along with consumer expectations. There was no clear signal from the other components; some were actually up and others were little changed. Essentially, component analysis suggested that a recession was not certain given that weakness was concentrated in the financial sector. Weakness in consumer expectations probably reflected concern over financial markets specifically. A more in-depth look at the leading index once the three-month rule was met would have indicated that a wait-and-see attitude was still appropriate in terms of gauging whether a recession was imminent.

Helping to address the shortcomings of the three-month rule, the Conference Board publishes a diffusion index for each of the composite indicators. The diffusion indexes indicate to what degree the component series moved in the same direction without actually having to examine each component.

Deriving Net Contributions to the Index

Net contributions are an important focus for analyzing changes in the leading index, since the breadth of gains or losses across components is of interest in determining if the economy is strengthening or weakening. Net contributions are how components of the composite indexes are analyzed and are a major portion of the methodology of deriving the composite indexes. They can be derived from raw data for components that are put into either symmetrical percent change form or in first differences. Component data are then adjusted for component weights and index standardization. These "adjusted" percentage changes for the components are essentially added together to get the percent change in the overall index. Before looking at these calculations in detail, let us examine the concepts that are involved.

Monthly Symmetrical Percentage Changes and First Differences
The percent changes used in deriving component contributions are symmetrical percent changes using both the current month and previous month for the denominator. This has the desirable quality of producing percent changes of equal magnitude when a component rises and then falls (or falls and then rises) by the same absolute amount. Standard percentage changes are biased in that decreases tend to be smaller than increases since the base period for decreases is naturally larger than for subsequent increases (this bias also holds for increases that are followed by a decrease). Symmetrical percent changes are defined as the difference between the current month, M_0, and the previous month, M_{-1}, divided by the sum of the two months and then multiplied by 200:

$$PC_{\text{symmetrical}} = \frac{(M_0 - M_{-1})}{(M_0 + M_{-1})} \times 200$$

First differences (the current month less the previous month) are used for series that contain zero or negative values or are already in percentage change or ratio form. For the index of leading indicators, the component that is put in first difference form is the interest rate spread. For the coincident index, all components use symmetrical percent changes, while for the lagging index, first differences are used for two of the seven series: the change in index of unit labor costs and the change in consumer prices for services.

Component Weights
When a composite index is designed, there must be a decision as to how much each series "counts" toward deriving the total. That is, what is each component's share or weight of the total? The Conference Board weights each series in a given composite indicator equally but adjusted by component volatility. As shown below, weights are implicit in the derivation of the component standardization factors. Should a component not be available, weights are based on available data.

Component Standardization Factors
Components are standardized because they have varying degrees of volatility. Some series have significantly larger monthly percent changes (without regard to sign) than others. Without standardizing components, those with larger mean absolute percent changes or standard deviations would dominate the overall composite indexes. The component standardization factor is based on standard deviations (v_x) for each series. These standard deviations are inverted ($w_x = 1/v_x$) and component standard deviations are summed ($k = \Sigma_x w_x$). The sum is re-

calculated so that the sum of the index's component standardization factors $(r_x = 1/k \times v_x)$ sum to 1. The "equal" but adjusted weights of the components are implicit in the recalculated component standardization factors. Component standardization factors are revised only with comprehensive revisions; there are no annual revisions to these factors.

Index Standardization Factors

In order to make the movement in the three composite indexes consistent with each other, the weighted percent changes calculated in the preceding step for the leading and lagging indexes are standardized. This is done so that the leading and coincident indexes' standard deviations of percent changes equal that of the coincident index. The index standardization factor for the leading index is the ratio of the standard deviation of the percent changes in the coincident index to the standard deviation of the unadjusted percent changes in the leading index. For the lagging index, the index standardization factor is calculated similarly. For the leading index, the index standardization factor as currently calculated over the 1959–1995 period is 0.654; for the lagging index, 0.825. These values below 1 indicate that before standardization, these indexes had greater monthly volatility than the coincident index. For the coincident index, the index standardization value, of course, is 1. These values are updated annually.

Calculating the Net Contributions

For an example of calculating the net contribution for a component, we can use the initial claims data in the initial release for the statistical month of December 1996 as shown in Table 14–4. December initial claims were 353,800 while November's were 336,700. First, the symmetrical percent change is calculated in thousands:

$$(353.8 - 336.7)/(353.8 + 336.7) \times 200 = 4.953$$

This is then multiplied by the component standardization factor (0.025) and then by the index standardization factor (0.654):

$$4.953 \times 0.025 \times 0.654 = 0.08.$$

The 0.08 would be the net contribution for the initial claims series except that it must be inverted (multiplied by -1) to take into account that a decline in claims is a positive.

Basically, each component's *net contribution* is derived by (1) taking the appropriate symmetrical percent change or first difference, (2) multiplying by the component standardization factor, and (3) multiplying by the index standardization factor.

To get the percent change (the symmetrical percent change—not the "standard percent change derived from the index in its final form) in the overall index, the net contributions are summed. Actually, *Business Cycle Indicators* describes the methodology as summing the adjusted month-to-month changes in the components and then multiplying by an index standardization factor. This is the equivalent of summing the net contributions (assuming no rounding differences). In contrast with versions of the leading index prior to the 1989 revision, no trend adjustment factor is added to the sum of the net contributions. See below for an

TABLE 14–4

Computation of the 10 Components of the Composite Index of Leading Indicators, 1996

Component	June	July	August	September	October	November	December
1 Average weekly hours, manufacturing	41.8	41.6	41.7	41.7	41.7	41.7	42.0
Symmetric percent change		−.480	.240	.000	.000	.000	.717
Standardized by a factor of .222		−.106	.053	.000	.000	.000	.159
Component contribution (index standardization factor: 0.654)		−.07	.03	.00	.00	.00	.10
2 Initial claims, unemployment insurance	355.6	337.9	323.1	334.9	333.8	336.7	353.8
Symmetric percent change		5.105	4.478	−3.587	.329	−.865	−4.953
Standardized by a factor of .025		.128	.112	−.090	.008	−.022	−.124
Component contribution (index standardization factor: 0.654)		−.08	.07	−.06	.01	−.01	−.08
3 Manufacturers' new orders, consumer goods and materials	142,773	145,444	143,586	144,521	145,252	143,345	140,718
Symmetric percent change		1.853	−1.286	.649	.505	−1.322	−1.850
Standardized by a factor of .047		.087	−.060	.031	.024	−.062	−.087
Component contribution (index stardardization factor: 0.654)		.06	−.04	.02	.02	−.04	−.06
4 Vendor performance, slower deliveries diffusion index	53.2	50.9	52.5	49.7	50.7	51.5	51.6
Symmetric percent change		−4.419	3.095	−5.479	1.992	1.566	.194
Standardized by a factor of .026		−.115	.080	−.142	.052	.041	.005
Component contribution (index standardization factor: 0.654)		−.08	.05	−.09	.03	.03	.00
5 Manufacturers' new orders, nondefense capital goods	40,535	43,348	38,824	44,799	44,703	41,300	41,074
Symmetric percent change		6.707	−11.011	14.290	−.215	−7.914	−.549
Standardized by a factor of .012		.080	−.132	.171	−.003	−.095	−.007
Component contribution (index stardardization factor: 0.654)		.05	−.09	.11	.00	−.06	.00

6 Building permits, new private housing units	1,415	1,457	1,423	1,399	1,362	1,418	1,422
Symmetric percent change		2.925	-2.361	-1.701	-2.680	4.029	.282
Standardized by a factor of .017		.050	-.040	-.029	-.046	.068	.005
Component contribution (index standardization factor: 0.654)		.03	-.03	-.02	-.03	.04	.00
7 Stock prices, 500 common stocks (S & P)	668.50	644.07	662.68	674.88	701.45	735.67	743.25
Symmetric percent change		-3.722	2.848	1.824	3.861	4.762	1.025
Standardized by a factor of .031		-.115	.088	.057	.120	.148	.032
Component contribution (index standardization factor: 0.654)		-.08	.06	.04	.08	.10	.02
8 Money supply, M2	3410.5	3409.0	3419.0	3422.6	3420.6	3435.9	3456.0
Symmetric percent change		-.044	.293	.105	-.058	.446	.583
Standardized by a factor of .293		-.013	.086	.031	-.017	.131	.171
Component contribution (index standardization factor: 0.654)		-.01	.06	.02	-.01	.09	.11
9 Interest rate spread, 10-year Treasury bonds less federal funds	1.64	1.47	1.42	1.53	1.29	.89	1.01
Symmetric percent change		-.170	-.050	.110	-.240	-.400	.120
Standardized by a factor of .310		-.053	-.016	.034	-.074	-.124	.037
Component contribution (index standardization factor: 0.654)		-.03	-.01	.02	-.05	-.08	.02
10 Index of consumer expectations (University of Michigan)	84.0	86.5	87.3	90.1	89.9	93.9	91.8
Symmetric percent change		2.933	.921	3.157	-.222	4.353	-2.262
Standardized by a factor of .017		.050	.016	.054	-.004	.074	-.038
Component contribution (index standardization factor: 0.654)		.03	.01	.04	.00	.05	-.03

Source: The Conference Board, Business Cycle Indicators, February 1997.

explanation of trend adjustment factors. To finish the process of calculating the composite indexes, the levels are "backed out" of the symmetrical percent changes. The history of the index is then rebased so that the 12-month average level for 1992 equals 100, completing the process of deriving the composite index.

Trend Adjustment Factors

Historical artifacts, the trend adjustment factors for the leading, coincident, and lagging indexes were derived in earlier versions of the composite indexes so as to make their trends equal to the trend for real GNP (the main aggregate at that time). The long-term growth rate in real GNP was the target trend and the trend adjustment factor was defined as the target trend minus the trend in the raw index. The raw index was an index derived from converting symmetrical percent changes of the component contribution sums to normal percent changes. These were then used to create raw index levels. In the immediate pre-1989 versions of the composite indexes, the target trend was the average of the trends of the components of the coincident index. The switch to targeting the trend in real GNP was made because economists generally focus on real GNP as a measure of long-run economic activity.[13] The current version (and 1989 version) of composite indicators does not use a trend adjustment factor because it tends to temporarily mask turning points at the peak of a business cycle: the trend-adjusted leading index would still be positive while the raw index might be declining.

CHART 14–1
Leading Indicator versus Real GDP

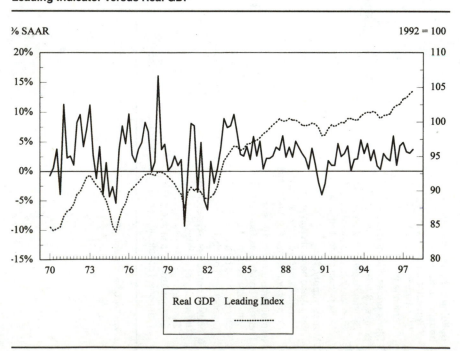

Dating the Business Cycle Using the Coincident and Lagging Indexes

The coincident index is primarily used as a tool for dating the business cycle; the lagging index plays an ancillary role. The NBER is generally acknowledged by economists as the official arbiter for determining cyclical peaks and troughs in the United States. While there are no set rules for "measuring" turning points, historical decisions by this group strongly suggest rules of thumb that involve the coincident index.

Once monthly economic data are persuasive that a recent turning point has occurred, the appropriate NBER committee meets. Each economist on the committee presents his or her argument for the specific month for the turning point based on various economic indicators. If there is disagreement over the month, then there is further discussion leading to a compromise position. Importantly, the economic indicators used in this evaluation are primarily those in the coincident index—even though others can and do enter into the debate.[14]

In the post–World War II period, business cycle peaks and troughs have usually been officially pegged to peaks and troughs in the coincident index although revisions have shifted turning points in the coincident index by one month in several cases. Historically, a turning point has been pegged as official when a given peak or trough in the coincident index is followed by six consecutive months that are a reversal of the previous trend.

If there is not a reversal of trend for six consecutive months, then usually movement in real GDP (or real GNP prior to 1992) is the other primary consideration. Two consecutive *quarterly* reversals of trend in real GDP is then the complementary determining factor to movement in the coincident index. A peak is usually placed in the last quarter with positive real GDP growth, and, similarly, a trough is put in the last negative quarter before the reversal of trend. If there are six consecutive months of reversal of the coincident index, then there is no compelling need for either two quarters of reversal in real GDP; nor is there a need to place the peak or trough in the same quarter that real GDP peaked or troughed.

If a recovery is weak and wavering, then the committee usually waits to date a trough after the level of economic activity (usually in terms of real GDP) surpasses its previous peak. Once real GDP exceeds the previous peak, any subsequent downturn would be classified as a separate and new recession. The NBER announced the March 1991 trough on December 22, 1992, when it was apparent that real GDP for the third quarter of 1992 exceeded the peak of the second quarter of 1990 and would not be revised below this level.

The main reason that the coincident index, and not real GDP, may turn one quarter is that the coincident index is still dominated by manufacturing components while real GDP has a greater share in nonmanufacturing sectors (services and construction). This can keep growth positive if the manufacturing sector is only mildly negative. The coincident index does have components other than industrial production, but for employment and personal income, manufacturing still creates the greatest cyclical movement. This is also somewhat true for business sales.

On a final note in the determination of peaks and troughs, the NBER also looks at leading (and lagging) indicators (the composites and components) to see if they have peaked (or troughed) prior to and after the prospective peak (trough) of the coincident index. If the coincident index is well bracketed, then this helps to confirm and define business cycle turning points. Essentially, the primary purpose of the lagging index is to help confirm turning points in the business cycle.

KEYS TO ANALYZING THE MONTHLY REPORTS

First, one should remember that the leading index is primarily designed to predict turning points. It is only a moderately good measure of the strength of the current economy. However, there is a strong correlation between the coincident index and real GDP, as measured with quarterly growth rates. One of the primary reasons that the coincident index does reasonably well in this regard is the inclusion of real personal income (excluding transfers) in the coincident index. Personal income is a large component of GDP on the income side of the ledger for the national income and production accounts.

The leading index is primarily useful during times of uncertainty. However, in order to judge if a turning point is imminent, one should not focus solely on the number of months of decline or rebound. One should use the three Ds—depth, duration, and diffusion—to see if a change from trend is widespread and significant in magnitude. To examine these factors, one can look at component contributions to see whether a turning point is likely. As discussed earlier, component contributions take into account normal differences in the size of monthly percent changes between the various components. Furthermore, one can look at the diffusion indexes published by the Conference Board.

As is shown in Table 14–2, the leading index has a shorter lead in predicting turning points in recovery than in downturns. Therefore, whenever the index strengthens, one should expect to see improvement in the economy relatively quickly.

Finally, the leading index is a better indicator for turning points in manufacturing than for real GDP. This is due to the inclusion of leading indicators for manufacturing (the orders series, the manufacturing workweek, and vendor performance), the lack of indicators covering services, and the fact that manufacturing is more cyclical than real GDP.

KEY QUESTIONS IN INTERPRETING THE NEWS RELEASES

Leading Index

- Does the latest figure for the index represent a continuation of a trend, or is it near a possible turning point? Over how many months has the current trend continued?
- How large was the change in the index?
- How many components moved in the same direction?

- What did its diffusion index do?
- Has recent movement in the overall index been dominated by just one or two components (perhaps the stock market component or money supply), or are most components moving together?

Defining a Turning Point

- Has the leading index had six consecutive moves in the direction opposite the most recently established trend *or* has real GDP reversed course for two consecutive quarters?
- What month is the turning point for the coincident index?
- To help define the turning point, for the apparent peak or trough as depicted by the coincident index, does the lagging index turn similarly within the following 12 months?

NOTES FOR CHAPTER 14

1. In addition to the composite indexes, the Conference Board also produces other economic statistics: consumer confidence, business confidence, and help wanted indexes.
2. Barry Beckman and Tracy Tapscott, "Composite Indexes of Leading, Coincident, and Lagging Indicators," *Survey of Current Business,* U.S. Department of Commerce, November 1987, p. 24.
3. Gary Gorton, "Forecasting with the Index of Leading Indicators," *Business Review,* Federal Reserve Bank of Philadelphia, November-December 1982, p. 16.
4. *Business Cycle Indicators,* New York, the Conference Board. See also Beckman and Tapscott, op. cit.
5. These categories were employment and unemployment; production and income; consumption, trade, orders, and deliveries; fixed capital investment; inventories and inventory investment; prices, costs, and profits; and money and credit.
6. There is an additional indicators grouping in *Business Cycle Indicators* for international comparisons but it is not relevant for sectoral coverage of domestic composite indicators.
7. The NBER and BEA give ratings (in terms of being leading, coincident, or lagging) to each cyclical indicator relative to peak, trough, and overall. If the ratings for peak and trough activity differ, then a series is given an overall rating of "unclassified." This is discussed further in the business cycle indicators section of Commerce's publication, *Survey of Current Business.*
8. See U.S. Department of Commerce, *Composite Indexes of Leading, Coincident, and Lagging Indicators, September 1992,* November 3, 1992, p. 1.
9. For details on the revisions, see two publications of the Conference Board: "Forthcoming Revisions to the Composite Indexes," *Business Cycle Indicators,* November 1996, pp. 3–4, and "Details on the Revisions to the Composite Indexes," *Business Cycle Indicators,* December 1996, pp. 3–4 and A–1.
10. For more explicit detail on the changes in the composite indicators, see *Business Cycle Indicators,* December 1996.

11. However, the actual turning point of the leading index did precede that of the coincident index on two of these late three-month rule-of-thumb forecasts. The turning point comparison is basically a one-month rule.

12. The latest historical revisions (as of early 1997) do not show three consecutive declines in the index of leading indicators from June through August 1984—"merely" a decline in June, no change in July, and then declines in August and September. Earlier versions of the index told differing stories. An old 12-component composite actually revised the data after invoking the three-month rule so that there were no three consecutive declines.

13. The January 1989 comprehensive revision to the composite indicators occurred prior to the BEA's completion of the December 1991 benchmark revision of the national income and product accounts, which included a shift in emphasis from gross national product to gross domestic product as the key measure of aggregate production.

14. For more detailed discussion of the considerations involved, see Geoffrey H. Moore, *Business Cycles, Inflation, and Forecasting,* 2nd ed., Ballinger, Cambridge, Mass., 1983, pp. 5–9.

BIBLIOGRAPHY

Beckman, Barry A., and Tracy R. Tapscott. "Composite Indexes of Leading, Coincident, and Lagging Indicators," *Survey of Current Business,* U.S. Department of Commerce, November 1987, pp. 24–28.

U.S. Department of Commerce, Bureau of Economic Analysis, *Handbook of Cyclical Indicators: A Supplement to the Business Conditions Digest,* 1984.

Conference Board. "The Cyclical Indicator Approach," and "Forthcoming Revisions to the Composite Indexes,"*Business Cycle Indicators,* November 1996, pp. 2–4.

———. Details on the Revisions to the Composite Indexes," *Business Cycle Indicators,* December 1996, pp. 3–4 and A–1.

———. "Using the Individual Leading Indicators to Predict Growth," *Business Cycle Indicators,* April 1997.

Gorton, Gary. "Forecasting with the Index of Leading Indicators," *Business Review,* Federal Reserve Bank of Philadelphia, November-December 1982, pp. 15–27.

Green, George R., and Barry A. Beckman. "The Composite Index of Coincident Indicators and Alternative Coincident Indexes," *Survey of Current Business,* U.S. Department of Commerce, June 1992, pp. 42–45.

Hertzberg, Marie P., and Barry A. Beckman. "Business Cycle Indicators: Revised Composite Indexes," *Survey of Current Business,* U.S. Department of Commerce, January 1989, pp. 23–28.

Moore, Geoffrey H. *Business Cycles, Inflation, and Forecasting,* 2nd ed., Ballinger, Cambridge, Mass., 1983.

Ortner, Robert, and Theodore S. Torda. "Leading Index: A Useful Guide but Not an Automatic Indicator," *Business America,* August 6, 1984, pp. 22–23.

Ratti, Ronald A. "A Descriptive Analysis of Economic Indicators," *Review,* Federal Reserve Bank of St. Louis, January 1985, pp. 14–24.

CHAPTER 15

THE PRODUCTIVITY AND UNIT LABOR COSTS REPORT AND THE EMPLOYMENT COST INDEX

Financial market analysts often focus on measures of labor cost because labor costs are a significant portion of the production costs of most goods and services; essentially, labor costs are viewed as indicative of inflation pressures. Productivity is often viewed as an inflation indicator since it has an inverse relationship to unit labor costs: higher productivity implies lower unit labor costs. Productivity is also important as a long-term determinant of wages. Firms are willing to pay a wage that is commensurate with labor productivity, and as productivity rises, so does labor's earnings capacity. Of course, the roles of productivity in inflation and wage determination are more complex than this simple explanation, since capital equipment and entrepreneurial contributors have their own demands for return on investment which are competitive with labor.

The two broad measures of labor costs are unit labor costs and the employment cost index. Unit labor cost data are part of the same report in which productivity data are released, while the employment cost index falls under a separate report.

PRODUCTIVITY AND UNIT LABOR COSTS

The productivity and unit labor costs report contains data on a quarterly basis, produced by the Bureau of Labor Statistics. Data are released and revised eight times a year and are published in the report *Productivity and Costs*.

Productivity is a measure of output relative to some input measure. Therefore, productivity is the ratio of output to a unit of input. Productivity is *usually* in reference to a unit of *labor* input, for example, hours worked. Analysis of productivity is almost always in reference to labor productivity. However, there is a relatively new measure of productivity known as multifactor productivity—that is, output compared to *combined* units of inputs. There are two measures of multifactor productivity produced by BLS:

1. For labor and capital inputs
2. For capital (K), labor (L), energy (E), materials (M), and purchased business services (S)—otherwise known as KLEMS. Multifactor productivity numbers are published only on an annual basis and are not regularly tracked by financial markets.

With the release of data for the third quarter of 1995 in February 1996, the BLS switched to annual weighted indexes for computations underlying productivity and costs data series. These series are now based on output data constructed in the same manner as chain-dollar GDP. The base year for these series is now 1992, which is equal to 100. Also, output is expressed in terms of various sectors within the economy, and as such, output is measured as gross product originating (GPO) in a sector. This is a value-added concept.

Productivity: Data Sources and Adjustments to Source Data

To estimate productivity, separate measures are needed for output and for the labor input. Output measures for business and nonfarm business sectors are based primarily on measures of GDP from the BEA. BLS's output measure is now based on the product (expenditure) side of GDP rather than the income side, as in the past. The intent of this switch was to reduce the size of revisions of productivity and other measures.

Estimates for employment and average weekly hours are derived primarily from BLS's Current Employment Statistics (CES) and Current Population Survey (CPS) programs. Establishment data are adjusted from an "hours paid" basis to an "hours worked" basis. These adjustments are largely based on BLS's Hours at Work Survey. The CPS employment data are mainly used for estimates of farm employment and for proprietors and unpaid family workers.

There are several sectoral measures used for reporting, but the three primary sectors are the business sector, the nonfarm business sector, and manufacturing. To derive business sector output from GDP, BLS subtracts from GDP:

1. The product of general government, private households, and nonprofit institutions
2. The rental value of owner-occupied dwellings

Nonfarm business sector output also excludes farm output. For the manufacturing sector, quarterly output measures reflect independent indexes of industrial production prepared by the Federal Reserve. The annual output measures for the manufacturing sector are still GPO based.

Compensation and Unit Labor Cost Measures in the Productivity Report

A measure for unit labor costs requires not only a measure for labor input—such as hours worked—but also a measure of compensation. This is a concept not covered by the productivity measure, which is the ratio of output to labor input.

By definition, the unit labor cost series measures the cost of labor input required to produce one unit of output and is derived by dividing compensation in current dollars by output in chained dollars.

The compensation measure used to calculate unit labor costs is a special, broad measure of labor costs. In particular, this measure is based on the definitional needs for data used within the National Income and Product Accounts (NIPA) on the income side of GDP. This compensation concept is expanded beyond the establishment employment data for earnings and covers more than just wage and salary workers. This compensation measure includes estimates for farmworkers, government enterprise workers, and proprietors as well as imputations for unpaid family workers. Proprietors' compensation can be a large share of overall labor compensation for some sectors. For example, proprietors compensation is a substantial part of labor compensation in the retail sector. To estimate proprietors' compensation, BLS assumes that the labor compensation per hour (separate from return on entrepreneurial contributions) is the same as that of the average employee in that sector.

This report also includes indexes of compensation per hour that measure the hourly cost to employers for wages and salaries, supplemental payments, which include employers' contributions to Social Security, unemployment insurance taxes, and payments for private health insurance and pension plans. Compensation is defined broadly and as a measure from the GDP accounts includes some estimated components. It includes tips and bonuses. This is in contrast to the employment cost index, which specifically excludes tips and largely misses bonuses. The compensation series is not based on a constant labor force.

Analysis of Productivity Data

The information content of productivity and unit labor cost data vary significantly in the long run compared to short-run movements in the data. Long-term trends have a greater tendency to reflect "textbook" definitions, especially for productivity. Since productivity is defined as output per unit of labor, the focus of discussions of long-term trends generally are in terms of growth in the output capability of labor—a type of "quality of labor" issue.

Long-term trends in productivity reflect a variety of underlying trends, including:

- Technological improvements in production processes
- Increases in capital per worker
- Improvements in workers' skills
- Improvements in efficiency of production
- Increases in the share of output in "higher-productivity" industries

Based on these factors, growth in productivity leads to increases in consumer buying power and higher average standards of living.

In the short run, however, productivity growth rates follow the business cycle. Both the output measure and the labor hours input are cyclically sensitive, but the output component is even more so. In fact, productivity will often lead the economy during recoveries as output picks up faster than the workweek and number of employees. Going into recession, however, productivity is about coincident with the economy.

On a quarterly basis, productivity numbers are very volatile owing to volatility in both output and labor hours. As seen in Chart 15–1, quarterly numbers are largely "noise." Over any business cycle, it is not uncommon for output to surge or pause either in anticipation of stronger demand or in reaction to unforeseen weakness in demand. Similarly, over the business cycle, hiring is not entirely smooth, depending upon business expectations and how closely those expectations are met. If firms "overhire" one quarter, they will simply slow down the following quarter. In any of these situations, productivity growth rates will vary sharply on a quarterly basis. These quarterly deviations have no implications for any long-term trends in productivity and may have little meaning even for cyclical movement. Basically, quarterly changes in productivity overwhelm both cyclical and secular movement. Similarly, cyclical movement overshadows secular movement. Importantly, quarterly changes in productivity have nothing to do with changes in the quality of the workforce. Cyclical changes, however, over long expansions can reflect changes in the quality of the average worker if labor supplies become scarce and less-productive workers are in demand. It is during these cyclical circumstances that low productivity numbers can be a concern as an indicator of building inflation pressures. Table 15–1 shows data for productivity and costs from 1980 to 1997.

CHART 15–1
Nonfarm Business Productivity, Labor Costs, and Output

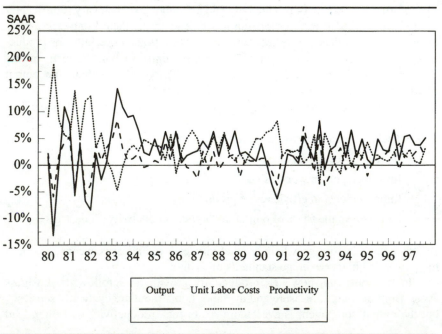

TABLE 15–1

Productivity and Costs: Annual Changes in Productivity and Related Measures

Measure	1980	1981	1982	1983	1984	1985	1986	1987	1988	1989	1990	1991	1992	1993	1994	1995	1996	1997
Nonfarm business																		
Productivity	−0.4	1.1	−0.7	4.1	1.8	1.0	2.6	−0.2	0.8	0.5	0.5	0.7	3.2	0.1	0.4	0.1	1.9	1.7
Output	−1.2	1.9	−3.2	6.1	7.8	3.6	3.4	3.0	4.1	3.2	0.7	−1.7	3.0	3.0	3.9	2.6	3.5	4.5
Hours	−0.8	0.7	−2.5	1.8	6.0	2.6	0.8	3.2	3.3	2.6	0.2	−2.5	−0.1	2.8	3.4	2.5	1.6	2.7
Hourly compensation	10.8	9.6	7.4	4.3	4.2	4.6	5.1	3.8	4.5	2.7	5.5	5.0	5.1	2.3	1.9	2.4	3.8	3.8
Real hourly compensation	−2.4	−0.6	1.2	1.0	−0.1	1.1	3.2	0.1	0.4	−2.0	0.1	0.7	2.0	−0.6	−0.7	−0.3	0.9	1.5
Unit labor costs	11.2	8.4	8.2	0.1	2.4	3.6	2.5	4.0	3.6	2.1	5.0	4.2	1.9	2.2	1.4	2.3	1.9	2.1
Manufacturing																		
Productivity	0.5	1.3	5.5	3.5	3.0	3.8	4.5	2.8	1.6	1.3	1.8	2.3	3.6	2.2	2.7	3.1	3.9	4.4
Output	−4.1	0.8	−3.6	4.6	9.7	3.0	2.9	3.5	4.4	1.7	−0.4	−1.9	3.2	3.6	4.9	3.5	3.2	5.6
Hours	−4.6	−0.5	−8.5	1.0	6.5	−0.7	−1.5	0.8	2.7	0.4	−2.1	−4.2	−0.4	1.4	2.2	0.4	−0.6	1.1
Hourly compensation	12.0	9.9	9.7	2.7	3.4	5.4	4.5	2.8	4.1	3.3	4.7	5.3	4.3	2.9	2.8	2.8	3.3	3.5
Real hourly compensation	−1.4	−0.4	3.3	−0.4	−0.9	1.8	2.4	−0.8	0.0	−1.4	−0.7	1.1	1.2	−0.1	0.2	0.0	0.3	1.2
Unit labor costs	11.4	8.4	4.1	−0.8	0.5	1.5	0.0	0.0	2.4	2.0	2.9	2.9	0.7	0.7	0.1	−0.3	−0.5	−0.9

Source: U.S. Department of Labor, Bureau of Labor Statistics, various years.

THE EMPLOYMENT COST INDEX

The employment cost index is another labor series that is an important measure of cost pressures in the economy:

> The employment cost index (ECI), published quarterly by the U.S. Bureau of Labor Statistics (BLS), measures changes in the price of labor—defined as total compensation per employee hour worked. As a fixed-weight or Laspeyres index, the ECI controls for changes occurring over time in the industrial-occupational composition of employment.[1]

This quarterly series is released the last week of the month following the reference quarter. The data are available in the U.S. Department of Labor's *Monthly Labor Review* and *Current Wage Developments.* As noted, the ECI is a measure of the change in the cost of labor, free from the influence of employment shifts among occupations and industries.

The importance of the ECI is not only that it is a measure of underlying inflation on the cost side, but it is also used in labor negotiations and, sometimes, as a cost-of-living adjustment (COLA) escalator. Data are available by industry and by occupation. The two key components of the employment cost indexes are wages and salaries and employer costs for employee benefits. The key shortcoming of ECI data is that the series do not go back far historically.

Definition and Methodology

The ECI is a Laspeyres—or fixed-weight index—at the occupational level. However, the index is not for a fixed basket of benefits for workers. It is a measure of the employer's cost for a fixed labor pool. As such, the weights given to various worker groups are fixed, based on Census Bureau counts. Weights are fixed at the occupational level. The ECI is defined by specific occupation: a promotion and higher salary do not affect the data unless the changes in wages and benefits for the job reflecting the promotion are affected according to what was paid for that specific job. The Census counts used are the 1990 Census for March 1995 data and since; 1980 Census for June 1986 through December 1994; and 1970 Census for data prior to June 1986. The base period is June 1989, which equals 100. Most ECI series only go back to 1980 to 1982.

The ECI is based on data from a sample of about 4,100 private industry employers and about 900 establishments in state and local government (including schools and public hospitals). The ECI data cover only civilian workers and currently do not cover federal civilian employees. Initial data are collected by a visiting BLS field agent, and subsequent reports are made by mail, fax, or telephone.

The ECI specifically excludes farms, households, the federal government, self-employed, owner-managers, and unpaid family workers.

TABLE 15–2

Employment Cost Index by Industry and Occupational Group (Seasonally Adjusted)

Series	June 1997	September 1997	Percent changes for 3-months ended							
			December 1995	March 1996	June 1996	September 1996	December 1996	March 1997	June 1997	September 1997
Civilian workers	132.8	133.8	.6	.6	.9	.6	.8	.6	.8	.8
State and local government	133.8	134.5	.7	.6	.6	.6	.8	.5	.5	.5
Private industry workers	132.5	133.6	.7	.6	.9	.7	.7	.6	.8	.8
White-collar occupations	134.0	135.1	.7	.9	.8	.8	.7	.8	.8	.8
Blue-collar occupations	130.7	131.6	.6	.6	.7	.4	.9	.3	.8	.7
Service occupations	130.6	132.8	.3	.5	.7	.6	.9	.9	.8	1.7
Goods-producing industries	132.7	133.7	.8	.4	.9	.7	.6	.2	1.0	.8
Construction	128.5	129.4	.7	.6	.5	.4	.9	.6	.9	.7
Manufacturing	133.6	134.6	.8	.5	.9	.8	.7	.2	.9	.7
Durables	134.0	135.0	.8	.3	1.2	.6	.7	.1	.8	.7
Nondurables	132.8	133.9	1.0	.7	.5	1.2	.7	.3	1.0	.8
Service-producing industries	132.4	133.6	.6	.8	.8	.7	.8	.8	.7	.9
Transportation and public utilities	131.8	132.9	.7	.6	.7	.6	1.0	.3	.6	.8
Wholesale trade	133.5	134.6	.8	.6	.9	.7	.8	1.7	.2	.8
Retail trade	129.5	130.9	.4	1.5	–.1	1.1	1.3	.9	.6	1.1
Finance, insurance, and real estate*	129.4	130.5	.3	1.1	1.4	.3	–.6	2.1	.6	.9
Services	135.7	136.9	.5	.8	.8	.7	.8	.7	.9	.9
Nonmanufacturing industries	132.0	133.1	.6	.7	.8	.7	.9	.7	.8	.8

* No identifiable seasonality was found for this series.

Source: U.S. Department of Labor, "Employment Cost Index," News Release, September 1997.

Key Series and Types of ECI Data

As already mentioned, ECI data cover only civilian workers. The primary components for state and local government and for private industry workers with the component breakdown for wages and salaries and for benefits cost are also important. As used for the ECI, wages and salaries are based on an hourly straight-time wage rate. For nonhourly workers, straight-time earnings are divided by corresponding hours.

The definition of straight-time earnings is based on:

- Payroll before deductions
- Exclusion of premium pay for overtime on weekends and holidays, shift differentials, and nonproduction bonuses (lump sum in lieu of wage increases)
- Inclusion of production bonuses, incentive earnings, commissions, and COLAs in straight-time earnings

Benefits covered include:

- Paid leave (vacations, holidays, sick leave, etc.)
- Supplemental pay (premium pay for overtime and work on holidays, shift differentials, nonproduction bonuses)
- Insurance benefits (life, health, sickness, and accident)
- Retirement and savings benefits
- Legally required benefits, including (1) social security, railroad retirement and supplemental retirement, railroad unemployment insurance, federal and state unemployment insurance, workers' compensation, and other such as state temporary disability; and (2) other benefits, such as severance pay

While the list of benefits covered generally remains constant, that is not the same as an employer providing a constant level of benefits. For example, an employer may choose to change a contract for medical insurance provided and increase copayments by employees. This would tend to lower the cost to the employer and would show up as part of the measured ECI.

Data are available by occupation, industry group, bargaining status (union versus nonunion), region, and area size. Also, data are available in seasonally adjusted or not seasonally adjusted form.

Finally, once a year BLS publishes employment cost data in dollar—not index—form. These numbers are useful for individual firms wanting to make cost comparisons with national cost data. The annual publication is usually released in March of each year and is entitled *Employer Costs for Employee Compensation*. Table 15–3 lists employment costs for 1976 to 1997. As seen in Chart 15–2, employment cost inflation has come down dramatically since the early 1980s. In contrast to the late 1980s, compensation growth in the mid-1990s was dampened by weak growth in benefits costs.

INDEX